TOtaL DeVotiOn

Selected Books by Kevin Johnson

Early Teen Devotionals
Can I Be a Christian Without Being Weird?
Could Someone Wake Me Up Before I Drool on the Desk?
Total Devotion: 365 Days to Hang Tight With Jesus

Early Teen Discipleship
Get God: Make Friends With the King of the Universe
Wise Up: Stand Clear of the Unsmartness of Sin
Get Smart: Unscramble Mind-Boggling Questions of Your Faith
Bust Loose: Become the Wild New Person You Are in Jesus

Books for Youth
Find Your Fit[1]
Find Your Fit Discovery Workbook[1]
Find Your Fit Leader's Guide[1]
God's Will God's Best[2]
What Do Ya Know?
Where Ya Gonna Go?

*To find out more about Kevin Johnson's books
visit his Web site:
www.thewave.org*

[1]with Jane Kise   [2]with Josh McDowell

Kevin
Johnson

TOtaL
DeVOtiOn

BETHANYHOUSE
MINNEAPOLIS, MINNESOTA

Total Devotion: 365 Days
Copyright © 2004 by Kevin Johnson

Cover and interior design by Lookout Design Group, Inc.

Unless otherwise noted, Scripture quotations are from the HOLY BIBLE, NEW INTERNATIONAL VERSION®. Copyright © 1973, 1978, 1984 by International Bible Society. Used by permission of Zondervan Publishing House. All rights reserved.

Scripture quotations identified NLT are from the *Holy Bible*, New Living Translation. Copyright © 1996. Used by permission of Tyndale House Publishers, Inc., Wheaton, Illinois 60189. All rights reserved.

Scripture quotations identified NCV are from *The Holy Bible*, New Century Version. Copyright © 1987, 1988, 1991 by Word Publishing, Dallas, Texas 75039. Used by permission.

Scripture quotations identified TLB are from *The Living Bible* © 1971 owned by assignment by Illinois Regional Bank N.A. (as trustee). Used by permission of Tyndale House Publishers, Inc., Wheaton, IL 60189. All rights reserved.

The Scripture quotation marked NKJV is taken from the New King James Version of the Bible. Copyright © 1979, 1980, 1982, Thomas Nelson, Inc., Publishers.

Scripture quotations identified TEV are from the Bible in Today's English Version (Good News Bible). Copyright © American Bible Society 1966, 1971, 1976, 1992.

Scripture quotations identified GW are from God's Word. Copyright © 1995 God's Word to the Nation's Bible Society.

Published by Bethany House Publishers
11400 Hampshire Avenue South
Bloomington, Minnesota 55438

Bethany House Publishers is a division of
Baker Publishing Group, Grand Rapids, Michigan.

Printed in the United States of America.

Library of Congress Cataloging-in-Publication Data

Johnson, Kevin (Kevin Walter)
   Total Devotion : 365 days to hang tight with Jesus / Kevin Johnson.
      p. cm.
Summary: A collection of daily devotional readings to help teenagers deal with common problems and concerns.
   ISBN 0-7642-2884-6 (pbk.)
1. Teenagers—Prayer-books and devotions—English. 2. Devotional calendars. [1. Prayer books and devotions. 2. Devotional calendars. 3. Christian life. 4. Conduct of life.] I. Title.
   BV4850.J64 2004
   242'.63—dc22   2003021870

To Lyn
The Love of My Life

To Nate, Karin, and Elise
The Lights in My Smile

Kevin Johnson in the bestselling author or coauthor of almost thirty books, including *Can I Be a Christian Without Being Weird?* and *Catch the Wave!* Pastor to children, youth, and families at Calvary Lutheran Church in Golden Valley, Minnesota, he has also served as senior editor for adult non-fiction at Bethany House Publishers and as associate pastor for middle schoolers at Elmbrook Church in metro Milwaukee. While his training includes an M.Div. from Fuller Theological Seminary and a B.A. in English and Print Journalism from the University of Wisconsin—River Falls, his current interests include cycling, trail running, and world music. Kevin and his wife, Lyn, live in Minnesota with their three children.

CONTENTS

Total Devotion

Until the day you expire—or at least until some far-off future point when you misplace all your mental marbles—you'll remember the date 9-11-2001. Deeply scratched in the memories of you and your every peer is the day nineteen hijackers—driven by a wickedly twisted dedication—killed thousands.

Don't mistake what the terrorists did for *total devotion*. A way better name for it is *full-blown deviation*. The terrorists aimed to show the world why their cause was worth murdering and dying for. But they couldn't have made clearer to us why Christ is worth living for.

Read Romans 12:1

What kind of commitment does Jesus want from you?

The 9/11 terrorists lived out such a warped style of commitment that you can just look at what they did, then do the exact opposite:

- You aren't trying to earn heaven as a suicide killer. God offers you eternal life as a free gift.
- You aren't aflame with viciousness. Your commitment to Jesus overwhelms you with compassion.
- You don't slog for a faraway, foreboding God. You lovingly serve the Savior who walked in your shoes and died in your place.
- You don't unleash death on the innocent. You usher the guilty into life.

Total devotion isn't a one-shot suicide mission. It's an attitude you can adopt this instant and apply moment by moment. It's a joy-jazzed offering of your whole self to God. It's clinging tight to the Lord of the universe and letting him reign over every square inch of your life.

And when you consider what Jesus has done for you—giving you breath, eternal life, and everything in between—you know in your heart he deserves nothing less.

You're no dead fool. You're a living sacrifice. That's total devotion.

Dear Christian friends, I plead with you to give your bodies to God. Let them be a living and holy sacrifice—the kind he will accept. When you think of what he has done for you, is this too much to ask? ROMANS 12:1 NLT

If You Snooze You Lose

Just as Keri slapped the snooze button on her alarm clock for the third time, her mom knocked on her bedroom door and hollered to see if she was awake. "It's eight o'clock, Keri. We leave for church in half an hour."

By the time Keri dragged herself into the kitchen, she was primed to whine. "Why do we have to do this? Can't we take a few Sundays off? You and Dad should go by yourselves. You like it." Keri thought Sunday school was okay. She just chatted with her friends while the teacher droned on. But a second hour in a church service made her bonkers. Keri's parents weren't amused by her organ imitation—moaning like a cow in labor—and Keri couldn't figure out why the pastor got so worked up about everything.

One of these days, she told herself, *I'm staying home. And I'm not going back.*

Read Colossians 1:10

Why would anyone want to "please God in every way"?

Before we decide to trust God, we figure that knowing, following, and enjoying God ranks in value right up there with a stash of Happy Meal toys lost in a backyard sandbox. So instead of recognizing God as King of the universe, we rule our own lives. We're God's enemies, rebels against him.

You probably know the facts on how God figured out a way to bring us back to himself. Though we deserve to die for our sins (Romans 6:23), Christ suffered our punishment for us. He died on the cross in our place so we can be forgiven (Colossians 1:21–23).

Once you're sure of those facts, you have a colossal reason to choose total devotion to Jesus. You've admitted, *I've been wrong, God. I thought you weren't worth it. I disobeyed you. I accept the gift of forgiveness and life you offer through Christ.* You've become God's friend. Now you can choose daily to follow God because you realize the infinite value of being tight with him. He's rescued you and brought you into his kingdom of love. And he's worth every bit of your life.

And we pray this in order that you may live a life worthy of the Lord and may please him in every way: bearing fruit in every good work, growing in the knowledge of God.
COLOSSIANS 1:10

To Die or to Die

"Quit stalling! Get him!"

Tadd's friends had made a deal—a dare each guy had to do to keep hanging with their group. The test started out as a joke. One by one Tadd's friends had done the deed and passed.

Now it was Tadd's turn to beat someone up for no reason—other than to join the group, that is. His friends got to choose whose head he would turn inside out. They picked Pat.

"He won't even fight back," they reminded Tadd. "He's a wuss."

Tadd more or less agreed with them. Pat played the flute. He was strange. He walked, talked, and giggled like a girl. But Tadd had known Pat since kindergarten. He didn't deserve this. But now a bunch of people were waiting for Tadd's first punch.

Read Mark 8:31–38

What did Jesus say was the toughest thing about following him?

When you choose to follow Jesus, you might get caught between a rock and *the* Rock (Isaiah 26:4). If you ignore the demands of your friends, you face humiliation and rejection. Yet if you do wrong—abusing yourself, others, and Jesus—you know God will be less than thrilled.

Either way you die. So what's the use of picking sides?

Jesus bluntly told his disciples that obeying God's plan would mean he would be mocked and killed on the cross. He was still determined to obey God.

And Jesus said that anyone devoted to him must imitate him. Deny oneself and take up the cross. Swap your way for his way—totally. Obey him even when it hurts—even when you feel like you've been pierced with nails and all you can do is twist in pain.

Daring to stick with Jesus sometimes feels like you've been hung up to die. Tough stuff. But Jesus promises that his way leads to life.

Then he called the crowd to him along with his disciples and said: "If anyone would come after me, he must deny himself and take up his cross and follow me." MARK 8:34

Look Out Below

From your perch atop your office tower—all 110 stories of it—you ponder your quick ride to the top. A little lawn-mowing service, a few baby-sitting jobs, some lucrative investments, and *whammo*—you own a sizable chunk of the world.

You bought a city block. You built a building. It's yours. Downstairs you have a garage packed with cars—Bimmers and Humvees and Ferraris. They're yours. And every one of the thousands of workers in the tower below answers to you. All yours.

Your feet? Propped up on the desk. Your nose? Sky-high. Your bank account? Bigger than the gross national product of Bulgaria. You call the shots. You run the show. You're your own boss. And you're only fifteen.

Just wait until you get your driver's license and move away from Mom and Dad.

Read John 12:25–26

Who runs your life when you're out and about on your own?

Even if you perch at the tip of the tallest office tower in the world, there still is Someone above you.

Whether your kingdom consists of half a bedroom, a bunk bed, and a few video games—or a dorm room, a microwave, and an '88 Honda—or condos, cars, corporations, techno-toys beyond imagination, and the largest CD collection in the world—you're not the master of the universe. You don't even rule your own life.

There's no escape: You serve *somebody*. The Bible says you're a slave either to what's wrong or to what's right (Romans 6:19), either to death or to life (Romans 8:6), either to Satan or to God (Ephesians 2:1–10).

Trying to run your own life is like leaping off your office tower. You won't fly. Life without God is a death spiral as sure as gravity. But to "hate" life and give yourself back to God—that means to stick close to him, obeying his commands—sends you soaring.

Growing up isn't getting free to finally rule the roost. It's your chance to choose for yourself to follow Jesus—to fly with the real Master of the universe.

Whoever serves me must follow me; and where I am,
my servant also will be. JOHN 12:26

On Your Mark

You waddle to the line for the ten-thousand-meter race wearing generously padded hockey bibs. You eyeball the runners next to you through your helmet's face cage. *Why is everyone dressed funny?* You struggle to bend over to take your mark, catching yourself with your thick gloves as you topple into position.

The starting gun fires. As you shuffle off and your blades slice into the dirt track, you observe that it's hard to run in skates. And as the pack of runners pulls away, you look down and detect one more problem. Your skates are laced together.

Read Hebrews 12:1–3
How should you dress for the race to follow Jesus?

Bibs, jersey, pads, gloves, helmet, and skates are great if you want to jam on ice. But they make you a clod if you're running a race. If you hope to run well, you strip to essentials and slip on the lightest shoes you can find.

As Christians we have a race marked out for us, with an eternity in heaven with God and his people on the far side of the finish line. Our racecourse—a life lived tight with Jesus—isn't a sprint. It's a marathon run that demands determination and devotion. To run well we toss off anything not necessary for the race.

Sometimes, though, we lumber along with loads as out of place as hockey gear at a track meet—like a social calendar that crowds out time with Christian friends, or a sports schedule too busy for time alone with God. Those are good things out of control.

Even worse is when bad things grab hold of our lives. Sin takes us out of the race. Doing wrong leaves us wadded in a knot and sprawled on the track until we ask God for forgiveness and let him pick us up.

Your Christian life might feel like you've shown up wearing skates to a track meet. Now is the time to toss off everything that tangles up your run.

Let us throw off everything that hinders and the sin that so easily entangles, and let us run with perseverance the race marked out for us. HEBREWS 12:1b

The Finest Thing in Life

With the entire contents of her closet spread out on her bed, Shawna plots party wear with Charise over the phone. "I don't know. Sweaters make me look pudgy—especially with a turtleneck.... Huh? I can't wear *that*. I'll never wear that again. Don't you remember? The last time I did, David called me 'bubble butt'.... Sure, I suppose we could both dress up. That would really make Jill look bad.... Yeah, I guess the green outfit would be okay.... Yeah, I know. It's kind of cute. You don't think it makes me look like a leprechaun, do you? I don't want anyone to laugh at me this time."

Read Matthew 6:25–34

When you're aiming to be totally devoted to Jesus, what goal should you keep in the front of your mind?

Girls aren't the only ones who get intense about their wardrobes. And clothes aren't the only things in life that can consume us. The problem? Hunting down the ultimate snowboard gear, drilling to make the all-city soccer team, or mastering level 643 of your favorite video game—all these things aren't bad, but they can squeeze something even better out of your brain.

You *need* clothes and food and a few other things. You *want* fun and money and lots of other things. Yet God wants to help you think about bigger things.

Jesus says to seek *first* God's kingdom and righteousness. To seek God's kingdom is to want what he wants. That's giving God your heart. To seek his righteousness is to look for ways to love him and others. That's giving God your life. And when you chase God hard, he promises to take care of everything else.

That doesn't mean you never think about those other things. Birds dig worms and flowers drink, and it's not a bad idea for people to lay out clothes for the next day so they aren't late for school. But you're running toward the wrong goal if you perpetually panic about what to wear without ever pondering how to live.

For the pagans run after all these things, and your heavenly Father knows that you need them. But seek first his kingdom and his righteousness, and all these things will be given to you as well. MATTHEW 6:32-33

Marshmallows

The campfire flared, lighting up a dozen sweaty faces.

"So what are you in to? What makes you happy?" someone asked Vicki. No one had been able to figure her out. Nothing seemed to thrill her.

"Money makes me happy," Vicki said. "I want to be rich."

"How come?"

"I like to go to the mall." She flashed a look that meant, *Isn't that obvious, you stupid people?* She did dress like she knew her malls.

"What do you do when the malls close?" someone prodded.

"Not much."

"And that's fun?" someone else asked.

Vicki could tell no one was impressed. "Marshmallows!" she said suddenly. "I like marshmallows." She oozed a marshmallow between her fingers to demonstrate her sincerity. "Marshmallows make me happy."

The last question to her fell unanswered as she looked away, into the fire. "So what happens when the marshmallows are gone?"

Read 1 Corinthians 3:10–15
What parts of life last forever?

Think of all of life's thrills and peak moments: an afternoon kicking around with friends, a whoosh down a water slide, a new tune in your headphones, winning at sports, your dog jumping at the door for you after school—they're marshmallows. Sweet. Fast yet delicious. Sugar roasted hot on a stick. Lick your lips to get it all.

But is that *all* there is? If you admit there is more to life than marshmallows, peers might think you're weird. Too serious. Too much on the fringe. They might leave you sitting alone at the campfire.

God made marshmallows to enjoy. But he also points out that only things connected to him last forever. Anything built on Jesus—enjoying things his way, doing his will, following him—matters for eternity. Anything done without him—jumping out-of-bounds, leaping into sin, doing your own thing—will be gone in a flash.

God wants to have more than a fluffy friendship with you. He invites you to total devotion.

If any man builds on this foundation using gold, silver, costly stones, wood, hay or straw, his work will be shown for what it is.
1 CORINTHIANS 3:12–13

At the Pearly Gates

Standing outside the gates of heaven, you scope out the ticket booth with the shortest line. When you reach the front of the line, you pull stacks of yellow sticky notes from your pockets.

"What are these?" the ticket lady asks.

"It's everything nice I've ever done," you say. "I've been keeping track."

"I'm sorry, but you can't get in with these."

The girl behind you nudges past you to the counter. She hands the lady a ticket with big letters that say *Admit One*.

You push back to the ticket lady. "You've made a mistake," you plead. "I've got all the proof I need right here. I've been really good."

The ticket lady turns back to the girl. "Welcome, Anita. Go on in.

The lady glances back at you. "You can't buy tickets here," she says. "The tickets were free. Back on earth."

You rip the girl's ticket from her hands and stare at it, looking for a secret code or a hint of where it came from. "Where did you get this? Who could possibly give you a free pass to heaven? I've been good my whole life just to get here."

"Didn't you hear?" the girl replies. "Jesus was giving them away."

Read Ephesians 2:8–9

What gets you friendship with Jesus—and eternal life in heaven?

There's a danger in total devotion. It's this: You might begin to think that your spiritual goodness scores you friendship with God.

No, Jesus doesn't hand out cheesy tickets to heaven that say *Admit One*—or even *Get Out of Hell Free* cards. But he wants you to be sure of one fact: He's the only way you can know God and get into heaven.

Get it straight: Your total devotion doesn't earn you squat. Your love for God is your thanks for everything God has done for you.

God already loves you completely. When you trust Christ, he "saves" you, forgiving you and promising you life in heaven. You can't take credit for that salvation.

God saved you by his special favor when you believed. And you can't take credit for this; it is a gift from God. Salvation is not a reward for the good things we have done, so none of us can boast about it. EPHESIANS 2:8-9 NLT

Lost and Alone

As Sue ran deeper into the forest, tree branches whipped her face and scratched her arms and legs. She'd been running down a logging trail in a thick woods when she realized the path no longer looked familiar. Scared, she ran faster but recognized even less. She turned and headed the other direction, then bolted off the path. As darkness grew, she was overwhelmed with confusion and fright. She crumpled from exhaustion on the shore of a lonely, isolated lake, totally lost.

Ever been lost? How did you get unlost?

Some people panic—like Sue. Other people refuse to admit they're in a sad spot. (Just recall a snapshot moment from your last family road trip—with Dad or Mom driving farther and farther down the wrong road to avoid the total embarrassment of stopping to ask directions.)

But some lost people stay calm and get directions. They backtrack in the woods. They find a sign. Or they pull into a gas station. They admit they need help figuring out exactly where they are and how to get where they want to go.

Read 2 Timothy 3:14–17
How does the Bible help you find your way when you want to follow God?

If you want to get un-lost in the woods or on a road, you've got to stop to get directions. Because some hikers found Sue and led her out of the forest, she didn't die. Because drivers gulp down their pride and ask directions, a lot of family vacations are rescued. If you want to get un-lost in life, the Bible is the place to look. It teaches you to know God and helps you mature. It shows you the way to real life.

Getting directions doesn't work if the directions you get aren't clear. But the Bible is "breathed by God"; it provides perfect directions from the perfect God. If you look to God's Word, the Bible, for directions, you can trust what it says. It's your unique guidebook written by the ultimate guide, God himself.

All Scripture is inspired by God and is useful to teach us what is true and to make us realize what is wrong in our lives. It straightens us out and teaches us to do what is right.

2 TIMOTHY 3:16 NLT

Hunger Pains

"My Sunday school class decided to read the Bible from cover to cover this year," Scott moaned. "I flew until January 23—all the way through Leviticus and halfway into Numbers. Then I crashed. I suppose I should feel good. That's three and a half books. But I still think God is mad I didn't do way better."

Know what? Getting to know God isn't supposed to be such a pain.

Read John 6:28–35
What do you think drew people to Jesus?

No one forces you to eat. You eat because you're hungry. Your stomach growls and you stuff something into it.

Hunger is what pulls you to God. Your questions, problems, doubts, triumphs, failures, your dreams about things you want to be or do, the things you love and hate—know it or not, those are hunger pains poking you to get tight with God by spending time with him and his Word.

When you go out to eat you never say, "Give me one of everything, please," then try to eat it all. And you don't have to gulp down the Bible all at once. Start with a few of the Bible's choicest morsels, and later you can eat your way through the rest of the menu.

And while you're at it, don't just focus on the load of spiritual vitamins, amino acids, and complex carbohydrates you're getting. Who wants a plateful of *that*? You might as well ask a preacher to jab you with an intravenous needle and inject you with sermons. In the same way, if you come to your Bible always telling yourself, "I'm doing this because I have to" or "I need to finish the Bible by next month, or else," you'll lose your appetite for God.

Food that tastes good lures you closer. Jesus promises that he's that kind of food—food that satisfies better than anything else. *He* is what makes Bible reading something you do because you want to, not because you have to.

Then Jesus declared, "I am the bread of life. He who comes to me will never go hungry, and he who believes in me will never be thirsty." JOHN 6:35

Out on a Limb

The man's spotless business suit became rumpled and grimy as he heaved himself into the tree. His pants caught on a sharp twig and ripped. After grunting loudly and sweating through his suit coat, he settled on a branch that sagged under his weight. People on the ground burst out laughing as they recognized the guy.

The people? Your friends. The tree-climbing dude? Your dad, trying to get a better shot with his camcorder at your first soccer game of the season.

Why would your dad—or your mom, or whoever—do that? Because he wants to see you—and show you off to anyone who will sit through the video.

Read Luke 19:1–10

Why would anyone want to see Jesus so bad?

Zacchaeus (Zack-KEY-us) scaled a tree to see Jesus because he had heard that Jesus loved the unlovable—and Zach wasn't exactly adored by the masses. A corrupt tax collector, he cheated his countrymen and aided the occupying enemy, the Romans. He was slime, the baddest of the bad.

But Jesus picked Zacchaeus to share dinner with him. Why?

Jesus strolled right by the people who stood on the ground laughing at Zacchaeus—people who thought they were good enough to deserve Jesus' friendship. Zacchaeus had a need and showed it by climbing the tree, and he went out on a limb because he knew he really needed Jesus. People laughed at his honesty, but every person in the crowd also needed Jesus as forgiver, master, and friend. They *all* should have climbed a tree.

You are special to God. He sent his Son, Jesus, to live and die and rise again for you. And he comes now. "Here I am!" he says. "I stand at the door and knock. If anyone hears my voice and opens the door, I will come in and eat [fellowship] with him, and he with me" (Revelation 3:20).

Your spiritual starting point is to be like Zacchaeus. Admit you need Jesus—and don't give a rip who sees you.

When Jesus reached the spot, he looked up and said to him, "Zacchaeus, come down immediately. I must stay at your house today." So he came down at once and welcomed him gladly.
LUKE 19:5-6

The Wall

For nearly thirty years, eastern Germany was walled off from western Germany—city from city, family from family, friend from friend. East Germans suffered through pollution, poverty, and brutal control of politics and religion, barely able to dream of the freedoms enjoyed in the West, outside the wall. Anyone who tried to escape the East faced razor wire, killer dogs, land mines, and machine guns.

You would never willingly choose to live locked inside a wall, separated from everything you enjoy, in a country that doubles as a prison cell. Yet you and I and every person who has ever lived are expert wall builders. We choose to separate ourselves from God and his goodness.

Read Luke 15:11–24

How does the son distance himself from his dad?

Deep inside we're all a lot like that son (Romans 3:23). Some of us battle openly to do things our way. Others of us are scared to step out of line—though if we thought we could sin and live to tell about it, we might act a lot more like this wandering son.

Each time we disobey—when we sin by what we think, say, or do—we lay a brick between ourselves and God. He doesn't build the wall; *we* do each time we choose to sin. Sin separates us from God as we build that wall brick by brick; sin makes it impossible for us to be God's friends.

Separation starts now, but it can last forever. If we refuse God's way of demolishing the wall, we will discover that when we die, the wall cements for eternity (Romans 6:23). We'll find ourselves cut off from God and everything good he has made. No phone, TV, radio, or satellite dish will tie us to family or friends or God on the other side of the wall. Being cemented inside the wall—in hell—isn't a fairy tale off a heavy-metal album cover. It's real.

The son came home to his waiting father. Our Father is waiting for us, too, so that we can be friends again with him. He sent his son, Jesus Christ, to tear down the wall we've built. It's a job only he can do.

But while he was still a long way off, his father saw him and was filled with compassion for him; he ran to his son, threw his arms around him and kissed him. LUKE 15:20

Demolishing the Wall

Imagine the Beaver—the kid on the old TV show, not the furry wood-land creature playing ball in the living room while his parents are gone. *Whizzz* flies the ball, curving right. *Craash* goes his mother's lovely vase. Eddie, wily friend of Beaver's brother, helps Beaver glue the vase back together and rearrange the flowers. Then Eddie exits.

Enter Ward and June, Beaver's parents. June refills the vase with water. It leaks. With fatherly brilliance, Ward concludes someone has broken the vase. Wally, Beaver's older brother, takes the blame, telling his mother and father that he, not Beaver, broke the vase. Wally is grounded for a *looong* time.

That happens only in the world of black-and-white reruns, doesn't it? No one in real life ever takes the punishment like that, does he?

Yep. Someone did.

Read Isaiah 53:4–12

These verses predict that Jesus will take the punishment others deserve. Whose blame does he take?

Jesus had never sinned. He deserved no punishment. Yet he chose to suf-fer for *our* sin: pierced for our evil, crushed for the wrong we did. Jesus was perfect, yet he took God's punishment for sin—death—so we wouldn't have to.

He did what Wally did but many billion times better.

Jesus died for everyone, but God requires each of us to accept that fact personally. The Beaver needed to tell the truth about the vase, and we need to take responsibility for our sin. You can do that by praying, "God, I've sinned. I've broken your rules and disappointed you. God, I know that Jesus died in my place." That's the beginning of being a Christian.

If you accept the fact that Jesus suffered your punishment, you stick tight with God now and forever: "When people sin, they earn what sin pays—death. But God gives us a free gift—life forever in Christ Jesus our Lord" (Romans 6:23 NCV). Christ demolishes the wall of sin between you and God. Not a brick stands. Not a pebble is left—not even a speck of dust. It's all been washed away by Christ's blood.

But he was pierced for our transgressions, he was crushed for our iniquities; the punishment that brought us peace was upon him, and by his wounds we are healed. ISAIAH 53:5

The Principal's Office

Ponder for a moment your feelings upon receiving an invitation to your principal's office.

As you skip happily down the hall, you anticipate hearty congratulations for your outstanding scholarship and behavior. You look forward to sparkling conversation with the person who inspires your love of learning and all your intellectual pursuits. You're already composing the thank-you note for the teacher who recommended you for this time of warm sharing with your friend of friends, your principal.

Maybe not. Unless your past has been sparkling clean, warmth is the last thing you feel when you get recommended for a trip to the principal's office. You go with anger flaring like drawn guns, certain that you're entering enemy territory.

Read Hebrews 10:19–22

How is getting close to God different from heading to the principal's office?

If the principal were your good friend you'd have a radical change of attitude about your invitation to the school office. You might need a blimpful of imagination to picture this one, but try. Your principal—emphasis on the *pal*—is an incredible teacher, counselor, enforcer, and friend rolled into one. Whatever the problem—homework, relationships, the school bully, loneliness—he gets you through.

If the principal were your best friend, instead of getting *sent* to the principal, you would *run* to the principal. This same radical change happens between you and God when the wall of sin and separation crumbles. You go to God's presence without fear because Jesus won you total friendship with God.

Before becoming a Christian, we rebel, hate rules, make excuses for sin, and fear death and hell—the ultimate detention. After accepting Jesus as Savior and Lord, we learn friendship, trust, forgiveness, and openness to correction. We look forward to eternity in heaven with God, our best friend.

Don't be afraid to go to God. His door is always open. Jesus flung it open with his blood.

We have confidence to enter the Most Holy Place by the blood of Jesus.... HEBREWS 10:19

Eleven Against One

Holly didn't quite know what to say to Mrs. Kim. "I have piano on Mondays, ballet on Tuesdays, community theater on Thursdays," she rattled off. "I baby-sit most Saturday nights, and I have gymnastics three days a week after school. And I get lots of homework too."

"So you're saying you can't work on the yearbook just one night a week," Mrs. Kim replied. "You know that means you're blowing your chance to be editor next year, don't you? We'll be looking for *experience*."

"I know," Holly said. Then she decided to tell Mrs. Kim the real reason. "It's just that it's the only night of the week I can go to youth group."

Holly said no to a good activity so she could say yes to a better one— staying involved with her Christian friends.

Read Hebrews 10:23–25

How can you keep your friendship with God fresh?

The writer of Hebrews just explained to his readers their wild new friendship with God through Christ. Now he tells how to keep it going—and the key is to keep getting together with other followers of Jesus.

Loads of influences try to rip down your faith. So you need to reinforce and rebuild yourself and your Christian friends through encouragement—talking, praying, just sharing the coolness of being a Christian. Missing church or youth group hurts both you and the Christians you could be helping.

When church conflicts with another activity, maybe you can reschedule one or the other. When you can't, church shouldn't lose, even when that means disappointing advisors or friends, or missing future opportunities. Get the picture? Getting and giving encouragement is that important.

You would have to be a fool to walk out on a football field to take on a whole team by yourself. You would look up, see eleven mammoths charging to stomp your body, and run crying off the field. Why do you think you can stay in the game alone as a Christian—where the opponent intends to kill you (1 Peter 5:8)? You need your team or you won't survive.

Let us consider how we may spur one another on toward love and good deeds. Let us not give up meeting together, as some are in the habit of doing, but let us encourage one another.
HEBREWS 10:24–25

Cow Pies

It's tough to outdo this all-time huge gross-out: You're playing Frisbee barefoot in a park when something cold and wet oozes between your toes. You shriek. You do a funky one-foot dance. You scramble to find a hose to blast off the duck or doggy doo.

The apostle Paul had something like that in mind when he wrote this next chunk to the Philippian Christians.

Read Philippians 3:7–11

What's the most important thing in life—and what does Paul call everything else?

Paul is blunt: The things Paul once thought were important he calls "rubbish." The word he uses means "worthless trash" or "garbage" or, to be more vivid, "dung." Compared with knowing Christ, everything else is like dancing on a cow pie. Paul shocks us with the truth that the *best* thing in life isn't what we have or what we do but who we know: Christ.

That may sound like over-the-top devotion, like spiritual weirdness made for parents and pastors but not for you. But here's what it looks like in real life:

It's wanting one thing more than anything else: to hang tight with God. It's doing things the way God wants, whether that brings suffering or success. Being a believer is more than following rules, going to church, and trying hard not to beat up your little brother. It's being best friends with the Lord of the universe—but aiming to know, enjoy, and serve God completely in everything you do.

Thinking you can actually get close to God isn't a cotton-candy dream that dissolves when wind and rain pelt it—when you try to make it work at home, in school, or with friends. Paul's faith was tested by beatings, stonings, shipwrecks, and persecutions, yet he (and lots of other believers) agree with the Bible when it says that it's better to live one short day close to God than a thousand without him (Psalm 84:10).

I consider everything a loss compared to the surpassing greatness of knowing Christ Jesus my Lord....I consider them rubbish, that I may gain Christ and be found in him.
PHILIPPIANS 3:8–9

Get Up and Go On

"I QUIT," Carlie screamed from halfway up a scary element in a high ropes course. From the ground it was hard to tell whether her face was wet from tears or sweat, but she shook as she clung to a pole. "I can't find anyplace to put my feet. I keep slipping! I can't do this anymore. Lower me down!"

Climbers don't always make it to the top. Not many students pull straight A's. Few musicians never miss a note. And being a Christian isn't any different—except that *no one* pulls it off perfectly. *No one* lives a flawless Christian life. If we think we live without sinning, we're fooling ourselves (1 John 1:8).

Paul admitted that. Just after he wrote that everything was a cow pie compared to knowing Jesus, he told his readers he wasn't perfect. He was totally devoted to God, but sometimes he missed his step.

Read Philippians 3:12–14

How can you overcome your mistakes and mess-ups?

Mistakes make you want to quit. Botch a few assignments in a class at school, and it's tough to keep trying. You figure you're no good, that working harder won't change your grade anyway, and there's no way to start over. Mess up a few classes or a few semesters and you might start to think school isn't for you.

When you blow it as a Christian you can't take back hurt you've caused. You have to live with the consequences of messing up. Sin still offends God. But God makes a way to repair your relationship with him and start over *right now*. A verse in 1 John tells how: "If we confess our sins, he is faithful and just and will forgive us our sins and purify us from all unrighteousness" (1:9).

That's part of what Paul meant by "forgetting what is behind." When you admit your sin to God, he forgives you and picks you up so you can press on toward the goal of knowing Christ completely. Don't ever give up on following Christ just because you fall down. There's no such thing as a Christian who never stumbles. Real Christians are the ones who get up and go on.

But one thing I do: Forgetting what is behind and straining toward what is ahead, I press on toward the goal to win the prize for which God has called me heavenward in Christ Jesus.
PHILIPPIANS 3:13–14

- DAY 18 -

Look-Alikes

Check this out in a mall mob or church crowd: How many couples or friends can you spot who look alike—same hair, same clothes, same glasses, same expressions and gestures?

Before you mock those folks, think about you and your friends. You might sport the identical haircut, clothes, jackets and shirts and hats, earrings or watches. You walk the same and talk the same. Don't believe it? Spy on your group through the eyes of other clans at school. It's easy for you to pick out other cliques where members are clones of one another. Guess what? You and your friends look just as cookie-cutter to them as they look to you.

It's a fact: When you spend time with someone, you gradually resemble each other in how you dress and act. And the same thing happens spiritually. Who you hang around with shapes what your character looks like. When you spend time with Christ—talking with him, reading his Word, and hanging with his friends—you start to look like him.

Read Galatians 5:19–26

What qualities are rubbing off on you, thanks to the Holy Spirit, as you get to know God?

The passage begins by telling what you would look like *without* God—full of rebellion, from sexual immorality to idolatry to drunkenness, jealousy, and selfishness. Not that all non-Christians sport all those grotesque features—but since they hang out with God's enemies, that's what they look like more and more. If instead you choose to live close to Jesus, you begin to pick up all his good qualities, some of which are listed in verses 22 and 23.

That's the cool part of the look-alike thing. As you know Jesus better, people will see that you look more and more like him (1 Corinthians 3:18). No one can fault you for being his look-alike ("against such things there is no law"). People can't criticize you for being loving, joyful, peaceful, patient, kind, good, faithful, gentle, and self-controlled. And if they do, that just says how messed up they are.

But the fruit of the Spirit is love, joy, peace, patience, kindness, goodness, faithfulness, gentleness and self-control.
GALATIANS 5:22-23

Total Healing

Minutes after the collision, paramedics wheeled fourteen-year-old Alec into the emergency room, where a doctor washed the boy's wounds and sent him home. The doctor didn't sew up the still-bleeding cuts; he didn't set Alec's broken bones or treat his internal injuries. Alec was left brain damaged, bent, and twisted until death.

If a doctor ever actually gave such terrible treatment to someone you love, you would scream with fury and sue for billions. But some people get upset when God starts to go beyond washing our sins to treat the root of our problems. We like having our sins forgiven and knowing that we'll go to heaven, but we get angry when God wants to do surgery on our sin.

If sin is awful enough for Jesus to have to die for it, then it's awful enough for us to want to get rid of it. God saves us not just from the punishment for sin but from the power of sin to rule and wreck us.

Read 2 Corinthians 5:14–15
Why did Jesus die for you?

God is the great doctor who wants to heal us totally, and forgiveness is only the first part of his cure for sin. Getting us to stop living for self and start following Christ is the second part. God won't let us have one without the other. Because Christ has died, our old sinful lives have died—and we have been born anew to live a better life.

You might wonder how some people manage to live lives totally devoted to God. But there's nothing mysterious about how God works to change us. Once forgiven, we become friends with God. He uses that friendship to remake us. His Holy Spirit lives in us, teaches us through the Bible, and empowers us beyond our natural abilities (Romans 8:1–17). That takes time, and sometimes it hurts, like surgery. But in the end, we're closer to becoming who God wants us to be.

God loves us too much to leave us twisting in pain, our sin and selfishness untreated.

For Christ's love compels us, because we are convinced that one died for all, and therefore all died. And he died for all, that those who live should no longer live for themselves but for him who died for them and was raised again.

2 CORINTHIANS 5:14–15

Total Weirdness?

Hand a crowd of non-Christian youth a wad of pens and paper and invite them to sketch a prototypical Christian youth, and the picture might not be pretty. *Bizarre looks*—hoisted pants, yuck hair, and thick glasses, accessorized with a pocket protector or a funny little purse. *Strange talk*—they ask if you "know God," they always quote from the Bible, and they say "Praise Jesus" a lot. *Unbelievable actions*—they do stuff like running up to the lunchroom supervisor to explain who started the food fight.

As a Christian you know you're supposed to be different. But how weird do you have to be?

Read Matthew 22:34–40

What does Jesus say are the two huge ways you show you are totally devoted to him?

Jesus doesn't tell Christians to wear funny hats or shave their heads. They don't necessarily go door-to-door to hand out magazines. Their words don't always come out with "chapter 4, verse 12" attached. What makes a Christian different from other people is that he or she is (1) learning to love God totally ("love God with all your heart, soul and mind") and (2) learning to love others unselfishly ("love your neighbor as you love yourself").

That really *is* a wild kind of weird—because you won't find tons of people—kids or adults—following Jesus' command.

It's obvious that most people don't try hard to love God radically. They claim they try to be good to others, yet most people's lives, much of the time—at school, home, with friends, at work—gush selfishness. They consistently think of their own interests first. In that crowd, a Christian living as Jesus expects really stands out.

Even so, being a believer may actually help you make friends. True, your love for God may make others think you're strange. But your love for people may convince them that you're not. If your actions and words show that you care about others as much as you care about yourself, not everyone will call you *weird*. A lot of them may call you *friend*.

Jesus replied: "Love the Lord your God with all your heart and with all your soul and with all your mind...." And the second is like it: "Love your neighbor as yourself." MATTHEW 22:37, 39

Saved From the Drain

When Ellen sobbed and ran into the rest room, Steve looked pleased with himself. His cruel words about Ellen were dead-on funny. But Janika was fed up with Steve's thermonuclear sarcasm.

"I hate the way you treat people. Can't you see what you did to Ellen? Don't you feel bad? What's wrong with you?"

Matt rushed to Steve's rescue. "Don't blame him. He can't help it. It's just the way he is. Mr. Jackson says it's his personality."

"Actually, it's his biochemistry," Martina suggested. "Perhaps Steve should see my psychiatrist for a prescription."

"What's wrong with *you*, girl?" Liz butted in. "He has a sarcastic, nasty, obnoxious tongue. He needs to say he's sorry and glue those lips shut."

Read Ephesians 4:17–24
Can you help it if you're bad?

It's tough to drown in a bathtub. Sure, you might slip and bonk your head. But if you drew a scalding hot bath and lay there lazily until your skin wrinkled—and then soaked longer until your skin rotted—and then lingered in the tub still longer until one day you dissolved into quivering bits of flesh and whooshed down the drain—now, that would be *your* fault.

Paul uses some big words in this passage to say that apart from God, you want to stay stuck in a tub of sin. You lose your grip on what's right. You lounge in sin so long that your heart becomes numb with hatred, your mind dead with rebellion.

But God made a way for you to get unstuck. Christ lived so you could see what God is like; he died and rose so you could be made right with God. When you accept the fact that Christ rescued you, you want no more of sin (Titus 2:11–12). As you soak in God's truth—the Bible—you start to think differently. God works in you. You hate sin. You chase what's good. And it starts to show in how you act.

You get out of the tub before you wash down the drain.

You were taught, with regard to your former way of life, to put off your old self, which is being corrupted by its deceitful desires; to be made new in the attitude of your minds....
EPHESIANS 4:22-23

Busted Again

"We take these reports *very* seriously," Bianca's school counselor scolded. Bianca thought back to her essay on "What I want to be when I grow up." What did she write that got her handcuffed to a chair and wired to a lie detector? Why the blinding lights?

Her counselor zeroed in. "Miss Bratvold, in response to the question 'Would you rather be good, bad, or ugly?' you wrote 'I want to be good.' Really, now. Do you mean that? HMMM?"

"Yes," Bianca stammered. "Yes, I do."

"I'm sure you do," her counselor sneered. "But there's this little matter of cheating. We know that you peeked at Tim Ford's math homework back in third grade."

Bianca gasped. "I didn't mean to!"

"And just last week—did you or did you not make rude and false remarks about Lindsey Rich?" her counselor pressed. Bianca started to cry. "Need I continue?" inquired her counselor. "We have a *long* list of instances when you were in fact *not* good."

Read Romans 7:21–25

What's your problem when you can't seem to do what's right?

Blinded by a spotlight, cuffed like a criminal, plugged into a lie detector—forced to be honest—none of us lacks shortcomings. We know the rules. Yet we fail to keep them perfectly—no matter how hard we try.

It's like an annoying hunk of hair that always curls wrong. Slick it down, gel it up, as soon as you drop your guard: *fuh-wang!* Some curls in our character, though, aren't small. And they matter even more than doofy hair.

Even after we've decided to follow Jesus, sin still hounds us (Hebrews 12:1). Part of us wants to do what's right. Part of us doesn't. We can blame others, make excuses, or hide our faults, but it always comes back to one fact: There's something wrong with *us*. We're at war within ourselves.

But admitting we're a tangled mess opens the way for God to fix us. Being a Christian isn't just knowing the rules. It's not even knowing when you've broken them. It's relying on the Master to bust us loose.

What a wretched man I am! Who will rescue me from this body of death? ROMANS 7:24

The Living Dead

"It's okay," Norman sighs, unfurling his homework after the neighbor's cat ate it and hacked it up four days later like a hairball. "It was due yesterday, but at least I'll have something to turn in."

Such was Norman's life. When Norman goes to school the next day, he finds his principal has thrown everything out of his locker and given the spot to a new kid. "It's just what I would have done," Norman sighs. And when he goes to English class, he finds the new kid has taken his desk. "I'll sit up front on the floor. It's cold and hard, but I'll be fine."

"Don't be dense, Norman," remarks Norman's teacher. "The custodians can bring in another desk."

And after school Norman discovers his dog has been run over by a car, his parents kidnapped by terrorists, and his house blown up by the bully across the street. "Oh well," Norman sighs. "It's okay. Really it is."

Read Romans 8:9–17

Does having the Holy Spirit living inside you make you disappear as a person?

As you become more and more like Jesus, you don't exactly become less and less like you. God doesn't erase your personality. He doesn't overwhelm your emotions with perpetual bliss and good cheer. He doesn't vacuum out your brain. And he doesn't convert you into a satellite-guided RoboChristian that acts holy at the flip of some heavenly switch.

You still feel. You still think. You still act. You still react.

Here's what really happens. You have a new relationship with the God of the universe. You no longer dread God. You can, in fact, call him "Abba" ("Father," or even "Daddy"). He isn't simply "out there" somewhere. God himself lives *in* you through his Spirit.

The Bible says the Spirit produces love, joy, peace, patience, kindness, goodness, faithfulness, gentleness, and self-control in you (Galatians 5:22–23). He helps you understand God's commands. And as you listen and obey, the part of you that hates God's ways dies away.

And if the Spirit of him who raised Jesus from the dead is living in you, he who raised Christ from the dead will also give life to your mortal bodies through his Spirit, who lives in you.
ROMANS 8:11

Stayin' Alive

"These—they're cool. Get some." Micah grabbed a shoe off the shelf and shoved it in Eric's face. Eric peered at the price inside the heel and put the shoe down. "My parents said they'll only pay half. I have to save the rest."

"So you're gonna wait?" Micah scoffed.

"I only have half of my half. Are *you* going to pay for them?"

Micah pointed at his own shoes. "How do you think I got these?" Eric shrugged. "I put them on and walked out." Micah started to rummage through the shoe boxes under the display. "What size you want?"

Eric grabbed Micah's arm to stop his digging. "What about my parents? I'd get three feet inside the house and they'd want to know where I got them."

"Your parents don't have to see them," Micah reasoned. "Stick them in your locker and change at school. You want the shoes or not?"

Read Romans 6:11–14

So when did you decide to ditch evil?

Some guy with biceps bigger than your head tries to drag you into a boxing ring to knock your block off. What's the best strategy to stay safe? (a) Throw a right jab and a left hook and hope you don't break your hand; (b) jump on the guy's back and attempt to tear his ear off; (c) bark like a seal to arouse pity; (d) stay out of the ring in the first place.

Smart choice.

Just before the passage you read, Paul says that all Christians have "died with Christ." When you became a Christian—whether that process was quick, slow, yesterday, or a long time ago—God acted in you. Christ died *for* your sin, but you also died *with* Christ *to* sin. You said "No!" to evil. Besides that, God brought you "from death to life." God raised you with Christ, forgiving you, wiping your conscience clean, giving you a heart that's alive toward him.

Here's the point: You died to sin—so stay dead. You committed yourself to following God—so grow in that commitment to him. You made up your mind back then to ditch evil—so keep it made up. You decided to get out of the ring—so stay out.

Do not offer the parts of your body to sin, as instruments of wickedness, but rather offer yourselves to God....
ROMANS 6:13

Being Good in a Bad World

You jab your friends. This is the best part of the movie. The alien being from Planet Zorgon is oozing out of town toward the mother ship, having eaten a quaint little town in southern Minnesota. The town's lone survivor rigs a nuclear photon ray bazooka from cornstalks and a rusty muffler—something he learned watching old MacGyver reruns. One shot and the alien explodes into a gazillion globs—until the sequel, anyway. You and your friends sigh and leave the theater, relieved that evil has been crushed. But after your eyes get used to the light outside, you realize your bikes are gone, ripped off during the movie.

In the real world, evil isn't terminated within the span of a movie. And sometimes you wonder if God cares at all about stopping evil.

Read Malachi 3:13—4:3

What does God promise you when it's tough being good in a bad world?

The people in the book of Malachi noticed the same things you see every day: cheaters getting A's, drug dealers getting rich, snotty girls getting all the trendy clothes and all the cute guys.

The believers survived by reminding one another that the success of bad people isn't the whole story. In God's judgment at the end of time, evildoers will be punished, but those who follow God will romp like frisky calves set free from their pen.

So it isn't that God doesn't notice wrongs or that he doesn't feel your pain. Just the opposite. That's why he sent Christ—to end evil, to give people a chance to turn to him. However, God is patient and holds off his scorching punishment (2 Peter 2:9; 3:9).

That doesn't mean you relax and tolerate evil. Change what you can in your life and all around you. Work together with peers and parents and authorities to confront larger evils like drugs and abortion and poverty. But when you feel overcome by evil, be patient. Remind yourself that God sees you. He won't forget your faithfulness.

But for you who revere my name, the sun of righteousness will rise with healing in its wings. And you will go out and leap like calves released from the stall. MALACHI 4:2

Bondservant of God

Shivering with fright in the corner of a closet, you wonder, *Will they find me?* Big men rip open the door and drag you out. They toss you in the back of a truck, then into a rough cargo plane for a jarring ride to a jungle hideout. Finally the men make it clear that either you will work long days in the hot sun or you will starve to death.

Attitude check: How glad would you be to serve your captors?

Read Exodus 21:1–7

Why would a slave ever choose to stay with his master?

In Bible times people sold themselves to pay back money they owed. Not long ago Africans were brutalized and forced to serve against their wills.

But Exodus 21 shows a whole different kind of slave, one who voluntarily said "no" to freedom so he could stay with his master. His master took the slave to a doorpost and pierced the slave's ear. (Don't try that at home. Your mom won't like a hole in the doorframe.) That pierced ear showed that the slave was forever his "bondservant," someone who serves a master because he *wants* to.

That's some wild devotion. But crazy? The bondservant didn't think so. He wanted to work hard for his master because he was thankful for what the master had given him—security, love, a family, food, a home.

Later in the Bible Paul proudly called himself a bondservant of Jesus Christ (check an example in Romans 1:1). Paul was so sure of God's love that he chose to obey God in every way he knew—with unflinching willingness and excitement. Paul knew that unlike human masters, God is a righteous and good master. God gives us "every good and perfect gift" (James 1:17), from life itself to his never-ending love.

God doesn't twist your arm to make you serve him. He never beats you into submission. He earns your respect, trust, and love. Once you're sure that God loves you and wants the best for you, then it's never crazy—or hard—to love him back.

His master must take him before the judges. He shall take him to the door or the doorpost and pierce his ear with an awl. Then he will be his servant for life. EXODUS 21:6

Swine Diving

Who knows—maybe it's the sugar. Or maybe it's your expectation that sugar sends you into warp drive. Either way, you think you're funny. Hilarious. When you and sugar get together, you're a legend in your own mind.

At your friend's party you didn't stop after the chocolate chip cookie dough and two liters of Mountain Dew. You tried to set a personal best for the number of sugar packets consumed in one sitting. You were close to beating the record when someone yelled, "SWINE DIVE!" and the whole party headed upstairs.

Over and over you oh-so-elegantly leapt off a dresser and belly flopped on the bed across the room. But when you tipped the dresser and the bed crashed through the frame to the floor, your friend's dad sent you home. He said enough was enough. You were out of control.

You said you weren't to blame. It was the sugar.

Read Proverbs 25:28
What good is self-control?

Getting a sugar buzz sure isn't the only way to lose control of yourself. A guy who misuses drugs has misplaced his brain. A girl who gets drunk and winds up in bed with a stranger loses her body—and maybe her health or her life.

Letting your emotions or hormones run wild can destroy you. When you lose self-control, you're like an ancient city with broken-down walls. You have no protection. You have no power over who comes in or who goes out or what they do.

God respects you enough to make *you* ultimately responsible for yourself. He gives you parents and teachers and other authorities to instruct and shape you. But in the end, you answer to God for yourself. Having authority over yourself is God's gift that allows you to follow him—not because you have to, but because you want to.

But you abuse God's gift whenever you surrender control of yourself to anything or anyone other than God. You might as well bind your hands, gag your mouth, and unplug your brain. If you don't control yourself, some other nasty thing will.

Like a city whose walls are broken down is a man who lacks self-control. PROVERBS 25:28

Hose Out Your Heart

Jeremy and his science partner both torched holes in their desks with Bunsen burners, but it wasn't Jeremy who got caught. "You're in charge, Jeremy," his teacher called out as he escorted Jeremy's pyro pal to the principal. Jeremy congratulated himself on his promotion to teacher. *Not bad.*

After school Jeremy scored points at a quickmart by turning in his brother for shoplifting three candy bars and a soda—for him. "Come back in a couple years and I'll give you a job, son," the manager said. Jeremy patted himself on the back. *Impressive.*

And that evening Jeremy's confirmation teacher frowned as she picked glass from the shattered classroom window. "We're going to sit here until someone claims responsibility," she scowled, "except for Jeremy. You may go." *I'm too good,* Jeremy thought as he exited class.

Read Matthew 23:25–28
What does God think of spiritual fakes?

The Bible doesn't blow smoke when it says that all of us sin (1 John 1:8). It makes equally clear that forgiveness is always and immediately available to us when we confess our wrongdoing to God (1 John 1:9). So being a Christian means we're in process. We're not perfect.

Yet Jesus had a huge problem with people who strained to look good on the outside while evil ran rampant on their insides. He called them "hypocrites," a word that comes from the masks worn by actors in ancient Greek theatres. Jesus aimed his harshest words at these fakes.

While ripping into the hypocrites, however, Jesus also offered a stunning dishwashing tip that explains how God remakes us. Our lives are like cups, and scrubbing the outside of a cup doesn't guarantee the inside is clean. But if we wash the inside, the outside sparkles as well.

Do you want a life where your outsides match your insides? Then let Jesus hose out your heart. You won't be perfect this side of heaven, but you won't be a hypocrite.

On the outside you appear to people as righteous but on the inside you are full of hypocrisy and wickedness.
MATTHEW 23:28

Bowser

Standing on a little hill across the street from school, Kim puffed a cigarette as Bus 93 pulled by. *Losers. They're all staring at me. I know it. I hope they like what they see.* Kim never took the bus with the kids from her neighborhood anymore. She walked early to hang with friends on the hill.

In elementary school kids called her "Crybaby Kimberly" because she wailed when nailed in dodgeball. And in middle school the boys twisted her last name, Bowers, into the nickname "Bowser," as in *woof, woof, doggie.* Kids picked on her because she always knew the answers, always finished on time, always did what she was supposed to do.

One day she decided she was tired of being so obnoxiously good. Kimberly the Pastel Priss transformed herself into Kim the chain-smoking, pot-puffing, attitude-spewing Makeup Monster.

Read Galatians 6:9
What do you do when you're sick of being good?

You don't know if you can hold out any longer. *I should get suspended so I fit in better. If I do too well I'll get called a "brain." If I laugh at their jokes they'll like me. If I answer teachers' questions kids will think I'm a kiss-up.* So you give up and give in.

But being bad and being obnoxiously good aren't your only options. You can choose to be good God's way.

You're obnoxiously good if you remind people how good you are. Or if you do good to make others look bad. Or if you live to keep rules instead of keeping rules to live.

Being good God's way is an altered attitude and approach. You choose God's way because you trust that sooner or later it leads to life. You do what's right quietly and steadily because you believe God's promise that good behavior has good results.

God commands you to do good not to wreck life but to give life. Being bad is tossing your life away. Being obnoxiously good is asking to be boring and friendless. Being good—being obedient God's way—is getting set for God's best.

Let us not become weary in doing good, for at the proper time we will reap a harvest if we do not give up. GALATIANS 6:9

Invisibility

Mary couldn't recall how long she had been invisible. There were moments, of course, when people saw *parts* of her—bad parts, usually. Like the day Mary caused shrieks at school when kids saw a faceless nose topped by a gigantic zit floating through the hall.

Sometimes teachers saw her hand raised in class, usually after she scored well on a test. The teachers wondered how a hand could wave without being connected to a body. They didn't wonder long. After a couple days the hand faded from their sight.

And once Mary was eating in the cafeteria at a table full of people, though no one knew she was there. She was leaning forward on her chair when the chair shot out from under her and skidded across the lunchroom. Mary splattered on the floor, and for a split second *everyone* saw her.

Midyear Mary and her family moved. Her old school transferred the records requested by her new school, teachers crossed her name off class lists, and another student took over her locker to be closer to friends. But no one at school could remember what the kid who had moved away looked like.

Read Psalm 25:16–21
What hope do you have when you feel lonely?

God didn't design you to float through life alone. He created you to be friends with other people and with himself. He built you a brain, injected feelings, placed you in a horde of humans instead of sending you out to live solo, and set you loose to help and be helped by others and to worship him. Everything about the way God made you shows that he destined you to know and love him and others.

But there's a problem. While God made us for outrageously intense friendships, we've messed up. We've strained our relationships with both God and people. That's why at times everybody feels like Mary—invisible, distant, and friendless.

When you feel alone, God hears your every cry. And he has a plan to usher you into the friendships he designed for you to enjoy. He wants to show you how to be a friend worth having—and find friends who count.

Turn to me and have mercy on me, because I am lonely and hurting. PSALM 25:16 NCV

Rolling Boulder Test

You knew you were in trouble when Kris, Shelly, and Kathy interrupted your lunch. "We have a simple test," Kris announced with a strange grin. "If a boulder the size of a house were rolling down a hill and was about to kill all three of us—and if you could save only one of us—who would it be?"

You think, *Hmmm ... that's not so hard. I could live without Shelly.* But you're not stupid. *This is a trap. Two of them will hate me. And the one I save will think I'm a jerk for letting the other two get squished.* You're not so sure that saving someone from a boulder is what friendship is really about, but the threesome isn't looking for a philosophical discussion. So you stall for time. "Ah, could you rephrase the question?" you ask.

Read 1 John 3:11–16
How do we know what love is like?

Life without friendship is like life without air. That's why you feel as if your umbilical cord has been cut when you can't IM or use the phone. It's why being grounded is no fun. It explains why you feel awful when you eat lunch alone or when everyone seems paired off and you're not, and why the first thing you do when you enter a classroom is look around to see who you know. It's true: Next to knowing God, having good human relationships is the most important thing in the world (Matthew 22:35–39).

If you belong to God, it changes how you treat people. In fact, love is the big test of whether or not you know God (1 John 4:7–8).

Love is only love when it's demonstrated in real life. You don't get many chances to be a hero. You do get chances every day to love in less showy ways—chances to be kind, to encourage, to admit you're wrong, or to halt jealousy, lust, anger, and selfishness.

Jesus' death passed the true-life friendship test. That mushy promise to save a friend from a rock that will never roll? Not a chance.

This is how we know what love is: Jesus Christ laid down his life for us. And we ought to lay down our lives for our brothers.
1 JOHN 3:16

Friend-O-Rama!

You're not a kid anymore. And your life is like an all-school rummage sale. Just like stuff you lived with for so long—toys, clothes, games, vacation souvenirs, whatever—old friends go on the table cheap. A few are hard to part with, but you figure you can buy better stuff from another table.

Some friends, after all, don't fit anymore. They've shrunk to gossiping and nastiness, and you've outgrown that. Others resemble clothes you never wear—nothing wrong with them but your tastes have changed. A few friends, like most garage sale items, are boring and broken—like childhood buddies you played Barbies or baseball with who now toy with cigarettes and beer, or worse.

At a rummage sale it's not always easy to know what to sell and what to keep—or, if you're buying, what's a bargain and what's a rip-off. It's the same way when you're shopping for friends.

Read Philippians 2:19–24
What kind of friends should you hunt for?

Paul didn't make the Christians in the city of Philippi go garage-sale shopping for a high-quality friend. He crated up his buddy Timothy and shipped him off. Well, he probably didn't put Tim in a box. But he did want to send his friend Timothy to meet his great friends in Philippi.

Timothy was a rare friend. While everyone else was worried only about their own lives and interests, what mattered most to Timothy was doing what Christ wanted.

You don't need friends who make evil attractive to you—friends who like you when you do wrong. You don't need people who tell you that you're comical when you drink or that you look grown-up when you have a joint hanging off your lip. You want friends who are totally devoted to God and who totally want you close to him.

The nearer you get to being an adult the less your new friends will have to do with where you live or a school seating chart—and more to do with interests you share, like sports, music, clothes, school subjects, or hobbies. When you go shopping for friends, the ones who are interested in God are your best buy.

For everyone looks out for his own interests, not those of Jesus Christ. PHILIPPIANS 2:21

Think Small to Think Big

Alisha elbowed Bill. "Isn't that the boy who moved in across the street from you?" The guy she pointed out moped all alone down the hallway at school. He didn't look at anyone—he looked afraid.

"I guess so," Bill answered. "He was at the bus stop this morning. He sat a couple seats away from me—would you quit looking over there? He'll see us." He turned the other way so the new kid wouldn't spot him.

Alisha glared at Bill. "You're pathetic. I'm going to go say hi and welcome him to school."

"Just leave him alone," Bill argued. "I'm sure he'll make friends. He's fine. He has to fend for himself like everyone else."

Bill pulled at Alisha when she started to head in the new kid's direction. "Let's *go*," Bill begged. "He'll think I want to be his best friend or something."

Read Mark 9:30–32

What does it mean to be "like Christ" in how you treat people?

Why are you here on planet earth? To consume oxygen? To master video games? To inhale the contents of your parents' refrigerator? To rule the world?

Think bigger. You're here to become like Christ (2 Corinthians 3:18). You're destined to do the things he did (Ephesians 2:10). You're here to be a servant like your Master (Mark 9:35). But what does *that* look like?

As his death on the cross loomed only days away, Jesus bluntly told his disciples that he was about to suffer and die. They didn't get it. They thought that Jesus would rule the world and crush the opposition. They thought that being his follower meant ruling with him and squishing people they detested. They didn't understand that being like Jesus means laying down your life.

Jesus-style servanthood is putting your love into action for all people. Like little siblings. And enemies. And losers. People you know and people you don't. And sometimes your acts of servanthood cost you everything.

The Son of Man is going to be betrayed into the hands of men. They will kill him, and after three days he will rise. MARK 9:31

Redo Your Attitude

Michelle rolled over, glanced at the clock, groaned, and bolted out of bed. *Not again!* She had eight minutes to master a disaster. Nothing clean to wear—everything was in the washer, sopping wet. She pulled her wangy sleep hair into a ponytail and tugged on a baseball cap.

A sprint to the bus stop saved her a long, late walk to school, and she dropped panting into the first open seat. Bad choice. Kaytlin smiled sweetly at Michelle. "Sleep through your alarm again, Shelly?" she inquired. "That's twice this week, isn't it?"

Kaytlin had once loaned a stack of teen magazines to Michelle. Michelle toiled to follow their beauty tips, but it was like trying to follow a blueprint to build a bomber. And today Michelle once again felt woefully average. She dreamed what it would be like to have Kaytlin's flawless face and bikini body. She wanted plastic surgery on her life.

Read Titus 3:3–8
How do you put a stop to jealousy?

Miss Americas claw and whine to get their own talk shows, and Super Bowl winners turn into armchair-quarterbacking couch potatoes. Jealousy doesn't end when you get what someone else has, because you'll always find someone else who still has more.

Your only hope is to be happy with what *you* have.

God doesn't do plastic surgery to make you into someone else. He does a heart transplant to redo your attitude. Paul told Titus that before we know God, we're wrapped up in malice (a desire to harm or spite others) and envy (unhappiness at what someone else has or can do). Yet when we accept God's kindness we begin to see we have everything we need most—God's acceptance, his forgiveness, the promise of living in eternal paradise with God, and friendship right now with his Holy Spirit.

Compared to that, the stuff that others have—that we don't—is nothing.

We lived in malice and envy, being hated and hating one another. But when the kindness and love of God our Savior appeared, he saved us.... TITUS 3:3-5

Bragging Rights

"Strike three! That's the game!" the umpire hollered. Runners trotted in from first and third, and the scorekeeper recorded another loss for the Panthers. "You're out, son," the ump said a bit more gently as Troy stood stuck in the batter's box, still trying to figure out what had blown by him. "Next time."

Troy was barely out of the box when David pounced on him. "You whiffed! You always whiff! You lost the game!"

"Me? I wasn't the only one who got out," Troy shot back.

"But you're a loser. Almost the whole team is a bunch of losers. I don't know why I play on this team. I hit, I run, I score—then you whiff."

Jake joined David in walloping Troy, and others trotted over to see what the noise was about. "The two of us," Jake bragged, "could beat the rest of you put together."

Read Jeremiah 9:23–24
When is it okay to brag?

You can argue with a friend about who's taller. But you both look short next to the starting center for the Lakers. You can debate who's smarter, but Einstein wouldn't have asked either of you for help with his homework. Likewise, God reminds us that next to him we don't measure up. "To whom will you compare me?" God asks in Isaiah 40:25, "Or who is my equal?"

God's goal isn't to pound us into the ground like a kid hunting ants with a baseball bat. Here's his point: The things we brag about are imperfect, powerless, and broken down. It's silly to feel overly proud of brains that leak, beauty that gets baggy, muscles that go flabby, and money that whooshes down the drain in ways we can't predict.

It's right to enjoy the good things God gives us. Even so, our confidence and security is God himself—not some nasty brute of a God, but One perfect in kindness and goodness. God is "righteous in all his ways and loving toward all he has made" (Psalm 145:17).

And having a friend like that *is* something worth bragging about.

Let him who boasts boast about this: that he understands and knows me, that I am the LORD.
JEREMIAH 9:24

Don't Apologize for You

"That isn't the Little Dipper. It's *those*," Jamie argued. "Over *there*."

"Actually, it's that set of stars up there," Eileen said quietly. "See the handle? And the dipper?" Eileen was surprised. *They didn't laugh at me.* Dazzled by the night sky outside the city, kids on the church retreat actually seemed to listen to her. So Eileen pointed out other constellations. Then Mars and Jupiter. One of the kids, though, said she was making stuff up. Eileen got quiet again.

"Ignore him," one of the adult leaders advised. Then he asked how she knew so much. Eileen never told anyone she was into astronomy because it would only make her feel even more like an alien. She didn't care about clothes, got bored putting on makeup, and thought most boys needed to grow up. But this time she let some of her enthusiasm out. The leader thought Eileen should bring her telescope on the next retreat.

Maybe she would.

Read Psalm 138
How can you learn to be bold about who you are?

"Different" probably isn't high on your list of what you want to be when you grow up. You might like someone no one else likes, so you pretend to like a popular person who really makes you retch. Or you know that people are about to bad-mouth your music or your hobbies, so you slam them before they slam you. True, sometimes it's socially acceptable to be strange—but only if the crowd says so.

That's what the "gods" and "goddesses" around you think. But God has some amazing news about who you are.

You are the work of God's hands—and he won't abandon you. He made you unique—and he will show you his purpose for you. His heart is with you wherever you go—and when you ask for help, he will make you bold.

God delights in nothing more than seeing you live as the masterpiece he made you (Ephesians 2:10). He is worth praising for how he designed you—no matter what others think. When you're shy about revealing the real you, he is your source of power to crack out of your shell.

*When I called, you answered me; you made me bold
and stouthearted.* PSALM 138:3

Don't Roll Over, Rover

Sabina knew something was wrong as soon as she picked up her book bag. *This is too light*, she thought. She kicked herself for forgetting her homework. But it took Sabina only a few seconds to recall she *had* put her homework in the bag.

Someone's been in my stuff. Fumbling to unzip her bag, she dumped it upside down. Only two library books fell out—none of her spiral notebooks. Worst of all, her typed-up oral report and all the notes she used to put it together were gone.

The next day Mr. Grady wouldn't buy Sabina's story about a stolen paper— even when a girl named Jessica stood up and read Sabina's report, word for word. With all her notes and everything gone, Sabina had no way to prove Jessica had read *her* paper.

Sabina was dead.

Read 1 Peter 4:8

Do you have to roll over and play dead after someone hurts you?

When someone does you wrong, it's natural to moan to your friends. It's simple to start a rumor. You long to let loose the Dobermans.

Jesus gave you a better way to confront wrong. He said to start by talking to the person who hurt you. If getting face-to-face doesn't resolve the situation, take someone with you to back up what you say. And if that doesn't work you can appeal to people in authority like parents, teachers, principals, or pastors (Matthew 18:15–17).

However those tactics turn out, there's one more step to take. When you've done all you can do to set a situation straight, it's time to let love "cover" the wrongs you have suffered.

To cover a pile of sins doesn't mean act like wrongs never happened, or Jesus would never have given you that script for fighting wrongs. But it does mean you forgive others as God has forgiven you (Colossians 3:13). You quit broadcasting blame (Proverbs 17:9). You do your best to live at peace (Romans 12:16).

You don't have to roll over when someone wrongs you. But you do need to call off the Dobermans.

Above all, love each other deeply, because love covers over a multitude of sins. 1 PETER 4:8

Right Place, Right Time

Chad joked with a clump of friends as they waited to buy movie tickets. When a group of guys from church walked up and spotted him, they looked less than jovial. They seemed to be watching him.

Sitting in the movie, Chad couldn't figure out why his Christian friends were irate. He couldn't do everything with them. And he wasn't sneaking into some ghastly movie he shouldn't see. In fact, Chad knew his parents would never let him see the movie his Christian friends headed into.

When Chad darted out to get a bucket of popcorn, one of his church friends followed him to the lobby. Jake pounced on him. "What are you doing with those guys?"

"They're my friends from down the block," Chad explained.

Jake wasn't convinced. "You shouldn't hang around with them. They're going to ruin you. You're going to turn into one of them."

Read Luke 15:1–2
Should Christians have non-Christian friends?

You'd know you were in the wrong place at the wrong time with the wrong crowd if cops busted down the doors and shot in tear gas.

People and places and situations don't have to be so unmistakably evil to be just as risky. The Bible, for example, makes clear that Christians shouldn't be "unequally yoked," roped together with non-Christians. Clinging totally to people cold toward God sooner or later will keep you from obeying God (2 Corinthians 6:14).

But that doesn't mean you should run and hide from non-Christians. When the Pharisees criticized Jesus for spending time with sinners—including the lowest life-form of that society, tax collectors—Jesus retorted that he was like a doctor rushing to help the wounded and dying.

Jesus went where he was needed most. He wasn't making an excuse to have out-of-bounds fun. His goal was to invite people to meet God. What's yours?

The Pharisees and the teachers of the law muttered, "This man welcomes sinners and eats with them." LUKE 15:2

O Play-Doh Day

Oh noooooo! Not again!

Splat. A fist slams you, shimmies and squooshes you this way and that, rolling you into a ball.

Oh noooooo! Not that!

It's intense tucked inside the Play-Doh press. Tiny holes dead ahead!

Oh noooooo! Not the stringy thingy!

You struggle uselessly as you're forced through itty-bitty holes, shredded into a dozen strands—one big-time split personality, not to mention the splitting headache.

You're pinched and pressed and sliced with a plastic knife. You've been turned into hair and plastered onto a Play-Doh dog.

Read Galatians 1:3–12
When is it worst to give in to peer fear?

You don't live in this world by yourself. It's crowded. You bump people. They shove you. They gang up and squish you. You inevitably get molded into a new shape.

So? You've heard that before. Parents, teachers, and dim TV commercials have been telling you since you were two that peers can crush you.

But peer pressure isn't all bad. If it weren't for peer fear, you'd still pick your nose in public. You can't live isolated from your peers, and a lot of times it's fine to fit in. A true nerd is someone who lives in a wee little world, clueless of when it's *okay* to conform.

Yet you can never be all that your peers want you to be. In one area—your faith as a Christian—it's never right to be squashed by the forces that surround you. The facts that Christ died and rose for you, forgives you, and deserves total obedience aren't ideas open for negotiation. You don't swap them to win points with people.

Sometimes you can act, talk, dress, and think in a way that is wonderful both to God and people. Other times you can't. It's a choice. But it's no contest whose opinion matters more.

Am I now trying to win the approval of men, or of God? Or am I trying to please men? If I were still trying to please men, I would not be a servant of Christ. GALATIANS 1:10

Cable Surfing All Alone

There wasn't even anything on TV. A hundred and sixty-two cable stations, and Nina's best choices were a demo of the lesser-known features of spreadsheet software, a shopping network hawking ceramic kittens, and a local-access rerun of a third-grade boys' basketball game.

Nina agreed with her parents that her school's dances weren't the best place to be. She'd been there. She'd seen what went on. So she didn't go. Normally she didn't feel left out because she always found something else to do. This time her friends weren't around, her dad was away on business, and her mom was busy with Nina's sick little brother.

So at seven o'clock that evening when the dance was starting, Nina curled up on her bed and stared at the wall, imagining the fun she was missing.

Read Psalm 1:1–6

What does God promise you when you feel like a reject because of him?

Some days you might feel like a tree stuck by your lonesome on the prairie, bent by the wind, scraggly for lack of water. No one lops a gushing hose at your roots. No one trims you to look like a giraffe or a flamingo. You fear you're going to lose your leaves, shrivel up, then tumble away in the wind.

You may have convinced yourself that's what you are. Or you might worry that's what you'll become if you refuse to wallow with the wicked or saddle up with sinners or mesh with those who mock God. Your imagination roars with all the fun you'll miss.

It's time to remember reality. You're not the one who needs to worry about wilting. Here's what God promises his people: They drink from God's streams. They sprout fruit. They stand in God's presence. God watches over every detail of their lives. And here's what happens to those who distance themselves from God: They lack roots—no water, no food, no life. They're dried-out "chaff" (the husks left over from threshing wheat). They're blown away in the hurricane of God's judgment. It doesn't sound like you're missing much.

Blessed is the man who does not walk in the counsel of the wicked or stand in the way of sinners or sit in the seat of mockers. PSALM 1:1

You Make Me Gag

Megan gagged when her new science partner walked up and bobbed her hair from side to side. "I was, like, so glad when I found out you were my partner, ooh yeah!" Felicia twirped. "Like, I was gonna flunk if I hadn't gotten paired up with *you*. Everyone knows that you have a brain, you know."

Each day Megan slaved over the Bunsen burner while Felicia giggled with her friends at another table. Felicia explained that helping would mean wearing goggles, and that wearing goggles would necessitate major hair repair—which was out of the question. So Megan was stuck. If she didn't do the work, she and Felicia would be partners again at summer school.

Read Matthew 18:15–17

What can Christians do when someone treats them badly?

Christians are supposed to "turn the other cheek," aren't they? Yep, Jesus himself spoke those familiar words (Matthew 5:38–39). But Jesus was talking about not taking tooth-for-tooth revenge—like shattering a rack of test tubes over Felicia's head. He never said you shouldn't work to solve problems.

If you've given a wrongdoer the same room to be imperfect that you give yourself, and you still find a wrong too big to just let go, Jesus says to tell the person directly. That takes a brave heart and gentle words. It's harder than moaning about the problem or gossiping, but it's also more effective, especially if you're also ready to repair any wrongs you might have done.

If speaking to the person doesn't work, Jesus gives further steps—like taking a friend or two with you, not to gang up on the person but to back up your accusations. After you've done your best with the first two steps, you can go to your pastor (or a teacher or parent or someone in authority) for help.

Jesus' solution squashes whining, stewing, tattling, bashing, and behind-the-back complaining. It's also realistic: You can't fix every problem, and—as a last resort—sometimes you need to avoid people who mistreat you.

If your brother sins against you, go and show him his fault, just between the two of you. If he listens to you, you have won your brother over. MATTHEW 18:15

Girlyman

Nick wasn't trying to be mean on purpose. As he watched a game-winning soccer goal thump in the net, he boiled so bad that he exploded. "You clod! How could you have let the ball by?" he screamed at Chris. "At least we would have gone into overtime if it weren't for you. And Blake! He could have stopped the ball back at midfield. I thought Blake was the only girlyman on the team. I guess there are two."

KaBOOM. Chris walked away, trying not to cough from the smoke of the explosion. (Real men don't cough.) When Nick turned to go, he nearly tripped over Blake. He had heard it all. He was holding back a cough too.

Read 1 Peter 5:5
What can you do to put friendship back together when you've blown it apart?

When you fight with a friend it's like you've dynamited a pit—but not before you jumped in too.

Still, you might wonder why you need to repair the damage when you've hit, bit, spat upon, betrayed, cheated, lied to, gossiped about, or otherwise hurt someone around you.

For starters, fighting leaves you friendless, and it gets lonely in the pit you've dug. And there's another huge reason. You have been accepted by Christ, flaws and all. As Christians, we need to accept others the same way God accepted us (Romans 15:7).

Peter points out your only good way out of the pit. It's humility.

The first foothold in putting humility into practice is asking forgiveness from God (1 John 1:9) and from the one you hurt (Matthew 5:23–24). You could avoid the problem, pretending you did nothing wrong. But if you never admit your wrong, you only dig deeper into the pit.

There's a bunch more footholds that let you climb out of the pit little by little: See a situation through others' eyes. Deflate your big head. Remember others' needs, not just your own. Change how you act.

When you do those things, your friends just might see your humility. They might even help you out of the pit.

All of you, clothe yourselves with humility toward one another, because, "God opposes the proud but gives grace to the humble."
1 PETER 5:5

Over the Edge

"I'm going over. It looks like fun." With that your friend climbs over the edge of a cliff—a brainless, stupid stunt—bungee-jumping without the bungee. Within a second she's headed for the bottom of a gorge unless you do something.

You throw her a rope. What do you do next? Do you (a) let go of the rope and yell, "Hasta la bye-bye"; (b) heroically wedge yourself into a tree and pray you don't get rope burn; (c) run to your youth group and preach a sermon detailing your friend's stupidity; or (d) tie the rope to an enormous rock and find some people to help you pull your friend to safety?

You can't help but notice friends and classmates jumping over spiritual, moral, and emotional cliffs—they quit church, drink, do drugs, shoplift, become sexually active, or just waste away. But what can you do about it?

Read Galatians 6:1–2
How can you help hurting friends?

Abandoning friends isn't cool. You've got a relationship—a rope attached to your friend. Galatians says we should try to pull people back up by helping carry their burdens. (The word for "burdens" in verse two means a load too big for one person to lift.)

But helping friends out of danger is tricky. They may need more help than you alone can provide—like with depression or substance abuse. And being a helper often puts you in danger. If your friends' problems are moral or spiritual, you could fall over the same cliff. Just when you think your spiritual heft will keep you anchored on top of the cliff, that's the moment their weight will *fwang* you over the edge (1 Corinthians 10:12).

Any choice but (d) is unwise. You've got an unbudgeable Rock to which you can anchor your fallen friends: Christ. Pray for them. Ask God to help you to encourage, persuade, and befriend, and to know how to model faith for the person who needs more of Jesus.

And find help. Rescuing your friends single-handedly may seem heroic, but it's stupid. You don't get a second chance if your friends smack the bottom of the gorge—and take you with them.

Brothers, if someone is caught in a sin, you who are spiritual
should restore him gently. But watch yourself, or you
also may be tempted. GALATIANS 6:1

Dear—or Dork?

Radar sweeps the horizon. *Zzzt. Zzzt. Zzzt.* Beautiful girl at two o'clock, floating through the lunchroom. She looks good—she looks fine—as she gets into the line. Every guy at the table notices her, but no one knows her name. She's a UFO (Unidentified Female Object). Guys dare each other to talk to the babe o' de day.

Meanwhile, at another table, girls have their turn. Fresh from study hall, Amanda eagerly reports on Josh Hormone. "His smile is so cute!" Amanda squeals. "He even said hi to me. He's so nice." Hearts go *pa-thump, pa-thump, pa-thump*, and the girls conclude that Josh is everything a girl could want in a guy—friendly, funny, considerate, and a hunk.

Read 1 Corinthians 13:4–7
What qualities should you look for in a guy or a girl?

When you go deer hunting you make sure you know what you're looking at before you take aim. *I heard something ... over there ... the bush moved. BLAM BLAM* isn't good strategy. Only after you kill something would you know what you hit—maybe a deer, maybe a bear, maybe a tree, maybe your hunting partner.

The same is true for hunting guys or girls. Don't aim your heart at someone you're not sure you want to hit. And it does matter who you set your sights on now. The kind of person you get crushes on becomes the kind of person you want to date. And the one you date becomes the kind of person you want to spend your life with.

The "Love Chapter" of the Bible—1 Corinthians 13—tells what to hunt for in a guy or girl: patience, kindness, humility, good manners, unselfishness, an even temper. You want to aim at someone who forgives, who does right, and who never stops wanting God's best for you and your relationship. That describes someone totally devoted to Christ. That's your target. Don't waste your love ammo on anything less.

And you can't spot those qualities from across the lunchroom or from a syllable and a smile in study hall. You have to watch for a long time to know for sure whether you're aiming at a dear...or a dork.

Love does not delight in evil but rejoices with the truth.
1 CORINTHIANS 13:6

Bladder Buster

The movie was about half over when you felt a tiny jab. You decided, *I can wait. I can make it.* But later—with a half hour of movie left—there's no ignoring the pressure. You try not to think about the two-liter bladder buster you guzzled before the movie started.

You cross your legs and uncross them. You try to relax. Your back screams pain and your feet tap-dance.

You lose it.

Wrong time. Wrong place. And if you had been more careful about what you had to drink, you would have been able to wait.

Read Genesis 2:19–25

Why is marriage a big deal?

Way back at the beginning of time, God watched Adam in the Garden of Eden. Even though Adam had a zooful of friends, God knew that being alone was a bad deal for Adam. So God made Adam someone he would stick with forever, sharing life at the deepest level of both body and soul.

Marriage is the same big deal now. It's a man-and-woman promise in front of God to love each other for the rest of life. To couples who commit themselves to that unending friendship with each other, God gives an incredible wedding present: the gift of sexual love. Hebrews 13:4 says, "Marriage should be honored by all, and the marriage bed kept pure."

To keep marriage pure means to save sex and the things that lead up to it for God's time and place. Your body and emotions get more and more impatient, though, as you get older. So if you're going to follow God's best for your life—if you're going to wait for sexual love until marriage—you can't be dumb about what you take into your life right now. Movies, videos, music, pornography, dirty jokes, starting to date, daydreaming, giving a friend even a casual kiss—all these things add to the pressure you feel.

Some of those things are sips. Some are gallon gulps of poison. All add up. Yet you have a choice about what you drink—what you look at, listen to, and think about. It's better to watch what you drink than to wait in misery or to lose it all.

The man said, "This is now bone of my bones and flesh of my flesh." GENESIS 2:23

Which Row to Hoe

Jason and Amy met in Mr. Hoff's social studies class. It was a magical combination. Jason was funny, Amy was shy, and Mr. Hoff was nearsighted and hard of hearing, so he couldn't see or hear them sitting next to each other in the back of the room. Jason and Amy wrote notes, whispered, and laughed all semester.

Jason wasn't a Christian and Amy was, but Amy liked Jason because he paid attention to her. He said she was pretty. She couldn't understand why he hung out with the people he did—they looked kind of wild—but...

What do you think of Jason and Amy's relationship?

Make no mistake: Jesus told Christians to reach out and enlarge God's family, and that only happens if you make friends with non-Christians. Yet getting entangled with non-Christians can trip you up.

Read 2 Corinthians 6:14–7:1
Are guy-girl relationships between Christians and non-Christians a hot idea?

A tug-of-war starts when a Christian is "yoked" to an unbeliever, lashed together like two horses joined to plow a field. Two things can happen. You can fight about how and where to plow (and rip each other's heads off), or you can give in and let the non-Christian drag you down a row where you shouldn't go. (Forcing a non-Christian to go down your row isn't an option. Jesus doesn't *make* us come to him. He invites us.)

Going together, being best friends, dating, or marrying are all relationships that yoke. But other things can yoke you too. Sports teams, jobs, clubs, or activities that demand total commitment can also control you in a bad way.

No non-Christian will join with you completely in living your faith—in belonging to God and making him the most important thing in your life. You won't head toward the same goals and standards. God wants your closest friends to be ones you can pull together with to know and follow him better.

For what do righteousness and wickedness have in common? Or what fellowship can light have with darkness? What does a believer have in common with an unbeliever?

2 CORINTHIANS 6:14–15

In This Corner

Jake hated baby-sitting his younger brother and sister. Tuesday was always grocery day, and once again Jake's mom reminded him to come straight home from school so she could run to the store. At lunch, Jake's friends had other after-school plans—nothing big, just playing basketball—and they bugged him about going home to play Mommy.

That afternoon Jake's mind bounced back and forth: *Go. Don't go. Go. Don't go.* It would have gone on forever—except that the last bell rang and his friends were leaving. He had to decide.

Being stuck between friends and parents is a boxing match—friends in one corner, parents in another. At the bell they dance out of their corners. But they don't fight each other. They come after *you:* Listen to parents, and some friends sock you. Listen to the wrong friends, and parents rampage.

Read Proverbs 1:8–19

What big bad influences does the father warn his son against?

The bad guys in Proverbs wanted the son to help ambush an innocent man. Jake's friends wanted him to shoot hoops, not humans, but they still encouraged him to do something wrong by breaking his mom's trust. Friends, enemies, and everyone in between can pressure you the same way. They try to tell you how to talk, think, feel, and act. Sometimes what they suggest doesn't agree with what your parents expect.

Like Jake and the son listening to his dad in Proverbs, you need to figure out what's true and right—what's really best for you. The "sinners" offered the son easy-to-grasp stuff: membership in their group and part of the plunder, enough to meet any need. Your peers might promise big pay-offs too: immediate popularity, excitement, or adventure. Parents argue that it's really a sucker punch—a wallop that catches you by surprise when you're not looking.

Who's right? What's best? You're in the middle of the boxing ring and both sides are coming at you. It's time to think hard about your parents and the job God gives them.

My son, if sinners entice you, do not give in to them.
PROVERBS 1:10

From Mars With Love

Suspicions bubble inside your brain the first time you flip through your parents' high school yearbooks and see all those pointy heads and spaced-out faces. Your parents, you notice, aren't the only ones who looked like Martians. So did most of their classmates.

You brace yourself. *My parents were part of a massive alien invasion.*

Your theory explains a lot. You've always wondered why your parents argue about the pros and cons of various warp drives when they watch *Star Trek.* You've got answers to your truly deep life questions—like why hair sprouts in your dad's nose and why your mom constantly fibs about her age and moans about her weight. *If she were back on Mars*, you calculate, *she'd be 47 percent younger—and tons lighter!* Only one question still begs for an answer—how your parents could pilot a flying saucer forty million miles but not grasp how to set the clock on the VCR.

Read Psalm 68:6

What's God's plan for you to get along in your family?

It's weird. You can be in the middle of a perfectly normal conversation with your parents when suddenly you're sucked into a Martian Moment, a throbbing instant when their utter weirdness convinces you they're from another planet.

But if your parents are Martians, what does that make you? You're a chip off the old planetoid. When your parents blurt, "You'll understand when you have kids," you actually get what they mean—sometimes. There's a lot of them in you and a lot of you in them. You'll probably be a parent someday. And your parents definitely were once kids—although it may have been long ago in a distant galaxy.

You're not as alien to one another as you might think.

God knows exactly where your parents came from. He wants to help you figure out how to get along when they're around. And he wants to teach you to follow him when they're not.

God sets the lonely in families, he leads forth the prisoners with singing; but the rebellious live in a sun-scorched land.

PSALM 68:6

The Parental Mind

Attempt to understand your parents and you may feel as if you're at the helm of a galactic starship blasting into an uncharted sector of the universe. Intelligence reports show no known intelligence. Other explorers, you have heard, have died trying to squeeze their vessels into so tiny a space. Contrary to all previous data, however, you discover the mind of your parents isn't empty. Actually, it's bigger than it looks from the outside, and you bump into quite a bit of stuff once you figure a way in.

Lots of days your parents are pretty okay. You may wonder, at other times, if your parents have anything at all in their heads besides a slow computer program with one command: MAKE CHILD MISERABLE.

That's not wholly wrong. The truth is that your parents *are* programmed at the factory to follow one command.

Read Proverbs 22:6
What job does God give to parents?

Parents understand that they have one goal: to help their child become an adult who can survive and thrive on his or her own. They aim to move their child from dirtying diapers to changing them, from spending money to earning it, from being mothered to being a mom or a dad. All parents have that programmed into their brains—and you do too, as you'll discover when you have kids. Even more than that, Christian parents understand that training a kid in "the way he should go" ultimately means raising that child to follow Christ in every area of life.

That one job has countless duties. God expects parents to
protect their children (Hebrews 11:24),
provide for them (1 Timothy 5:8), and
discipline them (Hebrews 12:7, 11).

Besides that, he expects all parents to love him and teach their children to do the same (Deuteronomy 6:5–7).

Those four assignments alone probably make you nervous. But that's because *you* are programmed to want to grow up and survive on your own.

That's what makes the voyage so interesting.

Train a child in the way he should go, and when he is old he will not turn from it. PROVERBS 22:6

Waiting Up

Picture this: Jennifer's parents are anxiously waiting for her to walk through the door. *She was supposed to be home an hour ago. Where is she? Jenni always calls if she's late. We shouldn't have let her go with Sharon.*

Now answer this: When Jennifer gets home, sees the lights on, and finds her dad pacing the living room and her mom nervously stuffing herself with chips, how will she react? If she had been home on time, she might have thought their waiting up was cute and comforting. Tonight, though, she'll probably get angry when her parents ask why she was late.

Parents are people who wait up for you to make sure you get home safely. They're the ones who keep the lights on. But you don't always like the lights shining bright. Some days, in fact, you want to turn your parents on and off like a light switch. You want them on when you can use them, and you want them off when they're a hassle.

Read Ephesians 6:1–3
What does it mean to "honor your parents"?

No doubt your parents will embarrass you at times. Your dad might wear his white T-shirt, Hawaiian shorts, dark socks, and dress shoes to a school event. Other times they'll make you angry. But you've done the same to your parents. Think back to the time you barfed on the check-out stand at the supermarket or when the police brought you home for throwing rocks at cars. Your parents didn't stop caring for you. They kept the lights on.

Honor is a lot like the way you treat your parents when you want something from them. You show respect. You hear their side. You obey. But there's a world of difference between wanting to honor and just wanting something your parents can provide. Honoring your parents is acting kind out of thankfulness, with no expectation of a payoff.

Parents deserve nothing less than that honor, even when you disagree or they embarrass you. And as you learn to show them honor day after day, they will learn to trust you enough to not wait up. Or at least they'll pretend to go to sleep. They've kept the lights on for you. Don't shut the lights off on them.

Children, obey your parents in the Lord, for this is right.
EPHESIANS 6:1

Nuttin' Like a Hound Dog

All Jamal wanted to do was hang out with some friends. All his dad wanted to know was what they would be doing. "You never trust me!" Jamal yelled. When his dad told him to go to his room because he was grounded for the weekend, Jamal just glared at him. Then he grabbed his jacket and headed out the door.

Jamal was right. His parents don't trust him.

But he didn't spot something else. He doesn't trust his parents. Once he thought his parents knew everything. Now he calls them idiots. Once he thought they were caring. Now he says they're snoops.

Read Proverbs 4:3–4
Do parents know anything about anything?

It's normal for your gut to churn when your parents start with "I expect you to..." or "You'd better not..." or "When I was your age...." But get this: Parents know *lots* about, well, *lots of things.* And they know *something* about *pretty much everything.* Most parents are more than happy to spout advice. But what do you do when that advice sprays all over you?

Trust is when you believe that (1) your parents have wisdom you can learn from; (2) they want what's best for you; and (3) God uses your parents to guide you. Trust means hearing and obeying your parents even when you're convinced you're right and they're wrong.

When you trust your parents enough to obey, an amazing thing happens. In time you gain more freedom than you ever imagined. Your parents will notice you don't need a leash to control you.

If you don't trust your parents, you're like a rabid animal. Ignoring your parents' advice so you can make your own mistakes makes you like a dog that needs to be tied up–not the mature young adult you want to be. If your parents figure out that you don't listen to them, don't be surprised if they tie you to the doghouse with a short leash. And don't yell when you try to gnaw through the leash and end up chewing off your leg.

When I was a boy in my father's house, still tender, and an only child of my mother, he taught me and said, "Lay hold of my words with all your heart; keep my commands and you will live." PROVERBS 4:3–4

Parents Get So Obnoxious

Trish sprawled on the floor, surrounded by a dozen half-finished party invitations. "Okay, Mom. Everything's filled in except the time and what to bring." Then she brought it up again: "Can they sleep over or not?"

"I've heard enough about that," her mom retorted. "I told you no. You're completely obnoxious when your friends sleep over. Remember the last time? Screaming through the house and running into walls at four in the morning!"

What's Trish's next move?

Does honoring and obeying her parents mean she gives up and plays dead? It's hard to tell who's right—maybe Trish, maybe her mom—but here's a great tidbit: God doesn't just tell kids what to do and how to act. He has some rules for parents too.

Read Ephesians 6:4
What big thing does God tell parents not to do?

Parents should provide and guide with firm love. Kids should listen and obey. Face it: Sometimes you mess up.

But sometimes you'll feel your parents are the ones who mess up. They may embarrass you or be too busy for you. They may pay more attention to the TV than to what you say. You might think they're too strict about your friends, music, attitude, bedtime, schoolwork, or social life. Exasperation is what you feel when you've pulled out your hair and still want to pull out your parents' hair. What do you do when your parents irk you?

It won't work to run to your mom or dad with a finger jabbed in your Bible to tell them not to annoy you. You can, however, learn to speak up—not to kiss up or scream or plot your escape from their control. Your best approach is to respectfully *appeal* to a parent the way you would bring a well-prepared case to a judge. You offer reasons: "I think I should be able to...and this is why." You present evidence: "I've proven myself in these instances." You ask for a decision: "What do you think?"

Then accept your parents' decision, as you do the authority of a judge. Parents have the final say. But what *you* say impacts that decision.

Fathers, do not exasperate your children; instead, bring them up in the training and instruction of the Lord. EPHESIANS 6:4

Guess I'll Keep Them

It looked as if a refrigerator had dropped on Nate and swallowed him. When the pile cleared, Nate still lay pretzel-shaped on the football field.

In the stands his parents could see something was wrong. When Nate didn't get up, his coach ran in from the sideline. Nate writhed in pain, his leg broken.

"Where's my dad?" Nate cried as they took him off the field. "Get my dad and mom!"

Since the day you were born your parents have been letting go—little by little allowing you to grow more independent. Once they held your hand wherever you went. Now they're content to watch you from the stands.

Sometimes you're glad to spot them in the front row. Other times you want them to get lost at the snack table. But they're the first ones who come running when you need them. And they're probably the people you want the most.

Read Luke 2:40–52

Did Jesus ever mess up his parents? How did he work it out?

Jesus never sinned (Hebrews 4:15). He never strayed from God's plan, never disobeyed God's commands. That doesn't mean he never perplexed Ma and Pa.

It wasn't as if the Joseph Carpenter family of Nazareth drove off and forgot twelve-year-old Jesus at a rest area. Joseph didn't glance in the backseat and turn to Mary and say, "Have you seen Jesus? Whoops!" Traveling to the Passover Feast caravan style, Joseph and Mary likely assumed Jesus was with friends or cousins. It took a day to realize he was gone, a day to travel back, and a day to search. What a pain!

Jesus was fine. He wasn't sleeping on a sewer grate or spray-painting graffiti on camels. That wasn't the point. Mary and Joseph knew it was their job for a few more years to keep track of their son. And Jesus knew he still needed his parents. He went home.

"Son, why have you treated us like this? Your father and I have been anxiously searching for you."...Then he went down to Nazareth with them and was obedient to them. LUKE 2:48, 51

Cinderfella

Just like every Saturday morning, Trigg did a good job washing his mom's car. He picked bug gunk off the grille and hood, hand-dried the car, and polished the windows. Then he went back inside his family's apartment to do a pile of dishes and dust the furniture.

He finished his chores by vacuuming dust bunnies from under the couch—and from under his snoozing brother. Trigg kicked hard at the end of the couch, but his brother barely stirred. *I'm going to change my name to Cinderfella,* Trigg moaned to himself. *I do all the work around here.*

If you have brothers or sisters, you probably get mad at them more than you do anyone else.

That's nothing new.

Read Genesis 4:1–9
Why do siblings sometimes not get along?

The first family feud was no pillow fight. It started when God disapproved of Cain's attitude in worship. Cain blamed everyone but himself: *God—what a slave driver. See if I ever bring him another offering. And Abel—that kiss-up gets to play with the sheep while I bust my back farming. Dad and Mom always loved him more.* Instead of straightening things out with God, Cain took his anger out on Abel.

Cain's fight with his brother really began as a fight with God. God had warned Cain that if Cain pushed Him away, sin was ready to break in and pounce on him. The instant he stopped wanting to please God, he flung open the door to a family fight.

Cain thought Abel made him look bad. Your brothers and sisters will give you lots of real and imagined reasons to get mad—laziness, meanness, slugging, swiping, and sniveling. You have a choice between striking back or obeying God.

You wham the door shut on sin when you decide to do what's right and ask God to help you to love your unlovable brothers and sisters. Make your home God's home, and crush sin's fingers in the door.

But if you do not do what is right, sin is crouching at your door; it desires to have you, but you must master it.
GENESIS 4:7

Don't Blame Me

Krystal and Jamie had a deal. Everyone else in their group of friends had high-priced team jackets, which made Krystal and Jamie feel stupid. So they agreed that neither would buy a coat until they both could.

When Jamie broke her promise and came to school wearing a new coat, Krystal got desperate. The next day she showed up wearing a team jacket she swiped from her brother. He'd forgotten it when he left for college and wasn't coming home for a month. By then Krystal could buy her own coat.

Everything went fine until Krystal snagged the jacket on a car door and ripped off half the back. She shrugged. "Oh well. It's my brother's anyway." After school Krystal stashed the jacket back in Nick's closet.

When Nick came home and discovered his ripped coat, he immediately blamed Krystal's sister. Krystal breathed a sigh of relief. She was off the hook.

Read Proverbs 28:13
What good thing happens when you 'fess up to wrongdoing?

Ever done something wrong at a friend's house? You maybe felt too embarrassed to ever go back. Well, multiply that discomfort times 24/7 and you realize you're in for real trouble when you don't 'fess up at home—a mess only gets messier. Take Krystal. She took a jacket without asking, laughed off the damage she'd done, hid the evidence, and let her older sister take the heat. She also let fitting in with her friends become more important than fitting in with her family. She had a lot to admit to both God and her family.

It's never fun to admit you've blown it. At home, saying "I did it" instead of "Not me! Not me!" can be awful.

But it's a guaranteed bad time if you hide wrong.

How come? Because God sees—and won't let you succeed as long as you hide your sin. But he promises that you'll find his great forgiveness when you admit your wrong and resolve to do right.

In the short run your family might rub your wrongdoing in your face. But sooner or later mercy shows up at home too. Your family will be far easier on you if you 'fess up now than if someday they dig up your hidden sin.

If you hide your sins, you will not succeed. If you confess and reject them, you will receive mercy. PROVERBS 28:13 NCV

Nightmare Coaster

Justin lounged in the family room, scarfing chips and flipping TV channels with the remote. Nothing much was on, but he pushed the volume up to drown out his parents' fight in the next room. A few shows later his dad rushed out the door with a suitcase.

"Hey, Dad!" Justin yelled. "Where—?" He didn't finish because he knew his dad hadn't heard him. *Another business trip?* Justin wondered.

Two days later Justin found out his dad hadn't left on business. He had left for good.

Having parents separate or divorce is like being dragged onto a roller coaster thundering out of your nightmares. No one checks to see if you're big enough to handle the ride or if you're safely buckled in. You loop, twist, and plunge, hanging on to whatever you can. Even when it's a biblical response to an awful problem, divorce is no kiddie ride.

Read Psalm 62:1–8
What good is God when family life gets that scary?

The best amusement park roller coasters worry you enough to wonder, *What if...? What if I fall out? A rail breaks? I blow chunks?* Yet deep down you're sure you're safe—or you wouldn't ride it. On the nightmare coaster of divorce, however, you don't have a choice whether to ride or not, and you're seldom sure of what's ahead: *Who will I live with? Will we have enough money? What will happen to me?*

You do, however, have a promise that you'll survive the ride: God will keep you safe. When you're weak, God is a fort to hide in. You can tell him what you think and feel, and you can even yell at him when you need to. God doesn't promise to halt the roller coaster, so you'll still face surprising dips and turns. But he can make you peaceful and confident in him.

The one thing worse than being on the nightmare coaster is riding alone—having no one to scream with, lock arms with, or sigh relief with. Friends and a supportive parent, pastor, or counselor can ride part of the way. And God has the stomach and endurance to stick with you for the whole ride (Hebrews 13:5).

God is my mighty rock, my refuge. Trust in him at all times, O people; pour out your hearts to him, for God is our refuge. PSALM 62:7-8

In the Trunk

Cassie and her younger brother, Brent, stood at the front of the church while the organ oozed a jazzed version of "Here Comes the Bride." Bride? Cassie had never thought of her mom as a bride. When Cassie's mom got to the altar they all stood at attention—Cassie by her mom, Brent next to Ryan, his step-brother-to-be.

Brent thought everything was great. He was getting a new playmate, plus a new dad to do fun stuff with.

Cassie's outsides smiled pretty, but her insides knotted. She despised Ryan—*little brat*. She would deal with him quickly enough. Cassie's bigger fear was losing her mom. As long as Cassie could remember, they had been best friends. It was bad enough when her mom started dating. Now Cassie would have to share her all the time.

It's hard to know what to expect of a new family arrangement. Cassie's mom and Brent both hoped that their new family would be better than being alone, but Cassie dreaded losing the one relationship she knew she could count on. Same situation, different expectations.

Some blended families turn out almost as bubbly as the Brady Brunch. Others don't.

Read Romans 12:18

What's your job when you have to get along with people you're not sure you like?

Relationships are like driving a car. When it comes to friends, you're usually in the driver's seat. Within limits, you can pick your friends. With people around you at school or on a team, you get some choice. That's like being a backseat driver. But when it comes to family, you don't get any control. You're all stuffed in the trunk together, like it or not.

Still, you help determine whether the trunk is cozy or crunched. Any family will get cramped at times, but you can at least control whether it's *you* that's elbowing, shoving, and kicking everyone else. You can choose not to bang on the inside of the trunk or drill into the gas tank and drop in a match.

You can't control who's in the trunk. But you can control yourself.

If it is possible, as far as it depends on you, live at peace with everyone. ROMANS 12:18

Never-Ending Love

"My dad keeps trying to push his way into my life. I can't take it anymore," Steven fumed. "Until a few months ago he was never around. Now he's having some mid-life crisis thing, and it hits him that he's been a workaholic. He wants to take me to ball games like I'm a little kid. He always went to work before I got up and came home after I was in bed. He never knew when I needed anything, so I got a paper route to pay for clothes and a bike and everything else. I'm sorry, but I don't need him now."

It's easy to forget to feed a fish—it doesn't make noise. It's harder to forget to feed a dog—it scratches and yelps for food. It should be impossible to forget to care for a kid—it can use words and actions to scream for what it needs. But it happens. Some parents neglect their children.

Read Lamentations 3:22–24
Does God's love for you ever run out?

At some time or other almost everyone feels ignored by his or her parents. And it's easy to think a friend's parents are nicer, more understanding, and softer judges. In better moments, though, your parents seem pretty good. You can talk things over and work problems out.

But in some families relationships are totally neglected. A parent may work outside the home too much for no reason. They give lots of stuff but never time or attention. Others escape into hobbies or into too much activity at church. A mom or dad may up and leave. And a few parents are just cold. It's as if their answering machine says, "I'm sorry, but we're unavailable. We don't plan to return your call."

God never forgets his children (Isaiah 49:16). His comfort and compassion never quit (Lamentations 3:22–23). His love "reaches to the heavens" (Psalm 36:5). And nothing in all of creation "will be able to separate us from the love of God that is in Christ Jesus our Lord" (Romans 8:39).

God loves you now. And his love lasts forever.

Because of the LORD's great love we are not consumed, for his compassions never fail. They are new every morning; great is your faithfulness. LAMENTATIONS 3:22-23

Outta Here!

Jill hid behind the doorway when her eighteen-year-old brother punched his fist through the living room wall. "I hate you!" Jeremy screamed at his parents. "I'm sick of your stupid rules. You never listen to me. You treat me like I'm a baby. Haven't you noticed that I'm eighteen? I can run my own life!" The front door slammed hard after Jeremy, and his motorcycle roared as he drove off.

Jeremy spent the next couple of weeks at a friend's house, then moved in with some older guys. Jill couldn't believe the hole in the wall or the way Jeremy treated their parents, but she was a little jealous that her brother got to be out on his own.

It's normal to dream about moving out. It's a fantasy, though, to think being out from under your parents makes everything perfect.

Read Joshua 24:14–21

What does Joshua vow his family will do?

Life isn't a game. That's why parents usually shelter you from the cold facts of life: If you're sassy you get fired. If you're a jerk you get bounced out of your apartment. If you're lazy you starve. More than that, when you leave home you don't escape rules. Instead of parents you get professors and roommates and bosses—and then a spouse and kids to answer to.

In fact, there's no such thing as "running your own life." When you get to be out on your own, maybe with a family to care for, you actually get only two choices: *I will follow and obey God,* or *I will choose another god.* Look out: Picking another god means signing up to be locked up (Romans 6:20–23). You leave what you think is a prison and go to what turns out to be a zoo. It might look like a nice place to visit, but you wouldn't want to live there.

Happiness and freedom aren't found in busting loose but in choosing to enjoy God and his will for you (Psalm 37:3–4). It's better to enjoy your place in God's family than to be a baboon locked up in a zoo.

But as for me and my household, we will serve the Lord.
JOSHUA 24:15

The (Im) Perfect Family

Sitting behind the Hoffstats in church, you'd think they had pranced out of an ad for a trendy department store—perfectly dressed with their spiritual smiles, fresh haircuts, and stylish clothes. Every family in church wishes they could be the Hoffstats. They're so cute you could pinch their cheeks.

But no one saw them on the way to church, when Tina once again mangled Brandon's fingers until he cried, all because he said that a boy she likes resembles one of those wart-covered goldfish. And when the family sings a hymn, no one can tell that Mom and Dad haven't spoken to each other since they fought three days ago.

If you compare your family to the *image* of a family like the Hoffstats, you might feel cheated.

So join their family for a while. Want to be Brandon? It's wonderful to have your fingers torqued until they touch your wrist. Or how about trading places with Tina the Terrible? She doesn't know any better way to handle her brother. She must be very unhappy. And what fun for both kids to wonder why Mom and Dad can't agree on anything.

If you were able to see *inside* the families that you think are so much better than yours, you'd find that no family is perfect. And you can't swap families anyway. So what do you do?

Read Galatians 5:14
How can you make your home a happier place?

God gives a simple rule that can turn the people in your family into some of your best friends: Love your neighbor—your mom, dad, sisters, brothers, whoever else lives in your house—just as you love yourself.

The family is a bunch of relationships you can't escape. It forces you to learn to love, to forgive, to talk about what hurts, to put God and others first, to get help when the family breaks. What you refuse to learn now will become problems that, until you learn to solve them, will hurt all your relationships.

If you want your family to work well, you have to work hard at working together. Your closest neighbors share the same roof.

The entire law is summed up in a single command: "Love your neighbor as yourself." GALATIANS 5:14

The Facts of Life

Five minutes into the test you're still staring at the first question. *I know this one*, you tell yourself. *X equals Y squared plus 4.* You plug in the numbers. No go. You try again. *X equals the square root of the inverse of Y.* El humungo blanko. More minutes pass. You're still stuck. You chew the end off your pencil and swallow the eraser.

Breathe. It's in there somewhere. You close your eyes, rock back and forth, and try to remember your teacher working the problem on the board. Your brain happily spits facts. *Abraham Lincoln. December 7, 1941. Sacagawea.*

You're not even hitting the right sector of the hard drive. You need one measly bit of data. It's lost. You freeze.

You know that as soon as you slap your blank test on the teacher's desk, the misplaced factoids will come whooshing back. You consider slamming your head onto the desk. Maybe it'll crack open and leak brain onto your paper.

Read Exodus 20:1–3

What one task does God put at the top of your to-do list?

Life is dazzling. Frazzling. Your head is full of things you'd better remember. Test stuff. Street smarts. Life skills. Details about friends, fractions, and facial scrubs. How do you keep it all straight?

When God wanted his people to understand the biggest facts about obeying him, he didn't send his list in an instant message. He didn't broadcast it on TV or even write it in a newspaper. He carved it on stone. And at the top of the list is one unforgettable thought: *God is Lord over all.* And because he's all that, you are to put no person or thing above him in your life. He's worth your total devotion.

That's the ultimate command of the Living God. You can forget a lot of stuff—but not this, the big fact of life. Whether you're at home or out on your own, it's at the top of your to-do list.

When life squeezes, your brain freezes. But stuff your mind full of that fact.

I am the LORD your God, who rescued you from slavery in Egypt. Do not worship any other gods besides me.
EXODUS 20:2–3 NLT

Busting Loose

"Mom and Dad," Trent confessed, "I'm sorry."

The umpteen other times Trent had gone on a church retreat he'd listened to the youth pastor's Bible talks and figured they were for the gothic kids next to him. God was rapping on *their* heads, not his.

This time, though, God took a wrecking ball to Trent, knocking some spiritual sense into him. He felt shock waves rumble through as he recognized his Sunday school snottery—how he thought he was better than other people, how he had a mighty swirly potty mouth, how at home he'd been on a six-month rampage about homework and chores, and how his sneaking out of the house had betrayed his parents.

When he got home to talk to his mom and dad, it all dumped out again.

"Hey, tough guy," his dad said, trying to brush the sorrys aside. "It's okay."

"No, Dad, it's not okay," Trent persisted. "I've been hurting *me*. I've been hurting *you*. And I don't want to be that way anymore."

Read Colossians 3:5–9

Why is God so big on changing you?

The wrong stuff you do deserves God's punishment. But it also causes staggering pain. So you can have a pretty sad spasm when you realize how bad sin really is. Psalm 107 says it well: "Some sat in darkness and the deepest gloom, prisoners suffering in iron chains, for they had rebelled against the words of God and despised the counsel of the Most High."

All sin chains you. Even if you think your sin is "not so bad." Yet God aims to set you free. Listen again to the psalm: "He brought them out of darkness and the deepest gloom and broke away their chains" (verse 14).

Saying "yes" to God's offer of forgiveness in Jesus frees you from the *penalty* of sin. But there's a second chain God wants to smash: the *pain* of sin.

Get God's forgiveness. But let him also lead you into his cool freedom from hurting yourself and others. Busting that second chain starts with knowing you need to get free. That's when you let God cut you loose to obey him totally.

Because of these, the wrath of God is coming. You used to walk in these ways, in the life you once lived. COLOSSIANS 3:6–7

Defused

When Aimee sat down in front of Scott at the school musical—right where he could stare at her while pretending to study the stage—his heart climbed into his throat and choked him. *An hour and a half,* he gargled, *of watching Aimee watch the show.*

God—thanks to a blunt youth pastor—had taught Scott the Bible's principles about guy-girl stuff: Control yourself (1 Thessalonians 4:3–5). Keep your thoughts clean (Matthew 5:28). Sex is for marriage (Hebrews 13:4). And don't hook yourself to non-Christians (2 Corinthians 6:14). Once Scott even thought he'd heard God say, "Don't go near Aimee." *Thanks, God,* his thoughts sassed back. *You didn't have to say that. She looks at me like I look at meat loaf. I can't get near her.*

A few months later everyone discovered Aimee's well-hidden secret: Her friends had pulled her into a serious drinking habit. That had led to a load of other ugly situations. Scott felt sorry for her. But suddenly he was also glad he hadn't gotten her as his girl.

Read Psalm 119:43–48
Why obey God?

It seemed like a strange game. Each day a total stranger sent you a tiny electronic gizmo and some assembly directions in the mail. Day by day, piece by piece, you were supposed to put the parts together. One day, after you've followed all the steps, you wake up. You've got a bomb taped to your chest. It turns out the parts and directions came from an enemy. The bomb ticks, ready to explode. You're not sure when.

Life blows up in your face when you follow the wrong directions.

Good thing: God is head of the bomb squad, and he keeps you from detonating your life in a couple of ways. Sometimes he arranges your circumstances to keep harm out of your life.

God has also given you the Bible. His commands are like instructions for spotting a bomb as it's being built. His rules steer away from stupid, unnecessary pain—and into life (John 10:10). And if you trust that God wants what's best for you, you follow his good instructions.

I will always obey your law, for ever and ever. I will walk about in freedom, for I have sought out your precepts.
PSALM 119:44–45

Stand, Walk, Run

Derek waves to his parents as they drive off. "See you later! Have fun!" Derek knows *he'll* have fun. As he shuts the front door he wonders why his parents said not to have anyone over. *What are they worried about? Don't they trust me?*

A few minutes later the half dozen friends he invited arrive—followed a few minutes later by a dozen he didn't invite. A guy Derek barely recognizes carries in a case of beer and asks directions to the fridge. A girl passes around a flask. Things get loud. Stuff starts to fall off walls.

Derek runs to the bathroom and locks himself in. *What to do? Call the cops on my own party?* Don't bother. The neighbors already made the call. Red and blue lights flash in the driveway. Derek hears a knock at the front door and a scramble at the back. The officers are nice enough, but they promise to come back and chat with Derek's parents.

As Derek shuts the door he wonders if maybe his parents had a point.

Read Psalm 119:30–32
Does obeying God ever get easy?

If you listen to your parents solely because they can ground you for life, then you'll always struggle with obeying. You'll concentrate hard on how to bust boundaries—not how to keep them.

It's the same with obeying God. You'll only eagerly chase his best when you trust him above anything else. That doesn't happen all at once, but *how* it happens isn't hard to understand: *You stand.* You "choose the way of truth" (verse 30). You tell God you want him and his way. You read the Bible to remind yourself what God has done for you (Romans 10:17). *You walk.* You "hold fast to God's statutes" (verse 31). You obey—even though you worry that you'll fall and grind your face in the dirt. But you don't. Over and over God shows that his ways work. He's kind and wise. Your trust grows. *So you run.* You "run in the path of God's commands" (verse 32). Your heart is "set free" or "enlarged," which means "swollen with joy" (Isaiah 60:5), and "increased in understanding" (1 Kings 4:29).

You obey because you want to, not because you have to.

I run in the path of your commands, for you have set my heart free. PSALM 119:32

It's Funny Until You . . .

With dual dart guns set to shoot, Andrew charged from behind the couch, put a dart gun on each side of Nick's head, and pulled the triggers. *Fwank! Thunk!* Andrew laughed as he retreated to reload while Nick faked pain. Then from the living room came a yell that halted the dart gun war: "It's funny until you put an eye out! Stop it right now."

We ignore rules that we think are too harsh: "Cross the street only at crosswalks." "Don't run in the hall." "Don't shoot dart guns at people's heads." Breaking those rules doesn't always carry the big bad consequences the rulemakers seem to threaten, so we take our chances.

Some people treat God's rules the same way, ignoring his warnings about right and wrong because they think they're too hard or too old-fashioned to be obeyed. Not only that, but they laugh at you when you take God seriously and don't join their activities.

Read Psalm 119:89–96
What makes God worth obeying?

Sooner or later many believers wonder why they bother to obey God.

Well, it doesn't hurt to remember that God spoke and created heaven and earth, so he gets to make the rules and set consequences for breaking them. But there are bigger reasons to obey than the fact that God can roast his enemies.

Of all the rulemakers in your world, only God puts together earth-shaking power, flawless wisdom, and total love. The result? Perfect judgment about what's right and what's wrong, what builds up and what rips down. Not one of his rules is dumb or out-of-date, and not a single one is meant for anything less than your good.

That's what God's faithfulness is all about. People's nastiness won't destroy you if you grasp the perfection of God's ways—his "laws," "precepts," "statutes," and "commands." Threats, teasing, and laughter loom over you only until you see their puniness compared to God's boundless wise care.

If your law had not been my delight, I would have perished in my affliction. PSALM 119:92

You and the Beanstalk

"Klass, ve are here to make zis boy big and schtrong, to give him superhuman schpiritual schtrength, to make him a good Christian who obeyz God allvayz."

Strapped to a glistening steel operating table, Michael was finding that his church's Sunday school superintendent had a unique way of fixing anyone who goofed off in class.

The man waved his arm at Michael. "Yah," he said, "zis is vhat happens to boys who do not pay attention in Sunday school. Ve vill first sew shut hiss big mouth. Next, ve vill give him bigger ears—zo he listens. Ve vill place tiny bits of tape above ze eyes to keep zem open. And zen—and zis is important—ve vill inject him vith special solution to make him schpiritually alert. Any qvestions?"

Read Mark 4:1–9 and 15–20
What makes a Christian strong?

Growing spiritually doesn't mean you never get bored in Sunday school—or snooze during a sermon—or forget to read your Bible. But if you want to get closer to Christ, it shows in how hard you listen.

How you respond to Jesus resembles the way seed grows—or doesn't—when it lands on different dirts. The word of God—the message of his care for us, Christ's death for us, and his commands for us—is like seed. God flings seed in all directions. Some drops on hard paths, where it settles on the surface and is snatched away. Other seed lands in rocky outcroppings. The seed springs up but dies for lack of roots, unable to reach water in the heat. Still other seed grows up among thorns—worries and distractions that choke a young plant.

But some seed falls on good soil—on those who pay attention to God's words, accept them, and act on them. Their lives explode with growth, producing a hundred times the amount of the first seed.

Each time you hear God's Word it's your chance to be rich, dark dirt. You can choose to listen or not, believe or not, obey or not. Live up to what you know and you'll grow. Don't and you won't.

Other seed fell on good soil. It came up, grew and produced a crop, multiplying thirty, sixty, or even a hundred times.
MARK 4:8

A Crying Game

One hundred yards. Five-iron if I'm lucky. You tee up the ball. *This time I'm going to put it on the green. I'm sick of them making fun of me.*

Smack! *Sounded nice.* But the ball hooks into the woods lining the fairway. *For sure I'll never find that one.* Your friends snicker. You blush.

You grab a new ball and it dribbles fifty yards into a stream. You stuff back a scream. Your friends grew up on this course with their father, Mr. Golf Instructor. They're practically pros. You? Once again you're wondering why you golf with them.

This ball-in-water situation, however, you know how to handle. You've watched golf on TV. Real golfers hit it out. With both feet in six inches of stream, you swing hard. *Swash.* You connect—with the water. The ball that went in doesn't come out. The splash that goes up comes down. All over you.

Read Matthew 4:1–11
Did Jesus ever struggle to do right?

Here's how we picture this passage: Devil pounces. Jesus flexes muscles and flashes an orthodontically flawless smile. Jesus fires Bible bits at devil. Devil whimpers away in defeat. No fuss, no agony. Temptation bounces off Jesus like a bullet off Superman's chest.

That isn't how it happened.

Jesus fought temptation the same way we have to—the hard way—by clinging to the truth. Satan didn't tempt Jesus with trinkets and a toy crown. He offered to make Jesus king of the world. And Satan didn't depart for good (Luke 4:13). The battle went on. Before Jesus went to the cross, for example, he asked his Father whether there was an easier way to save the world (Luke 22:41–46).

Struggling against temptation never feels good. When the temptation bullet comes your way, it hits, rips, rattles around inside, and goes out your backside. But Jesus knew hurt. He understands your hurt. When he sees you struggle, he doesn't sneer, snicker, stand by and do nothing, or fake a pout with a big lip and crying eyes. He wades in to help (Hebrews 4:16).

Then Jesus was led by the Spirit into the desert to be tempted by the devil. MATTHEW 4:1

Pop Quiz

Mom and Dad looked sympathetic. "We know how you feel, Hanna," they explained. "But we don't have any choice about moving. It will be okay. God's going with us, you know. You'll see."

I'm going to die, Hanna thought. *It's not even summer. If we have to move, why do we have to do it in the middle of the year?*

While Hanna's family packed up their stuff and she said good-byes to her friends, she hatched a plan. She'd walk to her new school so no one would see her sitting by herself on the bus. Then she'd dart from class to class—if she walked fast and looked like she knew where she was going then no one would notice she was totally friendless. She'd skip lunch and hide in a corner of the library. She steeled herself to face a new school all alone.

God? she said to herself. *What does He care?*

Read John 6:5–13
What does Jesus want most from you?

Jesus has a situation on his hands. A crowd of five thousand men—plus women and children—swarms toward him and his disciples. Jesus sees it's time to eat. And time for a pop quiz: "Where's lunch coming from?" Jesus asks. "For the whole hillside!" he adds. But he's not wondering where he can find the nearest Taco Tom's or looking for volunteers to cough up a spare year of salary. What he really wants is to know what the disciples think about him.

None of Jesus' disciples answer the quiz question right. Philip mumbles about the price. Andrew finds a kid toting what he regards as a useless little snack of fish and chips. The disciples all think Jesus means the lunch problem is *their* problem. To solve. To survive. And on their own they don't see solutions.

All Jesus wants them to do is to ask for his help. "Crack the bread in half, Jesus," he wants them to say. "Start passing it around. You're able to do what we can't." What he wants from his disciples—from his followers back then and from us now—is trust. It wasn't supposed to be a trick question. It was a trust question.

"Where shall we buy bread for these people to eat?" [Jesus] asked this only to test him, for he already had in mind what he was going to do. JOHN 6:5-6

God in a Box

You and your lab-coated friends gloat over your victim, awed by your own genius.

"It still looks strong," one worries. "Think the cage will hold?"

"The cage is fine." You'd spent months stalking your victim. But capturing and caging it was only the first step of your plan. The next step was to put its cosmic powers in a portable package.

Two friends twiddle the dials on the transmogrifier. One question left—how small to shrink your victim. Six inches high and it would fit in a box. A foot high and you could lead it around on a leash.

But before you can decide, the phone rings. "It's someone who says *he's* God. It sounds for real."

"We made a mistake," you mumble. "The thing in the cage isn't God."

Read Mark 6:45–52
Why trust Jesus?

Jesus walks across the waves to the boat. *That can't be Jesus,* they think. They imagine he's a ghost. He reaches them and the wind dies down. The disciples are bewildered.

They didn't get it. They didn't figure out Jesus' real identity. They couldn't fathom his power over *everything.* When he did things only God could do they stayed clueless. Sure, they knew Jesus was a cut above them. But he was infinitely greater. He was God himself, all-powerful, come to earth as a human being. They had Jesus in a too-tight box.

Power alone, though, doesn't make Jesus a hero. You'd fear him if he threatened to evaporate you with a blast from his finger. You wouldn't willingly like, love, or obey him.

But Jesus is total power paired with perfect goodness. That's what makes him worth trusting—obeying. He isn't just able to feed the crowds. He offers bread that satisfies forever (John 6:35). He doesn't just walk on water. He's the One who says, "It's me! Don't be scared!"

Immediately he spoke to them and said, "Take courage! It is I.
Don't be afraid." MARK 6:50

Booked Solid

"I can't—really," Tina protested. "Here—look at my calendar." Tina popped open her locker and flopped out a scheduler. Mary flipped through month by month. Tuesday—the night Mary's youth group met—was scribbled full for weeks.

"See?" Tina poked at the Tuesdays. "I volunteer at the animal shelter every Tuesday evening for the next eight weeks. I'll put you down for February 17."

Mary counted on her fingers. "That's *twelve* weeks."

"I help at Children's Hospital two Tuesdays after that," Tina explained, "and I need to keep a couple weeks open for emergencies."

"Sure," Mary said. "I understand. You just said you wanted to come to a Bible study sometime. You know—all those questions you had when your grandpa died.... We have stuff on other nights sometimes."

"Sorry!" Tina apologized. "It wouldn't matter. I'm booked solid."

Read Matthew 19:16–22

What can you do when good stuff gets in the way of Jesus?

Lots of things in life are good. But they aren't good anymore if they go extreme and keep you from following Jesus—like trying too hard to be popular (Galatians 1:10), overestimating the size of your brain (1 Corinthians 1:28–29), doing what's right—but to show off for others (Matthew 6:2–4), or getting too busy for God (Luke 10:40–42).

Jesus said there's something more important than the good things we often change. It's getting hold of God himself (Matthew 6:19–34). And Jesus pointed out that the young man had done everything right—except love God above anything else. The man didn't strangle anyone, steal anything, or spew at his mother. But when Jesus invited him to follow—but to ditch his luggage first—he couldn't bear to leave his hoard of wealth behind.

You became God's friend not because of what you *do* but because of what Jesus *did*. Yet obeying lets you experience God's care. To follow Jesus, you have to let go of what's good when it keeps you from grabbing what's best.

Sell your possessions and give to the poor, and you will have treasure in heaven. Then come, follow me." MATTHEW 19:21

Deepest Regrets

"Mitch is a Jesus-lover!" Scott taunted. "Christians are wusses. That's why Mitch won't kick butt on the rink."

Mitch knew he dug as hard as any other player on his hockey team. He just didn't love to break opponents' legs to stop shots. But that didn't stop the team from joining Scott in pouncing on Mitch.

"It's true. He prays at lunch." *How could he tell?* Mitch wondered. *I don't stand up and yodel.*

"And he reads a Bible in the library." *Not that much....*

"It's why he's a suck-up to all the teachers." *I just pay attention.*

"So?" Mitch finally spoke up. "Those things don't make me a Christian." *Well, technically not. They don't* make *me a Christian. But I do them because I'm a Christian.*

The dodge didn't distract them. "So are you or aren't you?"

Read Luke 22:54–62

What did Peter do when people accused him of being Jesus' friend?

When you make it your aim to obey Jesus, sooner or later someone won't like it. They laugh at you or slam you or just ignore you.

You don't have to hang yourself out for them to hate you. The Bible doesn't say, "Go ye forth and rub thy faith in thy neighbor's face." But it does coach you to be honest and unashamed: "Live such good lives among the pagans that, though they accuse you of doing wrong, they may see your good deeds and glorify God...." (1 Peter 2:12).

Those are words from the guy who three times denied he knew Jesus only hours after swearing he would go with Jesus to prison and death (Luke 22:31–34). When soldiers swept in and captured Jesus, Peter feared for his life and tried to hide. Just as Jesus had predicted, Peter claimed three times not to know him.

One look from Jesus was enough for Peter to understand what he had done.

The Lord turned and looked straight at Peter. Then Peter remembered the word the Lord had spoken to him: "Before the rooster crows today, you will disown me three times." And he went outside and wept bitterly. LUKE 22:61–62

Sob Stories

Adrianna buried her face in her pillow. *Sobs.*

She could count her close Christian friends on her two big toes after her church's third youth pastor in four years resigned and her youth group imploded. *Lonely sobs.*

Everyone she knew was into school or sports. She liked drama and music. Her social life was pathetic. *Bored sobs.*

One of her best friends even quit coming to church after a pastor told him that "following Jesus" was optional for Christians. Adrianna kept telling herself what she'd memorized from 2 Timothy 2:22—to "*pursue* righteousness, faith, love and peace, along with those who call on the Lord out of a pure heart." But where was everyone else? *Angry sobs.*

And she'd heard that the guy she liked at church thought of her as his sister. Barf. She'd uncovered a profound truth: No one ever asks his sister to a movie. Not that her parents would let her go. But it would be nice to be asked. *Shattered heart sobs.*

Read 2 Samuel 22:32–37

How do you keep obeying God when you feel like quitting?

Anyone who claims your Christian life will be stress free obviously missed Jesus' words in John 16:33: "Here on earth you will have many trials and sorrows" (NLT). But packed in the Bible along with that straight-up truth are hordes of promises that God will help you obey him even when you're bawling in your pillow.

Sift through this passage for some awe-striking promises: God is your Rock. He arms you with strength. He makes your way perfect. He gives you biceps that can curve a bronze bow. And he makes your feet dance like a deer on the tip-tops of mountain peaks.

And all through the Bible are more assurances. Some of the choicest: God points you "in paths of righteousness for his name's sake" (Psalm 23:3). He gives "the desire to obey him and the power to do what pleases him" (Philippians 2:13 NLT). And "he is able to accomplish infinitely more than we would ever dare to ask or hope" (Ephesians 3:20 NLT).

You have reasons to cry. But you also have reasons to dance.

He makes my feet like the feet of a deer; he enables me to stand on the heights. 2 SAMUEL 22:34

Don't Go Solo

As his home for the next seventy-two hours, Bob picked a strip of land jutting into a backwoods lake. If he could live with nothing more than a sleeping bag—building his own shelter, starting his own fire, snaring his own food—he would pass his survival skills test.

Halfway through Bob's second day a swarm of biting flies attacked him. He almost cried. He ducked into his sleeping bag for protection—head and all—but he baked like a pig in a blanket. So he crawled back out.

Later that night when Bob was back in the bag wishing he had found more to eat, a storm blew up and the wind nearly rolled him off the point. Bob yelled. He ran through the rain to rocks not far away. As he slid into a crevice he knew he had broken the rules for the solo. He had left his solo site. He hadn't passed the test. But he was safe.

Read Luke 1:26–38

Where can you run when you feel overwhelmed?

Obeying Jesus doesn't make your life a cushy motor-home campout. Flies will still bite at your eyes and storms will still blow your way. You're smart when you know enough to run for cover when you know you can't make it alone.

When an angel knocked at Mary's door and said that God had an astounding plan for her life, Mary had a big question: *How can I have a son? I've never been with a man.* But her baby wouldn't be made the ordinary way. He would be formed by the Holy Spirit. And Jesus wouldn't be an ordinary baby. He was God's Son, Savior of the world.

People will still talk, Mary must have thought. *I'll be an outcast.* Even Joseph decided to break their engagement until God told him the plan (Matthew 1:19).

Mary saw in God's plans for her life both wonder and terror. But she knew where to run for safety. She was tough—even though she was possibly barely a teenager—because she hid in the Rock (Isaiah 26:3–4). Mary knew whom to trust.

You won't earn a merit badge for trying to survive life solo. You've only failed if you don't hide in the Rock and end up getting blown away.

"I am the Lord's servant," Mary answered. "May it be to me as you have said." LUKE 1:38

Honest to God

"It's not fair!" Sandy was ticked. "He failed half of us." When she saw Mr. Denter's office empty and unlocked before school, she rampaged. Sandy cleared the top of his desk and yanked the desk drawers onto the floor.

Then her friend Kendra joined in by feeding a jelly sandwich to a VCR stored behind Mr. Denter's desk. Sandy froze. "Kendra! What are you doing?"

"They'll never figure out we did it. They'll think it was the guys."

That day Sandy told Mr. Denter she needed to talk after class. "I messed up your desk," she confessed. "I'll help you pick stuff up, and then I'll go see the principal."

"You're going to be hungry at lunch today, aren't you?" he prodded.

"I didn't do that!" Sandy argued. "Honest!"

"You'll have to explain that at the office, Sandy. I don't believe you."

Read Psalm 51:1–12
What good does it do to admit that you're wrong?

David wrote Psalm 51 after he had an affair with Bathsheba and ordered her husband killed so he could take her as his wife. That's big sin. But to God there's not much difference between David's sin and ours. All sin builds a wall between us and God.

Sin hurts everyone, but God more than anyone. He's the "you" in "against you, you only have I sinned." David could not make excuses with God, the ultimate judge. His only hope was to come clean and plead for mercy.

David wanted God to forget his "transgressions," to stop being angry with him, and to fix their friendship. God answers that request. He forgives those who admit what they've done wrong (1 John 1:8–9). And David knew it would be dishonest to grab God's forgiveness, then go and sin more. So he asked God to help him be happy doing what God required.

Little kids can pretend to be things that they're not—a pirate, a princess, a pro athlete. But to grow up you need to see yourself as you are. Growing a devoted heart begins when you're truthful to God and yourself.

Against you, you only, have I sinned and done what is evil in your sight, so that you are proved right when you speak and justified when you judge. PSALM 51:4

The Secret Service

Why the president wanted to visit your school no one knew. But one day your principal announced he was coming. *The* president. Of the United States. And your principal launched a school-wide essay contest: "What I Want to Ask the President."

Whoever won the contest would get lunch with the president. You wanted to win bad—not so you could discuss the finer points of foreign policy but to chum with the big cheese. So you titled your entry "Why I Want to Yuck It Up With the Yo-Yo."

When you lost the contest you plotted ways to get the president's attention. Then bomb-sniffing dogs checked lockers and secret service agents with burp guns under their suit coats banged through ventilation ducts. You decided that sitting in the front row and playing "Hail to the Chief" on your armpit wasn't such a hot idea. You didn't want the president to target a nuclear missile on your locker or snap a spy-satellite picture of you picking your nose. It's not good to mess with the president.

Read Proverbs 9:10

You know you're supposed to be good for God.
But does that mean you're afraid of him?

God calls Christians closer to himself than you'll ever get to a president. He offers to be your friend (Revelation 3:20). Because Christ died for your sins, you have a constant relationship with the God of the universe (Hebrews 10:19–22). That beats any invitation to the Oval Office. But knowing God is more than just hanging with the head honcho.

To "fear God" doesn't exactly mean you're scared spitless. God is totally powerful. That might push you away in fear. Yet God is totally loving. That pulls you toward him. Put those together: You're drawn to God in awe.

The book of Nahum illustrates how to think about God. There *are* reasons to dread him. He's a "jealous and avenging God" (1:2) and he "will not leave the guilty unpunished" (1:3). But God is also "a refuge in times of trouble" (1:7). He "cares for those who trust in Him" (1:7).

You're a fool to play with a fire. But you're a bigger fool not to come close and be warmed by its heat.

The fear of the LORD is the beginning of wisdom, and knowledge of the Holy One is understanding. PROVERBS 9:10

I've Had Enough

"Everyone at school lives in big houses," Brett yelled at his dad. "None of them wear stupid clothes like mine. They won't hang around with people like me." Brett wanted a spending spree. *Now*.

A few days later Brett piled into the car with his dad. When Brett noticed they were taking a long detour on the way to the mall, his dad waved off his questions.

"Brett," his dad finally said, "before we go shopping, I want you to see something. Not so you feel guilty, but so you know what we've got." They stopped in front of a run-down house, hardly bigger than Brett's friends' playhouses. A guy sat on the front stoop cleaning a handgun. Garages were sprayed with gang graffiti.

"I know we don't have a huge house," Brett's dad said, "but we have a lot to thank God for. I haven't been by here since you were little. This is where your grandpa and grandma lived when I was born."

Read Matthew 5:3
How can you be wildly happy, no matter what?

Matthew 5:3–11 contains what Bible buffs call the "Beatitudes" (say it like "be" plus "attitudes"). In some Bibles these bites of truth start with the word *Blessed*, as in "*Blessed* are the poor in spirit." But it's just as correct to use the word *Happy*, like other Bibles do, as in "*Happy* are the poor in spirit." If being blessed sounds gaggy to you, being happy probably sounds a whopper more appetizing.

In the verse you just read, Jesus is saying more than "Have an attitude of gratitude," though that's crucial (1 Timothy 6:17).

His point is this: When you think you've got nothing, you've got everything you need. You might feel short on friends. You might be truly penniless. Either way, you've got God. People who are poor in spirit—or just plain poor (Luke 6:20)—possess the kingdom of heaven.

Having a gargantuan house or a stunning wardrobe won't make your life perfect. When all you hold in your hands is God, you've got the stuff that really counts.

Blessed are the poor in spirit, for theirs is the kingdom of heaven. MATTHEW 5:3

Spiritual Belly Buttons

SHWOOP! FINGAFINGAFINGA! SPRANKkank kank!

Stunned, you stare at a sewer lid that's blown off the street, caught air like a Frisbee, and landed at your feet. You only look at the lid for a second. Intergalactic aliens dead ahead!

You've been strutting down your home street when a couple real sewer-cloggers block your path. Suddenly thankful for all the stranger-danger and self-defense stuff you've gotten in school, you punt the aliens back to where they came from, thereby preserving life as we know it on planet earth.

Not unexpectedly, you're recruited into the government's ultrasecret alien-fighting corps. You get the standard-issue dark suit and shades. Your identity is erased. You're invisible. You've attained ultimate cool. You're a one-person, alien-busting army.

Read John 15:1–4
Why do you need God in order to be good?

If you could single-handedly spank aliens right out of the galaxy, you'd think you were pretty good. But you still couldn't get by all by your lonesome. You'd still need a paycheck. Groceries. Electricity to charge your laser blaster. And you'd probably expect Mom to wash your dirty underwear.

Next time you think you're ultra-competent and totally self-sufficient, put your finger on your belly button and ponder this: Once upon a time, you were tucked inside your mom's tummy, kept alive through a cord.

Nowadays—know it or not—you're just as dependent. You're designed to draw life from God.

God will never scissors your spiritual umbilical cord and announce, "Won't be needing that anymore. Might as well knot it off and let it dry up and fall off." You'll never outgrow your spiritual umbilical cord—your connection to God. You're connected to him like a branch to a vine, and disconnected from him you can't do *anything*.

Your belly button is a distant memory of physical dependence. And you'll never sprout such a thing as a spiritual belly button. Because you'll never stop needing God.

A branch cannot produce fruit alone.
JOHN 15:4 NCV

Rocky Mountain High

You stash your rental board in a slot on the gondola and jump inside for your ride to the top of the mountain. "You know," says one of your gondola buddies, "an air force jet plowed into a lift just like this in Italy. Dropped everybody three or four hundred feet. Twenty people died, and the pilot got off with nothing." You eye the horizon, hoping not to become the next bowl of fly-by pudding.

As you ascend, the town at the base of the mountain turns tiny. Then it disappears. Before you looms the top half of the mountain you couldn't even see from the bottom. You exit the gondola and glance around. Never mind that all the green signs scream "Beginner." You see a cliff around every curve as you buckle in.

You turn and face downhill. You squeak out one question: "Is this the only way down?"

Read Psalm 118:6

Can you really trust God to take care of you when you go his way?

Life is full of slopes you're not ready to snowboard right now. If you dive down a hill called "Do the Dew" unprepared, you can expect trouble. If you dive too early into life's steep stuff—like a sworn-for-life guy-girl relationship or a locked-in career choice—even God's help won't keep you from feeling you're in over your head.

Other slopes—the sinful runs of life—you don't want to board at all. True, God forgives. True, God restores. He may be able to retrieve you if you fly off the back side of a mountain. But not even God can scrape you off when you splat yourself to a tree.

There's only one way to get down the mountain of life. When you aim to live life tight with God, you can relax in the protection of the Grand Snowboard Instructor. When you obey God's commands and slice where you're supposed to, you can be sure you're hanging right next to him. You might be shocked when he shoots you down the steep runs. You might not be thrilled to ride every inch of the hill. But you'll survive with a smile.

If being totally devoted to God were easy, you wouldn't need to trust your Instructor. But if you're sure he protects you, you fear nothing.

The Lord is with me; I will not be afraid. PSALM 118:6

Only If You Do What We Want

It seemed so cruel. But Lindsey wanted to fit in. And everyone was watching. So she agreed to the dare.

Andy was so slimy that Lindsey worried she might slip on the floor if she got too close. Still, she strolled over to the table where Andy sat alone studying calculus. She put her arms around his neck from behind and whispered in his ear: "Andy, I'd love it if you asked me to the dance."

This was *truly* cruel. Lindsey had her arms around the nerdiest guy she had ever seen, and she was supposed to tell him this was a joke.

You pick the ending: (a) Lindsey jumps back, yells "Just kidding," and gains fourteen popular yet heartless friends; or (b) Andy turns to answer Lindsey, his hair smears grease across her face while he drools on her shoes, but Lindsey can't bear to break his heart. When they show up together at the dance, the school's social elite are not impressed.

Peer pressure usually isn't that obvious, but it might as well be. The crowd screams: "*If* you do what we want, *then* we'll like you."

Read Proverbs 29:6
Do you have to choose between friends and God?

Nope, you don't *always* have to choose between popularity with people or popularity with God. But it's a delusion to think that you *never* have to rebel against your peers to follow God.

Jesus was clear that those who trust in him are on a wildly different path from those who don't. "Wide is the gate and broad is the road that leads to destruction and many enter through it," he said. "But small is the gate and narrow the road that leads to life, and only a few find it" (Matthew 7:13–14).

Picture it like this: Loads of times you can reach across and grab the hand of someone on the wrong path. Non-Christians need your love—and so do Christians wandering off God's way. God doesn't want you to let go of those folks. But there are times when they try to pull you over to their path. You don't want to go there. They're headed into traps set by their own sin.

That's when you have a choice. You can wade into destruction—or you can keep whistling while you walk with Jesus.

An evil man is snared by his own sin, but a righteous one can sing and be glad. PROVERBS 29:6

Night-Light Fright

One dark and stormy night every scary movie that Marcus had ever watched came crawling into his nightmares. Vampires tiptoed up behind him and fanged him. Men with disfigured faces jumped from behind corners and slashed him. Mutated aliens hijacked his body and throbbed inside his chest. Dolls sprang to life and strangled him—after chasing him and kicking his shins. Terrorists kicked down his door and sprayed his room with bullets.

And those were just the previews. The main feature involved demons crawling out of sewer grates to snatch his soul to hell.

In a sweat, Marcus shook himself awake. For the next month, he slept with the lights on.

Read Philippians 4:6–7

What can you do when you're scared or worried—and what can result if you follow the Bible's instructions?

You have a choice about whether you watch terrifying movies and pump your brain full of freakish scenes that make you flip in the night. Yet plenty of other scary situations invade your life and terrorize you against your will.

You might be fizzling your life away worrying about bad stuff that will never happen. Jesus was smart when he said, "So don't worry about tomorrow, for tomorrow will bring its own worries" (Matthew 6:34 NLT). But other threats to your health and happiness are real and present dangers. They don't lurk in your tomorrows. They're in your face today. Maybe your life at home is tense. Or you have tests to study for and tryouts to endure. You face clashes with friends. And then there's that weird growing-up body stuff.

The outcome of all of these things is high anxiety. Yet God invites you to worry about nothing but tell him about everything. You can dump all your worries on him because he cares for you (1 Peter 5:7).

God's response to your prayers is so certain that you can thank him ahead of time for his answers. He won't fix every stressful thing in your life. But he'll suction the worry from your brain. He'll inject calm.

Sounds like another bad sci-fi movie. But you get the point.

Don't worry about anything; instead, pray about everything. Tell God what you need, and thank him for all he has done.
PHILIPPIANS 4:6 NLT

Breathe

You can survive maybe forty days without food.

You could live three or four days without water.

But you can go without air for only a few minutes before you permanently fuzz your brain.

A few minutes more and you're dead.

Get this: Your body can do three kinds of breathing. There's *breathing hard* —like when you haul your bod through phys ed class. Then there's *breathing for others*—mouth-to-mouth emergencies. There's also *breathing you do all the time*—short, sweet, automatic bursts.

Prayer is like breathing. Your spiritual life can't survive without it. And just like you do three kinds of breathing, you can fill your life with three kinds of prayer.

Read 1 Thessalonians 5:17
How often does God want you to pray?

You figure God must be joking when he says to pray continually. It sounds like an assignment for your mom—or Mother Teresa. So how can you pray all the time?

By praying different kinds of prayer at different times.

There's *praying hard*. That's setting aside time just to pray—for yourself, friends, family, your whole world! It's a spiritual workout that's easy to shove aside, but it causes you steady growth.

There's code-red *prayer for others*. Those are the big-time emergency prayers—like when a friend's parents are divorcing or a family member is critically ill. But mouth-to-mouth moments don't come every day.

When the Bible says to "pray continually," it's talking especially about a third kind, *prayer all the time*—talking to God wherever you go and whatever you do. It's a habit as normal and unsweaty as the twelve breaths you take every minute of every day.

If prayer isn't part of your moment-to-moment life, you can slap your back and jump-start your breathing: Just say, "God, I think..." or "God, I feel..." or "God, I need..." and tell him what's going on in your heart, as often as you want.

Pray continually. 1 THESSALONIANS 5:17

Talking Straight to a Star

Imagine you won a contest to meet a superstar—let's say your favorite actress. Your parents drive you to a gleaming hotel, and two bodyguards with no necks meet you and escort you to the star's room. Other bodyguards push back screaming fans. The door cracks open, you dart in, and you're standing just inches from a celebrity you would sell your best friend to meet. What do you say?

After scraping your jaw off the floor, you would probably hit three themes: "I'm glad to meet you." (You tell her you're happy to be her friend.) "You're the best actress in the whole world." (You tell her she's a great person.) "Your last movie was so cool." (You tell her specific things she does that you like.)

You may wonder what to say to God when you pray. Someone once said that the word *PRAY* is a reminder of four things to do in prayer: *P*raise ... *R*epent ... *A*sk ... *Y*ield. When you're at a loss for words to pray, *praise* is a great place to start.

Read Psalm 18:25–36
What sort of things does David praise God for?

Knowing that you might fumble your words if you met a movie star, you would probably think ahead of time what to say—maybe even write it out. Applauding God with praise might take that kind of practice for you. But you can start with the same three kinds of things you would say to a star: Express friendship ("God, I'm glad I know you"); worship God for who he is ("You're an awesome God"); and thank God for what he does ("Thanks for helping me get my homework done"). It may help to read passages in the book of Psalms or to learn worship songs to discover what to say.

That might make you squirm, though, if you start to think that praise has to be gushy poetry set to music that makes you retch. Your praise doesn't need to be stiff, elegant, soft, or formal. Praise at its simplest is just using your mouth to applaud God, telling him he's great, whatever that sounds like coming from you. It's words you mean, telling God what you think of him.

For who is God besides the Lord? And who is the Rock except our God? PSALM 18:31

First Church of True Believers

Holly, president of the youth group at the First Church of True Believers, strode to the front of the church to pray. "God, ahem. I'm speaking. I thank you that we are not like the teens of this world who indulge in early sex and illegal drugs. We have Bible studies three evenings a week. We go on summer missions trips. We witness at school. We're just exactly the way you want us to be—not like scum who don't know you." She thumped her Bible—it looked as big as a library dictionary—then she smiled and said, "Amen!"

Andy sat in the back row of the church with his face in his hands. He had slipped into the back pew late after having a whopper fight with his parents. "God, I don't think I can ever be what you want me to be. Please forgive me."

Read Luke 18:9–14

Is God happier when we act totally holy—or get totally honest?

God doesn't hear your prayers because you've racked up a bunch of points by doing good or not doing bad. God hears you because Christ died and rose for you. God isn't happy with sin. But he's even less happy if we're too proud to admit that we sin against him and others in what we think, say, and do.

The second ingredient in PRAY is the *R: Repentance*. Repentance means to admit sin is sin. If someone is "repentant," it means that person comes to God in humility, realizing that he or she needs forgiveness.

Think how uncomfortable you are talking to your parents if you've done something wrong that they don't know about. You avoid being with your parents or looking at them. You sweat if they start asking questions. But the relationship is repaired as soon as you open up. It's the same with God. The person who hides sin from God is miserable, but the one who admits sin is happy and forgiven (Psalm 32:1–6).

Remember how sin erects a wall between you and God? Asking for forgiveness keeps the wall torn down and communication open. When you pray, take time to remember if there's anything you need to clear up between you and God.

The tax collector stood at a distance. He would not even look up to heaven, but beat his breast and said, "God, have mercy on me, a sinner." LUKE 18:13

God Is No Grouch

What aggravation! You need help, but the person you ask won't give it. It's like having a teacher who calls your questions stupid or a friend who puts off working together on a project. Or how about a store clerk who won't help you find what you need but instead follows you around the store expecting you to shoplift—just because of your age? All of it makes you walk away feeling awful, mumbling to yourself, "Fine. You don't care? I don't need you. I'll do it myself."

Jesus used an example like that to teach about prayer.

Read Luke 11:5–13
How does God respond to requests?

Jesus tells a story about a man who has an unexpected visitor show up at his door in the middle of the night. The host, though obligated to feed the visitor, has nothing to serve. So he bangs on a friend's door to borrow bread. Upset, the friend grouches about the time of night and slams the door. But the man is persistent. He keeps banging. In the end the grumpy guy wears down and gives in, loaning the bread only so he can get rid of the pounding and go back to bed.

The *A* in PRAY is for *Ask*. It's the part of prayer where you ask God to provide for your needs and wants—and it's the part most of us know best. But you'll never ask if you feel you're bugging God to do something he doesn't want to do.

Jesus wants you to know that God is the total *opposite* of the midnight grouch—or a belittling teacher, flaky friend, or suspicious clerk. You aren't being a pain to God when you ask him to meet your needs. In fact, Jesus encourages you to ask, expecting an answer: "Whoever asks, receives."

Jesus uses a bizarre comparison to show God's eagerness to answer your prayers. No father, he says, would give his child a snake instead of a fish, or a scorpion instead of an egg. Jesus' point is that if earthly fathers who sin and make mistakes can muster that much compassion, then you can be sure that your perfect heavenly Father won't fail to give you good gifts.

Ask and it will be given to you; seek and you will find; knock and the door will be opened to you. LUKE 11:9

Lord, You Pick

"No. You can't get a new bike this year," Kyle's dad answered. "Next year."

"All my friends have new ones," Kyle countered. "I don't want to ride my old one anymore. I look like a dork on it." Kyle's dad gave him that look that said, "Discussion ended."

The next summer Kyle's dad kept his promise and bought him a new bike. Since Kyle had grown several inches over the winter, Kyle got an awesome adult-sized bike. His friends had grown too, and now their bikes were tiny. They were the ones who looked funny.

Kyle's dad evaluated whether or not he needed the bike and decided he did, but he also knew next year would be better timing. When you ask God for something, he does the same thing. You can't treat God like a cosmic candy machine—put in the right stuff, hit a button, and expect the sweet of your choice. In prayer, the final choice is up to God, not you.

Yield is the fourth part of PRAY. It means having an attitude that says, "God, answer this as you see best, according to your plan, not mine."

Read Luke 22:39–46

How does Jesus' prayer before he died on the cross show him yielding to God's choice?

Jesus knew that dying for the world's sins would be more painful than anyone could imagine. He even wondered aloud whether there was another way to save the world, saying, "Father, if it is possible, don't let me go through this." But he closed his prayer with an attitude that yielded to his Father's plan, leaving the choice to God. He prayed, "Not my will, but yours be done."

Jesus trusted that his Father knew best. He accepted his Father's answer without complaint. He said to God, "You pick. You decide." He trusted that whatever God's answer was, it would be the best. Not the easiest. Not the most comfortable. But the best.

God has an incredible plan for you (Jeremiah 29:11). Ask for what you want. Yet don't forget to let God have his perfect way.

[Jesus] withdrew about a stone's throw beyond them, knelt down and prayed. "Father, if you are willing, take this cup from me; yet not my will, but yours be done." LUKE 22:41-42

Prayer Abuse

Somewhere in the high channels on your TV—wedged between the shopping networks and the B-movie reruns—there exists the TV Preacher Zone. A few occupants of the zone are honest teachers of God's Word. Others pull off a common crime: prayer abuse. *Prayer: It will make your every dream come true! Just believe hard enough, use my formula, promise to be good, and SHAZAM! God answers every prayer. Think of the possibilities, folks! Get an A on every test, make pimples vanish, always play your violin in tune, and sink every just-as-the-buzzer-sounds shot from half-court. Keep your dog from dying, your parents from fighting, and your best friend from moving away.* Click.

Read John 15:7–14

Does Jesus agree with the over-the-top promises of TV preachers?

Jesus did say, "Ask whatever you wish, and it will be given you." But here's the crucial condition: *If* you remain in him and his words remain in you, *then* God will give what you ask. "To remain" means being like a branch that stays connected to the vine. Having Christ's words in you means you're shaped by his promises, values, and priorities.

That doesn't mean God answers only the prayers of super-spiritual people. It just means that if you live close to God, you'll want what God wants for you, and he'll gladly grant that request. You'll want things that make you more like Christ so you show God's greatness, his glory.

Even so, you don't always get what you want, because no one *always* prays perfectly within God's will. Sometimes it's easy to spot prayer abuse—like praying to score a fake ID so you can sneak into an R-rated movie. Get clear about those prayers: You don't get what you ask for because your motives stink (James 4:3).

Sometimes it won't make any sense to you why God didn't answer a prayer the way you thought he should. Remind yourself that only God sees the best possible answer to your every request—and trust him to give it to you.

If you remain in me and my words remain in you, ask whatever you wish, and it will be given you. JOHN 15:7

Jesus' Prayer

"O God, who reigneth in the heavenlies," Mr. Hannon prayed, "we thank thee for plucking us from the mire of iniquity and designating us your progeny." Translation? "God of the universe, thanks for freeing us from sin and for calling us your children."

Some people use weird words when they pray, words that they would never use any other time. It can confuse us and lose us, like it did Jesus' disciples. They heard religious leaders pray all the time, but they noticed that Jesus' prayers were different. So they asked Jesus to teach them to pray.

Read Matthew 6:5–13

What kind of prayer did Jesus teach his disciples to pray?

Jesus let his followers in on a couple of truths. He told them not to pray in public just to get attention, and he said long prayers don't get better answers from God than short ones. Then he gave his disciples a sort of pattern to follow. He didn't say "pray these words"—though there's nothing wrong with that—but "pray something like this."

What he taught them—the Lord's Prayer—has several parts: "Our Father in heaven, hallowed be your name." That's praise—saying people should recognize God as holy. "Forgive us our debts, as we forgive our debtors." That's repentance—asking forgiveness for sins.

The other petitions are examples of the *Ask* part of PRAY. Some are spiritual requests. "Your kingdom come, your will be done on earth as it is in heaven" asks that God would rule in our lives and in the world. "Lead us not into temptation" is similar. It asks that God would keep evil from luring us away from him. Another request is practical. "Give us today our daily bread" is asking for things we need for survival in this world—food, a place to live, clothing, work, help at school, family harmony, and solid friends.

Jesus' sample prayer is *straightforward*, meant for talking with God, not impressing people. His prayer is *sure*; He talks to God as Father, confident of an answer. And his prayer is *simple*. It skips the fancy words and asks straight up for the things we need.

This, then, is how you should pray: "Our Father in heaven,
hallowed be your name, your kingdom come,
your will be done on earth as it is in heaven...."
MATTHEW 6:9

Rip a Hole in the Roof

Teresa stood by the door to the girls' locker room after phys ed, looking pale and foggy. A friend spotted her and ran over. "What's wrong?"

"I think I broke my arm." Brilliant insight, considering her arm looked like a piece of hanger art, bent in three new directions. How Teresa managed to slip by the gym teacher no one could figure out, but she was in such a pained daze that her friends had to take her by the hand—the unbusted one—and lead her to the school nurse, who called Teresa's parents.

Read Mark 2:1–12

How did the paralyzed man's friends help him get healed?

Lots of people you know need help getting to Jesus. Even though Jesus doesn't tour around like he did in the Bible, we can still bring friends to him through prayer.

Like the paralytic on his stretcher, your friends may not be able to get to Jesus by themselves. They may be sick—too depressed or medicated to pray. Their need may be so big that no human being can handle it alone—like coping with their parents' divorce, a dad's heart attack, or a sibling's suicide. Or the friends, classmates, parents, or other people you care about may not even be Christians—and so unaware of their need for Christ and his help that they would never pray for themselves.

Jesus healed the paralytic physically and spiritually. You might not always see those results from your prayers—sometimes God has a better plan. At other times the person you pray for may continue to resist God—like a parent who has an affair and refuses to come home. God would like to fix the situation, but the person won't let him.

Even so, *your* faith allows God to act among even your non-Christian friends. Your prayers can help a friend get healed, find hope, or become a Christian. God won't force himself on anybody, but praying for your friends is like opening a crack in the door to let God into the situation or like ripping a hole in the roof and bringing your concerns right to God.

Some men came, bringing to [Jesus] a paralytic, carried by four of them. Since they could not get him to Jesus because of the crowd, they made an opening in the roof. MARK 2:3-4

Prayer Changes Things

The bumper sticker on the car read, *Prayer Changes Things.* But the car didn't exactly look like a reason to believe that prayer works. The beater was twenty-some years old and it coughed black smoke as it rumbled slightly sideways down the highway. Prayer hadn't miraculously gotten that guy a better car—or just a better job so he could get a better car. Besides that, a stick figure in a wheelchair on the car's license plate advertised that the car's driver was handicapped. If God answers prayer, why wasn't the driver healed?

Have you or a friend ever prayed and it seemed God didn't hear? You prayed for your parents—they still got divorced. You prayed for your grandparents—they got sick and died. You prayed for a friend—the one who moved away. Or you prayed for smaller things—good grades, a place on the team, a role in a play—and yet all of your prayers seemed to go unanswered.

Paul talked openly about all the times he prayed to God for help dealing with a "thorn in the flesh"—maybe an enemy, maybe an illness. Even though we don't know exactly what Paul's problem was, we know the result.

Read 2 Corinthians 12:7–10
What did Paul's prayer change?

Prayer didn't change Paul's circumstances. It changed Paul.

Paul's problem was so bad that he prayed three times for God to take it away. Finally God said no. But God told Paul He would strengthen him in the middle of his agony.

Get this: Paul says he needed the thorn to keep him from becoming proud of his great spiritual insights. The thorn made him depend on God and realize that God was closest when he struggled. That didn't make the thorn any less painful, but Paul learned that God could use the thorn for good.

When you don't see the answers you want for your prayers, try to see what God might be doing in you and your relationship with him. Prayer *always* changes the person who prays in faith *if* he or she trusts that God hears and cares. Prayer that seems to fail produces a Christian who succeeds.

Three times I pleaded with the Lord to take it away from me.
But he said to me, "My grace is sufficient for you, for my
power is made perfect in weakness." 2 CORINTHIANS 12:8–9

All Ears

"Not now!" Jill's dad barked. "I'm worn out and I have work to do!"

"But I need help with math," Jill repeated. "It's due tomorrow."

"You're going to have to figure it out yourself," Mr. Davidson came back. "Maybe if you and your sister didn't fight all the time I'd have energy to help you."

Jill's mom rushed to calm Dad down. "What do you think it's like for your father? He works all day long and comes home and hears you screaming at each other."

By then Jill's little sister was pulling at Mr. Davidson's pant leg. "Will you take me to the park?" Mr. Davidson flashed a tiny bit of tenderness, then flew off again.

"I have to work," he said, pulling his coat on. "I'm going back down to the office. Good night." Jill winced when the door slammed behind him. She wondered why she even tried to talk to her dad.

Read Psalm 27:7–14
Why does God sometimes seem hard of hearing?

Talking to a parent can be like talking to a rock. A big unbudgeable rock. Or a sharp stone flung hard at your head. Or an annoying little rock in your shoe. Some kids react by shutting up and only talking with their friends. You're fortunate if you can talk back and forth well with your parents. You probably know friends who can't.

God isn't like a parent who can't hear or won't talk.

Still, sometimes he seems far off. Even David begged God to hear him and respond. What David wrote in Psalm 27, though, hints at some reasons God goes quiet: (1) to teach you to seek him more; (2) to not treat him like an old toy you store on the shelf until you're in the mood; (3) to teach you to trust his acceptance of you, that if you admit your sin to him, he never holds it against you (Psalm 103:12); or (4) to test whether you want to know how to follow him badly enough to wait for him to show you how.

In the end God wants to see one thing built in you: faith that he is good and he is your God. He isn't teasing. He isn't too busy. He's teaching.

Wait for the Lord; be strong and take heart and
wait for the Lord. PSALM 27:14

Church Is Booooring

Whap! Your pastor slaps the pulpit—his usual habit when he reaches a key point. Everyone stops rustling. Only a gurgling baby disturbs the silence.

Until you shake the pew, that is, while reading the unusually funny note your best friend just passed you. Your face contorts. You try to laugh without making any noise. Suddenly you notice the silence, look up, and see the pastor glaring down at you and your friends with one eyebrow raised. You shut up and start rehearsing your excuse for later: *Church services are so boring....*

Church isn't always fun. It's often designed for adults. Part of its purpose is learning and correction. And all you might know about worship and praise is "Get up. Get dressed. Get in the car. Sit still and shut up." But assuming you're not a rebel who wants nothing to do with God or church, the biggest reason church services are boring is lack of understanding.

Read Deuteronomy 6:4–9
How can you get hyped about church?

Adults are supposed to explain what being a believer is all about. Some don't—not in a way that helps you grab hold. So you need to get answers for yourself.

For starters, *try to understand what's happening in the service.* Ask your parents what's going on. If you watch a sporting event without knowing the rules, you get bored. At church, if you don't understand who the players are, why you stand or sit, or what the words in the music or sermon mean, you'll shrivel up. If you can follow what's going on, you might learn to like it.

Then ask your parents why they go to church. Why aren't they bored? If you watch a football game on TV all by yourself with the sound turned down, it's a guaranteed snooze. You need to be part of the oomph of the crowd to feel interested. Find out why God matters to your parents. Why did they start going to church? Why do they keep going? Why is worshiping God so crucial that you have to get up, get dressed, get in the car, sit still, and shut up?

These commandments that I give you today are to be upon your hearts. Impress them on your children. DEUTERONOMY 6:6-7

Big Baby

Steffi got claustrophobic every time she heard it. Whenever she wondered out loud why she had to go to church, her mom tossed her the same line: "Because it's right! We go to church because it's the right thing to do."

To Steffi, "the right thing to do" was excruciatingly, painfully, agonizingly boring. She'd tried everything to escape. Some Sundays she screamed. Other Sundays she shot cold, ugly stares at her mom. And one Sunday she yanked the covers over her head and ignored her mom. (Bad choice. As much as Steffi disliked going to church, she *really* disliked getting dragged from bed and going to church with her hair and face all gnarled.)

Steffi wanted a real reason to show up at Sunday school and sit through a church service—something more than "just because."

Somehow Steffi's mom always won.

But pretty soon Steffi would be too big to be carried to the car and strapped in the seat belt.

Read Psalm 95:1–11
What does it mean to "worship" God?

God is all-powerful: Lord, Master, Judge. God is all-kind: the Giver of forgiveness through Christ. But if you don't perceive God's mind-boggling perfection, then worshiping him doesn't make sense. The cool parts of being a Christian—obeying God and getting together with other believers—become rules and ritual rather than a relationship with your God. It's nothing more than "the right thing to do."

God himself is the reason behind everything you do as a Christian. And church is a primo chance to bow before him. Your *mouth* worships. You tell God how great he is. You "shout aloud to the Rock," the one who rescues you from sin's power and penalty. No mumbling meaningless words, though—your *heart* worships too. You acknowledge that you belong to God. You agree that his will is good. And you worship with your *life*, giving yourself to him out of thankfulness for what he's done for you (Romans 12:1).

God doesn't drag you to church. He created church as a chance for you to grasp his greatness.

Come, let us bow down in worship, let us kneel before the Lord our Maker; for he is our God and we are the people of his pasture, the flock under his care. PSALM 95:6-7

No-Brainer

You watch your brain float overhead as you lie on an examination table. Your brain jumps and wriggles as lasers shoot from the walls to probe it.

"Basically empty, compared to ours," a space alien doctor says to his colleagues. *Great. They must have figured out that I flunked my last math test. My parents don't even know that.* As they tuck your brain painlessly back into your head, they scan the rest of your body. *I can't wait to hear the results of this one.*

"Muscular structure: Unremarkable. Molecular composition: Mostly water. Chemical value of creature in earth money: Six dollars and two cents."

"Note the bad haircut," another doctor interjects.

"Yes, of course. I think we all agree with my recommendation: Vaporize."

Read Colossians 3:5–14

What do you want people to notice when they look at you?

When God made us, he planned that people would see *him* when they saw us. Unfortunately, sin has deformed our features so that we no longer look like God.

Quiz time: If you gave God, who is utterly perfect, the chance to make you look like him again, which of the following would best describe you? (a) The wardrobe and plastic good looks of Ken or Barbie; (b) the musical talents of the Beach Boys; (c) the brains of Einstein; (d) the vertical jump of Michael Jordan; or (e) none of the above.

In heaven we will receive a new body that may or may not include choices a, b, c, and d. But for now, God's first concern is something else: He wants to remake your *character* so that you think, feel, speak, and act like him.

The "old self" is human nature deformed. It's all the things that make you ugly, unlike God. The "new self" is just the opposite. It looks more like God each day. Those are the things God sculpts in you when you let him. He remakes you to look like him.

You want people to notice more than brains, looks, or talent when they probe your life. They should see a new you looking more and more like God.

Therefore, as God's chosen people, holy and dearly loved, clothe yourselves with compassion, kindness, humility, gentleness and patience. COLOSSIANS 3:12

Don't Look Now

9:00 A.M.   Your principal announces over the school's intercom that your *Save the Ducklings* poster won first prize from the state Animal Humane Society.

9:02 A.M.   Your social studies teacher sends you to chat with the principal about the celebration dance you did on your desk.

10:00 A.M.   Between classes your best friend thanks you for helping her study for a math test.

10:02 A.M.   Your significant other dumps you like yesterday's trash.

12:00 A.M.   Sitting in a lunch-hour detention for your desk disco, you receive an after-school detention for passing notes.

3:00 A.M.   You ponder why half the world loves you and half the world thinks you're a mutant gnat. Which is it?

Read Psalm 19:7–14
How does the Bible tell you who you are?

Picture this: You blow your nose and miss the tissue, sliming your collar. Your own eyes can't quite twist to spot your problem. You could walk around looking stupid for a long time. Some people point, laugh, and walk away. Others figure you already know and don't want to interfere with your stylin' accessorizing. Still others might call you a trendsetter. Only a real friend would whisper in your ear and tell you the truth.

All of us have flaws we can't see. Yet the evaluations of others aren't always accurate. Their criticisms can be too harsh or their support too kind. They might not know right from wrong. Even our own consciences can goof.

What others think does matter. But above all else, you want to listen to God's opinion of you. God doesn't give you a satellite hookup to heaven, but you can hear God speak in the Bible, teaching you right from wrong through his "laws," "statutes," "precepts," and "commands." You listen to him because you know his opinion is more important than anyone else's, and what he says isn't meant to hurt you. He speaks out of love, to help you.

He's definitely the kind of friend who whispers in your ear.

The law of the LORD is perfect, reviving the soul. The statutes of the LORD are trustworthy, making wise the simple…. Who can discern his errors? Forgive my hidden faults. PSALM 19:7, 12

Price Tags

Maybe you've seen peers leave price tags dangling from hats and jackets. It's a handy way to dash any doubt about whose clothes are more expensive.

But there's an even more sinister comparison that goes on all day long. We're constantly comparing "price tags" with everyone else—and not just how much our clothes cost. We measure *people* and judge how much they're worth.

Some kids' price tags say that they're almost worthless. There's the kid who sits three seats behind you in math class. Everyone agrees he's the dumbest person in your grade. Or you might join your friends when they laugh at Mindy when her unemployed dad drives up in a junker car.

Other people's tags are so expensive that they make you feel like a clearance sale leftover. Certain cliques won't let you in because you fall short of their standards. Peers in phys ed class who are more developed than you may make you wonder if you'll ever grow up. Or your youth group might look so spiritual that you doubt you could ever matter to God.

Here's some good news: God puts a different price tag on people. And the tag says that you are infinitely valuable.

Read 1 Peter 1:18–19
How much did God pay for you?

God thinks that compared to you, even gold is worthless trash. When God wanted to reignite a friendship with you, it cost him the incalculable price of the death of his Son, Jesus. Cash registers can't count that high! Yet that's the price tag God glues on you and everyone else on earth. That's how much he thinks you're worth. Given that fact, no one ever deserves to be tagged as a reject. And you can shut out any voice that says you are anything less than God's prized son or daughter.

When God looks at the world, everyone is equally valuable to him. No one is on sale. No one is an ugly shirt with six markdowns on his price tag, one that says, "You're worthless. No one wants you." Your price tag says the same thing as all the others in the world: *Jesus loves me and died for me.*

You were bought, not with something that ruins like gold or silver, but with the precious blood of Christ, who was like a pure and perfect lamb. 1 PETER 1:18–19 NCV

Looking Good

Sarah frowned at her bedroom mirror. *Jab, lift* with the comb. *Tug, tweak* with a brush. *Fwoosh, fwoosh* with the hairspray. Then, for the seventh time that morning, she ran into the bathroom to wet down her hair so she could start all over. After all, her hair didn't *poof* just right.

Sound familiar? Okay, so you're not hung up on your hair, though that's doubtful. But maybe you try on multiple outfits every morning. Or you are magnetically drawn to mirrors throughout the day. Or you're addicted to breath mints or habitually double-check your deodorant by sniffing your armpits. Uh-huh. That's you.

Read Micah 6:8

What is God scoping out when he looks at human beings?

Even if the whole world were blind, you wouldn't go out in public unwashed and dressed in a trash bag. Face it: You primp not just to stay clean and healthy and to feel okay about yourself but to please others. You think you look good only when others think you look good. And guys worry as much as girls. They just worry about other things, like building whomping thighs, massive chests, and peaked biceps.

Some people *will* judge you by your looks. Your task is to decide how much you will let their view of you run your life.

The ugliest people in the world are the ones who have polished their surfaces but never gone deeper. God—and anyone worth impressing—knows that looks aren't everything. God will be pleased when he spies genuine righteousness, kindness, and humility in you. He doesn't wonder, "Did your hair turn out? Are your muscles gargantuan?" He's asking, "Do you work hard? Can your parents trust you? Do you have a good attitude? Has your head swollen too big to get through a door?"

God made you awesomely good-looking—and he wants you to take care of yourself. But he made you to please him in attitudes and actions, not to be a slave to a blow-dryer.

The Lord has told you, human, what is good; he has told you what he wants from you: to do what is right to other people, love being kind to others, and live humbly, obeying your God.
MICAH 6:8 NCV

Good for Something

By the middle of the school year Ben was treading deep water and gasping for breath. His grades were dismal. He was benched by the soccer coach when he tripped and sprained his toe in the season opener—and broke the leg of the team's star center. His boss at the nursing home where he volunteered told him he annoyed the residents—and that they would rather be lonely than listen to him blather. Teachers politely informed him he couldn't sing, act, or draw—and that he should try to find himself somewhere else. In a burst of explorative ingenuity, he signed up for a Chinese class at a community center—and found out "Ben" sounds like "stupid" in Mandarin.

"Everyone's good at something, dear," his mom cooed. "You'll find something."

"Quit it, Mom!" Ben moaned. "You're my mother. You have to like me. But I'm not good at anything."

At times everyone feels like a child only a mother could love.

Read Romans 12:1–8

How do you find your special gift in life?

Sometimes mothers are right: Everyone is good at something. The Bible says the same thing: God gives everyone gifts. But how do you find yours? Try these tactics:

Don't expect applause. Some gifts put you up front where people *ooh* and *aah*. People seldom clap if you're kind, giving, encouraging, or good at serving. Just because no one says "Wow!" doesn't mean you bombed.

Try it out. You don't figure out what you're good at by sitting around or by trying something only once.

Be yourself. Even Christians can rip on people with different gifts. Sometimes you'll feel odd even when you're doing the right thing.

You begin to find your gifts, though, when you *make yourself available to God.* For starters, that's the only right response to everything God gives you. And as you follow him you'll find your way.

Just as each of us has one body with many members, and these members do not all have the same function... We have different gifts. ROMANS 12:4, 6

Power Steering

Megan cracks a wicked smile as her aunt and uncle and cousins pull into the driveway. They live in a state where it never snows. Last summer her cousins nearly drowned her in the ocean. They called her a hick.

Now it's winter. And they're on her turf.

Megan tosses them some ice skates and herds them to a frozen pond out back. It's time to race.

Race? They can't stand up. Cold air burns their lungs. When their toes get cold and they want to go inside, Megan swoops in for the kill. She buzzes circles around them. They sprawl. She hip checks. They smack ice.

On the way inside she tells them she has one more cool thing to try—licking a flagpole. "Helffffph!" they yell, their tongues frozen to the pole.

"You deserve that," Megan screams as she heads inside. "I hate you!"

Read Judges 16:23–30

How can you get good at something without getting snotty?

Samson's conceit about his strength was the only thing bigger than his muscles. So when he let his Philistine girlfriend sweet-talk him into revealing the secret of his might, God let his enemies grab him, gouge out his eyes, and toss him in prison to grind wheat like a mule (Judges 16:21).

Samson became powerful again only when he was tamed—when he remembered that because his strength came *from* God it should be used *for* God. Instead of using his strength for himself alone, he handed the Philistines—a nation at war with Israel—a crushing defeat.

When you're smart or skilled you can gently clue people in on what you know—or smear brains in their faces. When you're strong you can use your strength to help people—or to break their thumbs. And when you're funny you choose between cheering people up—or pounding them down.

And when you make your choice about how to handle your great gift, remember this: The strongest people are the ones who don't have to prove their strength.

Then Samson prayed to the Lord, "O Sovereign Lord, remember me. O God, please strengthen me just once more."
JUDGES 16:28

I Was Here

The note left on the lunch table read: *"I was here. Did you even notice?"*

Feeling unnoticed, average, and expendable is massively un-fun. Being so-so at sports means standout players get all the attention. Doing average at school means you slip past both teachers and tutors. Being your age—not a kid, not an adult—guarantees that some people will ignore you. Having blazingly smart brothers or sisters can make you feel worthless to your family. You feel invisible—and it makes you wish you could change your looks, age, clothes, personality, talents, brains. You'd try anything to bust loose from the crowd, to feel unique and important!

Read Jeremiah 1:4–10

How did Jeremiah respond when God told him to speak up?

Jeremiah was a teenaged shepherd known to no one when God called him to preach. Jeremiah probably thought his sheep could do better speaking for God. He reminded God that he was a nobody, young and fumble-mouthed.

God didn't see Jeremiah that way. He wanted to use the young shepherd to challenge the kings and people of Israel with a piercing message. God told Jeremiah that he had made plans for Jeremiah's life even before the young man was born.

And when God got through with him, Jeremiah was anything but ordinary. God transformed him from a scared shepherd to a gutsy prophet. What made Jeremiah useful to God wasn't his abilities or lack of them but his total devotion to God's plan. Piles of people are talented and smart. Few are obedient and available to God like Jeremiah.

God chooses and uses ordinary people so that everyone will realize that skills and abilities and talents are gifts from God (1 Corinthians 1:26–31). Whether or not you stand out in a crowd isn't what makes you matter. It's having an obedient heart that lets God lead you in the unique plan he's crafted for you.

But the Lord said to me, "Do not say, 'I am only a child.' You must go to everyone I send you to and say whatever I command you. Do not be afraid of them, for I am with you and will rescue you," declares the Lord. JEREMIAH 1:7-8

In the Spotlight

"It's a long fly ball," Cory bellowed in a sportscaster voice as Vinnie rounded first base in the middle-of-the-street ball game. "The Big V really smashed that one! What power! What grace!" Cheers were buried by laughter and the smash hit forgotten, however, as Vinnie tripped over second base and skidded on the pavement, shredding his knees.

Some days you figure you'll never do any better than Vinnie. But you won't always fall on your face. Sooner or later—maybe just in little ways—you'll see the crowd, hear the applause, bask in the spotlight. You might discover a hobby or a job you excel at. You could score the highest in your class, grow up into a hunk or a beauty queen some summer, or sweat hard and finally make the basketball team.

Applause is fun. Compliments feel good. But they can also make you a nasty person who looks down on people, ignores old friends, and expects special treatment.

When things go well and people applaud, you have a huge task. You get to learn to be great without getting big-headed.

Read Philippians 2:3–8

How did Jesus practice humility?

If anyone ever had a right to applause, it was Jesus. He's God! He possessed the majesty and splendor of the King of the universe, yet he didn't draw attention to himself. Instead of rolling up in a limo and making a big splash, he came quietly as a helpless baby and grew up to be a servant who died on the cross for the sins of his creation.

When the glare of the spotlight blinds you, you see only yourself. Fight that temptation to think only of yourself by stepping out of the spotlight, like Jesus, through servanthood. Run away from selfishness by remembering other people's needs as much as your own.

You can also share the spotlight with your Lord. After all, God is the real source of your gifts, talents, and abilities (1 Corinthians 4:7). When people applaud you, applaud God! Tell him thanks for your success, and remember that he is more important than anything you achieve (Jeremiah 9:23-24).

Do nothing out of selfish ambition or vain conceit, but in humility consider others better than yourselves.
PHILIPPIANS 2:3-5

No-Stick Jesus

Jennifer whirled around and pretended to dig in the bottom of her locker. Her long hair hid her wet eyes. She didn't want anyone to see her cry. *ZIT FACE!* echoed in her head. *How could Ashley say that about me?* she thought. *She's supposed to be my friend. Everyone in the stupid hall heard!*

Jennifer walked home from school that day instead of taking the bus. She cut through some backyards so Ashley couldn't look out from her house across the street and see her walking alone. That night she lay in bed rehearsing all the things she wished she had said.

Sticks and stones may break our bones, but being called names hurts even worse. We're Teflon people. Food is supposed to slip right out of those coated pans, but it's never that easy. When careless cooks scratch Teflon, it doesn't work so well. When careless people scratch us, the insults that are supposed to slide off stick and stink like burnt food: *You're ugly. You're dumb. You'll never get a girlfriend. You'll never make the team.* Those words hurt. Like the Bible says, "Reckless words pierce like a sword" (Proverbs 12:18).

But Jesus knew how to let what people said slide right off.

Read 1 Peter 2:21–25
How did Jesus react to put-downs?

Jesus didn't insult in return—that would make him as bad as his tormentors. Instead, he trusted the Father who sees perfectly. He realized one opinion counted more than all of the others put together.

Do the people who shred you know you? Not as well as God does. Is what people say true? Maybe. But if you truly do have something wrong with you, God tells you constructively—gently, with great timing, helping you change.

You can let insults slide off by listening to what God says about you. You're his daughter or son. He loves you more than anyone else does. Listen for *God's* evaluation of your words, dress, looks, attitudes, actions, sins, faults, and skills. It's God's opinion that counts.

When they hurled their insults at [Jesus], he did not retaliate; when he suffered, he made no threats. Instead, he entrusted himself to him who judges justly. 1 PETER 2:23

We Are the Champions

Each spring, baseball fans try to predict that year's World Series winner. But how can you see the end of the season at the start? Wishful thinking doesn't win championships—ask any Chicago Cubs fan. Being picked to win doesn't do it—plenty can go wrong during the season. Even buying multimillion-dollar players doesn't always work. Trusting luck is a cop-out—every team gets good and bad breaks.

Baseball fans—and players—would be less uptight about the season if they knew from the start who would win at the end. Knowing the winners ahead of time, of course, kills the thrill of sports.

You're at the beginning of the season as far as your life is concerned. It isn't much fun wondering how your life will turn out. How will *you* finish at the end of the season? Are you going to win? How can you tell?

Read Philippians 1:3–6
How does God promise you'll turn out when you're devoted to Jesus?

Paul wrote to the Philippians that he was certain about one thing: Because they belonged to God, he would never let them go. He would keep perfecting their faith until the time Christ comes back to earth. At the end of the season, they would be winners.

That wasn't just a happy wish. Paul had seen God start his work in the Philippians. They had become believers and had begun to spread the good news about Jesus Christ. As they continued as Paul's partners, God's life grew in them. Because God keeps all his promises, even suffering and death could not rip victory out of their hands (1:22, 29).

Some days you'll feel like a batter in an endless slump in the game of life. You may feel like a social reject, unlikable, ugly, awful at everything. God will coach you out of those slumps. What's more, his eternal game plan means that even though you don't always win in those things, you'll win big at the end of the season in what matters the very most: your relationship with God. If you let God be your coach, he promises to make you a spiritual champion.

Being confident of this, that he who began a good work in you will carry it on to completion until the day of Christ Jesus.
PHILIPPIANS 1:6

Phlegmwad

Andre glanced around for a friendly face, then sat alone at a lunch table. A group of older girls came over, called him a phlegmwad, and said that he was getting their section slimy. He was new at school, but he took that as a hint he should move. No big deal. He had spotted Dan, a kid he recognized from math class.

Dan didn't look too barbaric, and Andre thought he had a good shot at making a new friend. When Andre went over to Dan's table and sat down, though, everyone ignored him. Andre ate his lunch next to Dan and his friends, but he felt even more lonely than when he had been alone.

You don't have to be new at school to feel lonely. When strangers trounce you, your friends act like enemies, or your parents and family don't understand you, you feel isolated, left out. And since you can't see God, even he can seem like he's nowhere near.

Read Psalm 73:21–26
What can you do when you feel like a phlegmwad?

One of King David's musicians, Asaph (AY-saf), wrote Psalm 73 when he felt cut off from everyone around him because he followed God. What he discovered can help your loneliness, whatever the cause.

Asaph expected that God would fix his situation instantly. He no doubt thought that as a follower of God he was a friend worth having. He should be liked, popular—and included. In time, God surely gave him friends, but for a while God let him be alone.

Asaph found that God sometimes lets you feel lonely to remind you that all you really have is God and that he is all you need. Family won't always be there—parents have lots to do, and someday you'll move out. Who will you depend on? Friends move, or you just change. Who will you hang out with?

In the middle of being lonely, Asaph came to a simple conclusion: *God is always near.*

When you have no one else, you have God, and he's enough.

Whom have I in heaven but you? And earth has nothing I desire besides you. My flesh and my heart may fail, but God is the strength of my heart and my portion forever. PSALM 73:25-26

Best Buy in the Mall

Heather opened the front door, then wished she had checked the peephole to see what was standing on her step. Too late.

A man in a lime green leisure suit stepped forward with a dismal "Hullo. We're from the Church of the Bozos down the block."

The lady with him wore a dress that resembled the curtains in Heather's grandma's house. She looked as if the tight bun in her hair had cut off blood to her brain. It had. "Oh, honey, let me talk to her." She pushed her husband to the side. "Would you like a balloon, little girl?" she asked.

"Do I look like I do balloons?" Heather snapped back. "Hey, you haven't been over to my grandma's, have you?" The couple stood looking stupid until a boy Heather's age poked his head around. He was a three-quarter-size replica of his dad, to the suit.

"You're *my* age!" he squealed. "Will you come to church? *Pleeeeeease?*"

Read Matthew 13:44–46

Why did the digger swap everything he had for a treasure?

Your world has more salespeople than a megamall. Each tries to sell you something supposed to make you totally goofy with happiness.

God isn't selling anything. What he offers is free: He wants to give you the gift of his friendship, greatness, presence, and guidance. He wants to be King of your life. Yet he lets you shop around, to choose for or against him, to love him or leave him. Bozos, though, don't exactly help God's pitch. If you think being a Christian means becoming a bozo, then you'll keep malling for a better deal.

But once you understand what God has for you—becoming part of the kingdom of heaven, knowing and following God—no one has to beg or force you to accept God's treasure. Nothing makes you say "Blecchhh!"

Being totally devoted to God won't make you weird. Christians just put trust and obedience to God first. Always. No matter what.

That's a price. But what you pay is nothing compared to what you gain.

The kingdom of heaven is like treasure hidden in a field. When a man found it, he hid it again, and then in his joy went and sold all he had and bought that field. MATTHEW 13:44

Earthshake

Play parent: Your family is buying a house. You must choose from a cat-alog featuring the only two houses for sale on the entire planet. House A is ready for immediate move-in. It's a mansion with striking features, like a party-ready pool and deck in back. The contract for House A says, however, that one day an earthquake will shake the house to the ground, with its owner in it. Nothing will be left—no house, no stuff, no you. No lie.

House B looks like a more modest dwelling, but the house promises to keep you snug and warm. Parts of the contract for House B, though, are unusual. It says that renovators are constantly upgrading the house—for free. And here's the strangest part: Once completed, House B will be transported to a stunning oceanside location.

You're in charge of the family dollar. Which house would you choose?

Read Hebrews 12:22–29

What will survive when God shakes the world? ("They" in verse 25 refers to Israel, mentioned back in verses 14–21.)

You wouldn't be a happy home buyer if you moved into a house and found yourself stuck with mildewed living room carpet, a leaky pool, and a termite-infested deck. You'd regret you hadn't examined the house up close. You'd be in one ugly mood when the house shook to toothpicks and you hadn't believed that the contract was legal, binding, and unalterable.

So don't buy a house God has said he will destroy.

God promises that in heaven you will share a home where you can rock with the angel choir and room with non-bozos, where you're eternally wel-come because Christ paid the bills and invited you in.

Living in God's house are the people who accepted Christ's great gift. Living at the only other address in the universe are people who laugh at God's warning and refuse his invitation to live with him. When God shakes all of creation—to keep what's worth keeping—only God's house and those in it will stand strong. The other house—sin, and everyone in it—will be demol-ished.

Sound scary? Not if you choose the right house.

Worship God acceptably with reverence and awe, for our "God is a consuming fire." HEBREWS 12:28-29

Waves Gone Gonzo

After loafing too long on the beach, Cassie started to name the sea-gulls that begged for lunch. While her friends surfed and swam and Boogie-boarded, Cassie twirled her toes in the sand and frequented the hot-dog stand. Cassie wouldn't go in the water. She knew how to swim, but hadn't grown up on the ocean like her friends had. Waves terrified her.

Until her friends finally threw her in.

Waaaaaah! she howled as a wave whapped her. *Woaaaaaah!* she laughed as she figured out how to bob to the top. *Haaaaaaaah!* Cassie shrieked as she bodysurfed in to shore.

Read Hebrews 4:14–16

Do real believers ever get tempted to do wrong stuff? How?

God doesn't command Christians to sit by themselves on the beach building grand sand castles. The riotous fun is in the water—living life, playing, enjoying friends, working, studying, watching Christ stomp on the waves. It's where you get to chuckle, smile, and cheer.

Most waves are great fun. But some are killers that knock down and drown people who play in them.

Evil is almost always a good thing out of control—a wave gone extreme, out of bounds, past God's plan. Evil is words (a good thing) twisted into a knife (a bad thing). Or a desire to fit with friends churned into a fear of your peers. It's self-esteem swollen into pride. Or sex breaking the boundary of marriage. Or using the power of drugs to hurt rather than heal.

Just like us, Jesus was tempted to swim out over his head. He lived in the same rollicking waves of life. He had the same opportunities we do to get outside God's boundaries. To each temptation Jesus said, "Good thing. But wrong time. Wrong way. No way." (See Matthew 4:1–11.)

Christians don't hide on the beach, because they know the real fun is out in the waves. But they're smart enough to watch out for waves that threaten to pound them.

For our high priest is able to understand our weaknesses. When he lived on earth, he was tempted in every way that we are, but he did not sin. HEBREWS 4:15 NCV

Tummy Toaster

"My feet are really cold!" Drew shouted to friends ahead on the trail. They kept skiing. "I mean it!"

"Whiner!" one yelled back.

A half hour later everyone rested at a fork in the trail. "Drew—I hear your feet are cold," said Jeff, their trail guide. "Slip a boot off."

"No, they're okay. Really. I'm fine." Drew didn't want to be a whiner.

"I want to see your feet," Jeff insisted. He looked at Drew's right foot, then yanked up his own jacket and shirt. He knelt down and put Drew's icy foot on his bare stomach.

"Yikes!" one of the girls yipped. "*That* has to feel good."

While Jeff thawed Drew's other foot he talked to the group. "Why didn't you stop earlier? Drew's feet are frostbitten. We'll have to cut our day short and ski Drew back to the lodge."

Read 2 Timothy 2:22
Why are Christian friends utterly important?

You show weakness, and a friend calls you a baby. You share a secret with someone you trust, and two hours later you read it scrawled on a bathroom stall. You ask for help, and forevermore you're treated like an idiot.

Big deal, you say. You can live without friends.

Wrong. You can't. At least not without the right kind of friends.

Deciding you want to chase hard after God—that you want to flee evil, do right, trust God, and love others—won't work unless you follow the rest of Paul's advice: Run alongside others who are running toward God.

When your aim is to follow Jesus, Christians are the only ones going the same direction you are. It's possible that even Christians who chase after God with all their hearts may ice you sometimes. But if they've truly been warmed by God, they can't help sharing that warmth with you. People who are continually cold don't know God.

You need help from other Christians. Search it out. Make the most of it. You can't thaw your own feet.

Flee the evil desires of youth, and pursue righteousness, faith, love and peace, along with those who call on the Lord out of a pure heart. 2 TIMOTHY 2:22

Upward Bound

Half a mile from Addy's house there was a mountain. Okay, the mountain didn't even equal the size of a zit on the face of a really rocky peak. But there was a ridge big enough to hold a seventy-meter ski jump, a notch below full Olympic size.

Addy had no desire to hurl her body off a ski jump a few hundred feet in the air. But she was fascinated by the jump's scary-steep landing zone. In a flash of wintertime brilliance, she set a goal. *Come spring, I'm running up that hill.*

As the temperature warmed and the frozen hill thawed, Addy prepared for the Big Run. *Try One*: She dashed up the hill. Fifty yards up, her lungs screamed and her eyeballs throbbed. She stopped. *Try Two*: She managed a dozen more yards. *Try Three*: A friend hiked the hill with Addy, wondering all the way why anyone would want to run it. *Try Four*: A couple of weeks later, Addy reached the halfway point. Aggravated, she spent a month getting stronger by pounding up and down smaller hills. *Try Five*: Addy still hadn't hit the top, but she was within spitting distance. *Try Six*: She did it! Addy sucked wind and wanted to stop, but she made it up the peak—step by step, breath by breath.

Read Psalm 18:29–33

What can you accomplish when you get God's power?

Know it or not, you have a mountain in your life God wants you to run up. It might not look like a mountain to anyone else, but it's an area where he challenges you to press on even when you feel like quitting. Maybe it's talking to a non-Christian friend who needs to meet Jesus... or getting study skills to pull a grade out of the gutter... or learning to consistently obey him by busting a bad habit... or figuring out what to do with your time and talents now or in the future.

You've got a challenge in front of you that requires you to follow God step by step, try after try. When you press on, your faith takes a huge leap upward. And if you stick with it, sooner or later you'll scramble to the top.

God arms me with strength; he has made my way safe. He makes me as surefooted as a deer, leading me safely along the mountain heights. PSALM 18:32–33 NLT

Vote for Me

"The printouts 1 am distributing," your guidance counselor drones, "suggest a number of occupations appropriate for you, based on your individual academic achievement, aptitude test scores, and personality profiles."

Just show us the sheets. We know what they are. For weeks you had taken tests meant to spark your interest in a career. Your test results, you're sure, will disclose your multitudinous gifts and career choices. You already know what you want to be: *Pro tennis player. CIA special agent. Movie producer. Jet pilot. Oceanographer.*

"Don't look at your sheets," your counselor cautions, "until 1 say."

You peek. You spy only two choices.

That's okay. It's probably president of the United States and treasury secretary.

Look again. You got *burger flipper and French-fry dipper.*

Read 2 Corinthians 11:23–33
What price did Paul pay to accomplish his goals?

Goals are way easier to dream about than to actually accomplish. Paul aimed for two things in life: to know Christ (Philippians 3:7–11) and to tell the world about him (2 Corinthians 5:18–20). Paul he considered it such a privilege to be a preacher that even shipwrecks and whippings didn't make him quit. He took a beating and rebounded off the ropes.

Paul knew that actions—what you do right now—matter more than boasting about what you'll be. You won't become a rocket scientist if you never shoot higher than C-minus. You won't play in the symphony if you don't rehearse for real. You won't ever practice medicine if you don't practice caring about people now.

The book of James says that when you have faith—when you trust God to lead your life—that you will "persevere," trampling over, around, or through obstacles. You'll rely on God to help you dig into your dream and then finish what you start.

Perseverance isn't pain without a purpose. It makes you "mature," "complete," and "lacking nothing" (James 1:2–4). So you can reach your dreams for real.

I have worked much harder. 2 CORINTHIANS 11:23

Bobbing Heads

You doh-on't ski-ee, you doh-on't ski-ee. With the taunts of her shrimpy six-year-old cousins reverberating in her ears since the last family reunion, Teresa wasn't going to let this chance to learn to water ski escape.

"Teresa," her dad said seriously, "you've got two rules to follow when—er, *if* you fall. First, let go of the rope—or you'll get dragged and get a snootful of water. Second, poke a ski up out of the water—it helps boats see you."

When Teresa wiped out, she forgot the rules. She gulped water. She thought about what might be living in the deep end of the lake and flailed wildly for help. Back in the boat, she shook. She coughed. But she felt safe. And she wanted to try again.

Read Hebrews 13:5–6
What helps you try tough stuff?

When you learn to water ski you might fall and torque your head. You might burn your legs on the tow rope. But body slaps and water swallows are usually the worst part of wipeouts. Except for getting mowed over by a boat.

You want to get your ski up to signal for help. But even when you can't muster that, God watches over you as you zig through life, always ready to swing the boat around and pick you up when you wipe out.

God wants you to push, to dare, to try bold new stuff. And he promises that you'll never face a situation too big: "You can trust God, who will not permit you to be tempted more than you can stand. But when you are tempted, he will also give you a way to escape so that you will be able to stand it" (1 Corinthians 10:13 NCV).

That verse isn't just about urges to misuse sex, do drugs, or murder your momma. It also fits temptations to despair, throw pity parties, and give up. The verse right before warns to never imagine you can rely solely on yourself. The verse right after cautions against depending on anything other than God. The verses you read in Hebrews says the same thing: You can face anything if you face it with God. When you know God is always with you, you're willing to try hard stuff.

God has said, "Never will I leave you; never will I forsake you."
So we say with confidence, "The Lord is my helper;
I will not be afraid." HEBREWS 13:5-6

Wax Worship

Jared ran to his house, flew to the family room, dug for the TV remote, and flipped on the cable sports channel.

It's true.

For the past half season, Charlie Denton—everyone's favorite wide receiver of all time—had crumpled in fear of defensive lines. He dropped passes Jared's dog could have caught. And without Denton's usual stellar performance, his team slid to last place.

But now Jared saw video clips of a dozen squad cars pulling up at Denton's home and police taking his hero into custody. Denton admitted to everything from drug addiction to fixing games.

Later that evening Jared ripped down all the Denton posters in his room and shredded them into tiny pieces—except for one. He kept that for a dart board.

Read 2 Timothy 3:10–14
How do you pick someone to model your life after?

Big and powerful people can make you do what they say. You may not like a president, but you listen. You have to follow, but you're no fan.

Other people don't need to force you to like them. They make you laugh. Or they're like superheroes in masks and tights out crushing evildoers. Or you dream of singing—or shooting hoops—or skiing—or skating—the way they do. They're too cool to contain your enthusiasm.

You don't consciously sit down and decide who your heroes will be. Maybe you should. Paul listed all the reasons why Timothy should imitate him and heed what he said. Paul was real. His coolness lasted a lifetime, through victories and catastrophes.

Most pop heroes turn out to be wax figures who melt in the heat. It's usually the heroes close by—like parents, grandparents, or teachers—who turn out to be eternal stars.

But as for you, continue in what you have learned and have
become convinced of, because you know those from whom
you learned it. 2 TIMOTHY 3:14

Shortcut to Disaster

On his thirteenth birthday Marc's parents gave him the keys to a rebuilt classic Mustang. It was his ticket to immediate and total coolness. Sure, it had to sit in the garage for three years until he got his driver's license, but how many other thirteen-year-olds owned a car?

Not that it was easy to wait to drive. Sometimes when his parents were gone Marc backed the car out on the driveway. When that became a bore he drove the car around the neighborhood. The risk made it exciting—state law said he would wait until eighteen to get a license if he was caught driving underage.

By the time Marc graduated from high school his Mustang was as hot as ever and he had indeed attained coolness. He had the right car, the right friends, the right looks. But he wasn't around to enjoy it for long. Just after graduation he died in an accident.

Read Psalm 73:27–28

How do you feel when bad people get to their goals before you do?

Some people get all the good stuff sooner than you do. A few get it by working hard and doing what's right. But lots of others get it by taking shortcuts: They talk behind people's backs and win friends. They impress others with their stuff. They give away their body to get a boyfriend or girlfriend. They're cool. They know it. Everyone knows it.

When everything goes right for them, you feel jealous. You want what they've got. You think, *Why can't that be me?* You wonder if you've been wasting your time following God. You start to plot shortcuts you could take.

It's easy to feel like that until you realize one thing: Success gained by doing wrong won't last long. God promises that people who do wrong will lose control and crack up, like a driver who skids off a cliff. One moment the cool ones cruise. The next moment they crash.

Having everything doesn't mean you have it made. Having it made is enjoying God—and what he gives you, when and how he chooses.

Those who are far from you will perish; you destroy all who are unfaithful to you. But as for me, it is good to be near God. I have made the Sovereign Lord my refuge. PSALM 73:27-28

Don't Just Stand There!

You rushed through a shower, swallowed an egg whole, and ran out the door wearing socks that didn't match. Now you're standing in the cold waiting for the school bus, and your still-wet hair is freezing into icicles. Could you help it you slept a little late? Well, yeah—but it's your parents' fault you had to get to the bus stop pronto. They told you they wouldn't drive you to school if you missed the bus again. They called it "taking responsibility for yourself," or something like that.

You're particularly perturbed because you're not thrilled about getting to school anyway. Besides, if the bus doesn't come you can go back home and goof off all day. But you know that sooner or later the bus will come, so you wait. And wait.

Read Titus 2:11–14

What big event are Christians waiting for—their ultimate goal?
What should you do in the meantime?

As Christians, we're waiting for Christ to come and transport us to God's kingdom. Christ died for us so we could again serve and worship God, be adopted into his family, be made new people, and spend eternity as friends. In heaven God will be King, and we will be his.

Sometimes that feels like waiting for a slow school bus. It seems a long way off (2 Peter 3:3–14). But it isn't: God's reign as King begins *now* in the lives of those who know him. Instead of killing time at the bus stop and wishing we were back home in bed, we spend every moment of life getting set for eternity, getting rid of things that destroy friendship, and getting better at loving God and other people. When Christ comes we'll be dressed and ready to go, a pure people belonging totally to God (Ephesians 4:22–24).

You have to make that choice to get to the bus stop—to become a Christian—for yourself. And you have to make the choice to do something worthwhile—to keep growing up spiritually, rather than wasting time—for yourself.

Don't let God's bus leave without you. And don't just wait around doing nothing.

We wait for the blessed hope—the glorious appearing of our great God and Savior, Jesus Christ. TITUS 2:13

Dream Vacation

The pictures in the tour brochure looked so pretty. But pictures lie.

Of course, not everything about your family's vacation was awful. Your bargain flight took off on time—at 2:38 A.M. And they did serve a meal in flight. Well, more of a snack. It looked like the pilot's leftovers from the airport lounge. Your rental car from Bob's Borrow-a-Bomb was good protection from carjackings. Your family was in no danger of looking like wealthy tourists.

Then again, your mom had to clean the hotel bathtub before you could use it, and all week you slept on top of the bedcovers—to avoid infectious diseases. And on the one day nice enough to go to the beach the only place left to lay your towel was downwind from the Porta Potties.

All week long a question whined in your mind: *Why is this happening?*

Read Psalm 22:1–11

Do believers ever wonder if God is worth trusting when things go wrong?

Deep down we expect first-class accommodations on our journey as Christians—posh hotels, fast cars, and discount tickets to all the big attractions. We trust our all-knowing, all-perfect God to make the weather sunny and lines short.

When things go wrong, we feel cheated. It feels like our Father above booked us on a nightmarish trip with a fourth-class travel agency.

Psalm 22 shows how David wondered about God's travel plans for his life: *I've heard all sorts of stories, God, about how great you are. I've seen you myself. So where are you? Haven't you heard me? My enemies surround me. People think I'm crazy to trust you. I don't feel like I'm yours, yet I know that I've trusted you for a long time. Please help soon!*

Even the best of believers wonder where God is when trouble hits.

Nope, your trip through life won't be perfect, because the world you travel through is no paradise. But the sooner you figure out this big truth the better you'll cope: God hangs tight with you all the way.

My God, my God, why have you forsaken me? Why are you so far from saving me, so far from the words of my groaning?
PSALM 22:1

Whipped Potatoes

The food fight was well underway before Mrs. Heffermeister ambled toward the student cafeteria to do duty as lunch supervisor. But when she entered the lunchroom, the fight escalated into war in an instant. Mrs. Heffermeister became the room's sole target. From every direction mashed potatoes whizzed and whirled and pelted her from head to toe. Kids hated Mrs. Heffermeister. She could whip any boy in the school—and most of the male teachers. No one was about to leave when she bellowed, "ENOUGH!" and made everyone sit still until the principal came.

Chad was innocent, of course. He had eaten his ammunition before the fight broke out. No one paid attention, though, when he argued that he didn't deserve to stay after school with the rest of the lunchroom. And he didn't think too hard about how many times he had flung food in the past without getting caught.

Read Psalm 36:1–9

Why is the world such a messy place?

Are food fights funny? Sure. Are they right? No. They're usually a mess we expect someone else to clean up. They always waste food while kids starve. So why are they funny? Deep down we love to fling mashed potatoes.

Our battles might be okay if they stopped there. But they get much worse. Human beings deceive, envy, tease, bash, and kill one another. We steal each other's dignity. We think violence and divorce are normal.

God intended the world to be a place where we believe in him enough to do right—not only because we fear his anger but because we trust his wisdom. We were meant to bask in his love, swim in his goodness, rest in the shade of his protection, feast at his beachside barbecue sloshing down cold sodas. Life was to be a summer vacation.

But humanity chooses to live in the lunchroom throwing food—scorning God, cooking up more ammunition, and high-fiving each other every time a target takes a hit.

We've spoiled paradise.

Your love, O Lord, reaches to the heavens, your faithfulness to the skies. Your righteousness is like the mighty mountains, your justice like the great deep. PSALM 36:5-6

Quit Gawking

Ooooooo... Stars swirl as you lie on the floor. "He slipped on a banana peel on his way to Sunday school," you hear a friend say. "He hit his head pretty hard."

Your youth pastor pokes his face into yours. "God did this to you," he smirks. "It's because you put cereal in my sleeping bag on our last retreat."

"It's a hormone thing," mumbles a doctor. "He's at that awkward age."

An elder casts demons out of the banana peel. A parent scolds your youth pastor for his carelessness in teaching the church's youth. Finally a lawyer walks by and whispers in your ear, "It's the church's fault. Let's sue them for waxing the floor."

Read John 9:1–12

Who's to blame when bad things happen to people?

Admit it. You're responsible for most of what happens in your life. You flipped the banana peel, then it flipped you. You cut class, so you flunked. You were lazy and got canned. You didn't hustle, so the other team scored. Peers and parents and hormones influence you. But they don't make your choices. You do. And you live with the consequences of your choices.

At other times you're slugged by a situation you didn't choose. You catch the flu. Your parents divorce. You're beaten up or abused. You discover you're dyslexic. You're not to blame, though you still control how you respond.

Jesus' disciples accepted popular opinion about the man born blind: Hardship hit because someone sinned. The only question was *who* had sinned—the man (before birth, they thought!) or his parents.

Jesus rejected both explanations. And he said the disciples missed the whole point: What was God going to do?

That's still the point. When bad things happen God wants to work through *us*—through our helpful actions. He can move through the *miraculous*—out-of-the-ordinary displays of his power. And he's even glorified through the *tenacious*—people who rely on his strength to whip bad situations that don't go away. In Jesus' eyes the blind man wasn't a puzzle to solve. He was a person to help.

This happened so that the work of God might be displayed in his life. JOHN 9:3

Heart Attack

How could God let this happen? If God really loved Jim, Jodi thought, *he wouldn't be lying in a coma. If God really cared, he would have kept that truck from plowing into Jim's car in the first place.*

Jodi was sure God could work wonders to put her brother back together. She just didn't know if he would.

Read Acts 20:17–24
Is it right to expect God to do miracles? How come?

People have no shortage of agonizing problems—crunched friendships, twisted minds, exploding families, sick bodies. Yet while our outsides fall apart, an even deadlier problem hides inside: We don't know God well. Our hearts have stopped beating for him.

Paul saw that God shaped all the experiences of his life, good and bad, miracles and failures, to address that one problem. God wanted Paul to know him well and others to know him too. Paul focused his whole life on God's rescue plan—staying close to God and completing the job God gave him to do, following God even when it looked like God's plans led to pain. Being part of God's rescue squad was more important to Paul than any pain he suffered (2 Corinthians 6:3–12).

From God's perspective, our need for him is the biggest emergency of life. God wants to jump-start our hearts. When we become friends with God through Christ, our hearts pump anew. When we help others become his friends as well, more hearts pump. We want God to fix our circumstances. God wants to fix us.

That doesn't mean God leaves us twisting in pain. We pray for what we believe is best—to have a brother back, for a friendship to heal, for parents to stick together. We act where we can and ask God to act where we can't. God does what he sees best to jump-start hearts and to accomplish all the other plans and purposes he has for us.

Sometimes God works unbelievable miracles for our outsides. When we let him, he always works miracles on our insides.

I consider my life worth nothing to me, if only I may finish the race and complete the task the Lord Jesus has given me—the task of testifying to the gospel of God's grace. ACTS 20:24

Big Bad Momma

Billy was walking to school minding his own business when Bruce and company jumped him for his lunch money. Bruce sat on Billy's chest and knuckled his forehead to make him whimper before really punishing him.

Suddenly a screech from the end of the block distracts Bruce. One of Bruce's lookouts yells, "Mother on a rampage! RUN!"

They fall over each other trying to escape as Billy's mom steams toward them in fatigues, face paint, and whomping black boots. She heaves the bullies over fences into their own backyards, but not before threatening to push their noses to the back of their brains the next time they touch Billy.

Billy gets up. "Thanks, Mom."

"No problem," says Billy's mom. "Anything for my baby."

Read Psalm 144:1–8

Does needing God's help make you a wimp? Why—or why not?

You would probably rather go home with a black eye than be rescued by your mother. But some battles you can't fight yourself.

Even David—the fierce warrior who wrote Psalm 144—admitted he needed God. Without God he was nothing—a "breath," a "fleeting shadow." He begged God not to stand by. He asked God to split the sky, toast the mountains, and shoot lightning at his enemies. David needed God to rescue him.

That doesn't mean believers are weak. Sometimes God does dash down the block to save you. But he also arms you to defend yourself.

Because David was king of Israel, a political country ruled by God, he saw his enemies as foreign nations who served other gods. *Your* biggest enemies aren't people. They're spiritual. And they don't want your lunch money. They want to bully you out of your faith. God gives you weapons to strike back: truth, righteousness, the good news of Christ, faith, prayer, sureness that you belong to God, and the Bible (Ephesians 6:10–18). God's weapons all defend and strengthen your trust in God.

Needing God doesn't make you a mamma's boy—or girl. You never grow out of your need for God.

He is my loving God and my fortress, my stronghold and my deliverer, my shield, in whom I take refuge, who subdues peoples under me. PSALM 144:2

Next Time I'll Floss

Gzzzzzzzzzer goes the drill into the surface of your tooth. You flinch. "Does that hurt?" your dentist inquires.

Hurt? Would it hurt if I twisted my finger in your eye at six thousand RPM? "Just a little," you respond politely. "Maybe I need another shot." When three shots of Novocaine do nothing for your agony, you stop contemplating how much money you'll get for pain and suffering when you sue your dentist. You start wishing you had paid more attention to your mom's childbirth stories. *How did she breathe? Hoo-hoo-hee?*

Your bleary mind makes a deal with the dentist. *Stop it! Stop it! Next time I'll floss!* Your dentist pauses—to let the filling dry, he says as he heads out the door. *So why does he keep bobbing in to check on me? To see if I'm dead?*

Read Isaiah 40:27–31

How do you know God hears you when you pray for help?

You would settle for less than a miracle. You just want a little something to take the edge off your pain. And you wonder why God doesn't respond to your generous offer to become a missionary to Ukarumpa in exchange for a little help now.

But nothing happens. You think God has said, "Forget it, slimeball. Chew dirt!" and you get aggravated. You're crying, *Hello, God! Can't you see I'm hurting? Quit ignoring me. Why won't you answer me?*

He has. God doesn't sleep or go to lunch. And he doesn't put a price on his services. He doesn't hear you because of *your* promises to him but because of *his* promise to you: You belong to him. He sees your problems and hears your prayers.

But he answers prayers the way he knows is best (1 John 5:14–15).

He doesn't always say "Yes." But he's not necessarily saying "No." Sometimes he says "Wait" or "I'll answer, but not the way you think." When you trust God he renews your strength—to walk, to run, to fly. Or to defy life's drills.

But those who hope in the Lord will renew their strength. They will soar on wings like eagles; they will run and not grow weary, they will walk and not be faint. ISAIAH 40:31

Out of Cash

Colleen's mom sat at the kitchen table with her checkbook and a stack of bills. After each bill she carefully figured how much money was left.

"I'm sorry, honey," she told Colleen when she got to the bottom of the pile. "There's not much left. Enough for a pair of pants when school starts and a shirt at the end of next month."

Only one pair of pants? Colleen thought. It was a good thing her mom hadn't noticed the hole in the bottom of Colleen's shoes, or she would be getting shoes instead of pants. Colleen knew she could hide the hole from the kids at school—at least until it rained and her feet got wet and stunk. She couldn't hide old, worn clothes.

Colleen knew that her mom was doing her best to provide for the family, but she still felt sick. *I'm going to look like a troll—like I crawled out from under a bridge. I'll be the only one not wearing new stuff!*

Read Psalm 31:1–5
Where is God when you suffer?

When you struggle—whatever your struggle—it's normal for questions to pour in: Why won't God fix my problem *now?* When will God punish the people who hurt me? Why do bad things happen to me? Where is God when I hurt?

When you ache you feel like a reject. You're sure you're the only one who botched the test. You assume you're the only one whose parents fight or work too much. You glance in the mirror on your way out the door and you convince yourself that you're the only one whose clothes are less than wonderful or whose bangs wanged.

When you suffer you feel like you're alone.

You're not. When God doesn't jam his hand into your life and immediately fix your problems, you might think he's left you to fend for yourself. He hasn't. You belong to him. For the sake of his name—his reputation and truthfulness—he will lead and guide you. He is your rock to hide behind and beefy protection from your enemies. And each bout of misery you face is an opportunity to cry out, "Protect me, God. I'm yours!"

Turn your ear to me, come quickly to my rescue; be my rock of refuge, a strong fortress to save me. PSALM 31:2

Okay to Hurt

Britney sat against the back wall of the church. She couldn't drag herself to the front, close to her best friend's open casket. Lakeesha was dead, and now Britney was dying on the inside. People said Lakeesha was in heaven. All Britney knew was that she wasn't here with her anymore.

What bugged Britney most was that hardly anyone talked about Lakeesha. The adults chitchatted about the weather and how tough it was to be a kid these days. The kids gabbed about school and mean teachers and stupid homework. It was like Lakeesha never existed. Just like how her locker was already cleaned out.

Britney's insides were screaming to talk about *all* of it. No one else wanted to talk about *any* of it. When it came to pain, her crowd had two rules: (1) guys aren't supposed to cry, and (2) girls are supposed to get over it.

Britney's mom suggested she tell God how bad she was hurting.

"Why God?" Britney said. "He doesn't have a clue what I'm feeling."

Read Matthew 5:4
What good is God when you're hurting?

You're probably good at faking tough. You learned to be tough when you tipped off your bike and ripped up your leg and forced yourself to stop crying. You got to practice toughness when you got a good scab going and someone came by and kicked your shin.

God doesn't make you fake toughness. When you cry to him, he comforts you. When you wail to him, you're talking to someone who's always listening. He's your always present help in times of trouble (Psalm 46:1).

God understands loss. He's watched his coolest creation—human beings—ditch friendship with him and devour one another. He witnessed the death of his Son, Jesus, for all the evil of the world.

God has hurt figured out.

There's more news: While God won't bash your sadness, he also won't let you wallow in it. He heals you, then lets you help heal others. Whenever God comforts you, you can pass that care on to other people facing tough problems (2 Corinthians 1:3-4). He heals you—and makes you his agent of healing in the lives of others.

Blessed are those who mourn, for they will be comforted.
MATTHEW 5:4

God Is Angry Too

You and your dad were so delirious after watching your favorite team clinch a playoff spot that you determined that post-game burger inhalation was the only way to wind down.

Halfway through your fast-food feeding frenzy, two men with nylons over their heads burst into the restaurant waving shotguns. They herded everyone into the store freezer and made you lie on boxes of food with your hands behind your head. They jabbed your dad in the back with the shotgun and threatened to blow away anyone who moved.

A few minutes later their noise out front stopped. The men were gone. But they aren't gone from your mind. When your best friend came over with a nylon stretched over his face you slammed the door and hid. Later that seemed funny. What isn't humorous is crying in the middle of the night or shivering when you remember the freezer. And what makes you want to punch walls is that the men got away. You can't understand why God hasn't put them on ice for good.

Read Habakkuk 3:3–16
When will God punish people who do wrong?

God is the one Being in the universe who is totally holy—totally powerful, wise, and good in everything he thinks, says, and does. He can't tolerate sin. Habakkuk's prayer recalls what God did to the Egyptians, Israel's slave masters, until Egypt finally let Israel go. Gory stuff.

God isn't just mad at Egyptians. He threatens eternal separation from himself and everything good for all who continue to fight him. The Bible pictures the place of punishment for rebels (called "hell" in the Bible) as unstoppable fire (Revelation 21:8), everlasting chains (Jude 6), and utter darkness (Matthew 8:12). People who do evil will get what they deserve, even if they don't get caught on earth.

God is only ferociously angry with really bad people, right? Not *us*, right?

Truth is, we all deserve separation from him. But God doesn't wish hell on anyone (2 Peter 3:9). He waits for people to admit their sin and accept his forgiveness.

That's why he doesn't always ice enemies now. When God seems slow to punish people who sin, be glad he wasn't quick to punish you.

In anger you threshed the nations. HABAKKUK 3:12

Get Real

"You gotta get over it." Steven tried to knock sense into Tom. "I know what you're thinking—that you can get your parents back together and make everything the way it used to be. Forget it, Tom. Stuff won't ever be the same. I should know. It's been six years since my parents divorced. They treat me like a video rental. They borrow me for a few days and take me back when they've seen enough."

Steven didn't hold back what he thought about Tom's situation. "You learn to survive on your own. Hey—if you're smart you can take advantage of this whole thing. My dad tries to buy me because he knows Mom can't afford to keep up. I keep upping the price. I get something new every weekend. You'll make it if you just remember one thing: When they trash you, you trash them back."

Read Romans 4:18–21

How did Abraham react when God promised to help him?

Back at the beginning of the Bible, God told Abraham he would be the start of a great nation, God's chosen people. He couldn't father a nation without first fathering a family, and he and Sarah didn't have any kids. When Sarah heard God's promise, she laughed (Genesis 18:10–15). She thought, *Aren't you a little late, God?*

Abraham wasn't stupid. He knew as well as Sarah that their bodies were out of fire, ready to expire. He didn't ignore the problem. He faced facts. Yet he had faith. He was sure God would do what he had sworn to do.

Here's reality: Life hurts. Here's a bigger reality: God keeps promises.

It's a fact: You're starting at a new school and you're totally alone. But *God says he will never leave you* (Hebrews 13:5–6). It's a fact: You want to tear off the eyebrows of people who hurt you. But *God promises to punish those who hurt you* (Romans 12:19). It's a fact: Life at home or school is falling apart and you don't think you can cope. But *God promises to work through any difficulty to bring good to your life* (Romans 8:28).

What we see and feel can make God's promises sound crazy. But he always keeps his word.

[Abraham] did not waver through unbelief regarding the promise of God. ROMANS 4:20

Waiting

Angela toweled off the steamy bathroom mirror so she could see to gently comb the few strands of hair left after her chemotherapy treatments. Her doctors hoped the drugs had killed her cancer, but everyone had still sighed relief when she made it to her birthday.

Now as she got ready for her party she mulled whether to wear her wig or to go with the chic bald look her friends teased her to try. *A year ago I worried about bad hair days,* she thought. *Now it's no-hair days.*

The mirror refogged. Angela wiped it again, this time to stare at her eyes. *I wonder if I'll be alive in a year.*

Read Romans 8:18–27
Why don't problems go away?

Life isn't a sitcom where every difficulty ends in hugs and smiles and apologies within a half hour. And the future is like a fogged-up mirror. It's hard to see anything clearly. But you have to try.

God promises an eternity in heaven with no danger, death, disease, discomfort, or displeasure (Revelation 21:1–8).

Life here, however, can be a disaster. The world is falling apart and filled with moaning. Believers groan as we wait for a perfect world. Creation itself—everything God made—groans like a woman in labor, screaming with frustration to give birth to a renewed, perfected planet. God's Holy Spirit groans as he prays ("intercedes") through us for God's perfect will for us.

That's foggy stuff. What we see, though, is that the world is out of whack. Life at its best is less than perfect. People sin, and creation produces things like mosquitoes, hurricanes, and cancer. Life at its worst is ghastly. And our best efforts to fix things are like wigs. They cover up the problem, but they don't grow new hair.

Our problems won't be solved completely until our "adoption as sons" (and daughters) at the end of time when God shakes the world, when he eliminates what is evil and perfects what belongs to him. That's what we hope for. That's what God promised us when we became believers.

And so we wait.

I consider that our present sufferings are not worth comparing with the glory that will be revealed in us. ROMANS 8:18

In the Meantime

Tasha and her pastor sat in the rec room of a mental health unit.

"They've got me locked up like I tried to kill someone!" Tasha blurted.

"Tasha, you *did*. You tried to hurt Tasha. We won't let you do that."

"Well, this place is humiliating. They took away my shoelaces and my belt and my—you know. Anything they think I can use to hurt myself. I can't use the phone. You're the first person I've seen other than Mom. It's like jail." She calmed. "They did let me go for a supervised walk outside today. That was kind of nice. I haven't gone for a walk in a long time. Dad and I used to walk together. You never met him, did you?"

"He died before I moved here, remember? Tasha—your dad—is his death what this is about?"

Tasha started to cry. "I don't know—it's about my dad and my mom and my sister and my friends! I just wanted to get away."

Read Habakkuk 3:17–19
What do you do when hurts don't go away?

Some tactics for dealing with pain are like prying the protective cage off a fan and inserting your face. People who make those choices—to rebel, drink, inhale, misuse sex, hide, weld headphones to their head, or quit life altogether—miss out on fingers and foreheads and noses. Or on life.

But there are choices that refresh, like plopping in front of a fan on a hot day. *You can choose to deal with your problem:* Change what you can. Talk with people who can find solutions—parents, teachers, counselors, and pastors. Memorize Bible passages that encourage you. *You can choose to keep busy:* Join a club. Exercise. Play sports. Goof off with your friends. Do homework. Help around the house. Find a hobby. Most of all, *you can choose to keep trusting God:* When everything goes wrong (when "the fig tree doesn't bud" or "the fields produce no food") God is still Lord—he still watches over you. He's still Savior. Even when everything else goes wrong, he is right there with you.

Though the fig tree does not bud and there are no grapes on the vines...yet I will rejoice in the Lord, I will be joyful in God my Savior. HABAKKUK 3:17-18

Hanging In

Almost a foot shorter than anyone else in his grade, Brian lived with a long and ugly *can't-do-that* list.

I can't reach the pull-up bar.
I can't come close to spiking a volleyball.
I can't dream of looking a classmate in the eye.
I can't see the blackboard unless I sit in the front row.
I can't stand getting laughed at in the locker room.

Trapped in the body of a lot-younger kid, Brian couldn't make himself grow. He couldn't change his situation. But he could choose to conquer it.

Read 1 Peter 1:3–9

What keeps life's tough stuff from being a waste?

If pain were pointless, people wouldn't beat their bodies in workout rooms or do waddle-till-they-wheeze marathons to stay fit. Adultish-types wouldn't willingly pull all-nighters to survive college, work graveyard shifts to save for a house, stay glued together in nasty marriages to jump-start love, or give up money to help people they've never met.

Painful Truth 1: You can choose pain to gain huge prizes.

Painful Truth 2: You can choose to find gain even in pain you don't pick.

No circumstance of your life outsmarts God's control. He can rearrange pain or remove it. But if he doesn't shoo away the troubles that tromp through your life, count those troubles as part of God's training to make your faith strong.

Pain only works its wonders if you submit to its training. Hardships strike out of nowhere and slap you upside the head. But God makes them into something useful. They'll make you righteous and peaceful. They prove that your devotion to God is real. And your faithfulness brings glory to God.

If you try to wiggle free from the weights in God's gym, though, what's supposed to be your spiritual workout is a waste—it just wastes *you*, that is. It becomes stupid suffering, not a sweaty but sweet workout for your soul.

You may have had to suffer grief in all kinds of trials. These
have come so that your faith may be proved genuine.
1 PETER 1:6–7

You Understand

Mrs. Bradley wanted Brian out of her class. He was a funny kid. But his defiance was catching on and destroying her class.

She had only one weapon left, one she saved for kids she hated: embarrassment. So, hoping to shame Brian into behaving, she sent him across the street to the elementary school—slamming Brian back to second grade.

She thought it was punishment. Brian loved it. It got him out of her class.

From his big desk in the back of the room Brian noticed a little boy named Sam. He acted exactly like Brian—no focus, zippo attention span.

One day Sam asked Brian for help, and Brian discovered he could explain the answer to Sam. Brian and Sam became study buddies. They understood each other. And when Brian watched Sam's teacher try to help Sam with his assignments, Brian realized how difficult he had made life for Mrs. Bradley.

Read 2 Corinthians 1:3–11
Can God make good come out of bad?

The last thing you want to hear when you hurt is that your experience will make you strong and wise—as if that makes you glad to get dumped, or happy that a friend died, or excited to struggle with math.

But it's true that you learn from tough stuff.

We're not exactly sure what Paul suffered in Asia. Whatever it was, Paul despaired intensely. He was as scared as if he were shackled in an electric chair and someone was about to flip the switch. His experience shattered his confidence in himself. Yet he found that God was "the God of all comfort." And he shared that comfort with the Corinthians.

Rough times teach you what God knows you need to learn: Trust. That's a sureness that God accepts you, cares for you, and ultimately will bring you to an eternity with himself in paradise (Romans 5:3–4). You learn to rely on God, not on yourself.

God didn't plan for bad things to happen in your world. But like a piece of clay that's been squished out of shape, God can spin your life into something good again. He heals your hurt. And he uses you to heal the hurts of others. Your pain isn't a waste.

[God] comforts us in all our troubles, so that we can comfort those in any trouble with the comfort we ourselves received from God. 2 CORINTHIANS 1:4

Heading Home

Bekah slouched in her chair, staring at her desk, sure that everyone around her was staring at *her*.

The school play had closed the night before. Bekah went to the cast party with instructions from her parents to be at the front door for her ride home at ten-thirty—an exceedingly generous school-night curfew, they said. When Bekah didn't come out to the car on time her dad strolled to the front door, rang the doorbell, and bellowed inside. There she was—Bekah Fischer, star of the school play, deserting the party right after it started, exiting hours earlier than anyone else.

In the car she protested to her dad that she wasn't tired at all. But a minute later she zonked. Her dad had to carry her into the house.

The next day at school all that anyone cared about was that she—and her dad—pooped out their party. That's why they were staring at her.

Read Hebrews 11:13–16

How did the big believers of the past feel about their home on planet earth?

This world has chosen to run from God. So if you're trying to run *toward* him you're going to bang heads with people going the other way. Big things, little things—you'll clash with your classmates. You won't always fit perfectly with your peers.

The problem isn't your parents—they just want what's best for you. It isn't God—what he commands is always good. It isn't you—provided you're trying to do what's right. It isn't even the people around you. It's bigger than that.

The real problem is that this planet isn't your home. As a Christian you're a citizen of heaven (Philippians 3:20). And that makes you an "alien" and "stranger" here.

When you follow God you always ache for something better. But it isn't until heaven that you receive *all* that God has promised: total happiness and utter protection.

It's where you belong. It's a long walk before you get there. But it's the one place where you'll feel totally at home.

They admitted that they were aliens and strangers on earth.
They were longing for a better country—a heavenly one.
HEBREWS 11:13, 16a

Jesus Does Your School

Suppose one day you decide to invite Jesus to your school. Sort of an experiment. People warn you that Jesus will act weird and humiliate you in front of your friends. So you're relieved that Jesus doesn't look odd when he meets you at the bus stop—none of that dusty ancient robe stuff. He dresses normal. He looks clued in. Pretty cool.

After English class Jesus says you're right—yes, Mr. Hefferman truly ranks among the driest teachers in the entire universe—and he's heard them all.

A couple of times classmates notice Jesus squished into the desk next to you. You don't introduce him to anyone. Jesus looks hurt. And once you dart off, leaving Jesus dangling. You run back. He's right where you left him, waiting patiently. You promise not to do that again.

By the end of the day you figure you've hit it off with Jesus, so you ask him to come back tomorrow to follow you around.

Jesus leans over and whispers in your ear.

"Huh?" You're bewildered. "You want *me* to follow *you*?"

Read Psalm 97:1–6

What would life be like if Jesus showed up at your school?

You might like school. You might hate it. However you feel, you'll spend more than a million minutes in classrooms before you graduate from high school. Not counting homework. And time doesn't fly when you're not having fun.

So what would happen if Jesus burst into those million minutes?

It's kind of you to take Jesus to school with you. But that's getting it backward. His job isn't to follow you around. It's your job to head after him.

Jesus calls you to go wherever he leads you. Right now, that happens to include school. But when he shows up at school, he isn't going to slouch around, take a last-row seat, and leave a grease spot on the back wall. Jesus is Lord of all. He owns every minute of it. And his goal is to show you his cool way to do school.

The mountains melt like wax before the Lord, before the Lord of all the earth. PSALM 97:5

Great Expectations

The night before Drew's first day at his new school, he tossed frantically in his sleep. "NO! NOT THERE!" he screamed as his old teachers dragged him toward the gaping mouth of a raging monster. And there at the monster's mouth stood Drew's parents, propping open the front doors. Drew's mom had that sorry look she got when he was little and he had to drop his drawers at the doctor's for a shot. His dad yelled encouragement as Drew's teachers tossed him in: "This hurts us more than it hurts you!"

The doors snapped shut behind Drew. Like a gargantuan tongue, the crowds inside swished him this way and that, and by the end of the day he felt as if he had been chewed to bits between overgrown molars.

He couldn't wait for the final bell to signal the school to spit him out.

Read Joshua 1:1–11
*What does God promise to do for you when
you head to school?*

God was prodding his people, the Israelites, to enter the incredible land he had promised to them. They knew all along that Moses, their leader, wouldn't go with them. But the people feared that with Moses gone their lives would never be the same. Not that they always liked Moses. Things just seemed normal—safe—when he was around.

The Israelites had nothing to fear. God, in fact, had promised success, provided they stuck close to him. It didn't matter that they had no idea where they were going. They knew their Lord. They knew his Law—the commandments he had given them. Three times God reminded Joshua and the people: "Be strong! Be strong! BE STRONG!"

When you grow into a new school, you leave your old school behind. And it's gone—except for a head busting with facts and a few fun memories of favorite classes, like recess. What made your life "normal" is dead.

Yet God says you have nothing to fear. He doesn't toss you all alone to the next stage in life. He swears to stay by your side and teach you *his* way to do school. And he'll show you how to conquer the monster.

*Have I not commanded you? Be strong and courageous. Do not
be terrified; do not be discouraged, for the Lord your God
will be with you wherever you go.* JOSHUA 1:9

Crawling the Walls

"Class, I'm going to step down to the office for twenty minutes," your teacher tells you and your cohorts. "I want you to remain at your desks, studying pages 643 to 678 of your social studies textbook."

Party! everyone thinks. *She didn't just say she was leaving. She said where she was going and how long she'll be gone!* As your teacher toddles down the hall, the lookouts scramble. *She's gone!* Chips and two-liter bottles of soda appear from nowhere. Guys break out cards. Girls disco on desks.

You, however, dutifully read your assignment as paper airplanes and footballs fly overhead. You pass page 678 and zoom toward page 700, until the rest of the class notices you. They pelt you with garbage.

Read Colossians 3:22–24

You're not supposed to crawl the walls at school. Why not?

Your class probably wouldn't riot if your teacher left the room. Then again, maybe it would. But if it did, you probably wouldn't be the only one not goofing off. Then again, maybe you would. Or maybe—just maybe—you would lead the revolt.

The choice you make all starts with one question: Does school rot or not?

The slaves Paul wrote to seldom suffered as badly as slaves in America did. More than half the people in major Roman cities were slaves, including most teachers and doctors. Still, the slaves were property controlled by owners. They couldn't do much about their bondage except alter their attitude.

Like you at school. You can *want* to do what you *have* to do anyway: When you do your work, you can make up your mind that you're working for God.

You don't do school for teachers who put you to sleep. God is the reason you struggle through your homework, listen in class, and stay clear of trouble. Doing school God's way starts with doing school for him.

Slaves, obey your earthly masters in everything; and do it, not only when their eye is on you and to win their favor, but with sincerity of heart and reverence for the Lord. COLOSSIANS 3:22

Blowin' in the Wind

They had a deal. Dirk, Ben, and Chester ate together. Every day. Then none of them would look stupid eating all by his lonesome.

At the opposite end of the lunchroom from where they usually sat was a table that oozed cool—occupied by girls who make guys gawk and guys who cause girls to flock.

One day when Dirk approached the cool table, its occupants stared him down. They might forgive him this once if he quickly crawled back where he belonged. Then they saw who he was with. One of their own. They let Dirk in—for today, anyway.

Ben and Chester stood up to watch Dirk and Theresa find seats. As Dirk eased into coolness they almost applauded. They waited for his signal inviting them over. But when Dirk sat down to eat they figured it out. They'd been forgotten. They'd been ditched. Dirk. What a jerk.

Read Romans 15:5–7

How do friends stay friends—and make more friends?

When you're friendless you blow through school like tumbleweed. You're barely part of the landscape. You feel dried up and ugly, and occasionally you get burned to keep other people warm.

With friends, you don't feel alone. You feel okay. Valuable. You belong.

Making great friends is a great thing. Except when it kills other friendships. Paul hints in the chapter before the passage you read that you make friends and stay friends (you have a "spirit of unity") when you work hard to pull people together instead of pushing them apart—especially if you pull together around Christ.

Paul says your goal is nothing less than to accept other people the way God accepts you—welcoming them into your group, onto your turf, treating them the way you want to be treated (Matthew 7:12). Dumping your musty old friends and chumming with the cool ones isn't your way to the top. It's hanging close to God. And he wants everyone in his mob of friends (2 Peter 3:9). He never forms a ring with his friends that's so tight there isn't room for more.

Accept one another, then, just as Christ accepted you,
in order to bring praise to God. ROMANS 15:7

Top Dog

Emily glanced at her grade, cracked a twisted smile, and looked around to see what everyone else got on the test. Her classmates hid their papers. They knew she did better. She always did better.

Emily snatched Eric's test. He was so nice—but so slow at school. "Give it back!" Eric begged, looking like he was going to bawl.

Emily sneered. "Maybe you should sit in the back with the druggies," she advised. "They could tutor you. Maybe you'd pass."

You don't have to look hard to see plenty of people better than you at a lot of things. Even so, it's usually not tough to find people worse than you—or to notice that when they look bad, you look good.

Read Psalm 26:1–2

How do you know when you've truly done well at something?

If you bust the curve, you might think you did your best on a test. If your brother catches the blame for everything bad, you might be content with how you act at home. Or if you know less about the Bible than your Christian friends, you might conclude you're a slug.

When you take a test, the curve counts. But grades don't tell the whole story—like whether anything lodged in your brain long-term. Dodging your parents' wrath might merely mean that you're good at hiding what you do behind their backs. Feeling less "spiritual" than your friends doesn't show whether you're getting to know God better.

If how you seem to stack up against others determines what you think or feel about yourself, then you're using a yardstick that's never the same length twice. And you'll either squish people with your huge head or feel tiny and worthless.

When you let God measure how to think and act by the yardsticks you find in the Bible, you see that all of us fall short of God's perfection (Romans 3:23). You feel congratulated when you truly do well (Matthew 25:21). Yet you also see what you're shooting for, and be assured that the same God who shows you the real you—the good, bad, and ugly—promises to remake you (Romans 14:4).

Then you can pat yourself on the back without putting other people down.

Test me, O Lord, and try me, examine my heart and my mind.
PSALM 26:2

Waiting for the Candy

I've read this sixteen times. With her head in her hands, Kendra peeked through her fingers at her math book. *I still don't get it.*

She knocked her book onto the floor. *Math is so stupid,* she steamed. What worried her most, however, was that *she* might be what was stupid. Seeing a math aide three days a week had helped Kendra keep up—until this year. She wanted to work hard and do well. Other subjects were tough, but nothing like math. Every study session was like starting over, as if each night someone stuck a syringe in her skull and sucked out her brains while she slept.

She mulled over her choices: Pretend school doesn't matter. Buy a bunch of makeup and hope she makes it as a model. Plan on bagging groceries for the rest of her life.

God, Kendra prayed, *you said you would be with me wherever I went. So where are you? Why is this so hard?*

Read Isaiah 41:8–16

If God is with you, why doesn't he make homework easier?

Worms. They spend life digging dirt. Then they get squashed on the sidewalk. Or bit in half by a bird. Or stuck with a fishhook. Or they just disappear into the ground. You're not a worm—God made you glorious (Psalm 8:3-9). But that doesn't mean you never feel a little slimy.

God is with you when school goes well. He's also there when things go awful and you feel wormish. Whatever you go through, God stays with you because you belong to him. And he's promised you his total help.

It's tense, though, in the time gap between your problem and God's provisions, between your hurt and God's help. God isn't a candy machine you can rock until the good stuff drops. But know this for sure: He also isn't a candy machine that swallows your money and leaves you empty-handed. He gives you what you need when you need it most.

Problems now. Provision in God's time. In the meantime? *Trust.*

So do not fear, for I am with you; do not be dismayed, for I am your God. I will strengthen you and help you; I will uphold you with my righteous right hand. ISAIAH 41:10

The Art of Endurance

Morning after morning you slam the alarm clock, crawl from bed, trudge to school, and take your seat in your first-hour art class.

Once you clocked your teacher saying "*Um*" forty-eight times in six minutes. At forty-eight you fell into a coma. After you regained consciousness, you killed time by plucking out your eyebrows hair by hair, but that only lasted a few days.

The way you see it, the system is taunting you. You feel you have no choice but to go deviant. While the class makes metal stick figures, you manufacture a miniature spring-loaded catapult to launch notes to a friend at another table. When the class builds a gargantuan log cabin out of tongue depressors to commemorate Abraham Lincoln's birthday, you hang sticks from your nose. And then one day you rewire the pottery wheel to pep it up. Your clay flies. It *thwonks* your teacher on the head. You get detention.

More excitement.

Read Galatians 6:7–8
How do you cope when school bores you silly?

Some days at school you feel like you should have unscrewed your brain and left it at home—you didn't need it. Or a teacher doesn't care about what he's teaching—so neither do you. Or you can't see what school has to do with real life because you have more important things knotting your mind—so you tune out.

Peers try anything to bust the boredom, from talking when it's time to zip lips, to arriving at school high. What will *you* do?

Doing good at school or anywhere else can be boring—until you see the reward. Doing what's right is like putting seed in the ground. Sooner or later plants sprout. In time you reap peace and a satisfaction that God is right and you did right (Hebrews 12:11). And that's no bore.

A man reaps what he sows. The one who sows to please his sinful nature, from that nature will reap destruction; the one who sows to please the Spirit, from the Spirit will reap eternal life.

GALATIANS 6:7-8

Spit Out Ze Bones

Girls looked up to her. Guys just stared at her. So when the seventeen-year-old Olympic hopeful stepped up to speak at the school assembly, everyone hushed.

"When I sprint, I imagine myself flying through the air," she told them. "In my mind, my feet barely touch the ground. You have the same power inside you to unlock all that you can be. What's the key? Believe in yourself. If you believe hard enough you make things happen. You can change what you become.

"In your mind you can picture yourself beating the person running in the lane next to you. You can think your way to straight A's. You can make yourself a millionaire by picturing it in your mind. You can even stop your little sister from being a brat. Just imagine it and you have it."

Read Proverbs 3:5–8
Can you be strong—or smart—without God?

There are other times you're not totally sure of yourself. You need a boost to keep you from crumbling.

Rehearsing the situation in your mind might help. But it doesn't change reality. If you could imagine your way to success, you'd be able to high jump fifty-three feet by now—not to mention pulling straight A's, dating a hottie, and driving a Ferrari.

You can have great confidence—through God. Think about it: "With your help I can advance against a troop; with my God I can scale a wall" (Psalm 18:29). Even so, God gently reminds us of this: "Without Me you can do nothing" (John 15:5 NKJV). Our brains aren't as big as we think. We're not as strong or wise as we tell ourselves.

No matter where you go to school you can't swallow whole what you hear and see: "Depend on yourself." "Just accept what I say. Trust me." "The Bible is full of myths." "Ignore your parents. Make your own decisions." God gave you the Bible to help you separate truth from lies (2 Timothy 3:14–16).

When you eat fish, you eat the meat and leave the bones. You'll survive if you swallow a few tiny bones. But if you don't strain out the big ones you'll gag. Or choke and die.

Trust in the Lord with all your heart and lean not on your own understanding. PROVERBS 3:5

School Smarts

While Neil's classmates spent five weeks in the library rifling through dusty books and encyclopedias to construct a paper that counted for half their grade, he studied back issues of *Sports Illustrated* and *Mad*. He snickered when the class egghead inquired how his research on the feeding habits of Galapagos tortoises was coming along. He roared when kids carried home piles of books. "You don't have to do all that," he informed them. "The teacher's just trying to scare us."

The night before the paper was due there was a good movie on TV, so Neil was glad his parents didn't know he had a whopper report to crank out. He ate popcorn and quaffed four cans of Mountain Dew. The next day everyone else turned in twenty-page reports with the required forty footnotes. Neil showed up with two pages scribbled in pencil off the top of his head.

Read Proverbs 4:5–13
What's the easiest way to get through school?

You'll have nightmares about school for the rest of your life. You forget to go to class—all semester. You lose your locker combination. You misplace your schedule, and a lady in the office with an AK-47 makes you pay fifty zillion dollars for a new one.

School can be scary. So how do you survive the nightmare right now?

Start by staying awake. Pay attention and take notes in class so you don't have to study so hard on your own. Listen to teachers. Laugh back at peers who slam you for studying hard. Do your own work and remind yourself that most of the time hard work still pays off.

Getting smart doesn't mean becoming a wise guy, memorizing encyclopedias, dining on dictionaries, or kissing up to teachers. It's knowing what your goal is and how to avoid the traps between you and your destination. It's figuring out the best way to get things done—following God's rules, staying within his boundaries of right and wrong and his guidelines of good, better, and best.

Those are the things you're supposed to do. They also happen to be the smart things to do. They're the easy way to get through school.

Do not forsake wisdom, and she will protect you. PROVERBS 4:6

Your Life in Pictures

You flip open your yearbook and spot your face spread on 22 of 36 pages. *You were magnificent.* You captained three teams, climbed your way to first-chair violin, and captured Student of the Year honors for your 4.0 grade-point average.

Or you've been bad—*really bad*—and you're splattered on just as many pages. Surprise! You were voted "Brat of the Year" and "Most likely to live in a home for juvenile delinquents."

Or you struggled along in the middle of the pack—and *no one knows you were there.* You didn't get voted "best dressed" or "best personality" or even "class brain." It takes three passes through the book to find a single tiny picture of you. Page 31, bottom inside corner, it's you with the flu. Even in black-and-white you look green.

Read 2 Corinthians 3:18

Why do you go to school? What will you be remembered for? What will you accomplish?

There are more efficient ways to do school if your sole reason for being there is to absorb facts. The custodians could hardwire you into a virtual reality system and give you a virtual brain. Or for a low-cost, low-tech education, teachers could lock you in solitary confinement with a textbook and give you something to eat only after you choked down algebra.

You need to learn school stuff so you don't spend your life refilling the burrito bar at Taco Tom's. And you pick up other skills at school too. Like how to get along with friends—and enemies. How to work with teachers—your bosses. How to keep going—when you'd rather quit.

God sends you to school for one more reason: to use the experience to remake you to look like Jesus, who knew God the Father totally (John 17:25–26), obeyed God willingly (John 6:38), and loved other people completely (John 15:13). People saw God's glory—God's greatness—reflected in Jesus, just like they can see it in you.

You may not rate a ton of pictures in the yearbook. But hopefully your classmates will always remember *who* you looked like.

We...are being transformed into his likeness with ever-increasing glory. 2 CORINTHIANS 3:18

No Lie

Mitch rounded the corner just as Caveman's fist pounded Steve's stomach. Mitch tried to backpedal, but Caveman—a gargantuan kid who spoke little and showered less—hoisted Mitch a foot off the ground and shoved him against a wall.

"Didn't see nuthin', did ya?" Caveman grunted. Mitch's feet tap-danced against the wall. Mitch shook his head *no*. "Tell anyone, you look like Stevie. Understand?" Steve was doubled over and holding his stomach, wheezing. Mitch nodded his head *yes*.

Later a teacher stopped Mitch to ask if he knew who hurt Steve. Mitch said he didn't and walked off to blend in with a crowd of students.

If God wanted to, he could act just like Caveman. He could be a knuckle-breaking brute, scaring us into believing *his* version of the story, no matter what we had seen with our own eyes. Or he could be a different kind of liar—a deceiving charmer, winning our love one moment only to drop us with a *splat* the next. Because he's bigger and smarter than any of us, God could out-maneuver, out-argue, and outwit us, making us believe lies. But he doesn't.

Read Isaiah 45:18–19
How do you know that God tells you the truth?

We don't always want the truth. We believe lies—and tell them—to keep life pleasant. Unlike us, however, God swears to be honest in everything he says. He makes some huge promises: (1) He speaks openly, for everyone to hear; (2) he doesn't tease—when he tells his people ("Jacob's descendants") that they can know him, he means it; (3) he speaks not just truth but *the* truth; and (4) he—and no one else—knows perfectly what is right.

Massive promises. But we can be sure they're not massive lies. We would be stupid to trust what God says if he were into busting knuckles or breaking hearts. He's not. His honest words are backed by honest actions.

God's ultimate promise is to be God for everyone who trusts him: "There is no God apart from me, a righteous God and a Savior" (verse 21). And when God sent Jesus, he gave you the ultimate proof that he means what he says.

Listen up.

I am the Lord, and there is no other. I have not spoken in secret.... I, the Lord, speak the truth; I declare what is right.
ISAIAH 45:18–19

Bewildered No More

This is so stupid. While all of Lisa's friends romped at the beach, she rotted in church. Lisa's mom had separated from her dad three years ago because he drank and beat up the family, and the divorce was finalized a few months back. About the time of the divorce, Lisa's mom started going to church. She said she had found God and he was putting her life back together.

Whoopee for her, Lisa thought. *But why drag me here? I've got a life. Besides, God's like Dad. Useless.*

Lisa's friends got her into trouble sometimes, but at least they stuck together. Lisa had never seen God, but she'd seen her friends. They were dependable. She wasn't so sure about God.

Read John 4:19–26
(The passage picks up in the middle of a conversation between Jesus and a woman getting water at a well.)
How do we know what God is like?

Lisa isn't the only one confused about God. Teachers may argue that God is a figment of your imagination. To a non-Christian friend, the cross is just jewelry dangling from her ear.

Confusion about God isn't new either. A long time ago Jesus told the woman at the well that she needed to get her facts straight. When she tried to pull him into an argument about the best spot to worship God, Jesus told her she was missing the point. Ceremonies and services and holy places are crusty, dusty religion if you don't "worship in spirit and truth"; that is, if your heart doesn't respond to God because you know whom you worship and why.

Jesus revealed to the woman that he wasn't merely a prophet, someone who speaks *on behalf* of God, but the "Messiah," God as a human, who came to speak *for himself* with the human race—and, even more than that, to save it from destroying itself.

Jesus came because God wanted to prove his power and trustworthiness to us. He wants us to understand clearly what he is like (John 1:14; Colossians 1:15). He wants us to see that he's the One worth listening to.

The woman said, "I know that Messiah" (called Christ) "is coming. When he comes, he will explain everything to us." Then Jesus declared, "I who speak to you am he." JOHN 4:25-26

Twinkies for Lunch

You woke when the waves sloshing against the shore tickled your toes. You remembered the storm, and being tossed overboard, but that's it. The fog in your brain starts to clear, and you realize you're on a deserted tropical island. *Panic!* You wonder whether you'll shrivel up from starvation or be mauled by wild animals.

Then you see it, a few yards up the beach: a boxcar-size crate of Twinkies.

"There is a God!" you shout. Sure, you're still shipwrecked, but you're the sole owner of an unlimited supply of your favorite food. You tan on the beach for the next day or two waiting to be rescued, humming reggae tunes and tossing down Twinkies. But when the rescue doesn't show, you discover something. You can't live on Twinkies alone. Better food, you figure, is behind you in the jungle.

Read John 6:30–40
What's the one thing that will sustain you for life?

Chowing down one or two—well, maybe three or four—Twinkies at a time is a delectable snack. But they're not something you could eat meal after meal. You need real food.

A few verses before this passage, Jesus had fed five thousand people with a few loaves and some fish. Some in the crowd claimed they would believe in him if he could produce another sign—like burgers and fries raining from heaven. Jesus knew that all they wanted was to satisfy their physical hunger. So he taught them about spiritual hunger.

Jesus said that they needed more than the first convenient crate of Twinkies. If the crowd would just look around, they would see a limitless feast awaiting them in the jungle. Jesus declared, "I am the bread of life." He's not a snack. He's the feast of life in the jungle. He alone can permanently satisfy people's deepest hunger and thirst.

Jesus didn't just want to treat the crowd to lunch; he wanted to give them eternal life. But for them to accept his gift of eternal life, they needed to want more than a meal. They needed to want him.

Then Jesus declared, "I am the bread of life. He who comes to me will never go hungry, and he who believes in me will never be thirsty." JOHN 6:35

Give Me the Light

Until the weather sirens blasted him awake, Caleb hadn't noticed the rain knuckling the roof or the wind tearing at the curtains on his open bedroom window. The storm had knocked out the power, so he bumped through the dark to his parents' room. His older sister was holding his sobbing younger sister. Socks landed at his feet as his dad ransacked a dresser drawer to find a flashlight.

Just as Caleb's mom shooed everyone downstairs to shelter, lightning exploded a tree in the backyard. Even Caleb's dad bolted down the stairs—minus a flashlight to light the way or a radio to tell them what was going on. With no light to tame the darkness, all the family could do was huddle in the blackness and wonder what more the storm could bring.

Read John 8:12
What's it mean that Jesus lights up your life?

On a stormy night when the lights go out you bump your way around your house or apartment. Sure, you can cope. But if the lights stay off and the storm keeps on, your life gets scary and confining. You wish for real sight.

Jesus came to shine into a world covered in spiritual darkness (John 1:4–5). Sin blocks out God's light. In its shadows, wrong looks right and good seems bad.

But Christ shines into the darkness. His light keeps you from getting lost in the dark. His life and words spotlight the difference between right and wrong. And the closer you stick to him, the better you see.

After stumbling around a dark house for a time, your eyes adjust to the lack of light. You get along better than before. But when the lights come back on, you realize how little you could actually see.

After a while you might get used to the lack of spiritual light in your world. You start to think you can see pretty well. But when Jesus shows up, you realize that the shapes you saw in the darkness weren't what you thought. The light is the place to be. In Jesus' light every move doesn't result in a bump and bruise. In him, you have light for life.

I am the light of the world. Whoever follows me will never walk in darkness, but will have the light of life. JOHN 8:12

Not That Dumb

Jill smelled trouble smoldering as soon as she walked in the door. As she tiptoed toward her bedroom, her mom stopped her short. She held out a small plastic bag and asked Jill what was in it.

"It's parsley." Jill shrugged. "I chew it for my breath. All the kids do. It just dried out."

Her mom wasn't *that* stupid. "Don't play games, Jill. It's not dried parsley. It's pot. What are you doing with drugs in your backpack?"

"You were in my backpack? You have no right to go through my things."

"I was looking for the makeup you borrowed and didn't return. Jill, I can't believe you'd do this. I'm too angry to talk now. You go to your room until your dad gets home."

Jill exploded. "I'll go where I want to! You can't tell me what to do."

Read John 8:21–30

What did Jesus mean when he said, "I am from above"?

Members of the Flat Earth Society want you to believe—*surprise*—that the earth is flat. From observations you make in everyday life, it's tough to disagree with them. One glance outside should cause you to say, "Yup. Flat like a pancake." But as soon as you get a bigger view—like the pictures of the earth astronauts take from space—you're forced to say, "Nope. Round like a ball."

A youth doing drugs doesn't want to admit that her parents or teachers or doctors have a better, bigger view of the danger of using drugs than she does. No one likes to be criticized, questioned, or condemned. But we have to admit that we don't have the ultimate understanding of ourselves and our world. It's God who has the big picture, a view of all people and all events for all time.

Jesus said his teaching wasn't something he made up on his own. He spoke as God's Son, who came "from above," from the Father in heaven. He repeated what he heard from his Father. He warned us for our own good.

Confusing? The crowds around Jesus thought so. But the point is that Jesus didn't speak as an ordinary human. He saw more than us. And he knows more than us.

If you do not believe that I am the one I claim to be, you will indeed die in your sins. JOHN 8:24

Pink Bunny Sheets

You stroll to school wrapped in the only bed sheets left in the linen closet—your little sister's pink bunny sheets. You would have preferred plain white, but no matter. *People will still recognize me*, you reassure yourself. You step into traffic, protected only by a raised hand, and tires screech as cars skid to a stop. You raise your hand again to bless a neighbor's poodle.

When you get to school you don't take your seat. Instead you walk to the front of homeroom and command the class to be silent. "I have an announcement," you say. They stop to listen only because you look so wacko. "I will be running class from now on. You see, I am God."

You're serious. But the snorts of your classmates echo in your ears as your teacher escorts you to the principal.

Read John 8:48–59
Why did the crowd want to kill Jesus?

If you told all your friends that you were God, they would offer you a ride to a rubber room—once they stopped laughing. Yet to many people back in Bible times, it was just as preposterous when *Jesus* announced he was God. He was their neighbor, the run-of-the-mill son of a carpenter (John 6:42).

The crowd's reaction to Jesus seems strange to us. He says, "Before Abraham was born, I am!" and they want to hurl rocks at his head. What could Jesus possibly have said that got them mad enough to kill him?

Whenever Jesus used the phrase "I am _____" ("the Messiah," "the Bread of Life," and so on), he echoed the name God had given himself in the Old Testament, "I am who I am" (Exodus 3:14), a name so revered that the Jews didn't dare speak it aloud. For a man to take that name for himself was a crime deserving death, according to Jewish law. In this passage Jesus' simple "I am" was a blunt claim to be the God who existed before time began.

Some people say Jesus was merely a good man, a respected teacher like Confucius or Thomas Jefferson. But other great teachers didn't claim to be God. Jesus did. He knew what he meant. The crowd sure knew what he meant. And Jesus was willing to die for what he said.

"I tell you the truth," Jesus answered, "before Abraham was born, I am!" At this, they picked up stones to stone him.
JOHN 8:58-59

He Treats You Right

Four-year-old Marty peeked one eye around the chips and dips on the aisle end. *Not here.* He looked around another corner. *Not there.*

Lost in a cavernous supermarket filled with strangers, Marty pulled the jacket hood tight to hide his crying eyes and quivering lip. He shook with lostness. He howled with misery. He'd lost his mommy.

He ran down aisle after aisle, farther from his mom. His mom, though, was already searching for him. Eventually she caught up to Marty and picked him up, holding him tight. Marty buried his face in her hugs. "I'm here, Marty," she whispered. "It's okay. Mommy's here."

Read John 10:1–11
How do you recognize Jesus' voice?

If a watchdog is well trained, it's suspicious of any stranger who comes near the house it protects. Nothing distracts it—throwing biscuits, cooing "Here, doggie, doggie," yelling "SHUT UP, YOU DUMB DOG" while waving your arms like a wild man. A good dog can't be tricked. If you're not the dog's master, it won't be your friend.

A little child loves his mom's voice, and a watchdog jumps when it hears its owner. As believers—like sheep—we learn to recognize our Shepherd's voice.

Sheep know their shepherd treats them right. He gives each a name. He provides for their needs—food during the day, shelter at night. The shepherd stands at the gate of the pen to check the sheep one by one, soothing wounds and providing security. The sheep know their shepherd's unique call and scatter at anyone else's voice.

By experiencing the shepherd's kindness, the sheep know that their shepherd isn't like others who might sneak into the pen and hurt them. The shepherd's one concern is the good of those in his care.

Once you know that Jesus' main concern is to lead you into the best life God has in mind for you, then you won't be fooled by violent or stealthy voices that want to turn you into a lamb chop. You know they don't sound like Jesus. Jesus' voice is kind. Jesus is your Good Shepherd.

The thief comes only to steal and kill and destroy; I have come that they may have life, and have it to the full. I am the good shepherd. The good shepherd lays down his life for the sheep.
JOHN 10:10–11

Don't They Get It?

Sweat beads on Scott's lip. He looks left. He looks right. Just like last time—they come at him from all directions. Suddenly a guy built like a walk-in freezer flies through the air and tackles him.

Scott screams, wakes up, and sits up in bed.

This time it was only a dream. Next time he would think twice about busting the curve on a biology test. Sometimes doing the right thing makes other people mad.

Read John 10:31–39

What would you do if people kept chasing you with rocks?

It was the same scene all over again. The religious leaders wanted to kill Jesus, this time because he called himself "the Son of God." Jesus didn't mean God had given birth to him. For Jesus to call himself "the Son of God" meant (1) that Jesus was God and (2) that Jesus had a unique relationship with the Father. They were separate yet one (verses 30 and 38).

Jesus didn't lie down and let his critics pelt him. He tried to persuade his enemies with Scripture. If they could accept that God honored mere human rulers with the title "gods" or "sons of the Most High" (Psalm 82:6), then his claim to be the Son of God was no crime. He was, after all, God's special representative to the world.

And he offered his life as proof: *The works I do*—healing disease, casting out demons, calming storms, feeding multitudes, raising the dead—*show that what I say is true. The miracles I do are what my Father does. I am who I claim to be.*

Jesus' claims and the good he did go hand in hand. He argued that his actions alone are proof enough to believe. And he wants you to be sure about one thing. He can't make it any clearer without slapping your face: *When you look at me, you're looking at God. If you reject me, you reject God. If you don't follow me, don't claim that you're God's child.*

Believe me, Jesus argued. Some didn't. *You can't kill me for doing what's right*. One day they would.

Even though you do not believe me, believe the miracles, that you may know and understand that the Father is in me, and I in the Father. JOHN 10:38

After the Funeral

Until Jamie's grandma got cancer, she lived two thousand miles away in Florida. Jamie's parents said they wanted Grandma to die at home, with family surrounding her. When her parents called a family meeting to decide whether Grandma should come to live with them, Jamie voted yes.

That sounded great a year ago.

Now it hurt. Jamie hardly knew her grandma before she moved in. If Grandma had died halfway across the country, her death wouldn't have mattered much. Jamie would have missed Grandma at Christmas and birthdays, but that was about it. Now Jamie knew her. Now she missed her. Jamie cried herself to sleep after the funeral. Her parents said they would see Grandma again someday. But that sounded like a fairy tale.

Read John 11:17–26
What happens to believers when they die? Why?

Time-warp yourself sixty or seventy years into the future. You're at a funeral, but no one notices you're there. The old photos of the deceased in the back of the church look familiar, like pictures of a long-lost childhood friend. To take your mind off the organ music warbling in the background, you line up to view the body.

When you look into the casket, you see *you*—drained of life, caked in makeup, laid out in your best clothes. All around you, family and friends are crying.

If you could be a guest at your own funeral, what would you say?

For Christians, saying "We'll see Grandma in heaven" isn't a sugary treat we suck on at funerals to make ourselves feel better. Death is a consequence of sin (Romans 6:23), but Jesus took the punishment for sin for all who believe in him. Believers die physically, but death can't keep us down. Jesus is the Resurrection and the Life, and what Jesus did for Lazarus temporarily—check out verses 38 through 44—he will do for us permanently (John 3:16).

"I know you miss me," you would say if you could speak. "But don't cry forever. I followed Jesus. I'll be in heaven. I hope you'll be there too."

Jesus said to her, "I am the resurrection and the life. He who believes in me will live, even though he dies." JOHN 11:25

Stinky Feet

"Look out!" someone yelled at the team's star batter. "Willie's behind you!"

Too late. Willie lay on the ground wondering what planet he was on, walloped in the forehead by a wild warm-up swing. The bench emptied and everyone crowded around the Panthers' bat boy.

"You weren't practicing where you were supposed to!" Willie's older brother yelled at Slugger.

"So?" Slugger shrugged and glanced at Willie, still moaning on the ground. "Big deal. He's okay. Don't worry about it." He kicked at Willie. "Hey, kid. Get me some water."

Read John 13:1–5, 12–15

Why did Jesus wash his disciples' feet?

Jesus picked a strange way to show strength. Politicians often stay on top by spewing lies and digging up muck. Gangs show who's boss by tagging turf and busting bodies. Some teachers keep control with threats of detention, suspension, and expulsion.

Jesus is the Master of the universe. All things are under his power. But you wouldn't have known any of that when he washed his disciples' feet. Rather than demanding honor and making his disciples suck up to him, Jesus did the job of the lowest household servant. He peeled off his shirt, wrapped a towel around himself, then unlaced the sandals and washed the feet of a dozen burly men who had spent the day tramping along dirt roads. Sweat, dust, and leather—imagine how bad it reeked. It would have been better to be a bat boy fetching water and chasing foul balls.

Jesus' disciples should have washed *his* feet. He washed theirs.

He didn't use his power to knock his disciples down but to lift them up.

To us, Jesus sometimes looks like a bat boy just flattened by a blow to the head. But don't mistake Jesus' servanthood for weakness or stupidity. He's really the King.

You call me "Teacher" and "Lord," and rightly so, for that is what I am. Now that I, your Lord and Teacher, have washed your feet, you also should wash one another's feet.

JOHN 13:13-14

Here, Kitty, Kitty

Blistered from scurrying down miles of backcountry gravel roads, your paws hurt. What a lousy vacation this turned out to be! You're a thousand miles from home, and after a week you've seen no trace of your owners, whom you misplaced when you ditched your kitty carrier to search for mice. Definitely bad judgment. The tasty feast never happened.

No one understands your lonely *meow*, so you can't ask directions. No one knows who you are or where you belong. Maybe if you keep searching you'll find your owners again.

Fat chance.

Stories of pets sniffing their way home across thousands of miles make for great tearjerker movies. But face facts: The only kitty that gets home is one whose owner tracks it down and carries it back.

Read John 14:1–7

Where does Jesus plan to take his followers someday?

As human beings we're lost—but not because our Owner decided he was tired of caring for us. We weren't flung out of a moving car in the middle of nowhere or stuck in a bag and sunk to the bottom of a lake. We wandered away from God (Isaiah 53:6). And we're a long ways away.

Asking people how to get back home isn't much help. They're lost too. *Look for the god inside yourself,* they say. *Work hard to be good enough for God. Trust cold, concrete data and nothing else. Accept fate. Make up your own beliefs. Look to spirits and stars. Pummel your body to perfection. Get rid of desire—care about nothing.*

Human thought can't lead you through life to an eternity of paradise with God. Its destinations are confused. Its routes are dead ends.

Jesus knows where to take you and how to get there. He's tracked you down. He says, "I am the way and the truth and the life. Want to come home?" Only Jesus is the Way—he died for you and opened the gate back to God. Only Jesus is the Truth—he gives a perfect picture of God. Only Jesus is the Life—he conquers death so you can live eternally.

He's the one road back to where you belong.

Jesus answered, "I am the way and the truth and the life. No one comes to the Father except through me." JOHN 14:6

Resolutions

The clock struck midnight. Everyone cheered and smooched, but Katie faked a smile. She thought about the past year—*what a wreck!* She had spent most of the year in her room, grounded from the phone and the TV and from getting together with friends. She had fought so much with her mother that her dad threatened to send her to boarding school.

Katie was even more depressed because she knew that deep down it was her fault. Her own stubbornness caused the problems with her parents. She told them she wanted to make her own mistakes. She did. The mistakes hurt. So in the first few hours of the new year, Katie resolved to obey her parents even before they opened their mouths. She closed her eyes and made her promise. When she opened her eyes she smiled, convinced things would be better.

They weren't.

If happy thoughts and resolutions were enough to make us better people, then the world would already be a paradise. Or at least fighting and nail-biting would be extinct.

Jesus came to make it clear, however, that it wasn't human promises but a divine Person—Jesus himself—who would make us new people. It's through *him* and everything he's done for us that we grow up spiritually.

Read John 15:4–5

What's up with Jesus calling himself a "vine"?

Horticulture lesson: Fruit doesn't appear in a grocery store out of nowhere. It comes from fruit-bearing plants. It starts on a vine, tree, or bush.

Christ taught that he is the one True Vine. We are the branches. If we want to bear good fruit—if we want to mature spiritually—we have to "abide" or "remain in" or "stay connected" to him.

Fruit won't grow on a branch that's not in total contact with the vine. So our human promises—the ones we make without tapping into his power—mean little. We break them. Trying on our own to be good—without Christ's help—gets us nowhere. We wear out. What matters is relying on God, through his promises, to forgive us, live in us, teach us, and encourage us—and to be close to us as we stay close to him.

I am the vine; you are the branches. If a man remains in me and I in him, he will bear much fruit; apart from me you can do nothing. JOHN 15:5

Promise or Threat?

It was a little like getting a fortune cookie written by Dad every morning for breakfast. Whenever Ryan's father went on business trips, he left a stack of dated envelopes on the kitchen table, each with a note inside for Ryan to read while he was gone.

Sometimes there were lists of things for Ryan to do. A few notes were warnings—like nudging Ryan to study ahead for an upcoming test. Once in a while an envelope contained money to treat the rest of the family to pizza or a movie.

The notes reminded Ryan that his dad cared about him. They also made it hard for Ryan to forget that his dad had high expectations of how he would act, even when Dad wasn't around.

Read Revelation 22:12–16

After Jesus ascended to heaven he appeared to his disciple John to reveal "what must soon take place" (Revelation 1:1). What did he promise?

Three times in the last chapter of the Bible Jesus said that he would return to earth (22:7,12, 20). That's a threat. It's also a promise.

When your parents leave you home alone and you do things you shouldn't, you might dupe them into thinking everything went swell—that you did your homework, that you didn't blast the stereo loud enough to rattle the dishes or invite friends over when they said not to.

Jesus can't be fooled like that. That's the threat.

But the promise is that Jesus is coming to remake the world the way he wants it to be—with God on the throne and no death or crying or pain (Revelation 21:1-5). Those who "wash their robes"—who accept forgiveness and new life in Christ—will spend eternity with God in paradise.

Sometimes you might feel like God is far away. Yet through the Bible he's written us notes to read daily—warnings, things to do, words meant to remind us of his love and to encourage us to do what's right until he comes.

Do you believe his notes? Is he the One you listen to?

Behold, I am coming soon!... I am the Alpha and Omega, the First and the Last, the Beginning and the End.
REVELATION 22:12-13

Whom Do You Listen To?

Flash forward through your day....

A teacher pats you on the head and says your history essay was outstanding. She claims you're way smarter than your peers.

A friend pulls on your sleeve and urges you to skip class.

Your sweetie runs fingers through your hair. Your parents want you to cool your relationship, but you're begged to meet after school.

Your mother smothers you with hugs and says your spat with the neighbor kid couldn't be your fault because you never do anything wrong.

Your dad rips into you for the C you got in math. When he was your age he did way better.

Your coach whacks you with a baseball hat. The throw was right on your glove. How could you miss the tag?

A TV flickers on. Beauteous guys and girls leap and dive in a game of beach volleyball. Everyone breaks to throw back a cold beer.

Battered by the noise, you collapse onto the floor.

Read Psalm 25:1–6

Whom can you count on to always tell you the truth?

You can't escape hearing dozens of voices—family, school, friends, media, even your maturing body and brain—telling you every day what to do.

You're surrounded. Maybe even crumpled on the ground in confusion.

With so many voices shouting at you, which ones do you believe? How do you know who is wrong—or who is right? Which voices speak truth? Which spouts lies? Whom should you listen to?

The easy way is to give up and follow whichever voice is the loudest. But that isn't the only way. God wants to lift you up, look you eyeball-to-eyeball, pull the wax from your ears, and utter pure truth to you. Jesus invites you to tune in to his voice and follow him. He promises to help you sort out the other voices, distinguishing truth from lies, good from bad, real from fake.

God's voice isn't the loudest, because he respects you too much to scream at you. But listen up. He's got life-altering stuff to say.

Show me your ways, O Lord, teach me your paths; guide me in your truth and teach me, for you are God my Savior, and my hope is in you all day long. PSALM 25:4-5

Truth in a Toilet

Ten seconds ago the couple on-screen was goo-gooing into each others' eyes—sappy but harmless. All of a sudden they're making out like a car wash during the scrub cycle. And it goes on and on. Your contact lenses fog. You didn't expect that in this movie.

Question: What do you do? Your choices: (a) Cover your eyes—but peek through your fingers; (b) gawk and take notes; (c) stomp out and never go to another movie; or (d) ponder excuses for watching something you know you shouldn't.

No good answers.

Better question: Why are you at the movie? What are you looking for?

Read Proverbs 2:1–15
How do you look for wisdom?

God's wisdom helps you "live in safety and be at ease, without fear of harm" (Proverbs 1:33). That sounds appealing—almost like the happiness and relaxation you want from entertainment. Sometimes a movie or some music provides a bit of what you're looking for. It says what you feel or expresses a truth about life. But it doesn't teach the knowledge of ultimate truth and reality that satisfies through and through. Only God's wisdom does.

Be honest. Lots of times you have to sit through a heap of bad to get a tiny bit of good. Trying to find wisdom in some places is like trying to find lost change in a toilet. It may be there, but it's not worth the dig.

Disgusting? You bet. But so is swishing through the swirl of waste served up on the Net as well as in many TV shows, videos, tunes, concerts, magazines, books, comics, and computer games—not just the violence, bad language, and "adult situations," but the sarcasm and selfishness.

That isn't smart stuff. If you're looking for wisdom—for truth, reality—which leads to life, there's a better place to look.

Wisdom is treasure worth searching for. It's worth crying out for. And God is *the* place to get it. Don't bother looking for gold in an outhouse.

If you call out for insight and cry aloud for understanding, and if you look for it as for silver and search for it as for hidden treasure, then you will understand the fear of the Lord and find the knowledge of God. For the Lord gives wisdom.
PROVERBS 2:3-6

Buena Contesta

You hate that Papa Smurf know-it-all look your older brother sometimes gets. "I'm worried about you," he says as he sits you down on the couch. "I've done some dumb stuff I don't want you to do." You wonder what stupid thing he just did to make him feel the need to straighten you out. *We knew all along that you were dumb. What's your point?*

"Some of those kids you're hanging around are trouble," he advises. You squirm. He's right. Then your brother gets an odd look. You see a tear form in the corner of his eye. That's never happened before. "I know I've treated you like a dirtball," he apologizes. "But I really care about you. You need to be smart. I hope you'll listen to what I say."

Read 1 Kings 3:5–15
Why did Solomon ask God to make him wise?

You thought God was supposed to tell *you* what to do. But suddenly he appears to you in a dream, asking what you want *him* to give you. You have phenomenal cosmic power at your fingertips.

What would you ask for? The ability to run a hundred yards in 3.6 seconds? To captain the starship *Enterprise*? For your worst enemy to die in a sudden freak accident? How about sole ownership of Microsoft?

Think bigger.

Asking for wisdom is as good as wishing for more wishes. Wisdom unlocks every part of total devotion—being close to God, steadfast, thoughtful, strong, loyal, unselfish, forgiving, honest, dependent on God, and free from peer fear.

Okay, okay. Wisdom is best.

But who should you ask to help you get wise? Not the parents of some of your friends—who aren't smart enough to ever say "no." Your older sister or brother? Maybe. Maybe not. A friend? Not likely. You may know people as cool as you but surely none as bright.

How about God? He's the one Being in the universe who knows everything.

Good answer.

I will give you a wise and discerning heart. 1 KINGS 3:12

Wise Guy

Pen and narrow-ruled notebook at the ready, you lean forward in your seat and strain to appear as intelligent as the other students in your first college class. Your professor strolls in, easy to spot in his tweed jacket, gray hair, and goatee. His accent informs everyone that he was born on the distant island of Academia.

As your professor explains his requirements for you to earn an A, B, or C, a guy waves his hand wildly. "Is this going to be on the test?" he asks. The professor sneers at him, and students look down their noses. "Leave now," your professor warns the class, "if you're not planning on *working* to earn a C. You will work, or you won't pass."

You wince.

"You will succeed," he continues, "if you remember two things: *I* am here because I know more than you. *You* are here to benefit from my wisdom."

You cringe. Yet you know he's right.

Read Proverbs 1:1–7
Where do you go to get smart?

Life is a string of events in which others do for you what you can't do—and teach you what you don't know—until you grow capable yourself.

So admit it: Sometimes, in some situations, you're helpless and dumb.

Don't feel bad. So is everyone else. We all need what God wants to teach: "wisdom" (knowing how to live skillfully), "discipline" (training in obeying God), "discretion" (choosing rightly between two ideas or two actions), and "prudence" (thinking through actions before you do them). God's wisdom rescues you from being simple or immature so you know how to act well toward yourself and others.

The incredible part is that the all-knowing God never treats you like an idiot. He isn't a professor parading his vastly superior knowledge.

But *he can only teach you as much as you want to know*. You get smart only when you "fear God"—when you respectfully submit to his teaching because you know that you need him to figure out life.

You'll always need to learn from the Father who knows best.

The proverbs of Solomon son of David, king of Israel...for giving prudence to the simple, knowledge and discretion to the young. PROVERBS 1:1, 4

What a Trip

Your social studies teacher was fresh from college, but she looked as if she'd found her bell-bottoms in a musty box in her dad's closet. You called her Moonmuffin.

A chia pet on Moonmuffin's desk daily blessed her tofu sandwich with fresh sprouts. Scattered around her desk were crystals she said kept her from getting sick. You said they were pretty. She said they were powerful.

And when the class studied the Salem Witch Trials she offered to read palms and brought in a "white witch" to speak. "She's wonderful," Moonmuffin gushed. "She harnesses the power of nature to do good." *Yeah, right*, you thought. *She tries to harness the power of rabid dogs and bat fangs and killer sharks. This is our role model?*

The last you heard, Moonmuffin had been nailed by a truck while meditating against air pollution on a freeway overpass.

Read Proverbs 1:20–33
What happens to people who refuse to get smart?

This is one section of Proverbs where you don't want to recognize yourself. You don't want to be *simple*—dimwitted, too stupid to watch where you're going. You don't want to be a *mocker*—sharp-tongued, too proud to accept advice. And you definitely don't want to be *foolish*—stubborn, too headstrong to be corrected, apt to repeat your mistakes like a dog that chomps its own vomit (Proverbs 26:11).

The simple, mockers, and foolish have a few things in common. They like themselves just the way they are. They live as if God didn't exist. And catastrophe will liquidate them because they continually reject wisdom.

Not smart.

You won't straighten out every person in the world who rejects God. But it's your job to not be duped when they try to sell you a different god—or no God—or rewritten rules of right and wrong. Understand what they say. But understand too where they go wrong. After all, you can be so open-minded that your brain falls out.

For the waywardness of the simple will kill them...but whoever
listens to me will live in safety and be at ease,
without fear of harm. PROVERBS 1:32-33

Dig It?

Phil had heard so much about high school being tough that he panicked his freshman and sophomore years. He studied hard. He pulled better grades than anyone expected. Then halfway through he decided to slack off.

At the end of one semester his counselor called him to his office. "At this rate you won't graduate on time," his counselor warned him. "You understand that, don't you? What are you going to do about it?"

Phil promised to work hard, but his promises got to be a joke. He goofed around in class and study halls and after school. *I'm just doing what my friends are doing,* he told himself. And spring semester of his senior year he didn't have enough credits to graduate.

Oops.

Read Ecclesiastes 7:23–25
Will you get smart if you just wait long enough?

Suppose you didn't quite hear your old neighbor when she leaned over the fence to whisper in your ear. But you think she said there was gold buried in your backyard. Your response wouldn't be "Did you say something?" or "Were you talking to me?" or "Excuse me, I didn't quite catch that. Would you be so kind as to repeat what you said a moment ago?" You would say, "Did you say GOLD? WHERE?" If you didn't understand the message the first time, you would scream for a clear answer. You would scoop, shovel, excavate, and detonate until you found gold.

It's not enough to want wisdom. You must search for it. It's how you get clear on the stupidity of sin and the insanity of going your own way. Just like graduation doesn't just happen—you don't get smart without studying—wisdom doesn't just drop in your lap.

Attaining wisdom might feel like it's as far-off and far-out as graduating from high school or college. True, not every nugget of wisdom you get from God by studying the Bible is something you always use that instant. That makes it tempting to slacken your search or give up altogether. But the only way to get wise is to keep at it, to store up wisdom so you have it when you need it.

So I turned my mind to understand, to investigate and to search out wisdom and the scheme of things and to understand the stupidity of wickedness and the madness of folly.
ECCLESIASTES 7:25

If You're So Smart...

Laura grimaced at the poster Adrianne and Paul were making for their youth group's Christmas musical. To be honest, the head on Adrianne's shepherd looked as if it had been crushed in an accident, and Paul had run out of room writing the date, time, and place.

"Can you make it any uglier?" Laura sassed. "Are you *trying* to scare people away? Anyone who looks at that will think we're doofs. Of course, that does fit most of you anyway. We sound awful. Most of the cast can't act. You should hear our school musical. That's a real group, of course. We had tryouts and Mr. Malone said I was the directors' first choice. We didn't take just anyone, of course."

"Of course," Paul mimicked. "Anything else, O Great One?"

"You don't have to get mad or anything. I just don't want anyone to think that this musical is all the better I can do."

Read James 3:13–18
What's the difference between real brains and fake brains?

Imagine a relay race with millions of runners on the track at one time, each caught up in catching and passing on a gigantic baton. Runners can enter the race at any time. Here's the really bizarre part: No one races against anyone else. The goal is to get everyone to the finish line in good time.

That's what being a believer is like. We're all in the race. We work together. James says that if you have real brains you help others along in the race. You do good with humility, deliberately accepting people who are less mature, skilled, or smart than you. You don't just look out for yourself. You show gentleness not because you're weak but because you're strong.

When you have fake brains, you're like Laura. You rush to defeat others. You cheat. You loosen other runners' cleats. You wallop people and trip them midstride to get to the front of the pack.

James says not to pretend you're trying to do good. You're just trying to look good.

Who is wise and understanding among you? Let him show it by his good life, by deeds done in the humility that comes from wisdom. JAMES 3:13

Nowhere to Go

Older guys surrounded Branston and his friends as they walked home from school. The biggest kid grabbed Branston. "I saw you sneaking around. You stay out of my face."

"Out of your face? I was just walking home. I wasn't anywhere near you." The thug hit Branston with a half-punch, half-slap, full wallop. Branston's head snapped to the side and his lip gushed blood.

Branston lived with both parents in a city apartment in a tough neighborhood. They never made enough money to move away. When his parents bussed him to a school in the 'burbs, kids mocked and harassed him.

He wanted a place where he fit. He wanted someplace safe. He didn't know where it was. He for sure didn't know how to get there.

Read 2 Chronicles 14:11
What is "trusting God"?

Some problems—at school, at home, with friends, with your health—get so big that you can't budge them. You feel like an old beater car stuck in a trash smasher. The walls are closing in. No escape routes. You know you're supposed to trust God—and you're supposed to know how. But how?

The verse you read picks up in the middle of a description of how King Asa of Judah and his troops squared off against a vast army of Cushites. Asa's actions show what to do when there's not much you *can* do: He prayed. And obeyed. That's trust.

Asa reminded God—and himself—that there was no one as powerful as God and that God alone was their hope. Then King Asa led the Israelite army into battle, confident that God was with them. God crushed the Cushites.

But the end of the story isn't so happy. Late in life Asa refused to depend on God and do what he knew was right. He bought help from an evil army and sought healing from occult doctors. Even when a prophet reminded Asa that "the eyes of the Lord range throughout the earth to strengthen those whose hearts are fully committed to him" (2 Chronicles 16:9), Asa refused to trust in God—to pray and obey. His nation remained at war. His illness got worse. Asa had something even better than *somewhere* safe to go. He had *Someone.* But he forgot.

Help us, O Lord our God, for we rely on you.
2 CHRONICLES 14:11

Walk on the Wild Side

"Whaddaya mean this wristband will let you track me wherever I go?" David quizzed. "What if a bear eats me? Will it still keep beeping in its stomach? Or what if it only eats my arm? How will you find the rest of me?"

"Trust me" was his scoutmaster's reply. "You have your map and compass and know how to use them. You have two days to get to our pick-up spot."

"This map—is it right?" David panicked. "Did you check this compass?"

"I picked your route carefully. And yes, that's my best one."

"But there's one more thing," David protested. "I've never been where I'm going."

"David," his scoutmaster explained, "that's the whole point. Now git!"

Read Genesis 12:1–5

Are you stupid if you trust God? Why—or why not?

God told Abram—later called Abraham—where to head to get to the land of his extreme blessings. God's directions were a treasure map Abram trusted enough to leave a comfy life in Ur and go where God had pointed.

Just like that, God wants to lead you places you've never even thunk of. He's given you a map and compass—his Word, the Bible—that's a hundred percent accurate. It's your total guide to getting along, growing up, and making the most of life.

Trouble is, even if a map is perfect and the path it charts exotically exciting, you'll never move from point A to point B if you don't *trust* the map. You won't ever wholeheartedly follow God if you don't *rely on* the excellence of your outfitter.

You could look at the Christian life and dream up all sorts of reasons *not* to go where God wants you to go: "I'd act more like a Christian if I had more Christian friends." "If I had a deadly illness—then I'd trust God." "Believing God would be easy if I had more time to read my Bible." "I wouldn't do stupid stuff if my friends didn't ride me so hard."

That's making up scary bear stories. God doesn't pass out messed-up maps. He doesn't deal in cracked compasses. He knows how to fend off killer animals. So be daring. If you believe God, you'll walk on the wild side.

So Abram left, as the Lord had told him. GENESIS 12:4

Is God a Wimp?

Tasha didn't mean to be nosy, but from what she could see there weren't many books in the locker across from hers, even though three people crammed their stuff into it. It seemed like the most popular locker in school. There was never a crowd, but someone was *always* there—before school, after school, between classes. The locker was a puzzle, but it didn't bother Tasha—except that sometimes she felt left out. Whatever was going on, she sure wasn't part of it.

Then one day she saw an argument at the locker. Faces tensed, pills spilled, a knife flashed. The dispute ended quietly, but that didn't calm Tasha. She felt unsafe. She felt guilty because now she knew why the locker was so busy. And most of all she was angry at the school. They must know what was going on. The people in charge were either stupid or they didn't care.

When you look around at the ugliness of our world—the sickness, hatred, divorce, abortion, starvation, genocide—it's easy to conclude that God is distant. Or stupid. Or uncaring. Or powerless.

Read Isaiah 46:3–13
Is God really powerful? If he is, why is the world a mess?

The Bible portrays God as all-knowing and all-powerful, big enough to direct the galaxies yet near enough to spin every atom of his creation. He guides his people from the beginning of life through old age. He creates, carries, and rescues. He predicts the end while at the beginning. He will accomplish all his goals. No one compares to him. He is God, and there is no other. God is in charge.

The world doesn't always look that way. God is Master of the universe, the Beginning and the End. But if he's so powerful and so loving, how can his world be so ugly?

Here's the catch: God intends the world to be a place of righteousness, where people accept his love and live together in peace the way he planned. Yet God gives people freedom, the chance to follow or disobey his commands.

God says that when everyone listens to him and trusts his authority, life will be heavenly.

Unfortunately, not everyone agrees.

I am God, and there is no other; I am God, and there is none like me. ISAIAH 46:9

The Jester

The gloomy clouds gathering over the kingdom fit the sour mood that had afflicted the king's subjects since they had heard the rumor about a country with no king. In that imaginary country no one told the people what to do or what not to do. People there, it was said, were exceedingly wise and happy, each having the freedom to do as he pleased.

The king's subjects supposed that their lives must be boring by comparison. Though they had been entirely pleased with the king's rule, they grumbled that their lives should belong to themselves, not to the king. Yet no one thought to do anything about their discontent until the king's jester made up a rhyme:

> *The king is bad and you are sad...Of course he is to blame.*
> *Just follow me and you will see...Your lives won't be so tame.*

The people decided that day to live as if they had no king, shutting out his provision and ignoring his commands.

Read Isaiah 14:12–14
What did the being Isaiah describes do wrong?

A human being who rules a country with total control is called an "absolute monarch" or a "dictator." No human being has the right or the ability to handle that much power.

But God does. God is no human being. He *is* ruler of all. He made everything and has complete authority over it (Psalm 24:1-2). That would be unbearable if God's love for us weren't perfect. God's total love, total knowledge, and total power make him worthy of our total devotion.

But not everyone agrees. The Bible talks in a hazy way about the beginning of a rebellion against God. Satan, whom God had made the most beautiful of all created beings (Ezekiel 28:12-19), decided *he* should be in charge. He believed he was wiser than God.

Satan is the jester who puts our fears into words. He spends his time trying to persuade the world that *he*, not God, is the one worth listening to.

He's wrong.

You said in your heart, "I will ascend to heaven; I will raise my throne above the stars of God.... I will make myself like the Most High." ISAIAH 14:13-14

Red Tights

Luke pulled out a Mercedes-Benz hood ornament strung on a long chain inside his shirt. "Cool, huh?!"

Toby was a little shocked. He was sure Luke hadn't found his latest fashion statement at an auto parts store.

"No big deal," Luke spouted. "That's why people have insurance. Besides, people who drive cars like that have plenty of money to fix them. A hundred bucks is like buying bubble gum to them. You want to go get one?"

"My parents would kill me if—" Toby tried to protest.

Luke just rolled his eyes with an expression that said, *Don't be such a doorknob.* "No one's gonna find out."

Read Genesis 3:1–7
How did Satan make rebellion against God look good?

The Garden of Eden apparently was the only place Satan wore a snakeskin suit to get human beings to listen to him. But he's still devious. He twists thoughts so that good seems bad and bad seems good.

In his chat with Eve ("the woman" in the passage), Satan questioned whether God had said anything at all about eating fruit. He wanted Eve to think that specifics about right and wrong didn't matter much, even to God. Satan and Eve both made God's rule tougher than God had. (Look at Genesis 2:16–17. God only forbade eating fruit from one tree.) Then Satan told Eve the consequence she feared was really just a fib. She wouldn't die, even though God said she would. And finally Satan lured Eve in with one last morsel: The reason God laid down the law was to deprive her of something wonderful.

Satan's tactics haven't changed. The fright and flash of devil worship and heavy-metal album covers are just a diversion from his widespread, everyday deceit. His voice hisses all around us: *You can run your own life. Nothing will happen. God just wants to rain on your party.* Don't expect Satan to pounce at you from behind a corner, sporting red tights and a tail, shouting, "*Hey, you! Wanna sin?*" Satan still slithers like a snake.

"You will not surely die," the serpent said to the woman.
GENESIS 3:4

The Art of Self-Defense

Joel rammed the joystick. His weapons display blinked WEAPONS LOCKED ON ENEMY TARGET. He fired. Hah! Four choppers and eight tanks blown to microbits. MISSION ACCOMPLISHED. RETURN TO BASE. Nothing better than zinging around in a helicopter gunboat shooting rockets and laser-guided missiles.

When Joel's parents told him they were divorcing he felt like he had been shot—except this was no video game. Joel tells himself and his friends that he's okay, but he spends most of his time alone, shooting up digital enemies. The rules are simple—kill or be killed. There's nothing to figure out. Vaporizing his enemy means he wins.

Joel hit the Play button again.

Read Ephesians 6:17

How can you defend yourself when your head feels attacked?

It's easy to believe God when things go well. You're certain: *God is good. God is powerful. God is right. God loves me. God tells the truth.*

It's not so easy to believe when life explodes.

You're in a fight to the finish. When tough stuff makes you wonder why people treat you rotten, why your family fights, why school is so hard. When you can't figure out why God doesn't fix it all, you're tempted to start thinking differently about him: *He's evil. He's weak. He's mistaken. He doesn't care. He's trying to trick me.*

When circumstances grew tough for Jesus and he was tempted to stop believing and stop obeying his Father, he fought back with Scripture. When Jesus was hard pressed in the wilderness, he countered Satan's statements point by point with verses from the Old Testament (from Deuteronomy 8:3; 6:16; and 6:13). Jesus applied Scripture to his life, and Satan fled.

You can't shoot laser missiles at your thoughts or at your enemies. But God's Word is your weapon. You build up your ammunition every time you study your Bible. You access that potent force when you learn to trust. You fire when you say, "Hey, brain. Don't listen to that lie. It's not true. God says..."

That's the only way you'll win.

Take the sword of the Spirit, which is the word of God.
EPHESIANS 6:17

Rock Your World

You struggled to keep your footing on the steep stairs. The canoe perched on your shoulders tipped forward and back and side to side, and each step tested your balance and tortured your already tired muscles. You'd paddled eighteen miles and portaged overland four more. But climbing Stairway Portage was the worst—a hundred yards straight up. Once you had the canoes at the top, you climbed down and up twice more to get all your other gear.

When you and your friends finally collapsed in camp that night, everyone opened up their packs. What you found wasn't just food and clothing. Your packs were full of rocks. Large rocks. Many large rocks.

You'd been sacked. Your supposed friends at base camp had snuck in and filled your packs with rocks.

Read Matthew 11:28–30

What does Christ ask you to carry when you follow him?

If the Christian life were a canoe trip, you would still face ridiculous portages, strong head winds, and crazed mosquitoes that zoom up your nose. Obstacles and opposition are part of life no one can escape. Life is often a toil. Being a Christian doesn't mean someone else will paddle your canoe while you kick back and duff.

But as a Christian you won't find back-busting rocks in your backpack. The One who maps your trip and packs your load wouldn't do that to you. The burden Christ calls you to carry is light. His authority—His "Lordship"—over you is kind and fair (Psalm 145:17). His love for you never ceases (Lamentations 3:22). He knows exactly how much you can lift (1 Corinthians 10:13). And he's there to unburden you when the weight becomes too much (1 Peter 5:7).

Contrast Christ with jokers who load your bags with boulders—some to be funny, some to be mean. Either way, you carry stuff you don't need to—heavy expectations, bad maps, bug repellent that doesn't repel, and sun block that doesn't block. That's what happens when you let anyone but Jesus pack your sack and guide you through life.

Come to me, all you who are weary and burdened, and I will give you rest.... For my yoke is easy and my burden is light.
MATTHEW 11:28, 30

In a Coffin

After spending a whole summer working at a Christian camp, Jenna had hoped for a little more enthusiasm from her friends when she passed around her summer photos. Her friends flipped quickly through the pictures. They looked bored even when they saw children's faces of every age and color. They stared into space when she shared her intense excitement for teaching kids about Christ. No one even perked up when she told how the camp staff had done a ropes course together—and how she'd hung upside down thirty feet off the ground.

One day, after yet another apathetic reaction from a good friend, she ran home to her room and thought horrible thoughts about her summer of service. She wanted to throw away the pictures. She wished she could throw away the whole experience.

Read John 12:23–28

What do you think it means to fall into the ground and die?

When Jesus said we should "hate life" and "die" like kernels of wheat, he spoke wildly to make a point—like "Don't have a cow" or "You eat like a pig." Jesus doesn't want you to kiss a speeding truck or gulp poison like a cult member. To "hate your life" or "to die," Jesus explained, is to be totally devoted to him. To boldly trust and obey him in every situation of life. To let him be your absolute Lord.

But doing all that can cause a heap of pain as you ditch sin, let go of selfish ambition, or feel rejected by others for following Jesus. That pain is what Jesus means by "death."

The pain that can result from obeying God, however, is only half the story. After death comes life. A seed sitting on a shelf in a shrink-wrapped package won't grow. Only when a seed is dropped into the ground does the soil's scratchiness and cold wetness force a plant to spring up.

In the midst of death God grows new life in you and in others. Suffering as a Christian—falling into the ground and dying—sometimes feels as fun as lying trapped in a coffin. But remind yourself of one thing. God promises that you won't be in there forever. He'll come and lift you out.

I tell you the truth, unless a kernel of wheat falls into the ground and dies, it remains only a single seed. But if it dies, it produces many seeds. JOHN 12:24

Wave Walking

He had told them to row to the other side of the lake. It sounded easy enough, but as Jesus' disciples bullied the boat into the wind, they must have thought his command was ridiculous. With oars flexing and hull groaning, the boat drifted backward almost as much as it lurched forward.

In the middle of the night they suddenly saw someone coming toward them. Without a boat. On *top* of the water. It was Jesus, but they didn't know that. They thought it could only be a ghost. Jesus calmed them before their terror could drive them overboard: "Take courage. It is I. Don't be afraid."

Read Matthew 14:22–33

What did Jesus' disciples learn in the middle of the storm?

Jesus' stroll on the sea gave his disciples courage. He saw them straining to follow his command to take their boat to the far side of the lake and wouldn't let them struggle alone. Jesus met them in the storm and overpowered it. He even let Peter stomp on the waves with him. When Peter's doubts caused him to sink, Jesus caught the disciple's hand and challenged him to trust his powerful care.

Being a Christian won't plop you into a calm sea tickled by a gentle breeze. It might stir up storms. And Jesus' daring invitation sounds even crazier than rowing across a stormy lake or walking on water: *Know me*, he says. *Live for me.*

But Jesus *never* leaves you to face the winds alone.

When darkness upsets your sense of direction, when winds scream and spray pokes your eyes, Jesus comes to you and says, "I'm not a ghost or a fantasy or too good to be true. I'm real. Don't be afraid! It's me! I'm here!" He cares for you, using his Holy Spirit, his Word, and other believers to lift you up.

Do you want to hang tight with God? He feels closest when you're with him on the waves, practicing prayer, courage, and action out in the winds, gaining a daring faith that transforms you into a worshiper and a wave walker. He's worth your total devotion.

Immediately Jesus reached out his hand and caught him.
"You of little faith," he said, "why did you doubt?"
MATTHEW 14:31

Saved From Sludgedom

"Swank, huh?" Papa Sludge says to his family as they spy the mansion high on a hill, lit up in the moonlight. "Toldja it'd be great." Pops maneuvers the family truckster past the front gate, running over a valet. Pops jams their rusted purple Lincoln into a tiny spot on the lawn, and out pile Pops, Mama, and fourteen little ones, dinging doors on both sides.

The greasy horde follows the hundreds of candles lighting the way up the driveway to the house, bursting into a ballroom of long-gowned ladies and tuxedoed gentlemen. Grabbing fistfuls of elegant appetizers, they flop on a couch in front of a TV the size of one of those walls at a mall. As they claw for the remote control, it drops and shatters, with the tube locked on *WWE Wrestling.*

"Poyfect," Pops exclaims. He kicks his shoes off onto a glass coffee table. "Hey yous," he yells to the host. "Hows about a foot rub?"

Read Psalm 15:1–5

What does God expect of you if you want to live close to him?

Pick a part at the party. As a Christian you are (a) the valet who gets run over; (b) one of the well-washed, well-heeled partygoers; or (c) a member of the family Sludge.

The right pick is *c*. We're all grungy before we get to know God.

But also *b*. We don't stay that way.

Getting to know God is like showing up at a party hideously underdressed, an object of sneers. Because each of us sins, none of us is good enough to approach God on our own—to live on God's "holy hill." Yet God loved us while we were filthy with sin (Romans 5:8). And God makes us good enough to be in his totally pure presence, making us right with himself through Christ's death, flinging open the gates and inviting us in (Hebrews 10:19–23).

God and his partygoers welcome the unwelcomable. Yet it isn't right to stay sludgy, to spew on God's kindness. We're no longer unaware of our mess of sin. It's fitting that those who live on the hill act like the one who owns the house. So we learn to stop running over people and insulting our Host. If we keep on being rude and crude we won't enjoy God's party.

Lord, who may dwell in your sanctuary? Who may live on your holy hill? He whose walk is blameless... PSALM 15:1–2

Zero Tolerance

Adam waited outside the school office while the principal talked to his mom. An hour earlier one of the school's counselors—the one in charge of discipline—had yanked him from class. As they stood in the hallway, the counselor and another teacher said someone saw a knife in Adam's backpack. They wanted to turn Adam's pack inside out.

They said he had it. Adam said he didn't. They opened up his backpack and there it was, a small pocketknife. It wasn't Adam's. He didn't put it there.

Adam went pale and started to explain, but he knew they wouldn't believe him. "Zero Tolerance" meant they didn't care who the knife belonged to or how it got there. They wouldn't even try to find out. It was in Adam's backpack, and he was automatically out for the rest of the school year, a three-month suspension. Lots of time to stew.

Read Psalm 26:1–12

Who knows you're right when everyone says you're wrong?

You've *fwopped* your little brother on the head plenty of times and haven't gotten caught. For once you were actually being nice, but that's not what your parents think. They ground you.

Your protests of innocence sound hollow. Get over it.

But there's another kind of false accusation that's harder to swallow. You walk into a clothing store. One glance from the manager and your age makes you an instant shoplifting suspect. You laugh at a story you overhear after school at practice. Then you figure out everyone's talking about you— and it's not true. Or you choose to hang out with one friend. Suddenly another friend thinks you're evil.

To be "blameless" in the Bible goes beyond being able to say you didn't do wrong—*this* time. It's being absolutely sure that your one goal has been to live tight with God, doing his will, obeying in the power of his truth and love. It means being able to say you didn't join those plotting to do wrong. You did your best to do right.

David was sure of his innocence. No one believed him, he claimed.

God did. He knows the truth. And he promises that one day everyone else will know it too (1 Corinthians 3:12–13).

Vindicate me, O Lord, for I have led a blameless life; I have trusted in the Lord without wavering. PSALM 26:1

Can't Run—Can't Hide

David woke at the noise of the VCR swallowing a tape and the TV flicking on. "What are you doing?" he asked, tangled in his sleeping bag. "What time is it?"

"*Shhh*," Cal hushed. "I brought some midnight entertainment."

By now the four other guys sleeping in David's basement were awake too. "What is it?" Billy begged. "Tell me it's the swimsuit edition."

"This is no swimsuit video. This is better," Cal promised.

For a second David saw the bodies onscreen. "My parents—!" was all his shocked brain could blurt out.

"Trust me," Cal said as he sat back to watch.

Read Psalm 32:1–11
What happens when you try to hide wrongdoing?

You've probably felt that sickening snarl in your stomach followed by the need to crawl in a corner and rot. You're embarrassed because you did something idiotic—or even ashamed because you did something wrong (what this psalm labels "sins" and "transgressions" and "iniquity"). You want no one to know. Not your friends, not your parents, not even God.

You can't live like that.

When you know you've done wrong and you haven't made it right with God, at least part of the pain you feel is from him. It's meant to prick you, to push you to him. You could choose to wallow in your badness or to clamp your conscience, but God would rather have you let him help you. You can't rescue yourself. You can't remake yourself. God can.

It's scary that God can see everything about you. You can't hide. Then again, you don't have to—God knows you inside and out. It's good to be known for who you are. No better, no worse, just the real you.

God hates when you suffer by yourself. Hanging tight with God means you hide *in* him, not *from* him.

When I kept silent, my bones wasted away through my groaning all day long.... Then I acknowledged my sin to you and did not cover up my iniquity. PSALM 32:3,5

Between Disasters

Katie's long bangs mostly hid the huge scar high on her forehead. She knew that the jagged mark wasn't pretty, but it reminded her what she had survived. Two years before she had been riding next to her dad in their pickup truck down a country highway. Another driver slid through a stop sign. The pickup slammed into the corner of that car, hitting hard enough that Katie put her head through the windshield.

At first she was so drugged she hardly knew who she was. When the doctors took her off pain-killers she had to fight to not scream.

Strange—Katie almost wished she could go back to that time. God seemed so close. People prayed for her and with her constantly. When she got tired of headaches and surgeries and shots, God was tough for her. She promised God that if she got well her whole life would belong to him.

Looking back, Katie wasn't sure how well she had kept her promise.

Read Psalm 40:1–10

How do you stay close to God when your life goes great?

When you fly through a windshield, you can hardly see God through the pain. You can't wait for him to yank you out of tough times, and you think it will get easier to obey God in every attitude and action once everything is okay. Yet when things go well you almost wonder if it takes a shattered skull to feel close to God.

You land quite naturally on God's lap when life sends you flying. It's not hard to figure out why you need him.

Between disasters, though, it's tempting to scurry away and ignore God. But there's still lots to do when life goes great: You can thank God today for what he did yesterday. You have a break to take time to better understand his "will," how he wants you to live. You can help people who now need your help. You can encourage other believers ("the great assembly") when they struggle. You can tell others what God has done and what he keeps on doing.

With each experience God pulls you through, he puts a "new song in your mouth." But the lyrics won't always tell how he plucked you out of a slimy, gator-infested pit. You can sing about the calm times too.

He put a new song in my mouth, a hymn of praise to our God.
PSALM 40:3

Have a Good Holler

"Why don't you look where you're going?" Lori spewed. She had enough to worry about without Tadd running into her and splattering her books and papers on the floor. She stooped down to pick up her things.

"Look where *I'm* going?" Tadd sassed. "Why don't you go where *you're* looking?"

Very original, Lori thought. *And I know—I'd look better if I wore a hat on my butt and walked backward.* With her crossed eyes wandering all over, no one knew where Lori was looking. Besides that, she walked a bit side-ways, like a crab.

At home in her room that night, Lori read her Bible the only way she could—a couple inches from her face. She broke down and cried. Then she did something she had never done before. She screamed it at God: "WHY DON'T YOU FIX ME?" Shocked at what had slipped out, Lori covered her mouth. And she waited for lightning to strike.

Read Psalm 13:1–6
Is it okay to yell at God?

How long until you show up? David prayed. *Remember me? Or have you forgotten who I am and what I need?* Those are pretty harsh words from the mouth of the guy the Bible applauds as "a man after [God's] own heart" (1 Samuel 13:14). But David spoke his mind and lived to tell about it.

Big feelings simmer inside when you have confused thoughts or painful emotions or a hurting body. Sometimes harsh words boil over onto yourself, people around you, even God—*especially* toward God, the one with ultimate power and complete control.

There are a lot of reasons why you can hurt even though God is in con-trol. (A few to gnaw on: God gives human beings the power of free choice, and humans, not God, cause pain. Jesus is God's plan to fix things. Heaven is God's total solution to pain.) But when you're hurting, you don't have to hide your pain. David wasn't afraid to tell God about his hurts. They were real. But he always got around to thinking about a bigger reality, that God's love never quits. David didn't stop at speaking his mind and his heart. He spouted until he was able to praise God again.

How long, O Lord? Will you forget me forever? How long will you hide your face from me? PSALM 13:1

Not So Fast

Judd had skipped enough grades to make it to Sandberg High School as a weasely little eleven-year-old. He was smarter than almost everyone else at school—including most of the teachers. He studied trigonometry with a tutor. He had won a nationwide writing contest for his science-fiction novel—a sparkling story of slime molds rampaging through the galaxy. He never got anything wrong on anything.

Everyone at school hated Judd.

Judd wished the kids in his neighborhood would be nice. Every day after school he dashed home, scurried up into his backyard tree house, yanked up the rope ladder, and hid. Neighborhood kids stood below and threatened to pound his head in. No one ever came to Judd's rescue. So he threw rocks at them until they went away.

Read Psalm 35:1–10

Will God ever deal with your enemies?

It's weird. Mumble something nasty to yourself about an enemy and it's a *bad attitude*. Say it to someone else and it's *gossip*. Shout it at your enemy and it's *picking a fight*. Tell it to God and suddenly it's *prayer*.

How can you get away with that?

Because it's *prayer*. It's pouring out all the thoughts and feelings of your heart to God. It's asking *God* to do his thing. It isn't dishing out justice with your own hands. And it isn't begging God to carry out your whims. It's pleading to him to halt evil and give evildoers the punishment they deserve.

Old Testament believers were a bit foggy about life after death, so their prayers against enemies usually scream "Crush them NOW, God. Don't miss your chance!" Yet the New Testament is clear that some of the payback for evil—God's judgment, or his "vengeance"—won't happen until the end of time (Revelation 19:11-21).

And that's okay. God gives even awful people a chance to respond to his kindness. His concern for now is more to reach them than to roast them (2 Peter 3:7-9).

Still impatient for God to toast your enemies this afternoon?

Not so fast. Think about it. Should he be so quick to punish you?

Contend, O Lord, with those who contend with me; fight against those who fight against me. PSALM 35:1

You Know How It Ends

You sit alone in your dimly lit family room, deeply into the final twelve minutes of your favorite show. This week's superevildoer just fired up a gigawatt laser beam to slice your show's hero into a zillion pieces.

Your heart stops. *Thumpa Thumpa. Thump....*

Commercial.

Back to unreality. It's ugly. The laser beam sweeps back and forth like a pendulum—*zzzzzt zzzzzt*—inches from your hero's head, frying a hole through everything it touches. You sweat. Your stomach knots.

"BOO!" your dad bursts in. "Scared you, didn't I? What's on? Oh—a rerun. In just a second his sidekick is going to—"

"Don't tell me!" you scream. You hate when someone tells you the end.

Don't be ridiculous. You already know.

Read Psalm 18:1–15
How do you feel while waiting for God to save you from a tough situation?

If you thought TV action- or mystery-show heroes were real you'd go insane. Producers can't kill off their main character, but week after week they make you wonder. They get you nervous. Then they let you hang through commercials. Worse yet, they flash "To be continued ..." just when the clock tells you danger will dissolve.

Suspense isn't so entertaining in real life.

You're ill—and you wonder when you'll get well. Your parents are planning to divorce—and you get weak waiting for court dates that drag on forever. Or you're waiting for a monster test, an important game, a big recital or concert or play—and you melt into a queasy goo. The instant before your frustration is relieved—the moment you don't know relief is right around the corner—can torture you into hopelessness.

And then it's over. You're okay. God came through for you.

He *always* does. Not always how you expect. Not always when you want. But in his time and in his way he always does. So stay loose. You know how your show will end.

I call to the Lord, who is worthy of praise, and I am saved from my enemies. PSALM 18:3

Waiting for the Pumpkin

Theresa flashed a smile at the finish of her balance beam routine. She'd nailed it. Her scores flipped up—her brain did quick math—first place!

Her coach swept her up in a huge hug. "Incredible!" Coach cried. Theresa's teammates crowded around her, proud of their star.

By the next morning back at school everyone had heard that Theresa won the state overall junior title. Her classmates looked at her with awe. They chatted about her chances of making it to the Olympics.

What a year. Six months ago Theresa had just moved. She was miserable. Now she could see what God had done—a new school, a new coach, and better friends than ever before. It was great!

When she got a letter awarding her a full scholarship to an elite gymnastics camp she started to fret. This all felt too good to be true.

Read Psalm 118:1–16

How are you supposed to react when everything goes well?

When life seems too good you might begin to feel like Cinderella—you're having a ball, but you're sure your carriage will turn back into a pumpkin.

Jesus himself warned that being a Christian would at times be tough. "In this world you will have trouble," he said (John 16:33). Paul reminded readers that suffering is part of being a Christian (Philippians 1:29). And James explained that bad times make us strong believers (James 1:2–4).

But when things go well—big things, little things, or everything—misery isn't the right response! Don't spoil your fun by convincing yourself it's going to blow apart in the next twelve seconds. And don't spoil yourself by thinking your success is totally your own. After all, every good gift comes straight from God (James 1:17). So celebrate good times, good things, and good friends by thanking God for what he's given.

But thanking God may not jump to mind when times are fine. When thanking him doesn't come easy, think hard about three things: *Your past—* that you were surrounded, swarmed, and squashed. *Your present—*that God's protection and help got you where you are. And *your future—*that God will always be your refuge. And say thanks.

> *Give thanks to the Lord, for he is good; his love endures forever.* PSALM 118:1

Remember When

Twice a year Luke and his dad drove to the country to visit the gravesite of Luke's mom. This time Luke's new stepmom went with them. Luke wondered what his mom would have thought of Denise. He liked her pretty much.

"You'd be just as tall as Mom now," Luke's dad told him. "She'd still whip you at arm wrestling, though."

"But I would crush her at hoops," Luke shot back. "Her jump shot was feeble."

Luke and his dad talked for a long time, while his stepmom mostly listened. It helped to sit and think—to remember the past. Before Luke's mom died of cancer three years ago, she had always said that God would take care of him.

Looking back, Luke could see that he had.

Read Psalm 77:1–20
What keeps your heart attached to God?

Because your favorite chair has never collapsed or let you down in the past, you plop down without thinking. When a friend is a proven secret-keeper, you rely on him or her. You're loyal to a restaurant because they've never dropped your burger on the floor or spit in your soda.

Trust. It's built on past reliability.

You trust God best when you remember what he's done for you.

Some days you'll wonder where God has gone. *Doesn't he love me anymore? Where are the friends he promised me? Did I do something to make him mad?* When Asaph, the author of Psalm 77, worried that God had forgotten him, he took courage from one thing: recalling God's acts in the past. He knew it was God who blew apart the Red Sea to let Israel escape slavery. He was certain it was God who led his people to freedom. He hadn't seen God's footprints, yet he recognized God by his kind and powerful acts.

God has acted with kindness and power for *you* too. The same God you read about in your Bible is *your* master and friend. He sent Jesus to die and rise again for you. He's energized your heart through his Holy Spirit. He's always with you, helping you conquer your circumstances. And he's remaking you to look like him.

Remember that. And trust.

I will remember the deeds of the Lord. PSALM 77:11

All You Have—All You Need

With two intense Christian friends always close by, Jon had it made. Jon, Josh, and Tim went to the same church, the same school, even lived on the same block.

But then Josh moved away. A few months later, Tim started making excuses for not showing up at church. Then he started dodging Jon altogether. When Jon called to go blading, Tim's older sister lied that he wasn't home. The last time they sort of talked, Tim answered the phone himself. When he recognized Jon on the other end—*click.*

Jon heard that Tim's dad had started telling him it was stupid to be a Christian. After a while Tim thought it was stupid too.

So Jon was stuck by himself.

He knew it wasn't supposed to be that way.

But that's how it was.

Read Psalm 142:1–7
What do you do when you feel alone?

It feels like you're lost a long way from home. You're alone—the only Christian your age you can spot. Or—pretty likely—your Christian friends attend other schools or at least have other teachers. Or maybe the Christian friends you did find have stopped being kind.

Sooner or later your Christian friends let you down. Sooner or later there's no one around. Christian friendships are supposed to be your shelter, and usually they are. But once in a while you get left out in the rain. That's the time to find your way to God.

God sometimes allows you to feel alone so you learn to hide in him.

The intro to Psalm 142 says that David wrote the psalm in a cave, possibly when Israel's King Saul had gone insane and wanted to kill him (1 Samuel 22:1–2). What exactly did David do in the cave? He hid from his enemies. He prayed. He learned to trust. He got to know the God who says over and over "I will never leave you nor forsake you" (Joshua 1:5; Hebrews 13:5). He got to know the God who sticks close when no one else does. And an odd thing happened. When David hid in the cave—in God—his family came and supported him. So did a bunch of friends.

I cry to you, O Lord; I say, "You are my refuge." PSALM 142:5

Open-Door Policy

"Remember what you said when I was in lockup?" Tasha asked her youth pastor quietly. "It was right after my attempt. I said, 'How come I'm locked up? They're treating me like I'm a murderer.' You said, 'It's because you tried to hurt Tasha.' "

"You didn't understand me then, did you?" he remembered.

"No. I didn't care about Tasha. I didn't know who I was or why I shouldn't hurt myself."

"So has this place helped you? It's got to beat lockup."

"Yeah. It's taken a few months, but I get what you meant. I don't want to hurt myself ever again. But I'm still stuck on something. I know I'm a Christian. And I know you keep telling me, 'God is *always* there for you, Tasha.' But how can God forgive me for how I treated myself—and what I did to my family? I'm afraid God doesn't want me anywhere near him."

Read Psalm 103:9–12

Does God ever get so mad at you he shuts you out?

Picture this. You never get mail, but one day you've got a FedEx envelope at your door. Inside? Membership documents for the poshest club in town—good for a lifetime, all expenses paid. You can't wait! You're gonna golf, swim, smash a racquetball, and twirl in a whirlpool, all on the first day.

You're supposed to get free entry at the front gate. But you're scared. What if the promise was a lie? What if the club secretly votes to boot you out? What if they're just teasing—and want to laugh at you when you show your face?

Most free gifts are scams. But God's offer of friendship is real.

You might not feel acceptable to God. But he hasn't shut you out. Through Jesus, God has fully dealt with your sin—past, present, and future. He's flung your sin farther than the ends of the universe.

Remember? When Jesus died for your sins, he opened the way for you back to God. If you've said, "Yes, God, I've sinned and need your gift of forgiveness," then you're forgiven, fit to hang with the King of the universe.

If God didn't want you close to himself, he wouldn't have sent his Son to open the door and invite you in. But he did. Walk on in.

As far as the east is from the west, so far has he removed our transgressions from us. PSALM 103:12

God Is the Crust

If life were a pizza, God would be the crust.

You toss a lot of toppings on your pizza—school, sports, clothes, sleeping, relaxing, shopping, lessons, clubs, parties, and more. God isn't just another topping on the menu you can pick or ignore. Nor can you ask for God on one part of the pizza and leave him off the rest. You can't slice up your life and say, "These are the pieces without God, and these are the pieces with God—church and youth group."

If Jesus is your Lord and Savior, he's a part of everything you do. He gives your life its shape and determines what fits on top and what doesn't. Without the crust, everything slides off.

Pizza crusts, however, are always in danger of being ignored because the toppings are so obvious. Because you *can't* see God, it's easy to forget him in the midst of all the things to do that you *can* see.

When you eat a pizza, you need to slow down and savor the crust. When you go through your week, you need to slow down and concentrate on God.

Read Mark 1:35
How did Jesus fix his attention on God?

You can spend time with God two ways: in a group or by yourself. You need both to grow spiritually.

In a group you're encouraged by the strong faith and support of other Christians. Groups allow you to get fired up and celebrate your friendship with God.

Being alone with God helps you get to know him personally, just like you need time one-on-one with someone to know what they're really like. That's what Jesus did. Even he needed time to talk with his Father alone.

Reading your Bible—and using Christian books and music to help you understand and apply the Bible—is part of that. Reading the Bible is how God speaks to you. Learning to talk *to* God—learning to pray—is the other part of spending time with God. God doesn't want to talk *at* you but *with* you.

Very early in the morning, while it was still dark,
Jesus got up, left the house and went off
to a solitary place, where he prayed.
MARK 1:35

Shopping at a Car Show

You've never seen such a sea of sculpted metal and glass. When your parents dart left into minivan and family sedan land, you dodge right in search of monster sports-utility vehicles and rocket-cockpit sports cars.

Suddenly in front of you is your all-time favorite auto. Unoccupied.

All mine—for a minute, you think. You settle into the seat, play with the mirrors, land your head on the headrest. You wrap your hands around the leather wheel, close your eyes, and dream about scooting a hundred miles an hour down a dirt road. *Wake me up when I've got my license. This is better than any racing game at the arcade. This is the real thing.* Well, only sort of. You can't test-drive a car at an auto show.

Read Psalm 34:8–22
What good does it do you to follow God?

Life is no car show. It's a speedway. A road rally. A demolition derby.

Good news: God doesn't just look hot on the show floor. He tests best in the real race of life. "Check me out," he says. "Take me for a spin. See how I do." Drive with him once, and you'll never settle for anything less than his quality closeness and care—and his pedal-to-the-floor, hang-tight-to-your-seat blessings.

And following God has what car salesfolk call "the intangible benefits of ownership." Believe it or don't, hanging with a zoomy Lord as leader of your life can bring you friendship when you least expect it—and for deeper reasons than why people flock to a beautiful car.

Here's why: Whenever you get on the path of following God, you find others on the same path (Psalm 119:63). As you do his will, you deepen friendships and help others (Ecclesiastes 4:10). You find still more friends as you share God's friendship (Matthew 11:19). But most of all, getting soaked in God's love strengthens you to spread his care (1 John 4:19).

God is worth following. If you let him, he makes you into a person who knows how to be a great friend. After all, it's like your mom says: If you want friends, you have to be a friend worth having.

Taste and see that the Lord is good; blessed is the man who takes refuge in him. PSALM 34:8

Popularity Bubbles

You skip down the hall, joyful to be at school. Well, you don't really skip. And you're not quite joyful or gleeful. You just mind your own business, shuffling from class to class, gliding with a glut of people down the hall.

Suddenly you feel a hand on each elbow—and another hand around each bicep—and your feet lift off the floor as your back slams against the wall. You hang against lockers, feet dangling. You've been hoisted.

You look to the left. You're held up by a square-headed brute, the human equivalent of one of those Stone Age coelacanth fish everyone thought had died off a few billion years ago. On the right you've got Squarehead's thin twin. He's weaselly. Wiry. With half a mustache.

"We're here to get rid of you," Squarehead informs you. "Everyone just took a vote, and you don't belong."

Read John 12:42–43

Whose vote counts most when it comes to being popular?

Even at the cruelest of schools, no one actually takes a vote to figure out who's in and who's out. But they might as well.

It's like this. You're minding your own business when life suddenly turns into a popularity contest. Everyone votes. And vote after vote, only a few popular kids come out on top. Maybe it's you. Maybe it's not.

The winners are the ones who get to tell others who to be—and push everyone places they don't want to go. That's the top-of-the-social-pile job the Pharisees grabbed for themselves. As the religious leaders of Jesus' day, the Pharisees pressured people to reject Jesus. They caused even other popular folks to crumple in fear, threatening to kick them out of the synagogue—their place of worship—for following Jesus. How come? "They were more concerned about what people thought of them than about what God thought of them" (John 12:43 GW).

It's natural to care what other people think about you. It's even normal to dash around looking for votes. But if you have to choose between being loved by the masses or pleasing your Master, there's only one vote that really counts. His.

They loved praise from men more than praise from God.
JOHN 12:43

Chat Chat, Blah Blah

Jay Leno leans over to pop the question everyone wants you to answer: "So," says talk-show host Jay, "what's it like being the most popular young person in the world?"

"Tough." You wink. "Been training for years. And it's like climbing Mount Everest. I knew if I wanted to scramble to the top, I needed the right stuff. "I've got everything I need in a bag right here." You dig in your book bag. "Look—my last IQ test—140. Genius, you know. You'd have to be stupid to think you don't need brains. Just be careful not to show 'em. I've got sculpted muscles swathed in just-right body fat. Hmm, then some other stuff: flawless clothes, hair, teeth. Oh—and I always keep a few ugly admirers next to me so I look good."

You rummage at the bottom. "But here's my coolest tool, Jay. It's an attitude I couldn't have gotten along without: I'll do *anything* to be liked by everybody."

Read Matthew 21:1–11
How did Jesus react when the crowds admired him?

People probably don't lay palm fronds in your path and shout "Hosanna! You the King!" Then again, since you're not God's Son, you probably don't expect the royal treatment that Jesus got on Palm Sunday.

Still, you've been told what it takes to survive the high winds, frigid cold, and lack of oxygen as you scramble to the top of Mount Popularity. People promise that big biceps or the right bra size or bowing to the crowd's wishes will make you likable.

Those things won't take you to the top. And they won't keep you on top. What you don't see in the Bible passage you read is how quickly the fans who crowned Jesus "Mr. Jerusalem" changed their minds. Five days later the people who praised Jesus became a pack of piranhas. They begged he be killed on a cross (Matthew 27:22–23).

Jesus knew that popularity scatters like snow flurries in a mountain wind. So he didn't play to the crowd. Instead, he made obeying his Father his ultimate aim (John 4:34). Jesus didn't pack for the popularity climb. He picked a path to please God.

The crowds that went ahead of him and those that followed shouted, "Hosanna to the Son of David!" MATTHEW 21:9

A Dog Ate My Arm

"We get voted 'Cutest Couple' at Fall Fest," Mira fumes, "and then he dumps me! He says he likes Nikki better. And he tells the whole school I'm a 'psychowoman.' Arrgh! I'll show him psychowoman, all right."

"Arrgh," adds Beth.

"And then he thinks I should like him again after *he* gets ditched," Mira laughs. "Well, now *he* looks pitiful in front of everyone. Why should I care? Too bad!"

"You're too right," Beth chimes. "Too bad."

"He's such a dog!" Mira wails.

"Totally," Beth agrees. "He's such a dog."

"It's like he bit me bad," Mira sneers. "He chomped off my arm, then ran down the street with it dangling from his mouth. He's been curled up under a porch somewhere gnawing on the bloody stump—and now he wants to shake my hand."

Read Galatians 5:14–15
What happens when people battle for popularity?

When you get caught up in *who-likes-whom* and *who-wins-what* and *who's-better-than-whom*, sooner or later you get clawed. Rubbing shoulders with some folks leaves you feeling ripped off. A few people, in fact, will bite off your other arm if you aren't looking. And watch out: Once they're done with your arms, they'll knock you over and gnaw on your legs.

Lots of people think life is a popularity contest. The battle to be the best is so huge it seems normal. But in God's way of doing things, love is the law.

It's stupid not to realize some people are poised to bite you as they claw their way to the top. It's foolish not to know that a few are so dangerous to your heart that you'd better scamper away when you see them coming (2 Timothy 3:2-5). But to love one another—that's the goal.

Being kinder and gentler may still feel weird.

Then again, what's really weird is gnawing on arms and legs.

When people fight to be popular, both sides wind up bitten. And they devour each other down to the last bite.

If you keep on biting and devouring each other, watch out or you will be destroyed by each other. GALATIANS 5:15

Bottom-Feeders

Dillan jumps up and down on the soccer field, pretending to warm up. Actually, he's checking his fan club. One glance and girls on the sideline wave and blow kisses. *This is so cool*, he thinks. *I've got groupies.*

Last season Dillan was lousy. Then he grew six inches. As Dillan and team thrashed his school's archenemies, he grew a fan club.

Dillan tells himself the girls know quality when they see it. After all, they all play too. He isn't the only guy with a cheerleading section. And hey, Dillan is no sexist pig. The guys go and cheer at the girls' games too.

Dillan's parents, though, are less than thrilled with his new friends, both guys and girls. Sure, they smell drug-free. But they constantly sass one another and slam everyone else. Dillan's parents suggest he hang out with his old church friends. But who needs those rejects when he has half the girls' team after him?

Read Proverbs 13:20
Why hang out with wise guys—and gals?

Get this one: Whole species of fish have figured out that there's always plenty of food if you're willing to suck the muck on the bottom of a lake.

Get this two: You'll always have lots of friends if you settle for less-than-best.

Get this three: Less-than-best may be even less than you think.

The Bible shows two kinds of wise guys and gals: James says that *real wise guys* are "pure; then peace-loving, considerate, submissive, full of mercy and good fruit, impartial and sincere." They live a "good life" full of "deeds done in the humility that comes from wisdom."

The scoop on *fake wise guys* is scary. James says that when people are full of "bitter envy and selfish ambition," life is full of "disorder and every evil practice." And a little bit of fake wisdom gets hugely nasty: it's "earthly, unspiritual, of the devil" (James 3:13-17).

Got it? Friends that seem "not so bad" can be really "not good at all."

You can be a bottom-feeder and grow bloated on cruddy friends. Or you can look for the best friends. But remember: You are what you eat.

He who walks with the wise grows wise, but a companion of fools suffers harm. PROVERBS 13:20

Scrape Away

"Dang!" Cody moans. "Paint chips in my eye again!"

"Where are your goggles?" Micah asks.

"They steam up and I can't see," Cody argued back. "Besides, I've got this crap stuck to my arms and face and everywhere. Look at my hair. This job is just stupid. What's the point of fixing this piece of trash house?"

Abby rolls her eyes. "Well, Mr. Handyman, we're here to help."

"Yeah, Cody," Micah adds. "They told us it would be like this."

"Whatever we fix," Cody argues, "is going to fall apart again anyway. These people can clean it up themselves. Why should we help them?"

Abby has an answer. "Because it's too big a job for them."

Cody plops down. "I quit. You guys are losers. I'm on a team with a bunch of nerds doing a hopeless job for people too lazy to do it themselves. This is a waste of my good talent."

Read Matthew 27:27–31

Was Jesus afraid to get his hair messed up to help people?

Jesus was totally God. But he didn't act like his Royal Too-High-to-Help-Out-ness. Born a baby and trained as a carpenter, he grew up and did good wherever he went—healing, feeding, making miracles, feeling people's joys and pains. In the end, Jesus got far more than his hair messed up. He was beaten, bloodied, and killed for our sake. Even when he died for *us*—witless people who'd wasted earth—he never grumbled that his unbeatable abilities were being splattered into nothingness like a kicked-over bucket of paint.

When you're too good to hang with or help certain people—with anyone, anywhere—you're claiming a superiority God's Son scorned. Jesus didn't deny his greatness. He didn't hide his goodness. Instead, he used that awestriking goodness to help people.

You don't have to bash yourself. But you can choose to count others better than yourself. To look out for more than your own interests. To serve people who need your help more than you need it yourself.

Just like Jesus.

They spit on him, and took the staff and struck him on the head again and again. After they had mocked him, they took off the robe and put his own clothes on him. Then they led him away to crucify him. MATTHEW 27:30-31

Did Her Head Just Pop?

"It's *kabloom*, sing!" Mr. Edstrom yelled at Marsella. "You hear the explosion stage right, then you burst into song. Can't make it easier! Got it?" The play's director whirled around and walked off. "Everyone—take ten!"

Marsella was aghast. She *never* got yelled at.

With opening night a week away, cast and crew were biting nails—and spitting some, too. An angry cast swarmed around Marsella. "Looks like Miss Everybody-Loves-Me froze up again," Jake mocked. "What's your problem?"

"I...I..." Marsella stammered.

"If you hadn't been worrying about your hair holding up under the stage lights, you wouldn't have biffed your cue. You're so stuck-up. Your head is the size of a—"

Marsella started to bawl.

"Poor baby," Jake jabbed, glad to make her cry. "Hey, everyone," he grinned. "Was that a balloon, or did her head just pop?"

Read 1 Samuel 16:1–13
How does God judge popularity?

Imagine Jesse's sons strutting their stuff for God's prophet. Son Eliab thinks, *I'm the biggest.* Abinadab hums, *I'm the baddest.* Shammah's going, *I'm the brainiest.* Four more sons get scrutinized. God whispers to Samuel, "Don't be wowed by their outsides. I look at a person's insides."

Samuel nixes all seven sons. Then in walks David, the baby of the family, who'd been out walking the family sheep. "Pick him!" God shouts. "He's the one!" So Samuel pours oil on David's head—a signal of God's blessing and a warm-up for getting crowned king.

David had been in the fields working out, so he was no ugly man. It wasn't long before he'd whup Goliath, so he was no wuss. And in time he'd run a country, so he was no dunce. But what counted to God was David's innards: David was "a man after [God's] own heart" (1 Samuel 13:14).

It's not your job to deflate others. But it *is* your job to put a pin in popularity bubbles by valuing what really counts. Beauty, brains, and brawn doesn't impress God. It's stuff on the inside that's worth a wow.

The Lord does not look at the things man looks at. Man looks at the outward appearance, but the Lord looks at the heart.
1 SAMUEL 16:7

Toe Jammin'

"Sign my yearbook?" Kathy asked sweetly. "And can I sign yours?"

Me? Huh? Scott blinked. *She wants what?* For two years Scott sat next to Kathy in math, slaving together on tough problems. But Kathy had evolved into the babe of the grade. Now she never noticed him.

"Here. Thanks!" Kathy handed back Scott's yearbook. "Gotta go. See ya!"

She just wanted all the signatures she could get, Scott thought. But she'd filled his whole back cover with stuff like "Your friendship means a lot to me" and "You're a special guy. Stay that way." Her "Call me!" and "Love, Kathy" almost made Scott pucker. Her phone number at the bottom about made him puke with excitement.

Maybe she writes that stuff in everyone's yearbook. But her phone number? Why that? A week after school quit for the summer, Scott had to find out. He called. Out fumbled "Helloit'sScottyougavemeyournumberand saidtocallhowsyoursummergoing?"

"Scott? Scott who?" she quizzed. "I don't know any Scotts." *Click.*

Read Galatians 3:26–28
What's it matter that we're all "one in Christ"?

Some people make you climb a mountain to lick dirt off their shoes.

True, God lets people take turns leading—as parents, teachers, bosses, police, and presidents. Some day it'll be your turn to lead too.

Leadership is how the world holds together (Romans 13:1). But God tells powerful people not to use their God-given authority to stomp on others (Matthew 20:25-28; Ephesians 6:4).

And the fact that God grants some people positions of authority doesn't alter this huge truth about humanity: God made all people equal. Being "one in Christ Jesus" means that whatever might make us special—as in privileged, prideful, stuck-up, and snotty—really means nothing. We're all equal before him—and nothing like race, gender, status, money, looks, or power decides how much we're worth or what treatment we deserve.

Christ makes us a community (people hanging together) of equality (where everyone is valuable). You don't have to lick anyone's shoes. And don't make anyone tongue-wash your toes.

There is neither Jew nor Greek, slave nor free, male nor female, for you are all one in Christ Jesus. GALATIANS 3:28

Lettuce Head

Richard stabbed the air with his pen to make his point. "I'm gonna be the next class president. Everybody knows I'm Mr. Howard's pick." Complete with bow tie and wangy hair, Richard looked like a three-quarter-size clone of Principal Howard. "I'll make a bunch of ridiculous promises." Richard was a shoo-in with all the students who thought he could actually shorten the school day. "And Lisa—she's gonna be dust in the wind."

"Don't be so sure," Lisa snarled. "You shouldn't hold your strategy sessions in the hall. And keep up that Mr. Howard look. I'll beat you for sure."

"Well, *your* posters," Richard laughed, "make you look like Marcia Brady."

"You're goin' down, Richard," Lisa stomped.

"Get ready to be buried, *Marcia*."

Read 1 Corinthians 9:24–27
What's the prize that matters most in life?

Paul and the people who got his letter in Corinth knew that athletes preparing for the Isthmian Games—a huge Olympics-type competition held in Corinth—went into brutal training. Athletes did it all to win a wreath of laurel or—believe it or not—celery. Paul is saying, "I'm one of those guys. I'm buff." But Paul had picked a different fight. He competed for a different prize. What Paul sought above all was to be totally devoted to God. He fought hard to live the message he taught about Jesus.

Paul's big competition wasn't against other people. He aimed his hardest shots at himself. He was like ancient fighters who boxed with leather straps tied to their knuckles—except he beat his *own* sin and selfishness black-and-blue.

Ancient athletes won prizes that wilted only a little more quickly than presidents get replaced, Miss Americas get ugly, or the rich and famous of the world get out-pizzazzed. Someone who's prettier, richer, or more popular always comes along.

But being your best for God is the one contest where winning lasts forever. Hanging tight with God beats hanging lettuce on your head.

Everyone who competes in the games goes into strict training. They do it to get a crown that will not last; but we do it to get a crown that will last forever. 1 CORINTHIANS 9:25

Belly Itches

Your letter to the ultrapowerful boss at Smartypants Software ("guaranteed to make you too bright for your britches") was so brilliant he flew you to his ultraluxury compound to critique his software's ultrasecret next release.

You feel like Little Red Riding Hood meeting the Big Bad Wolf when a pack of guard dogs surrounds you. *My, what big teeth you have.* But the dogs heel like well-trained pups. You feed them doggie treats. They fetch. You scratch their bellies. You can't believe they're killers.

"It all depends which side of the fence you're on," Mr. Smartypants explains. "Come here and I'll show you." You walk out the compound entrance, where metal gates clang shut behind you. "Try to reach inside," he instructs. Sixteen darling puppies suddenly bare fangs at you. They bark and spring wildly into the air. "See what I mean?" he says. "Inside, they're your friends. But try to get in from the outside uninvited, and they'll maul you."

Read 1 John 3:18
Is it okay to snarl at people not in your group?

Cliques are like packs of guard dogs. If you're inside their fence, they cuddle. But if you're outside, they're vicious. Depending on what the pack dogs think of you, they morph from Chihuahua to chomper—or from fang to friend.

You're probably protesting that no group you belong to is ferocious enough to deserve the name "clique." But then think hard about these pointed questions: What do people have to do to fit with you and your buddies? What do you do to shut people out of your group? What fangs do you flash? What fences do you put up? And exactly who don't you let in?

There are a million reasons to snarl at people. But know that God flashes a welcoming smile at people voted least likely to be welcomed in anyone's club. God makes shut-out people like widows, orphans, and aliens the focus of his care (Zechariah 7:10). His love reaches to all sorts of left-out people all around you. In fact, inviting into your group the people that others lock out is a sure sign of your total devotion to God (James 1:27).

Dear children, let us not love with words or tongue but with actions and in truth. 1 JOHN 3:18

Pass the Oxygen, Please

Alec heard basketballs pounding in the church gym. Each splat and slam echoed in his under-the-staircase cave. As people played hoops after youth group, Alec heard a hollered "Where's Alec? We need another player!" He smiled. *They'll never find me.* He had run out after youth group and ducked into his hiding spot. In a few minutes he would dart outside into the dark and his parents would pick him up. He'd get away unseen.

Alec thought back to what his pastor had said about "belonging to the body of Christ." *I don't think I can count on anyone here. No one cares about me. I don't feel welcome.* And then a thought shot through him: *But maybe I'm not trying.*

Read 1 Kings 19:9–18
What was Elijah's problem when he felt all alone?

Life is like living underwater. Christian friends are your hose to the surface—not just for a whiff of fresh air, but for the oxygen you need to survive.

Elijah—one of God's key prophets—counted his friends and got zero. He was hated by Queen Jezebel, for instance, and hunted by her armies. To get away, he hiked for forty days and then crawled into a cave.

God totally heard Elijah's lonely cries. But then he asked why Elijah was hiding.

Elijah thought someone evil was standing on his air hose. Truth was, he was suffocating because he'd unhooked himself from God's people. But actually, Elijah had a whole horde of friends he could count on (1 Kings 19:18).

There's no such thing as a scuba tank that lets you frolic through the deep waters of life all by your lonesome. You've got a lifeline, the air hose of friendship. That hose can kink, so you have to tend it carefully. When you feel alone, tell God you trust that he has Christian friends for you. Then get your backside out of whatever cave you've crawled into—and look around for his answer!

I am the only one left.
1 KINGS 19:10

Back on the Bus

Right after Jennifer's family moved to Asia for her dad's job, she spotted signs on the stoplight poles: "Pedestrians should huddle together and cross the street quickly." Niffer appreciated the heads-up, but she didn't have anyone to huddle with on the way to school. And where were the signs warning cars not to drive on the sidewalk?

Niffer got used to dodging through the city in taxis. But taxis were pricey. A few classmates had motor scooters. But after one skidded across her toes and slid under a truck, she stayed off "murder scooters." So Niffer settled on taking the city bus to school—a bus with a big tough shell and bunches of fellow riders. Sometimes buses bashed into storefronts. So she sat in the back to feel safer, because buses don't back into buildings.

But that didn't begin to deal with all the problems *inside* the bus....

Read Isaiah 43:1–3

Who rescues you when your big, safe crowd lets you down?

You'd like to think that traveling in a huddle protects you. But sometimes what should be a safe spot for you—a team, a youth group, a group of dependable friends—is more like a bad bus ride. You're caged with strangers. You have to watch where you sit. Whom you talk to. Who might pick your pockets. Or weird you out.

And that's still not the worst of what can happen when your herd hurts you. Sometimes the friendship bus crashes and burns.

So what happens to you then?

You have a Friend who's able to jump into the flames to rescue you. God, after all, isn't some sidewalk bystander who *might* dash to your aid. "Redeemer" means God owns the bus. And not just the bus. The people and packages and everything else on board belong to him (Exodus 6:6-8).

When you're riding along and your crowd blows up on you, God is there. He's promised to rush in, pack you up in his arms, and be your friend with a fireproof blanket of love. Looking for proof? He's already rescued you from the worst crash and burn of all: sin.

Jesus died to draw you close to God.

You belong to God. He won't leave you alone on the bus, *especially* when the bus flames.

I will be with you. ISAIAH 43:2

Total Toughness

What was supposed to be a tame all-girl sleepover for Laura's birthday was getting hyper. Obnoxious. And worse. Therese and Jill hadn't planned to sleep much, but this was beyond their foggiest expectations.

Therese and Jill were just beginning to figure out that the frothy pink birthday punch was causing the punchiness when a pack of guys from school tromped in. The two girls glanced at each other. Without a word they knew it was time to leave—at three in the morning—and found a phone in a back bedroom. Jill's dad groaned like a bear wakened from hibernation, but as soon as Jill whispered the words "alcohol" and "boys," he said he would be right there.

Stares pierced the girls as they rolled up their sleeping bags and headed for the door. They stood outside in the cold, their best friends inside laughing at them—their ex-best friends, probably.

Read 2 Timothy 1:7

You know you're supposed to resist peer fear. But how?

Nothing is scarier than facing a roomful of people who think you're a dork. You want to be friends, but something about you makes them hate you. They might not like what you do. They might not like *you.*

You could talk like them, act like them, mangle people like them, smoke or drink or inhale like them—all to keep from looking stupid and feeling alone. You could give up and give in. You could suck up and let people control you.

Or you can stick with the Friend who sticks with you and let him make you strong.

God promises that the same power that raised Christ from the dead lives inside you if you belong to him (Romans 8:11). His Holy Spirit remakes you to want and to be able to do what's right. That's a "spirit of power" and a "spirit of self-discipline." But he also promises to make you able to face others with a "spirit of love." It's what made Jesus' first followers fearless and forgiving even when others hated them (Acts 6:8–8:2).

Following God doesn't make you timid. It makes you tough.

For God did not give us a spirit of timidity, but a spirit of power, of love and of self-discipline. 2 TIMOTHY 1:7

Don't Ditch the Pitstick

You were dying to see your classmates again after summer vacation. You couldn't wait to unveil your spanking-new self-assurance.

The kid at the next locker backs away. "What happened to *you*?" he asks.

"Hiiiiiyaaaa," you breathe. He backs up farther. "So you noticed? I've decided to live completely above peer pressure. I've totally stopped caring what other people think."

"Well, you smell like you crawled out of a garbage pile."

"I'm happy to let you form your own opinion about me," you reassure him. "It won't change how I act. I haven't had a shower since June. Soap, shampoo, deodorant, toothbrush, toothpaste—I threw them all away. And I've taken up public burping. Just gotta be me. Did you know that in some cultures a hearty belch is appropriate appreciation for a tasty meal?"

Read 1 Timothy 4:12
What's good about peer pressure?

Peer fear. Teachers lecture you about it. Parents shield you from it. Anti-drug, anti-thug, anti-smoking, anti-drinking TV commercials try to scare you out of it. But not all *peer pressure* is *beer pressure*—a push to swill alcohol, drug your brain, or mouth off to your folks.

Everyone needs *good* peer pressure—a healthy dread of what other people think. Good peer pressure is the deodorant of life. It stops life's little stinks.

Still, there's an even better peer pressure, a kind that launches you way beyond keeping a lid on your public belching. The *best* peer pressure comes from Christian friends who help you choose God and his ways (2 Timothy 2:22).

In fact, you don't have to put up with being pressed. You can do the pushing. Not by becoming a drug dealer or going deodorant-free, but by modeling for the world what a totally devoted Christian looks like in how you talk, love, and hang tight to God and his commands.

No matter what your age, you have a faith that can influence people around you. The world wants you to cave to peer fear. It's time to start pushing the other way.

Don't let anyone look down on you because you are young,
but set an example for the believers in speech, in life,
in love, in faith and in purity. 1 TIMOTHY 4:12

Cannibal Lunch

You thought they were your friends, but now they're fixin' to have *fillet of you*. They've got you hog-tied and hanging over a boiling caldron.

You beg them to slow down. You try to buy time. All you want is a chance to wiggle around—and run away. But there's no chance of escape.

You try to remind them of all the times *they* said or did something *you* didn't like—and how you let them off the hook.

You can't convince them to converse.

They dip your toe in so you can feel the burn.

Then they get a hotter idea.

They don't even bother to cook you.

They eat you raw.

Read 1 Peter 4:12–19

What do you do when people pick on you?

People who bug you come and go. And come again. It's a fact of life: When one drifts away, in drifts another one just as annoying or bruising. The fact that people will irk you is permanent (John 16:33). Some folks may even hate you (1 John 3:13). And sometimes even best friends hang you over a hot pot (Psalm 41:9).

Peter separates the pain of those cannibal lunches—the peer-eat-peer of daily life—from an even bigger, tougher-to-endure kind of suffering.

Peter's saying this: When you get boiled for stuff like putting a fork in other people—murder—or putting your nose in other people's stuff—meddling—you can't blame your suffering on anyone but yourself. God won't let you wiggle free just because you belong to him.

But when you don't deserve to be boiled and you catch wrong for doing right, you're suffering for a bigger reason. You're suffering for Jesus.

That's when you'd really like God to help you off the hook. But it's also when God puts a huge choice to you: Will you turn tough, hate God, and try to boil those who boil you? Or will you keep doing good God's way?

So then, those who suffer according to God's will should commit themselves to their faithful Creator and continue to do good. 1 PETER 4:19

Leftovers

Leftover tuna hot dish stared at Megan from the refrigerator shelf—a heaping bowl of over-boiled noodles and oily tuna mixed in with a mound of mushy peas. *Blechhhhh. Not a chance.* Nothing against her mom's cooking—and she didn't want to be ungrateful for food—but a dish that was worth eating wouldn't be camping in such massive quantities in the fridge.

Megan dug behind the tuna, but the unidentifiable food farther back had sprouted legs and was plotting to escape. So Megan reached for stuff to make a trusty peanut butter sandwich. But the kitchen was bare of bread.

With her parents out at a movie and her older brother out with friends, Megan threw herself a pity party. *Just me, TV, and a hearty helping of tuna hotdish,* Megan pouted. She stabbed the hot dish with a fork. *This stuff's just like me. I'm a leftover.*

Read Psalm 84:10

How do you cope when life leaves you all alone?

Some days you feel like you've been tossed off a skyscraper. You're hanging by your fingernails like an over-the-edge cartoon character. You're alone. You're hurting. You scream for help. You wonder if a rescue squad will ever arrive.

Even though you're stabbed with fear, you're also smart. You're on your guard against people who pretend to help but don't. You don't want to be fooled by people who enjoy seeing you suffer.

When real help arrives and flings a rope down from above, however, you cling to it. You loop it around your waist and tie it tight.

When you holler for God, you're not calling into nothingness. You're not relying on someone dying to let you down. You're asking for real help.

God promises to meet your needs (Philippians 4:19). He promises—in his perfect way, in his perfect time—to come to your rescue (Psalm 72:12–14). And most of all, he promises to be with you no matter what (Hebrews 13:5).

When you're lonely, grab hold of God. Hanging tight with him is the best place you could ever be.

Better is one day in your courts than a thousand elsewhere; I would rather be a doorkeeper in the house of my God than dwell in the tents of the wicked. PSALM 84:10

Rip Your Buns Off

The name "Mr. Headcrusher" should have been a big clue. But the guy who emerged in a splash of fireworks as the night's next wrestler looked scary even from your seat in row seventy-eight.

The voice of the master of ceremonies reverberates through the arena. "The next match-*atch-atch*," he roars, "involves audience-*ence-ence* participation-*ation-ation*." You wonder what audience member would be fool enough to go to the mat with that thing. But *you* are about to be the fool. The crowd chants, "YOU! YOU! YOU!" You're bodysurfed to the front and heaved into the ring.

"I'm going to tear you to pieces," Mr. Headcrusher growls as he circles you. "And when I'm done, kid, I'm gonna rip your buns off and make 'em into earmuffs."

Read Matthew 10:28–31
Who's the most fearsome guy in the universe?

Right before the chunk of Bible you just read, Jesus told his disciples what to expect when they went out to talk about him. Some folks would welcome them warmly. Others would try to waste them.

The world can be a pressure-filled place when you follow Jesus. You *plus* a crowd *plus* the ring of life can *equal* a crushing experience.

Yet if the world is tough, God's even tougher. If you think peers can power-bomb you, wait until you see what God can do to his enemies. If you're not on God's side, you've picked a reserved seat in a hideous place where his Son never shines.

But God's goal isn't to shred you. While these are some of the Bible's most straight-talking words (verse 28), they're tag-teamed with some of its most tender (verses 29–31). God knows the flight plan of every sparrow on earth—those tiny speckled birds that wing outside your window. They sold in ancient markets for next to nothing—two for a penny. But God watches over you infinitely more closely. He knows the smallest details of who you are. He cares about the frailest parts of *you*.

That's a good reminder to stick on the right side.

Do not be afraid of those who kill the body but cannot kill the soul. Rather, be afraid of the One who can destroy both soul and body in hell. MATTHEW 10:28

Woof! Woof!

"She's still a dog," Melissa laughed. "But at least we taught her to heel. *Woof! Woof!*" Melissa and her summer-camp cabinmates laughed loudly. Sue was their project for the week to "woof proof." They showed her how to shave her legs. They talked her into letting them do her hair. They shoveled on makeup to smooth her skin. They each donated a shirt or a pair of shorts. And they coached her in maximum boy appeal. By the time they got done, Sue looked like a big-haired poodle at a dog show.

Suddenly Sue stood in the cabin door. She had shaken out the new hairdo and wiped off all the makeup. She wore her own clothes. And she looked like the same old Sue. "I appreciate what you did," she stammered. "But I liked myself the way I was. I'm not anything fancy, but I'm me."

Read Genesis 1:31
Who likes you no matter what other people think?

Name something that makes you unique, and people have no doubt poked fun at it. You're *geek of the week*: You're picked on for temporary flaws. You dropped the ball, tanked the test, inserted your foot in your mouth and chewed vigorously. Or you feel like the *lice of life*: You're teased about things that might never go away. If you're big like a truck, they say you beep when you back up. If you're bony like boards jutting from the trunk of a car, they tell you to tie a red flag to your backside.

God knows you inside and out. After all, he made you inside and out. And he loves what he sees. All the things that make you *you*—how you think and feel and look and act—he can't get enough of those.

And Genesis tells you exactly what he thinks when he looks at you. When God looked down at the rest of creation, he said it was "good." When he made humans, he proclaimed it *very* good. One Bible translation puts it like this: "Then God looked over all he had made, and he saw that it was excellent in every way" (Genesis 1:31 NLT). That verdict includes you—all of you—and everything unique God built into you.

You're no dog. A little wacky, maybe. Your own person, definitely. And in his eyes, wonderful, undoubtedly.

> *God saw all that he had made, and it was very good.*
> GENESIS 1:31

Your One Coach

The mother of the pitcher screams from the stands: "Come on! Blow it right by!" The catcher tries his hardest to tip your brain off balance: "Hey, *battah battah battah*, suh-wing, *battah battah battah*." The pitcher throws you a tough one. The ball seems to laugh: "I'm a sizzling loop-de-doop-knuckle-fisted-sidearm curve." And some guy yells from behind the backstop, mere feet from you. His words rattle in your helmet: "Look at me when I'm talking to you!"

You refuse to be distracted. You glance at your bench. Your coach watches you calmly. Nods encouragement. Claps hands to tell you, "Get going. Eyes on the ball."

You hear the backstop guy again: "I said *look at me when I'm talking to you!*" This time you spin in your spikes to look. He stares you straight in the eyes. *Huh? Who's he? And why's he yelling at me?*

Read Acts 4:13–21

What did Peter and John say when religious leaders tried to keep them from talking about Jesus?

If a backstop stranger says your stance is too wide or you need to square-up to the plate, he's hollering good advice probably worth taking. But if he says you should swing blindfolded or slide into home plate on your face, he's clearly not rooting for you.

But there's a bigger point. When you play ball, you answer to *one* voice: your coach. The water boy can't signal you to steal second. Your best friend can't tell you to swing for a home run if your coach calls a bunt. Bystanders aren't your boss.

By God's power, Peter and John had just healed a man who couldn't walk (Acts 3:1–10). They were giving credit to Jesus, and the religious leaders who had opposed Jesus wanted Peter and John to tape their mouths shut. That clearly contradicted God's command to speak up about faith (Acts 1:8), and God's guys had one response: "We've got *one* coach. We obey *his* voice" (see both Acts 4:19 and 5:29).

Jesus is the clear, calm voice calling to you above the roar of the crowd. And when you listen to him, you'll win.

But Peter and John replied, "Judge for yourselves whether it is right in God's sight to obey you rather than God." ACTS 4:19

No Fear

Everyone called them "the Dwarfs," but not because they were short. The seven girls got their nickname when they started playing basketball together in elementary school. By the end of middle school they were best friends— and the core of the best team around, sure to power their small high school to a state title.

And the Dwarfs were Dwarfs because they *hi-ho-hi-ho*ed everywhere together—on or off court. They dressed, talked, and did their hair the same. Whoever they liked was popular. Whoever they disliked was scum.

The clump fell apart when two Dwarfs became Christians. "That isn't what Dwarfs do," the other five told Kelli and Elise. "We're not into God." That started a tough game of five-on-two. On the court the other girls pushed Kelli and Elise out of plays. Off the court they turned their backs and walked away. Kelli and Elise didn't see any way to win that game.

Read Numbers 14:1-9

How did Joshua and Caleb stand up to the crowd when God's people refused to enter the good land God had promised them?

When peers try to force you to follow their rules, they usually don't toss you an exploding basketball. They don't press a gun to your head and shout, "Cheat! Cut people down! Slack off! Scream at your parents!"

They play mind games (Romans 12:2). They make you think your world will fall apart without them. And peers get power over you because you give it to them. They don't *force* you to follow—you *choose* to do what they want because you believe two lies: (1) doing wrong to please them is more important than doing right to please yourself; and (2) making them happy matters more than making God happy.

The people of Israel said God was mean and his followers idiots. They feared that giants in the promised land would slaughter them. Joshua and Caleb struck back with truth—that the God of might would do them right. They refused to rebel against God. They refused to fear the crowd.

Because Joshua and Caleb dared to be different, God blessed them (Numbers 14:30). They turned out to be the real giants.

Only do not rebel against the Lord. And do not be afraid of the people of the land, because we will swallow them up.
NUMBERS 14:9

Lemmings and Lerts

Mama Lemming had it written big on the family calendar. *March 20.* First day of spring. Annual Lemming Migration.

Like all other good Lemmings, the family packed up their Lemmingmobile and headed toward the sea. Why to the sea? They didn't know. Everyone was going.

A minute out of the driveway the Lemming children grew impatient.

"Are we there yet?" Sister Lemming cried.

"How much farther?" Brother Lemming whined.

Papa Lemming found the expressway clogged with other Lemmingmobiles. "Oh, this is just great." Papa Lemming banged the steering wheel. "Now we'll never get there."

When the Lemmingmobile arrived at the sea, the Lemming family ran with all the other Lemmings into the sea, where the Lemming family—as well as all the other Lemmings—did *not* live happily ever after.

Read 1 Peter 5:8–11
Would you rather be a Lemming or a Lert?

Lemmings are tough little ratlike rodents that live in northern Europe. When their colonies get too crowded, millions of lemmings leave their homes in spectacular mass migrations. Sometimes they run into the sea. None of them bothers to find the answer to the one question that really matters: Is this a good idea?

It's not. Lemmings can't swim.

They don't intend to drown themselves. They're just looking for a nicer, less crowded place to live. They think they're about to cross a river—keeping to the shallowest areas—when they wind up over their heads in the sea.

Lemmings are stupid. Lerts, on the other hand, ask smart questions.

If someone tries to lead a Lert along a line of living that looks like it lacks logic, a Lert likes to learn more: Who's leading this migration? Where are we going? Is it a good place to live? Lerts have learned to discern lies.

Unlike lemmings.

Don't be a lemming. Be alert.

Be self-controlled and alert. Your enemy the devil prowls around like a roaring lion looking for someone to devour.
1 PETER 5:8

Thugs "R" Us

"Here it is." Brenda flipped through the movie listings in the evening paper. "It's showing at nine o'clock. Let's go."

Terese moaned. "My parents said to be home at nine-thirty."

"So?" Linda practically told her parents when *they* should be home.

"Do the math, O brainy one," Terese shot back. "The movie is two hours long. I'd be a little late."

"Since when do you listen to your parents?" Linda inquired.

Brenda had an idea. "Can't you call your parents and tell them you'll be late?"

"They'll say no. We're leaving early in the morning for my grandparents' to—"

Brenda cut her off. "We're going. You can go home if you want."

"You know what your problem is?" Linda asked. "You're not any fun."

Read James 4:1–2
How do you spot a thug?

The thugs you know probably look nicer. They dress like you. They talk like you. They live in your neighborhood and go to your school. They want the same stuff you do.

The thugs you know most likely don't lie in ambush to burglarize and butcher innocent pedestrians. But they still aim to rob others to enrich themselves—to look good, feel big, be popular, set the rules, and get what they want. They move in cliques and pick easy targets. Even without weapons they leave a trash trail—busted feelings, broken promises, stolen property, disappointed parents, wounded bodies, and stabbed hearts.

You know enough to run from tough hoods who whisper at you from alleys. It's the thugs nearby that you have to beware of—the ones who stop calling, stop saying "Hi!" in the hall, and stop being your friend when you don't join them.

And there's a thug inside you that you have to guard against. It's the part of you that wants to take by force or by stealth what isn't yours.

Thugs aren't always strangers on the street. Sometimes the thugs are us.

You want something but don't get it. You kill and covet, but you cannot have what you want. You quarrel and fight. You do not have, because you do not ask God. JAMES 4:2

Pus-Brain

Tyler knew to step aside, just like he was shrewd enough to get out of the path of a raging steamroller.

All Tyler wanted was to get to his assigned school assembly seat in the auditorium's nosebleeds. But as he trudged upward, he saw "the Mob"—the six most popular guys in middle school, plus their girls—rushing up from below, ready to run him over. Smart boy: Tyler scampered out of the aisle and into a row of seats to let them pass. But the Mob stopped at the same spot.

"Hey, pus-brain," they steamed at Tyler. "Those are our seats."

That they were. And the Mob wasn't moving. So Tyler took the only way out—the long way down the other end of the row. Half the auditorium watched him bumble over twenty other yelping bodies already in their seats.

He lived. But he had to lick ground to do it.

Read Matthew 5:5
What's it mean to be meek?

You can't take it totally personally when people pick on you. Mean people are like a mosquito pack that buzzes away tanked up on your blood. You may feel like a particularly plump, juicy target. Truth is, they just suck blood anywhere they can get it.

Sometimes you can stand up for your rights by speaking truth (Ephesians 4:15), relying on the authorities God put in place to make things right (Romans 13:1-5), or running for help when you can't solve a problem yourself (Matthew 18:15-17).

But other times there's no escape. You get the stuffing beat out of you. You get stomped on your way to the cheap seats. Some days you get steamrollered. Other days you get sucked dry.

Meekness ain't weakness. Meekness is gentle, self-controlled strength. Meekness means being something better than the bullies who beat up the world. God is on the side of the gentle, and Jesus hints at who *won't* win the ultimate popularity and power contest—the proud, strong, aggressive, harsh, and tyrannical who suck life from others.

Inheriting the earth means God gives a prize—someday, some way—for every pint of blood you give up. So it's clear who the real losers are.

Blessed are the meek, for they will inherit the earth.
MATTHEW 5:5

Miss Snotdaughter

"Miss Snotdaughter," a member of the talent show committee finally says, "we want to make sure we understand you correctly. You're auditioning this group because they do *not* have talent?"

"Exactly!" Jaye Snotdaughter squeals. "It's really *my* talent on display. I'm a nerd collector. And this is simply the best set of nerds I've ever assembled. "For starters," Jaye chirps, "take Belinda. She's quite ugly. Everyone says so.

"And Charles has a lisp," she continues. "Say something, Charles."

"Hi. I'm Charelth."

"Jaqi just moved here from out of state," Jaye goes on gleefully. "She has no friends at all.

"Then there's Riley. He's only in seventh grade, but I can already tell he'll *never* get a girlfriend. He's really a fine specimen. He'll be with me a long time.

"And Ben's just flunking math," Jaye finishes. "I'll help him raise his grade, then throw him back. He's kind of a temporary nerd. He rounds out my collection nicely, don't you think?"

Read 1 John 4:19–21
What gives us the power to love people we don't like?

God could treat us like his nerd collection. After all, in our unforgiven and unfixed state we're pretty repulsive. And if our good points are dung—like Paul says in Philippians 3:8—then the bad stuff we do is a mountain of Ultrasauraus droppings. It takes a house-size pooper scooper to clean up after us.

Despite these failings, God doesn't put you and the rest of your species on display in a zoo for losers. He sees something special in you, because he made you (Psalm 100:3). Nothing can separate you from his love (Romans 8:38-39), which reaches to the heavens (Psalm 36:5). And don't forget this: God's colossal love for you and your fellow earthlings is why he sent his Son, Jesus, to live and die (John 3:16).

If God had wanted you to make pets of the less-than-likable people around you, they would have been born with collars. Seeing none, it's obvious he wants you to do more than collect nerds. He wants you to love them with the love he lavishes on you.

We love because he first loved us. 1 JOHN 4:19

Human Hockey Puck

Ching–thwipp. Another shot off the post and into the net behind Justin. "Sorry, guys," Justin apologized—again.

Where Justin grew up there was no ice. When his family moved, he found his new friends had feet with blades instead of toes. Well, more or less. Putting Justin in the goal kept him out of their way, but even shuffling in the net sent Justin skidding on the ice like a human hockey puck.

Most days no one cared. But this time his friends got mad. Justin came home with a cut–up lip and a blood–soaked jacket. Not that anyone had slugged him. He got bashed up when they shoved him and he slammed the ice.

"Justin, what are you trying to prove?" his older sister pleaded. "You're good at English. You're pretty great at chess. You thrash those guys at basketball and—"

"But nobody cares about any of that stuff," Justin moaned. "All they know is that I can't play hockey."

Read Romans 12:3–8

Why would God want you to understand what you're good at?

You can go back to back with your friends to see who's taller. You can flex your biceps to see whose are bigger. But the real measurement of who you are is the good gifts God has built inside you.

You may still be figuring out what makes you unique. That's okay. But know that God made you good at something. For sure.

You may recognize yourself in the list of "spiritual gifts" Paul put here (or in 1 Corinthians 12:7-10 and Ephesians 4:11-12). Or you may be the total math tutor. Or someone whose shoulder is soaked with the tears of hurting friends. You may be the tightest writer your classmates have ever read. Or you may be a rock–steady influence on one close friend. Celebrate that!

You can't quit everything you're no good at. No one gets out of serving or supporting others. No one gets a free pass out of school. But it's okay to boldly put to use your unique talents. What you're good at may not make you popular, but what you're good at is your gift to this world.

We have different gifts, according to the grace given us.
ROMANS 12:6a

Better Than Buff

"Try it again, Bekka. Like this." Natalie stepped into the blocks. At the sound of an imaginary starting gun, Natalie exploded. She screamed past Bekka and soared over three hurdles before jogging back.

"I can't do that!" Bekka moaned. "You look like a gazelle or something."

"A gazelle? Gazelles stink. Besides, they get stalked and eaten," Natalie protested. "But thanks. By the way, you do great too."

"By the way, I do *not*." Bekka got quiet. "Natalie, that's why I'm going to tell Coach you should take my spot as team captain. You're way better than I am. You're way better than the whole state. You never put anyone down, you listen to everyone, and you're great at helping people. Before you came over here, I was so frustrated I was ready to wrap a hurdle around someone's head."

"I'm glad I could help," Natalie said, "because I like to help people. But it's God who makes me run fast. You're making too big a deal of *me*."

Read 1 Corinthians 4:7
Where did you get all your great gifts?

You invite a new friend to your house. You'd be totally mannerless if: (a) you dragged her in the door and over the dog to see your best-ever report card—the one your mom enlarged to cover the whole front of the fridge; (b) you wildly arm-wrestled her until your superior musculature ripped her rotator cuff; (c) you beat her mercilessly on your billion-bit video game system; or, actually, (d) all of the above.

Brainiacs are bright. Body builders are buff. Millionaires are marvy. But all our knowledge, might, and money—and everything else we are or own—come from one source: God.

When you feel like bursting out in a song of praise, don't screech about yourself. Say stuff about God, who is absolutely kind, fair, and right. His faithfulness clears hurdles higher than the sky. His bright, shining glory races around the earth (Psalm 108:3–5). You may be a big deal, but God is way biggest.

What makes you better than anyone else? What do you have that God hasn't given you? And if all you have is from God, why boast as though you have accomplished something on your own? 1 CORINTHIANS 4:7 NLT

Slick or Slob

I can't believe Mick pays attention to them, Jake fumed. *They're wreck-ing everything.* Jake stared at his youth pastor as he talked to the newbies in his youth group. They goofed off. Some stunk of smoke. They looked like they crawled out from under the drum set at a heavy-metal concert.

A little later Mick rapped on Jake's head—and it was like he'd read Jake's mind. "They aren't going to get fixed all at once, you know. God's working on them. Jake, think about it. You used to be mouthy. Did you shut up right away—even when you got serious about following God?" Jake remembered it took him a while to break a bunch of bad habits. "Jake, most of these kids have gotten kicked around bad. Think about ways to help them up, not to push them down."

Read Galatians 6:4–5

How do you handle it when you're better at something than everyone else?

You might be embarrassed when report cards go home. You might hide from volleyballs or figure skates. You might cringe when people eye your less-than-stylish clothes. But sooner or later in life you will land on some-thing where you're slick—and most everyone else is a slob.

Take your faith, for example. If you pay attention in Sunday school, you may think you're a saint. Truth is, you are. But not because of anything *you* did. Because of Christ's death for you, you're truly a saint (Colossians 1:12). Because of his life in you, you've got gifts to help you change the world (1 Peter 4:10). And truth is, apart from God we're all spiritual slobs. And we're to use our spiritual strength to hoist people out of sin.

Whatever good things we possess, God gave us (1 Corinthians 4:7). You can always find someone badder—and feel better. You can always find someone better—and feel badder. What matters is what's up with you. Are you doing your best? If you're doing well, who got you there? And how are you using your gifts to help others?

When you're doing better than others, thank God for how *he's* helped you. And figure out who *you* can help too.

Each one should test his own actions. Then he can take pride in himself, without comparing himself to somebody else....
GALATIANS 6:4-5

The Leader of the Band

"You deserve it, dear," Tonya's mother coos. "Just push your way up to the front. It's where you belong. If you're ever going to win the Teenage Miss contest, you *have* to be in the front. Do you think those judges would pick a girl content to stand in the back?"

The next day at the gymnastics team photo eleven girls wait for instructions. *This'll be in the paper*—Tonya thinks—*and the yearbook—and plastered in the school showcase by the trophies.* Tonya inches forward. *And my entry! I've got to get to the front.*

Tonya pushes past the others and drops into the splits. *Idiots. They're just standing there. They don't know what really matters.*

Tonya's coach shakes her head. "Tonya, I want Linda to be the one in front."

"No!" Tonya protests. "Me! Me! Me! I *have* to be in *front*!"

Read Mark 9:33–37

What does someone who possesses "humility" look like?

"What were you arguing about?" Jesus asked politely.

He knew.

"Nothing," they blushed. "It's not important."

Jesus had just told his disciples he would be killed. Not that he'd get a star on Hollywood's Sunset Boulevard. Not that he'd received invites to all the hot talk shows. Not that he and his band would play to packed stadiums on a sold-out world tour.

He would soon be crucified.

You'd think the disciples would have understood that being the world's Savior—or being his follower—wasn't a glamorous job.

Jesus told his disciples that following him isn't about pushing yourself to the front of the crowd. To be first is to be last. But to be like him is to welcome the ones people label "nerds" and "rug rats" and "pests." To imitate him is to serve—even to suffer—to bring others life (Matthew 20:26-28).

Jesus was God himself (John 1:14). But he didn't push his way to the front. He was no brat.

Sitting down, Jesus called the Twelve and said, "If anyone wants to be first, he must be the very last, and the servant of all." MARK 9:35

Nothing Like Her Sister

Megan cringed when Mrs. Grozny's eyebrow arched. She recognized that look. "Megan?" her teacher had said cheerily as she called roll on the first day of class. Then Mrs. Grozny spotted Megan. When she got a good look at Megan she glanced down quickly at her class list. "Megan *Ronson*?" And the raised eyebrow said it all: *You look like Tina. You'd better not act like her.*

"She knows your sister, Megan," someone across the aisle teased. "She thinks you're Tina."

There wasn't a kid in school who hadn't heard of Megan's older sister. No one would ever forget that three years ago Tina was expelled for selling drugs and then had tried to torch the school. "She thinks you're Tina the Terrorist!"

I'm not my sister! Megan wanted to say. *Give me a chance!*

Read Psalm 139:1

Who knows the real you—and who you can be?

They don't see you. They see what they *think* you are. You remind them of an older brother who was so bad that you never get a chance to be good. Or they remember your sister who was so smart and sickly sweet that you can't compete. Even people who don't compare you to brothers or sisters want to label you and stuff you in a box. They remember every time you've embarrassed yourself from third grade on—they won't let you escape. They never forget your flubs—they don't let you change.

They want to define you. Design you. If you let them tell you who you are and who you can be, you're trapped. Boxed in.

But they don't understand you like God does. He's searched you and knows you—your every thought, word, and action. He saw you before you were born (Psalm 139:15-16). And he wants you to live without comparing yourself—or letting yourself be compared—to other people (Galatians 6:4).

You figure out who you are not by listening to people who pin you in but by seeing yourself through the eyes of the One who knows you best. God blows the tops off their boxes. He sets you loose to follow him and become what he made you to be.

O Lord, you have searched me and you know me. PSALM 139:1

Made for Friendship

Birth was scary, wasn't it? As you lay in a basket in the middle of a whizzing intersection, trucks coughed smelly smoke into your little face and jolted you up and down. A speeding car nicked your basket, spinning it topsy-turvy. After a few hours in the intersection, you crawled through traffic to search for food by the side of the road.

Your birth probably didn't happen that way.

You weren't assembled in a mad scientist's underground laboratory and popped into the world through a sewer lid, left to fend for yourself on the street. God had a better plan. You were given life by an act of love and snuggled tight in a mother's womb. When you were born you were caught by someone's caring arms, fed, clothed, and protected.

Read Genesis 2:18–25

Who were the world's first friends?

When God made the world's first man, Adam was alone with the animals and the rest of creation. But not just alone—*lonely*, without a friend. God saw that being alone was about as fun as being born into a traffic jam. So for Adam he created a friend—Eve. Adam and Eve were "flesh of flesh" and "bone of bone" and exactly what the other one needed. Man and woman lived as perfect friends in paradise, the Garden of Eden.

God didn't stop there. He wanted human beings to know their Creator. So he made them in his image (Genesis 1:27), able to relate to God in a way a rock or a raccoon never could. God and people knew each other up close. God is pictured as "walking" in the Garden and talking directly with Adam and Eve (Genesis 1–3). God's purpose was not only for people to know each other but to know him.

God had a big plan. Adam and Eve were just the start. God designed his world to be a paradise of relationships. Everyone would get along. No one would get hurt. Everyone would worship God and respect neighbors. God, men, women, girls, guys, parents, children, even animals and plants had a role.

That was the plan, anyway.

The Lord God said, "It is not good for the man to be alone. I will make a helper suitable for him...." GENESIS 2:18

The Drop-Kicked Top

"I'm not talking to Michelle ever again," Jenni said, her face burning red. "She told me she could keep a secret, but she blabbed to the whole school what I said. I took all my things out of our locker and moved in with Sue. I left Michelle's locker door hanging open. I hope someone steals her stuff."

God intended relationships to spin like a top, with everything in smooth balance. But it's obvious something went wrong. God made friendships and family, love and unselfishness, but instead we live with fights, cliques, divorce, racism, and hatred.

What happened?

Adam and Eve were the world's first friends. They were also the world's first enemies.

Read Genesis 3:1–13

What did Adam and Eve do wrong? What was the result?

God had put Adam and Eve in paradise, the Garden of Eden, and told them to take care of the Garden. He made one rule: "Don't eat fruit from the tree of the knowledge of good and evil." God said eating the fruit from this tree would cause them to die (Genesis 2:17). When the serpent said it would make them wise like God, they chose their own way rather than God's way. They picked what they *thought* was good rather than trusting what God—who will never lie—had *said* was true.

By breaking God's command, Adam and Eve drop-kicked the top that God had set whirring in perfect balance. They threw the first family feud. Then, knowing they had sinned against God and each other, they were ashamed of themselves and covered up with fig leaves. Adam and Eve blamed everyone but themselves. Even worse, they fought against God. Their actions said, "God, we don't need you." They hid from God, who sent them away from his presence in the Garden (Genesis 3:21–24). The friendships between Adam and Eve and God now wobbled and bobbed like a sputtering top.

God, though, didn't give up on the people he had created for friendships. He determined to get the top spinning right again.

They hid from the Lord God among the trees of the garden.
GENESIS 3:8

Wipers

Snoozing in the dark in the backseat of the car, you hadn't bothered to open your eyes until the noise on the roof told you rain was really bucketing down. Feeling the car slow down, you leaned forward from the backseat to try to see ahead. You could tell your dad was having a hard time seeing the road, but after a scary while you made it home.

Without windshield wipers and headlights you wouldn't have made it home through the storm.

After Adam and Eve (and Noah and others at the beginning of the Bible), the human race fell to the point where evil made the world a dark, stormy night. All they saw of God was a blob—like the view through a rain-splattered windshield when the wipers break—and they had crashed in a spiritual ditch without even knowing it. They were upside down with the gas pedal floored and the wheels whizzing, but they weren't getting anywhere (Genesis 6:5).

Read Genesis 17:1–8
What did God promise Abraham?

Even though the human race had raced away from God, he came up with a plan to get us home safely to himself. But God didn't wait for people to come to him. Even at our worst, he made the first move to be our friend and to help us understand him again (Romans 5:8). Abraham's story marks the beginning of God working to show himself again to a race who had forgotten him.

So God "covenanted" (promised) to build a new nation—Israel—starting from the descendants of Abraham, a man who believed in and obeyed God. He promised to be the God of that people and to give them a new land to live in. He would rule them fairly, and they were to worship him and love one another.

The evil wasn't going away. God wouldn't blow away the storm and force everything to be good and right, because he wants people to have freedom to choose for or against him. But by showing himself to Abraham, God flipped on the wipers and headlights so that we could see him through the storm. He was starting to show us the one road back to himself.

*I will establish my covenant as an everlasting covenant...
to be your God.* GENESIS 17:7

Name That Car

Your head snaps as a sweet convertible blows by. What a car! What was it?

If you want to tell one car from the next, you have to look at the shape of the hood, the outline of headlights and taillights, the slope of the roof line, the style of the door handles and the grill openings. More than that, car brands have marks—hood ornaments, emblems, or distinctive names for different models. Once you know what to look for, all it takes is a glance to tell a Ford from a Chevy, or a Porsche from a Ferrari.

Read Exodus 3:1–10
How can you know you've spotted God?

If you saw a burning bush, would you figure it was God? Maybe. But if that's the only way you could recognize God, you might have to look a long time. After all, when was the last time you heard God's voice while herding sheep? And when was the last time a shrub caught fire in your backyard but didn't burn up?

God did reveal himself in a burning bush. Once. At the bush, however, he waved a hood ornament in our faces to show how he would later reveal himself *many* times—to his people in Israel, through Christ, even to you.

The first wave: Moses knew immediately who it was when God said that he was the God who loved Abraham. Remember? This is the God who founded a new people and acted in real ways, as real in history as Elvis or George Washington. God repeated his promise to bring his people into a good land. *God is the God out looking for friends.*

The second wave: God felt his people's suffering and rescued them from slavery. He even used the blood of a lamb painted over a door to protect his people from his judgment on the Egyptians (Exodus 12:21–30). *God is the God with awesome saving power.*

In time, Jesus would die a bloody death so that we could be spared from God's anger and freed from sin and become God's friends forever. But God prepared the way for that event. He didn't want us to wonder what car just cruised by or to mistake anyone else for the only true God. He wants us to recognize him when he comes to us.

*There the angel of the Lord appeared to him in flames of fire
from within a bush. Moses saw that though the bush was
on fire it did not burn up.* EXODUS 3:2

Suited Up

Football would be tough to follow if both teams wore the same clothes. Uniforms show who's on which side. Besides that, uniforms and the insignia on them describe what the team is supposed to be like. The Chargers—faster than a crazed linebacker. The Giants—able to squash the opposition in a single down. The Packers—men who grind up enemy players and shove them into sausage skins.

Uniforms also tell what a team is trying to do. A football player, you've probably noticed, doesn't wear a baseball uniform or running togs. A baseball glove isn't much good for catching footballs, and a tank top and shorts don't protect from tackles. (Football might be more interesting, though, if all the smallish players got baseball bats.)

Read Exodus 20:1–17

What does God want his people to look like?

The uniform of God's team isn't something they wear, like nice Sunday clothes, Jesus pins, or Christian T-shirts. It's their thoughts, words, and actions toward God and toward one another. God owns the team and designs the uniform: He is the Lord their God. He is our Savior.

God gave ten commands that describe what his team looks like when we're totally devoted to him. The first few ensure everyone understands that God alone is God. Nothing is more all-important or trustworthy than him—not an old hunk of wood or stone, or new idols like music, clothes, sports, grades, or popularity. Even God's name deserves respect. It is something to say not in anger or surprise but in awe. God's team also sets aside time to rest and worship him.

The other part of the uniform covers how players treat one another. Rebellion, murder, unfaithfulness, lying, or wanting stuff that belongs to someone else—those things dirty the uniform and make the team look like clods.

Jesus said that these commands and all the other do's and don'ts in the Bible could be summed up this way: Love God and love your neighbors (Matthew 22:35–39). That's the uniform that shows whose team we're on—and what game we're trying to win.

I am the Lord your God....You shall have no other gods before me. EXODUS 20:1-3

Build-Your–Own-Burritos

"What's the big deal? It's a church." Paige was mad that her parents wouldn't let her go to church with Stacy, a Mormon friend. Paige didn't think it was any big deal whether she went to her own church or to Stacy's. "Besides, the kids are more into it there. Everyone talks. They don't just sit there, and they really know what they believe. Can't I go? Stacy's really nice."

Stacy might be totally nice, but that doesn't mean what she believes is at all true.

Read Deuteronomy 12:1–7
Why does God get so picky about what people believe?

Even when the human race angered God, he never gave us the silent treatment. He never stomped to his room to pout, leaving us to wonder who he was, what he was thinking, or what he wanted from us. Just as you want people to understand and accept the real you, God doesn't want you to misunderstand him.

Think of it this way: God is no build–your–own–burrito bar. You can't pick the guacamole but flick the onions, or choose the cheese but lose the beans, making God fit your taste. While you're free to build a burrito to *ooh* and *aah* over, it's not okay to make God into what you think is best—not on your own or with groups that create gods and religions different than what the true God has revealed in the Bible.

God wants you to know him exactly as he is.

God also determines the what, when, where, and how of following him. When it came to worship, for example, he told his people what to get rid of, where and how to build a temple, what to eat and how to sacrifice animals—in so much detail that it makes you want to tell God to calm down. Yet the rules helped God's people stand out from their neighbors and understand that God wants pure, obedient, disciplined followers.

And God made a big point: He's the one who determines what's important and what's not, what's right and what's wrong, what's real faith and what's fake.

He's in charge. He's God.

You must not worship the Lord your God in their way.
DEUTERONOMY 12:4

In Living Color

Joey's parents had warned their little son to stay clear of the street. But nothing seemed to stop him from edging nearer and nearer the curb to watch traffic, or even from chasing balls into the street.

Then a car hit his dog. Joey saw Spot flattened on the road, and he ran bawling into the house. After that, Joey seldom forgot to look both ways. Blood taught Joey what his parents' words could not. Now he understood the danger.

Just because God had told Israel how to act didn't mean they always obeyed. His people often did exactly the opposite. Because they didn't trust God's brains or goodness, they didn't like his rules or believe his warnings. They treated their evil—their sin—as if it didn't matter.

Read Leviticus 16:15–17, 20–22
How did God remind his people how bad sin is?

In the Old Testament God told his people to offer sacrifices that would make peace for (or "atone" for) their sin. On behalf of the people, priests killed bulls, goats, and sheep and spread the animals' blood on special tables in the temple to display in living color the seriousness of sin: Death is the penalty for breaking God's commands (Genesis 2:17; Romans 6:23).

Once a year a special ritual, called the "Day of Atonement," showed the two sides to God's view of sin. First, *God judges our sin.* It isn't right for wrongdoing to go unpunished, so God required that a goat be killed for the people's sins instead of putting the people to death. Second, *God wants to forgive.* So he told the priests to send a second goat—a "scapegoat"—into the wilderness, symbolizing how God removes and forgets our guilt (Psalm 103:12). Year by year these sacrifices reminded Israel of the horror of sin.

Sound awful? Disobeying God is even worse. Even the death of an animal couldn't fully show the badness or fix what was really wrong. An animal can't pay the penalty for anyone's sin—just as a lawbreaker today can't send his dog to take his place in the electric chair.

The penalty for human sin must be paid by a human being. Someone had to die for the sins of the human race in order for us to be friends with God again.

[The priest] shall then slaughter the goat for the sin offering for the people. LEVITICUS 16:15

Time Out

"You can't tell me what I can't do," John hissed at his principal. "My parents won't believe anything you say." Sure enough, when John's mom arrived she looked ready to slug Mr. Phillips.

"Mrs. Donovan, you're well aware of the problems we've had with John in the past," Mr. Phillips started. "This morning he hot-wired a custodian's utility cart and skidded around the basement of the school. Security cameras filmed everything."

"Not my son!" John's mom shrieked. "It must be someone who looks like Johnny."

"The custodians cornered him in an elevator," Mr. Phillips continued. "But your son stopped the elevator between floors and pretended he wasn't there."

"I didn't do it, Mom," John protested. "They just don't like me around here."

Mr. Phillips got to the point. "I'm sorry you don't want to admit what you did, John. But you've shown us over and over that you're not interested in being in class. You've endangered yourself and others. After a three-week suspension, you'll be transferred to another school."

Read Jeremiah 16:10–15

What does God do when his people won't stop doing wrong?

Like a parent who gives a child a time-out or a principal who hands out detentions, God disciplines his people to teach them right from wrong—not to be mean, but to make sure they learn what's best for them.

As time passed, Israel became so rebellious that they couldn't even see the wrong they were doing. They wanted anything and everything but God. God's only option was to give them what they wanted. He allowed them to be dragged from their homes and land to a distant country that obeyed other gods. Yet God promised to bring an end to the punishment they brought on themselves, just as he saved them from slavery in Egypt.

God disciplines his people not to demolish us but to shake us awake. God sets consequences for sin not because he hates us. It's because of his incredible love for us (Hebrews 12:5–6).

See how each of you is following the stubbornness of his evil heart instead of obeying me. JEREMIAH 16:12

The Heart of the Matter

It's the first day of school and you've heard the lecture four times already. This time it's Mrs. Hinchley's turn to read her class rules posted in the front of the room. As each rule is pronounced, your mind becomes more devious:

"Speak only when called upon." *Okay, so I won't talk—at least not while she's looking. But notes—she didn't say anything about not passing notes. Besides, writing wastes more time than whispering.*

"Remain in your seats." *Ha! I'll do what I did last year. I'll forge a note from my doctor saying I have a bladder problem.*

"And no food, drinks, gum, pets, weapons, hats, cassette players, CD players, electronic games or appliances, over-the-counter or prescription drugs in class." *Anything else? I'll show her—I won't bring my brain to class either.*

Read Jeremiah 31:31–34

How does God promise to change the way we react to rules?

Knowing a rule doesn't guarantee that you won't break it. Even if the rule is good and right, when someone posts a rule, we itch to rip it down. Rules, we feel, are made to break. One thing is clear: Rules aren't enough to rein us in. Something inside us needs to change.

From the giving of the Ten Commandments to the warnings of the prophets, God read rules to Israel for hundreds of years. Like reading rules at the beginning of a school year, it helped for a while. Then Israel returned to their normal behavior, or worse. After times of following God closely, the people went back to worshiping hunks of stone and hating one another.

Through the prophet Jeremiah, God promised a better time, when his people would no longer wander off. His people would get beyond plotting to escape rules and live under a new agreement with their God.

God promised that this new covenant would re-create a fresh, tight friendship that would begin with forgiveness and result in a new heart. God would write rules on the inside—on people's hearts, not on a blackboard or a stone tablet. Love would build from the inside out, so that his people would follow because their hearts were totally devoted to him.

I will put my law in their minds and write it on their hearts. I will be their God, and they will be my people. JEREMIAH 31:33

The Ultimate Faceplant

It took you a while to figure out where you were. Miles back you had ditched your group to pound your mountain bike to the top of an uninhabited bluff. There you howled like a caveman, flung your skid lid into the bushes—*who needs a helmet?*—and broke off the trail.

Riding close to the bluff's lip, you threaded down through rocks and underbrush. But halfway down, your front tire caught and stopped. You flew over your handlebars, airborne until your face hit a tree. *Thud.*

Actually, whamming the tree was a good thing. It kept you from rolling over the cliff.

After you came to, you struggled to stand up. You stumbled. Something was wrong with your leg. Got up again, stumbled. You couldn't see through your swollen face to find your way back home.

Bike broken, you can't walk, and now it's getting dark. Not good.

Read Isaiah 42:1–9
How did God promise to help his wounded people?

If you were lying half-conscious in the middle of a wilderness, you wouldn't need a pamphlet on bike safety. Instructions for skidding down a steep, twisting single-track wouldn't do you much good either. You'd need a paramedic or a doctor in a flight-for-life helicopter. You'd need someone who could save your life.

By the end of the Old Testament, God's people and the rest of the human race had done the all-time end-over-end, a total faceplant. They were spiritually broken, imprisoned in spiritual darkness. God promised help. But not more rules or rituals—instead, a Rescuer.

The Rescuer that God would send would heal the broken and give sight to the blind, setting people free from sin's guilt and power the same way God had saved his people from slavery in Egypt. His mission was to help not just Israel ("the people") but all of humanity ("the Gentiles").

God could have left the human race alone. After all, we made the mess all by ourselves, and God had done all he could for us (Isaiah 5:1-7). But God wouldn't give up. The Rescuer was his last-ditch effort to save us and bring us back to himself.

I will keep you and will make you to be a covenant for the people and a light for the Gentiles.... ISAIAH 42:6

Mummified

What a year! Six months post-faceplant, you're still in a body cast. Being plastered and bandaged and tractioned like a mummy hasn't been a party, although it's given you time to memorize the lines in every Mr. Ed rerun. What's made your experience incredibly worse, though, has been the weird behavior of your best friend.

She's sent everything ever made for a sick person—stupid sympathy cards, shiny balloons, stuffed animals, smelly flowers. But here's the strange part: It's been six months and she's never come to visit. You decide that your best friend is now an ex-friend when you get a postcard scribbled from Disneyland: *How are you? I am fine. Wish you were here.*

Read Luke 2:4–12
Why was Jesus born?

The prophecies and promises that were fuzzy in the Old Testament quickly become clear in the New Testament. God's Son was on his way to help a bashed-up humanity.

One second the Son of God was ruling the universe with the Father and Holy Spirit in the dazzling brightness of heaven. The next second he was born on earth—still totally God, but now also fully human. Angels proclaimed who he was: Savior, Messiah, Lord. He was called Emmanuel ("God with us") and Jesus ("the Lord saves") (Matthew 1:21-23). Think of it! God came to visit his creation. God knew that real friends don't just send sympathy cards. They come in person.

God saw that his critically injured world needed help. He didn't just gaze at us from a distance, where problems get lost in a haze. He came as a friend—up close and personal, right here.

And when he came to visit, he did more than sit in a chair next to our bed and pity us. By leaving his glory and coming to earth, it was as if he too climbed into a body cast, so we could be certain he knows what we go through (Hebrews 4:14–16). He felt the same temptations and limitations we do. He felt the craziness of itching where you can't scratch, beneath a cast.

He didn't leave us suffering alone.

I bring you good news of great joy that will be for all the people. Today in the town of David a Savior has been born to you; he is Christ the Lord. LUKE 2:10-11

Jesus in La-La Land

Scott's parents said he had to go to church this morning. *I wonder if Grandma and Grandpa know I haven't been to church since they visited last summer.* When they arrived at church, Scott looked around. *Same as last time. No one my age.* By the middle of the service, the music had made him drowsy. Then the sermon threatened to push him over the edge into la-la land. *I know my parents mean well, but this isn't for me.*

It's hard to know what a Christian your age should look like—or even whether it's possible to utter "teen" and "Christian" in the same breath. Most kids, like Scott, think going to church is buying a ticket to snoredom. It's slouching, snoozing, counting bricks. All 4,672 of them. One by one. By one. By one. Is that the best you can expect?

Or church may mean the opposite—messy games, riotous outings, running from ride to ride at amusement parks. The leaders gave up doing Bible studies because no one listens. Their goal is to entertain the kids and keep them from trashing the church. Is that all there is?

Read Luke 2:46–47
What was Jesus like at your age?

Jesus was the Son of God, but he was no abnormal, mutant teenager. He faced the same challenges you do, including the temptation to think that faith is only for parents and weirdos (Hebrews 4:14-16). But he chased neither snoredom nor youth-group wackiness. He chose growth.

The adults Jesus talked with didn't spend an hour of class begging him to listen. Instead, he amazed them by asking hard questions and discussing real answers. He made learning at the temple his priority, to the point that he didn't even notice his parents had left for home. The result? Jesus matured in a way that impressed both God and people.

You probably suspect that there's more to being young and Christian than youth-group parties or sleeper sermons. Even if no one else your age is demonstrating to you what you can be, Jesus shows what you are capable of. He's with you now to help you (John 15:5). You don't have to settle for anything less.

Everyone who heard him was amazed at his understanding and his answers. LUKE 2:47

Upside-Down World

Pull out your school yearbook or a magazine and flip it upside down. Now stare into the eyes of those upside-down faces.

After a while, foreheads become chins and chins turn into pointy coneheads. Girls have bushier beards than guys. Kids are bald and bald men don't have beards.

Smiles look like weird frowns, and you can see down everyone's nose.

Notice anything else? After a while, these grotesque, upside-down faces begin to look normal.

Read Matthew 5:1–12
*How can Jesus' words be true when they seem
wildly off the wall?*

The world is like your upside-down yearbook. Things that should look bizarre start to look acceptable. Actions we should recognize as evil begin to look good: Bullies who scare money out of smaller kids get free lunches, cheaters pull good grades, and loose girls get cute guys. The rebels, instead of God's friends, look like the ones who are happy.

Jesus' teaching was aimed to turn things right side up, to display how God sees the world. The people who show mercy (not bullies) will be happy, because God will show them kindness. Those who want to do right (not those who go looking to do wrong) should be happy, because God will satisfy them. The pure (not the loose or mean) will know God. Even if this world is upside down in the worst way—with people insulting you, hurting you, and lying behind your back—God's way is best. Sooner or later, he will make things right side up.

Fortunately for your yearbook, you know that heads go up, feet go down. Food should drip off chins, not into noses or eyes.

The teachings of Jesus—the whole Bible, in fact—show what life looks like right side up (2 Timothy 3:16). They define what *normal* actually is. No confusion—up is up and down is down.

*Blessed are those who hunger and thirst for righteousness,
for they will be filled. Blessed are the pure in heart,
for they will see God.* MATTHEW 5:6,8

This Man Is No Loser

As Clarence floated past the mob of girls scrunched against the gym wall at the school dance, he thought he was a love potion in motion—that is, at least until he curled his upper lip into a snarl in a useless attempt to look cool, and the girls snarled back and told him to quit blocking their view of the real men. Yet even the girls felt a flash of pity for Clarence when his shoelaces spontaneously knotted together, tossing him to the floor with an *ooof*. Then the captain of the football team hunked past, and the girls forgot all about Clarence as he wimped off into a corner.

God is looking for friends. But don't mistake God for the school geek, a guy desperate for a dance, someone to feel sorry for. He's more like a cosmic Prince Charming thundering through space on a war horse (Revelation 19:11-16). He's the only one who can save the princess. There's nothing wrong with the Prince. It's his love who is frozen in a coma.

Read Luke 23:32–46
Why did Jesus die?

God put Adam and Eve in paradise and told them to live happily ever after with him as Lord and each other as friends. But Adam and Eve stopped serving God and others and started serving themselves. They sinned and shattered their friendship with God.

So God started over. He created a new people and saved them from slavery. Yet when God explained his rules again and again, his people fought against him, even when God reminded them that the penalty for their hatred toward him was death. All humanity rebelled, and all were sentenced to die (Romans 3:23).

God's Son suffered that sentence. At the cross, though, one of the thieves dying next to Jesus noticed something: Jesus hadn't done anything wrong. He wasn't being punished for *his* sins. He was being punished for *our* sins. An Old Testament prophecy explains: "But he was wounded for the wrong we did; he was crushed for the evil we did" (Isaiah 53:5 NCV).

God sent his Son to die for our sins because no one else could. Only Jesus was perfect and sinless, the only human being never deserving death, and the only one who could take our sins upon himself.

He was no loser. He just loved us enough to come to die in our place.

But this man has done nothing wrong. LUKE 23:41

Part of the Family

"So what do you think, Audrey?" The Sutton family and Audrey's social worker all turned and smiled at her. Audrey's smile lit up her face. *This is going to be great!*

Until last year Audrey's life had felt like a bad game of basketball. She was juggled between foster families like a loose ball thrown from team to team, slipping through fingers and skittering out-of-bounds. Things got better when she went to live with the Suttons, the first caring family she'd ever had.

Now she was about to swish through the hoop in a game-saving three-point long shot. The Suttons wanted to adopt her.

Read John 1:10-13

The "he" in the passage is Jesus. Who does God adopt into his family?

Most kids grow up with the parents who gave them birth, maybe with stepparents added in. Adopted kids are usually adopted as babies. Either way, it's easy to take parents for granted—except when they divorce or die or when you think they're mean and wish you could trade them in for a new set.

Kids adopted when they're older get a unique view of family life. They get a choice to be adopted or not, to accept or reject a set of parents, to join a family or not. In effect, they have to say to their new parents, "I need you. I'll accept your love. I want to be part of your family." They must say yes to cement the relationship.

God promises to adopt all who say yes to him. Christ's death and resurrection is God's offer to adopt you. And the offer is free, no strings attached. Our sins made us God's enemies, but Christ's death made it possible for us to be his friends (Colossians 1:21–23).

Whether we've never been a part of God's family or have grown up taking our heavenly Father for granted, we need to say to God, "Because I've done wrong, I need you. I believe that Christ died for my sins. I accept your forgiving love. I want to be your child." That's how you become a Christian. That's how you become one of his people.

In God's family, *everyone* is adopted. It's the only way in.

Yet to all who received [Jesus], to those who believed in his name, he gave the right to become children of God. JOHN 1:12

Is This for Real?

"You're so stupid! How can you believe that stuff?"

All Anne did was invite Ben to a Friday night Bible study. She didn't expect him to blast her.

"Like Mr. Renstrom says in science class—corpses don't come back to life. Have you ever seen anyone jump out of a casket?"

"Well, no." Anne didn't know what to say.

"Then how can you believe in Jesus? Why go to church at all? It's all fake. I'd rather go to Rich's party than your Bible study."

Ben was right—sort of. Without the Resurrection, Jesus would be just another dead man to read about and forget, like Aristotle and Socrates. They're great guys with gargantuan brains, but it's hard to see what they have to do with you.

Read 1 Corinthians 15:1–8

What's so important about Jesus rising from the dead?

If we think Christ is stuck in a grave somewhere, our faith crumbles. The fact that Jesus arose is like the bottom piece in a stack of blocks. Pull it out, and everything crashes. The truth is, though, that it's harder to believe that Jesus *didn't* rise from the dead. After he'd been buried for three days, five hundred people saw Jesus alive—walking and talking—and his disciples risked death to spread that good news. There's no better explanation for the empty tomb than Jesus' rising from the dead. Jesus isn't a dead dude from history class. He is the risen Son of God, the world's Savior and Master.

The Resurrection is God's proof to us that Christ's death paid in full the penalty we deserved for our sins (Romans 4:25). Jesus' resurrection is also God's promise that he will raise *all* believers to eternal life. And when you know eternity will be a party for you, you won't feel so pulled to the wrong parties here on earth. Your faith will seem worthless if you think only about the guff you take now for being a Christian and not about the great stuff God has planned for later (1 Corinthians 15:19, 32).

But you don't have to wait for all the good stuff. God wants the friendships he has planned for eternity to start now!

For what I received I passed on to you as of first importance:
that Christ...was raised on the third day according
to the Scriptures. 1 CORINTHIANS 15:3-4

More Than a Party

Marc and Kora collapsed with a couple of cold sodas after a long, hot day of work. In a few days their short-term missions team would split up and return home.

"I can't go home," Marc complained. "My friends at home aren't like the team at all. They say they're Christians, but everything bad I've ever learned to do I learned from them. People here are pumped. They read their Bibles without being nagged. They try hard to be good to one another. Everyone wants to get closer to God."

"There's no one like that at home?"

"My parents are okay. But that's not the same. At school there's a few religious weirdos. There *is* a church, though, that I've visited a couple of times. The kids seem better there."

"Maybe your parents will let you go to a Bible study there or something."

"Yeah, maybe. I just don't want to go back to being like my old friends. I need something more than that. I'm going to miss everyone here."

Read Acts 2:42–47
How did the first Christians grow together?

A good baseball team doesn't result from a bunch of players colliding in a field to toss gloves into the air, run and slide in the outfield, or pitch and hit and spit in every direction. Players have to commit to the team and its goals, learn the game, and practice together.

At church or camp or on a retreat you may have glimpsed what can happen when Christians live for God. The incredible friendship in Acts—what the Bible calls "fellowship"—doesn't happen by accident. You have to pursue it by joining a team and sticking together to pray, study, worship, share, and care together. No one rides the bench. Everyone plays.

The Christians you know may not be your first choices for teammates. You might hate their clothes, music, hair, or humor. They may go to the wrong school. Those things are less important than the fact that you all belong to God's family. Fellowship isn't just good friends getting together to party. It's God's friends getting together to grow.

They devoted themselves to the apostles' teaching and to the fellowship, to the breaking of bread and to prayer. Everyone was filled with awe. ACTS 2:42-43

Keepers Weepers

You're walking with a group of friends when you spot it. *Is that a...?* It's a small piece of greenish-white paper by the curb, waving in the breeze. *It's gotta be a piece of a magazine or something.* A few steps nearer. *Well...it might be.*

You get close enough and you're sure. *Jackpot!* Money just meant to be yours. What happens next? You don't schmooze to your friends—*Hey look! It's a $20 bill. Let's share!* Instead, you artfully distract them. Slyly pulling coins from your pocket, you toss them behind you. Your friends hear an unmistakable *kerjink, kerjink* and whip around to search the road for the fallen coins. You dash to the cash, pick it up, and deposit it in your pocket. Finders keepers.

Read Acts 1:1–8

Why not hog God all for yourself?

Before Jesus was taken up into heaven, he didn't merely promise to write every day and make certain all his friends had his new address. He said he would stick with believers through his Spirit *living in us.* The Holy Spirit comforts and teaches us (John 14:16), enables us to obey God (Romans 8:11), and, as Acts 1:8 tells, gives us power to tell others about him.

Why tell others? Because God doesn't adopt anyone into his family to be an only child.

God wants a huge family, with people from all over the world (Revelation 5:9). He assigns us a simple role in helping to enlarge the family. We give to outsiders—to non-believers—the same love and friendship God gives us as members of his family. We explain that Christ died to fix their relationship with God, and we tell them how they can be adopted into the family.

If you're worried people might laugh at your faith, it's tempting to throw pennies to distract them from what you really possess—changing a conversation away from God, hiding the fact that you go to church, acting the same as whoever is around you. Yet meeting God as Savior and Lord is like unearthing a limitless, eternal treasure. You've found a Mount Everest of gold. Don't be too stingy to share it with your friends.

But you will receive power when the Holy Spirit comes on you; and you will be my witnesses in Jerusalem, and in all Judea and Samaria, and to the ends of the earth. ACTS 1:8

No More Mr. Yuck

You don't need Mr. Yuck stickers to know you shouldn't drink drain cleaner. When you go to lunch at school no one brings you a booster seat and spoon-feeds you cafeteria glop. Your parents don't hook you on a leash at the mall, nor do they call a baby-sitter every time they leave you at home. You don't have a squished little face or a hairless head, or wear a bib or sleep in a crib. You're way too old for that sort of thing.

You didn't stay a baby.

It would be just as abnormal to stay a spiritual baby.

Read Ephesians 4:11–16
How do Christians grow up?

You didn't get beyond drool and diaper disasters all by yourself. You won't grow up spiritually without other people either. And there's more: They won't grow without you.

Adults might think of you or your peers trying to help others grow—trying to minister to others—like the newborns in a nursery trying to run the hospital. But that isn't how God sees you. Through his Holy Spirit, God has given you and every believer a gift to help the body (the whole church, the believers that make up God's family all across the world).

You may not see yourself in the list of gifts in Ephesians (or in 1 Corinthians 12:7–11, or Romans 12:6–8). But here are more specific starters: God might have gifted you to work with younger kids, to use drama or music or puppets to tell people about Christ, or to teach from the Bible. You might be good at leading worship, serving food, encouraging struggling friends, welcoming strangers, or building houses for the poor. You might be a role model for other kids or even to older people at church. Having a gift doesn't mean you're the best at something, only that you do your best for God.

When all believers put their gifts into action, everyone knows God better and thinks, feels, and acts more like Christ. When they don't, believers are like babies bobbing on the raging seas, tossed by wrong values and ideas. You know the outcome of that—babies sink. You have to grow up to swim.

Then we will no longer be infants, tossed back and forth by the waves.... Instead, speaking the truth in love, we will in all things grow up into him who is the Head, that is, Christ.
EPHESIANS 4:14a, 15

Final Exam

Your English teacher smiled wide and clapped her hands together. "Class, you all possess a *fa-a-abulous* thirst to learn." She said this so fabulously that you almost believed her. "Because you are mature enough to monitor your own work," she paused and said the next part slowly, "you will not be graded this quarter. Isn't that *fa-a-abulous*?" She bobbed her head up and down as if your brain-dead class couldn't answer even *that* question without help. "And as a further sign of our *fa-a-abulous* faith in you, we will not grade your behavior or report to your parents."

With that, half the class bolted. You decided to stick with it, but as weeks passed you became bored. You couldn't tell if you were learning anything. Besides, class wasn't fair—kids who never showed up got the same credit you did. When you had a group project to do, no one else did any work. Then again, neither did you. But hey—at least you thought about it.

Read Matthew 25:31–41

How would you act if there were no heaven or hell?

Be honest. You wouldn't study long for a class with no grades. When good isn't rewarded and bad isn't punished, you figure out quick enough that it doesn't matter what you do. So you do what you want, not what you should. You do what *feels* good, not what *is* good.

God promises that your friendship with him won't be a waste. One day—the Bible doesn't say exactly when—Christ will come again, and everyone on earth will take a final exam with one question: *Were you God's friend?* Those who become God's friends through Christ's death will stand before God without a flaw, totally forgiven (Colossians 1:22), and live eternally with God. Those who fail the test will be judged guilty and receive unending punishment (Matthew 25:46).

God says this final exam is simple to grade because his friends are easy to spot. Because they trust Jesus they love the same way God loves, caring for the hungry, for strangers, for the needy, sick, and imprisoned. They're surprised they get a reward, since they know it was God's love, forgiveness, and power that changed them. God made them everything they are.

Come, you who are blessed by my Father; take your inheritance, the kingdom prepared for you since the creation of the world.
MATTHEW 25:34

It Beats a Harp

The line to get through the gate piled up behind two men clubbing each other with politeness: "You first." "No, you." "Really, I insist." "Thank you, but you first." It went on and on and on. *No big deal,* you told yourself. After all, you had all of eternity to wait.

The unisex white robe you received once inside was exactly like everyone else's—what a slap to your individuality—though you couldn't complain about the spring-fresh fabric softener and lack of static cling. Getting a heavenly body was a bit better. You liked the pearly white teeth and zitless skin, although getting hair like a TV evangelist caught you by surprise.

Looking back, you'd have to admit it took you a few centuries to figure out this was supposed to be heaven. It was probably hardest, all in all, to get used to broccoli for every meal and the gazillion cable channels with nothing on but religious talk shows.

Read Revelation 21:1–8
What will heaven really be like?

If you're even close to normal, you can think of better things to do with your eternity than squat on a cloud and strum a harp. Fortunately, God has better stuff planned for us.

The good things we've had here will be like baby mush compared to the unending feast of heaven. What we've enjoyed of God's creation—music, nature, color, beauty—will be given to us in abundance, with boggling intensity. We can expect incredible surprises, because our dreams now are warped by sin. But be sure of this: Whatever we find in heaven will totally satisfy.

Even better than the place will be the people. God's friends will live in his peace—no enemies, no popularity contests, no prejudice or jealousy, no ugly names or biting words. But the real life of this eternal party will be God himself. He'll live with us the way he's wanted to since he created this world—with no doubt, fear, or sin separating us from him. We'll begin to know God as well as he knows us, and celebrate him for giving us an eternity of friendship with himself and his people.

God wants *you* in heaven. And if God is your friend, there's no better place to be.

They will be his people, and God himself will be with them and be their God. REVELATION 21:3

The Big Ditch

"Mom!" Erin howled. "You said I could pick my own clothes!"

"I'm not just going to watch you empty my purse, silly," Erin's mom tried to joke. But Erin didn't think it was funny when her mom tagged along at the mall and trailed her in and out of every shop. Mom couldn't just walk in and whip out the checkbook. She had to help pick everything—down to every last pair of socks. Worse yet, Mom wouldn't dream of leaving Erin's dad and brother and sister at home. Erin's shopping trip had turned into family night at the mall.

For a while Erin's family didn't notice her walking faster and faster, always at least twenty steps in front of them. No one, that is, until Erin's brother gave her away. "Why won't she walk with us?" he whined.

Worm. She'd get him later.

"What's wrong?" her dad bellowed. "Don't you want to be seen with us?"

Read Proverbs 6:20–22
Why does God stick us in families?

In the beginning is Dad and Mom. They bring a baby home from the hospital, maybe from a foster home. It's cute—love, marriage, baby carriage. But families are more than cute. There's no better place to teach a drooly new human how to grow up.

Deep down inside you probably love your family. Some days you even like them. But growing up means you're in the process of leaving them.

That's where the problem starts. It's part of God's plan for you to have a family to guide you. But it's also part of God's plan for you to grow up, to learn to make your own choices, to live on your own—but most of all, to hang on to him and follow him for yourself. Your family has been there to care for you. But you're learning to care for yourself.

You're caught in the middle—you still depend on your family, but your family isn't always around. Already you have to fend for yourself with friends, with strangers, at school, out and about. You're not a baby anymore.

But your family isn't always so sure. And unless you want them to treat you like you're still stuck in a stroller, you need to figure out how to get along at home—and on your own.

My son, keep your father's commands and do not forsake your mother's teaching. PROVERBS 6:20

Squid Sauce

Marcus gags as he spoons a blop of creamed corn onto his plate. "Nate doesn't have to eat this stuff at his house," he moans. Marcus neglects to mention that he once ate Brussels sprouts in squid sauce at Nate's house—and liked it.

Dad glares. "You're being rude."

Marcus suddenly bursts. "I always have to do what you say!"

"What's the big deal? You just need to eat what we cook," Dad responds calmly. "Unless, of course, you want to cook instead. Or you could always spend your allowance and call for pizza."

Marcus slumps in his chair and stirs his creamed corn with his fork. *I always have to do what they say.*

Read Ephesians 6:1–3

What good does it do you to "honor your father and mother"?

Being good to your parents doesn't just mean keeping your culinary critiques to yourself when you think the food is crude—although that's a start. It means even *more* than swallowing hard and suffering through what you know you're supposed to do. Honoring your parents means *respecting them* and *obeying them willingly.*

When Paul wrote this passage to the Ephesians he was repeating one of the Ten Commandments, the laws God had given his followers hundreds of years before. God was never dumb about how hard obeying can be. He didn't even assume that parents are always right or perfectly worthy of respect. After all, God knew that the first parents he created—Adam and Eve—had pushed each other to rebel against him. And their home life wasn't exactly happy—one of their sons murdered the other (Genesis 3:1–4:16). Still, God said clearly how it's supposed to go: We're to obey our parents.

That's blunt. But God doesn't say that listening to your parents will merely steer you clear of fatty foods and gruesome table manners. As you obey your parents, he promises to guard your life. Parents aren't God, but God's caring hands reach out to you through your parents.

Honoring your parents is right. It's also smart.

"Honor your father and mother"—which is the first commandment with a promise—"that it may go well with you and that you may enjoy long life on the earth." EPHESIANS 6:2-3

Grounding Your Parents

"She'd be cute if it weren't for her ears," Allison's dad teased.

Allison's friends laughed. That just egged her dad on. "Did you know that when you call Allison you have to pick which ear you want to talk to? Her ears are so big they're in different area codes."

They all laughed again. Allison didn't. But Dad was on a roll. "We're thinking of taking up windsurfing," he grinned. "We won't need sails."

Why does he always have to joke about my ears?

Allison faked a smile and got up to refill her soda, then hid in the kitchen popping popcorn for her guests. Finally she told her friends she had homework to do and left to hide in her room. Allison wished her dad would shut up. Instead *she* did.

Read 1 Timothy 5:1

What can you do when your parents get way out of line?

God commands us to obey our parents. But he has an even longer list of commands for parents. It's your parents' job to guide, discipline, and encourage you—to direct you without driving you crazy.

Sooner or later parents goof. They love you but don't know how to show it. Or they know what to do but do it imperfectly. They say things that hurt. They pile on rules and demands but don't raise a finger to help. They snoop too much and listen too little. They cut you down instead of building you up. And so the Bible warns parents not to irritate or push their kids to anger: "Do not nag your children. If you are too hard to please, they may want to stop trying" (Colossians 3:21 NCV).

You wish you could ground your parents—but you can't. And it won't help to spit back or act up or scream at your parents—especially if you're telling them what God expects of them. But you can talk to them. Instead of sassing back or backing off, tell them how you feel and what you need. That isn't an excuse to clobber them. It's a chance to gently persuade them, to talk to them the way you want to be talked to—with respect.

Your parents can't change if they don't know what hurts or annoys you. If you don't learn to speak up, your only choice is to put up.

Never speak harshly to an older man, but appeal to him
respectfully as though he were your own father.
1 TIMOTHY 5:1 NLT

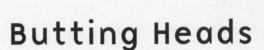

Butting Heads

Tyler did well at school. But he didn't want to.

When all his friends bragged about their bad grades—how low their quiz scores could actually go—Tyler began to plot. For as long as he could remember, he had studied hard. Now he figured he deserved time off for good behavior. So he decided that at the start of second semester he would slack off. He'd show up for school, but he'd leave his brain at home.

For nine weeks Tyler lounged in total slothdom. Then mid-semester notices went home and his parents found out he was flunking math and social studies.

Pick what Tyler's parents most likely would do: (a) applaud his desire to fail and get him ready for life on the streets by letting him camp in a refrigerator box in the backyard; (b) feed his need to kick back by jetting him to his own lush South Pacific island; or (c) ground him until he's thirty or until his grades improve, whichever comes first.

Easy pick.

Read Proverbs 3:12
Why do your parents discipline you?

You know how it goes when you butt heads with your parents. You act or think or feel one way. They make it known they want you to act or think or feel another way. They take it upon themselves to restrain your outsides and reshape your insides.

So does their knack for discipline ooze from an evil plan to ruin your life? Hebrews says it comes from a wish to make you the best you can be. You're hurting yourself, so your parents stop you. You're doing less than your best, so they push you to reach higher. You're doing something wrong, so they help you do what's right. Parents may differ about how and when to step in, but they're programmed at the factory to do discipline.

Their care reflects *God's* care.

Discipline hurts. Training is work. No football player or figure skater enjoys every rule or instruction breathed by a coach. But a coach isn't a coach if he doesn't drill his team. And parents aren't parents if they don't train their kids.

The Lord disciplines those he loves, as a father the son he delights in. PROVERBS 3:12

Horsing Around

"But you said I could go," Grant protested.

Grant's mom stood firm. "Grant, if you had finished your chores, you could go. But you didn't. And so you can't."

"I did my chores. I mowed the lawn."

"You munched two new shrubs because you were in a hurry. Then you ran out of gas and left half of the backyard undone. Remember? And you didn't weed-whack."

"I'll get it done," Grant seethed. "Can't I decide when I'll do it? You always treat me like I'm a little kid."

"I hate to say it, but right now you're acting like one."

Read Psalm 32:9

When will your parents treat you like you're grown up?

Horses are beautiful, but they're no match for your brains. Horses don't read maps. They can't follow directions. When you want a horse to go somewhere unfamiliar you put a bit in its mouth, hop on its back, and *steer*.

Sometimes your parents think they have to steer *you*.

Not long ago you needed your parents to feed, wipe, burp, and bathe you. You learned to walk, but it took a long time before you could cross the street by yourself. You learned to talk, but it was quite a wait before you made much sense.

Changes came gradually. Trust built slowly. The point? You can't fake maturity. You can't pry control away. To get freedom you have to prove yourself. Your parents may loosen the reins a bit if you conform on the outside—if you do what you're told. But you'll get even more freedom when your parents sense something good going on inside—when you *want* to do what's right. Playing the part of the perfect child isn't enough. Parents want to know you have a brain—good judgment. They need to see you have a pure heart—good character.

Your parents will always think of you as their baby. But if you don't act like one, you up the chance they won't treat you like one.

Do not be like the horse or the mule, which have no understanding but must be controlled by bit and bridle or they will not come to you. PSALM 32:9

Real Family

Halfway through their youth group's winter retreat, Chad decided to show Dana how much he liked her. He howled as he roared down the icy sledding run—straight at Dana. He hit. She flew. She body-slammed into the hard ground. What love.

Chad and Chelsea and some other friends carried a sore, dazed Dana back to the chalet, propped her in front of a fireplace, and brought her pizza.

Late that evening around a blazing fire, Dana bragged to the whole group about her shatterproof skull. She said her friends on the retreat were her real family. Friends were cool and home was horrible. Lots of kids nodded.

As Chelsea listened to other kids tell their stories and hint that *all* parents and brothers and sisters were awful, she felt like jumping up and yelling, "No! My family isn't like that!" Chelsea liked her family. Home was safe. Home was good. But she wondered if anyone would believe her.

Read Ephesians 4:29–5:2
Can a family ever be friends?

Some people say every family is a mess. Here's the truth: Some families get along most of the time. Many get along at least some of the time.

You may not live in one of those families. You may live with divorce, violence, or alcohol or drug abuse. Your parents may work too much. You may even have been beaten up or sexually abused—if that's you, find a counselor or pastor or teacher to talk to.

Whatever kind of family you live in you can still control how *you* act. It's easy to be nice to friends (Luke 6:31–35). But you no doubt let yourself do things to your parents and brothers and sisters you would never do to your friends.

It doesn't have to be that way. Paul says that the love and forgiveness God has for you is something you can pass on to the world around you—including your family. You don't have to sass, spew, or slug and turn your family into enemies. As far as it depends on you, you can be a friend (Romans 12:18). So you aren't weird if you get along with your family. You're weird if you don't try.

Be kind and compassionate to one another, forgiving each other, just as in Christ God forgave you.
EPHESIANS 4:32

Watch Your Head

Your four-year-old body lies on an emergency-room gurney. You gaze up through a sterile white sheet at the bright lights above you. Through a slit in the sheet, a doctor sews your scalp back together. The doctor asks how you cracked your head open. Technically, *you* didn't. Your six-year-old brother did it for you. He rammed your head into the corner of a chimney.

"What kind of kid would do that?" the doctor squawks. You wonder too. You're no psychologist, but you think what he did maybe had something to do with what you did to him a month earlier. At your grandparents' farm you swung open an old-fashioned garage door, caught your brother's mouth, and knocked out eight front teeth. Maybe he was mad about that. *I should have said I was sorry. Nah. It was an accident. Did anyone* make *him put his mouth there? Besides, they were baby teeth. They were going to fall out anyway.*

Maybe he was mad about that.

Read Ephesians 4:26–27
What's the best way to keep your family cool?

You can't help but get hot living in a family. You live close, share chores, battle over the TV and computer, fight for the phone, hog each other's space, and "borrow" each other's stuff. Living as a family always ignites strong feelings. That's normal.

The real problem is when you overheat.

Ephesians tells how to hose down the flames. "Don't let the sun go down while you're still angry" doesn't mean "Get even before it gets dark" or "Dish it out before dusk." It means this: Talk. Listen. Forgive. Forget. Before you go to bed. While problems are little. Before the flames flare up again.

Don't wait to fix things with your family. And don't forget that a few verses later Paul tells *how* you can get the guts to get over hurt: You can forgive others because God forgave us.

If you gash your hand, you don't wait days to clean it out and stitch it up. Ignore the wound for a while and you'll get a vicious infection. Take a year and it will kill off your arm. Wait a few years longer and it will eat away your head.

Do not let the sun go down while you are still angry, and do not give the devil a foothold.
EPHESIANS 4:26–27

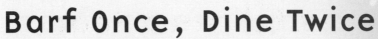
Barf Once, Dine Twice

As Mara time-warps through the wormhole, her cheeks and the corners of her eyes and mouth all slide toward her ears, peeled back like a rich lady's too-tight face-lift. Twenty-some years into the past she jolts to a stop. Suddenly Mara is watching her mom's life reel by in fast forward.

She sees her mom flirting. She's smoking and acting cool, laughing—drunk. Mara waves her hand in the face of her teenage mom. Her mom is startled. Mara speaks before her mother can. "See, you had your fun!" Mara accuses. "Now I want mine."

The wormhole begins to unravel, pulling Mara back to her own time. "You're not seeing all of me," her mom calls out as Mara blasts away. "You're not seeing what I really thought and felt. You can't see the pain!"

Read Proverbs 26:11–12

Why do as your parents say—and not as they maybe did?

When you were little your parents could say, "That's a stove. It's hot. It will burn you." You probably said, "No, it's not. No, it won't." But you were short enough that they had no problem putting you in your place to protect you.

Guess what? You're not so small anymore. And your parents' ability to keep your hands out of ovens and away from burners is almost gone.

Still, you've mastered the stove lesson. Your parents probably don't have to beat you back to keep you from broiling fingers for breakfast. Why? At some point you decided your parents aren't stupid. Sometimes you don't know best.

Adults have all done things they regret. What seemed fun at the time—and what might sound fun to you—doesn't look so good to them now. Like a whopper sunburn, the damage didn't show up until later. But they still got burned. Or maybe it caused a deadly case of cancer.

Your parents and other adults want you to learn from your mistakes—and from theirs. To do anything less is to be like a toddler too dumb to stay away from the stove—or like a dog that barfs once and eats twice. He goes back to chomp down what already made him sick, mistaking it for another meal.

As a dog returns to its vomit, so a fool repeats his folly.
PROVERBS 26:11

Noseprints on Glass

An hour after your parents were supposed to pick you up at the movie theater you're pressing your nose against a lobby window, staring into the distance, watching for their car. You sit down. You get up to look. You pace. You call home again. You try every cell phone number you can think of. No answer. You pace some more.

Your friends are long gone. The ushers stare at you half angry, half sorry like you're an orphan. Then you start to wonder if you are—if your parents are dead in a car crash somewhere. You push away that thought. *What could they be doing that's more important than picking me up?*

When they finally pull up you dart out, crawl into the car, and slam the door. Your parents gush about the deal they found on a new home entertainment system. They say it will shake walls and melt windows.

At the moment you're not impressed.

Read Isaiah 49:13–16
Does God ever forget about you? How can you be sure?

Some parents are messed up and hardly know who you are. Others are checked out—they've left, or they spend time on anything but their kids.

Most parents are just plain busy. Someone in your family has to make money, which means deadlines, trips, overtime, and stress. Besides that, you share your parents' attention with brothers and sisters and other relatives. Parents have to sleep and eat and collapse like everyone else.

Sometimes the reasons parents are unavailable are understandable. Sometimes they aren't. Either way, you're left feeling lost and alone.

When God's people worried he didn't care about them, he reminded them that no mother could fail to care for her child. But even if a mother could neglect her child, God wouldn't forget his people. Their names are written on his hands, just as you jot yourself reminders, only better. The forgotten are "engraved." *Very* noticeable. *Very* permanent.

When you feel your parents aren't there, God is. He hasn't, won't, and can't forget you.

Can a mother forget the baby at her breast and have no compassion on the child she has borne? Though she may forget, I will not forget you! See, I have engraved you on the palms of my hands. ISAIAH 49:15–16

Up on the Rooftop

Julie's parents stood in the driveway studying the snow on their garage roof. "They're not footprints," her dad said. "It's just the wind."

"It's strange how the wind makes little marks from Julie's window to the edge of the roof closest to the fence," her mom observed, "and knocks the snow off that one spot on the fence—and makes more of the little marks from the fence to the driveway."

"Well, maybe they are footprints. But they're not hers," her dad argued. "I asked her. She said she doesn't sneak out."

"Then how on earth do you think they got there?"

"I don't know."

"So we're not going to do anything about her sneaking out?"

"No."

Read 1 Samuel 2:12–17, 22–25

Who loses when your parents play stupid?

Eli's sons did unbelievable evil—the equivalent of skimming cash from the offering plate and sexually abusing women in the church. They got away with sin at least in part because their father knew what they were doing and refused to correct them. He was too foolish to believe what others told him—or at least too slow to stop them, even when God warned him.

Some days you can outwit your parents with half your brain tied behind your back. But taking advantage of their temporary denseness by doing wrong is like jumping at a chance to drink toilet cleaner. If a two-year-old's parents didn't childproof their house—if they didn't lock up poisons and hide medicine out of reach—you wouldn't cheer. You'd feel sad and scared. Freedom from sane boundaries isn't freedom at all.

You're no two-year-old. Ultimately *you* are in charge of yourself. When you choose to do wrong, it hurts your parents. It hurts others. But it hurts *you* worst. If your parents won't stop you, stop yourself. If they won't confront you when you head out a window, find someone who will.

Eli and his sons, by the way, didn't live happily ever after. They ignored God and died for their sins (1 Samuel 4:11–18).

This sin of the young men was very great in the Lord's sight.
1 SAMUEL 2:17

Start Your Engines

Mike's older brother Jared had been away at college for two whole months before he sent the letter he promised. The first part of the letter was about disgusting cafeteria food and enormous classes and stunning college women. Then Jared got a little more honest:

Mikey, there's a lot of drinking here. You can pray for me that I find friends. In high school I had friends who didn't drink. Now I live in a dorm wing with twenty-nine other guys. It seems like all of them drink.

I started going to a Bible study on campus. Good people there. Remember what Dad used to tell us when we were little and he went on business trips? "Be strong and courageous, because God is with you." That's helping me survive here. So many things are new.

I miss you. See you at Thanksgiving. Stay cool,

Jared

Read James 1:2–4
How do you get ready to survive on your own?

There's only one road to maturity. It's full of potholes.

Imagine a world where your parents aren't standing ready to whip out the wallet. Where you decide *when* you study or *if* you study—or *when* you go to bed or *if* you go to bed. Where you can choose your friends, your enemies, your roomies, and your church—or none of the above. Where you can bake brownies for breakfast or inhale tater tots three times a day. Where $1.50 is a fortune and you have to decide if your clothes will survive a spin in the washer if you mix colors with whites—or maybe you decide never to wash them at all.

Welcome to life on your own.

You'll grow up fast then. But you're getting ready now. How you spend the next few years determines whether you're prepared—or scared—to live on your own. Every rough spot in the road is a test. And every pothole you learn to steer around now is one less that can blow a tire later.

Perseverance must finish its work so that you may be mature and complete, not lacking anything. JAMES 1:4

Mom on a Milk Carton

Your teammates almost flatten you as they bound out of the locker room. Coach is sick, the assistant out of town. Practice canceled.

Your parents don't expect you home for two hours, so they'll never know you're not at practice. You have total freedom to slip away—to go anywhere, to do anything. Big question: What to do?

Bigger question: Who are you when your parents aren't around?

You spend quite a bit of your existence out of your parents' sight. But you never get out of their minds. They relax only when they know where you're going, what you're doing, and when you'll be home—and even then they're nervous. When you step out of their sight, you leap into another dimension: the danger zone.

You probably don't see it that way. You don't bow and scrape and thank your parents for the privileges of freedom. You just bolt. Being off on your own is no big deal.

Think again. It *is* a big deal.

Read Luke 2:42–52

How did Jesus act when he misplaced his parents?

When Jesus' parents headed home from Jerusalem they traveled with a caravan of relatives. They assumed he was somewhere with them.

Wrong. After three days, Jesus no doubt had noticed Mary and Joseph had left without him. But Jesus didn't exactly worry himself sick or pull down a cell phone from heaven or paint Mom and Dad's poor lost faces on goat-milk cartons. He sat tight. He was in the right place. He was doing the right thing. Even when his parents weren't around.

Whenever you step out it's *your* job to look after yourself—where you're going and what you're doing. Part of that job is keeping your parents informed so they don't have nervous fits. But the even bigger part is watching out for their number one concern: you.

None of us is brilliant enough to always make wise choices. None of us is upstanding enough to always make good choices. But God is both wise and good. And he's promised to lead the way (Proverbs 3:5–7).

"Why were you searching for me?" he asked. "Didn't you know I had to be in my Father's house?" LUKE 2:49

Once Upon a Tractor

Dane sat in the tractor's enclosed cab, howling with the stereo. But when he finished plowing the back forty of the family farm, he quieted down and watched the sun set over the rich black fields. *Maybe farming is okay.*

For eighth-grade graduation Dane had to give a speech describing what he would be doing ten years from now. Dane knew exactly what he was *supposed* to do—work the farm. Meeting each week with his youth pastor and going to a Bible study with dozens of other kids, though, had given Dane other ideas. But he was afraid everyone would laugh if he told his real dreams. Besides that, Dane didn't want a blowup like the one his sister and her husband set off when they left the farm. He'd never seen Dad so mad.

It's just a stupid speech. Maybe he could make up a story about being a farmer. *It's not really a lie. I can't talk about being a youth pastor. Dad will kill me.*

Read Psalm 139:13–16
Who sets the direction for your life?

Your parents hold you to a routine meant to make you an Olympic swimmer, but you dream of being an artist. You want to transplant brains, but your family tells you you're brainless. Your dad expects you to be his clone, but you'd sooner haul garbage. They laugh, they scold, and you get the message: Conform or face the consequences.

Conformity can be good. Without parental pressure you would ditch school, make armpit noises during sermons, and whine like a baby when you didn't get your way.

It would be wrong to obey your parents if they ever told you to do obvious evil (Acts 5:29). And it's wrong to disobey them when they tell you to do what's definitely right and good. But the solutions to some quarrels aren't that clear. Quiz yourself: *Why* do you want to break the mold? *Whom* do you want to please?

Your goal isn't to unnerve your parents or to pursue brathood but to run to what God wants. You're to listen to parents faithfully. But you're to obey God completely—and chase hard what he designed you to be. Your parents gave you birth, but God made you. You're his.

All the days ordained for me were written in your book before one of them came to be. PSALM 139:16

Been There, Done That

"Discussion ended," Paul's dad had announced. Paul crossed his arms and glared straight ahead.

As Paul's dad pulled the car to a stop at a red light, Paul undid his seat belt and climbed out of the car.

"What are you doing?" his dad demanded. "Where do you think you're going?"

"I can't stand this. I'll walk home—if I decide to come home." The traffic light turned green. Cars honked. Paul's dad flipped on his hazard lights. Angry cars sped around.

"You don't understand me!" Paul shouted above the traffic noise as he walked away. "You don't know what I face!"

Read Ecclesiastes 1:9–10

Is the world you live in different from what your parents faced when they were your age?

You cringe when your mom offers to help you pick school clothes. Your dad dies a quick digital death whenever he tries to play video games. They both fear computers. Your sister sets their digital watches, and you're still giving them lessons on how to run the home entertainment system.

So when your parents tell you how to dress, what to listen to, whom to hang out with, where to go, and when to be home, you're less than confident that they know what they're talking about.

Your parents don't go to your school. They might not have been born on this planet, but you can be sure that if they've lived on earth as long as you have, they understand at least a little of your world.

Even if your parents actually *were* born in the Stone Age they still understand trials and temptations. When they were younger they just got in trouble for different things—for not cleaning up the cave, driving the family dinosaur too fast, cutting their hair too short, or not piercing their nose.

There have always been opportunities to rebel against God. Everyone faces choices between right and wrong. There's nothing new under the sun.

There is nothing new under the sun. Is there anything of which one can say, "Look! This is something new"?
ECCLESIASTES 1:9-10

You Ain't Seen Nothin'

"These are the happiest times of your life," people say.

You hope not. In fact, you wish you could gleep over the past year. You started the year by growing four inches so all your clothes fit funny. In December your orthodontist said you had to get braces—unless you wanted teeth growing out of your nose. Merry Christmas.

Speaking of your face—it doesn't look like it used to. You stare in the mirror, worried that one eye is lower than the other. Maybe your head is attached crooked. Then there's that beachball-sized zit on your chin. And yesterday at church you had a major moment of adolescent clumsiness and dropped the offering plate—*KLANG KAjing gajing gajink.*

If this is as good as life gets, then you dread what's ahead.

Read Psalm 84:1–7

How do you keep your life cool and carefree—right here, right now?

Ancient Israelites went to the temple in Jerusalem—the "house of the Lord"—to feel close to God. But they never had an easy walk. To stand in the splendor of God's dwelling they endured dust and scorching heat.

Growing up is a trudge through the desert. God wants to mature your body, brain, and heart so that you look like him (2 Corinthians 3:18). But on the way you're hot and bothered. You face new challenges at school. You struggle with changing relationships with your parents and friends.

You may like being your age. You may hate it. Either way, two things are true: It won't last long, and God helps you get along.

When the Israelites "set their hearts on pilgrimage," when they chose to live close to God, even the "Valley of Baca" (the valley of "weeping" or "thirst") became a well-watered oasis, a spread of palm trees and ponds. But the best was always yet to come. When the Israelites reached the temple they couldn't imagine a better place to be.

When you're totally devoted to Jesus, a trudge through the desert becomes a stroll in the sun.

Blessed are those whose strength is in you, who have set their hearts on pilgrimage. As they pass through the Valley of Baca, they make it a place of springs. PSALM 84:5-6

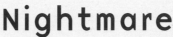

Nightmare

You shouldn't have watched the late news before you went to bed. You feel besieged: *Double murder-suicide. Flesh-eating streptococcus germs. Carjacking on the corner. Drugs in schoolyards. Satanists carving up animals in the country. Kidnappers crawling through windows. Terrorists and dirty bombs. Drug cartels flourishing in South America. Political dissidents oppressed in Asia. Bodies floating down rivers in Africa. Children starving everywhere.*

Solutions?

You could build an arsenal of megaplasma lasers and neutron grenades and hide under your bed.

Or you could be wise where you walk.

Read Proverbs 2:12–22
What dangers in life are worth worrying about?

Humans have always faced obvious outside threats. From woolly mammoths to the risk of worldwide thermonuclear war, history hasn't been wholly wonderful. Life has definitely been worse. But the world could surely be better. You want a long and happy life—emphasis on "long" and "happy." You expect circumstances to improve as you age. But maybe you worry that by the time you grow up there won't be anything left to enjoy.

Danger can feel like it's on your doorstep. TV thrusts you into terror attacks and wars and murder investigations and drug busts, and it drops dying children on your family room floor. You see the world's problems but become blind to the dangers most likely to do *you* in.

But get this: *You* are the biggest threat to you. The biggest factor in the safety and success of your future is how well *you* follow God's pattern for life. A night stalker crawling in through your window is far less a real threat than *you* crawling out at night, losing your moral and spiritual footing, and falling off the roof.

Growing up won't get easier. Yet when you trust in God you become a well-watered tree that doesn't fear when heat comes (Jeremiah 17:8). You not only survive, but you thrive—and get a chance to fix the world's nasty problems.

Wisdom will save you from the ways of wicked men.
PROVERBS 2:12

Nick Meets Dawn

"I guess we're partners. My name is Dawn."

Duh. I know who you are. Did you know that every guy in the grade likes you? "Hi. I'm Nick."

Dawn didn't have the best reputation. Everyone said she drank a lot. Everyone knew her boyfriend sold drugs out of his locker. *But she's beautiful. That stuff can't be true.*

One day when they were working together Nick needed Dawn's attention. He tapped her arm. His finger practically sizzled. Her arm was the softest thing he had ever felt! And once she grabbed his hand. "I'd be failing if it weren't for you" she said. "Thanks. You're really nice." Sweet—except Nick would be a corpse by morning if Dawn's boyfriend caught him looking twice at her.

But Nick decided he wanted a girlfriend just like Dawn.

Read Proverbs 6:23–29

What's the biggest reason we get lured into doing wrong?

The toughest temptations you face nearly always have a *face*.

But you aren't tempted by a flea-infested drug dealer driving a beat-up car. The people who tempt you have *cool* faces. They have *caring* faces. They laugh at your jokes. They think you're smart. They understand how you think and feel. They spend time with you.

In order to stay friends, you're tempted to do whatever they want—throwing out God's commands by ranking on the class dork, joining in at the party, dating a non-Christian, blowing off school, or blowing up at your parents. It feels right when you think those faces are cool and caring.

But coolness isn't a perfect complexion or clothes or car. And caring isn't about making you feel right when you're doing wrong. In a warped way pimps care for prostitutes and people care for their dogs. That doesn't mean you want to be a hooker or a hound.

Who's cool? Who cares for you? People who guide you into wisdom, watch to protect you, and remind you to stay on God's paths.

When you walk, they will guide you; when you sleep, they will watch over you; when you awake, they will speak to you. For these commands are a lamp. PROVERBS 6:22-23

Grumpy Burgers

"Emily, what's this?" Emily's boss holds open a cheeseburger. A line of ketchup forms a bright red smile, with two blops of mustard for the eyes.

"That's a happy face."

"See the sign? This is *Grumpy Burgers*. We don't do happy faces."

"I was just being creative," Emily explains. "Don't customers get bored with food that looks the same every time?"

"No. It's burger, onion, cheese on top, pickle, ketchup, mustard. In that order. Ketchup here, mustard there. Is that too hard for you?"

"Got it." Emily straightens her hat and dresses burgers oh-so-properly—until boredom hits again. Instead of smiley faces she makes frowny faces.

"Emily!" her boss yells a few minutes later. "What is *this*?"

Mr. Grumpy isn't amused.

Read Romans 13:1–2
Why would you want to do what people in charge say you should?

If you work for a jerk you could drop burgers on the floor, spit in the soda, and blow your nose in the French-fry vat. Or if a teacher goes demented you could ditch school, break every rule, and work hard to make him or her look like a fool.

But think twice. Bosses hire and fire. Teachers give grades. Police have handcuffs, tear gas, and jail cells. Acting up can land you on the wrong side of the boss, the principal, or the law.

But dodging the punishment that authorities dispense on evildoers is only half of why the Bible says you should submit to them—why you should obey them. Here's the other half: Authority is God's idea. He designed a world where bosses have bosses, teachers have principals, police have chiefs—and all answer to him. Without leaders containing us we would clobber each other.

Sometimes bosses and other authorities go ballistic over ketchup blops. But the only thing worse than living in a world where everyone seems to boss you around would be living in a world where no one does.

Consequently, he who rebels against the authority is rebelling against what God has instituted, and those who do so will bring judgment on themselves.... ROMANS 13:2

Time Warped

Fast forward your life twenty-five years.

You stare at your home computer, reviewing your monthly family finances. It looked simpler when you were little and your parents sat down with a stack of bills and the checkbook at the kitchen table.

"Honey, I don't know how we can do this!" you vent. "The mortgage, the car payment, and Becky's orthodontist bill are due at the same time. We can either live in the street or go hungry. Which would you prefer?" For the next three hours you and your spouse discuss ways to increase income and cut expenses.

What's the moral of the story? That you should rent a tent, ride bikes, and throw back any children with crooked teeth?

Nope. It's that no one is going to pay your bills for you.

Read Proverbs 6:6–11
Why work hard?

Whenever you just get by you always get behind. You might think you can take shortcuts on your schoolwork, for example—and flip to the back of the book to find the right answer. But you'll hit the fan when you take a test.

The admissions office at Harvard won't ask how you did in eighth-grade math. But they'll be able to guess. What you study now prepares you for high school, which fits you for even more serious stuff. If you waste away in middle school you'll be three years behind students who decided not to dangle on the edge of disaster.

When God gives you school, chores, or other jobs to do, learn to work *now* "with all your heart, as working for the Lord, not for men, since you know that you will receive an inheritance from the Lord as a reward. It is the Lord Christ you are serving" (Colossians 3:23–24).

You don't have to manage cars, kids, braces, bosses, bills, houses, or hassles for a while.

But you're in training.

Go to the ant, you sluggard; consider its ways and be wise!
It has no commander, no overseer or ruler, yet it
stores its provisions. PROVERBS 6:6-8

First Things First

"Anyone else do their homework?" Silence.

Mike's cool, Nicole thought. Her Sunday school teacher never blew up at the class, even though no one except two nerds in the front row ever handed in homework.

Nicole shyly held up her paper. "Mine's done." She slumped in her seat. *I am not a nerd*, she reassured herself. *Then again, maybe I am turning into a nerd. Or maybe the nerds aren't so nerdy.* All Nicole knew for sure was that she felt better when she read her Bible and talked to God, like Mike taught in class.

Anita grilled her after class. "I can't believe you actually did the homework. What's wrong with you? Don't you have anything better to do?"

"I don't know. I've done the last few. I might as well turn them in."

Then it occurred to Nicole that maybe she wasn't the one with a problem. "Don't *you* ever think about God?" she asked Anita.

Read Luke 10:38–42

What does Jesus say you need more than anything else?

You've seen the symptoms of terminal adulthood: sleepy reflexes. Saggy clothes. Not to mention petrification—brains as dense as rock. Or putrefaction—rotting attitudes.

The middle part of *adult*, you note, is *dull*. No one wants that.

But Mary—along with a bunch of other men and women in the Bible—shows how to mature without getting moldy. Mary's kind of stillness won't mellow you prematurely.

It's hard to talk to a friend when you're sprinting. You can't converse while blasting a hill on a mountain bike. If you want to get to know a friend there's no substitute for slowing down—talking over a gooey pizza or lounging next to a glassy lake or flopping on your bed with the phone.

Jesus wants you to be like Mary, to slow down and spend time with him. By reading his Word—the Bible—you "sit at his feet" and hear *from* him. By praying—by telling him what you think and feel, what you like about him, asking for his help—you can talk *to* him.

It's one kind of sitting still that doesn't mean you're dull.

She had a sister called Mary, who sat at the Lord's feet
listening to what he said. LUKE 10:39

Don't Waste Yourself

Brandon had made sure everyone knew: No socks or underwear this year. Just cash. *I hope they put the money they saved on bows and paper into the card.* A card from his parents. *Cash!* One from Aunt Bertha. *Cash!* He ripped into the rest. *Cash! Cash! Cash!*

In the end, Brandon had more money than he'd ever assembled in one spot, a tad more than the $128.38 he needed for a new video game deck.

Brandon headed for the mall but stalled at a carnival that had landed outside. He spotted a toss-the-football-through-the-tire game with you-know-what as a prize: the game deck. Twelve misses later Brandon went a few rounds on the *Whirl and Hurl* ride to prove he was still a real man. Brandon finally stepped into the mall, only to realize he no longer had enough money for the game deck.

He panicked. Before he knew what happened, he was back outside the mall, staring into a bag stuffed with a Thighmaster and a sixty-seven-piece ice-fishing ensemble autographed by Wayne the Walleye Guy.

He was broke. And not too bright.

Read Proverbs 2:6–11
What good is God's wisdom?

If you dash through a mall with a wad of cash bulging in your pocket—noseprinting windows, testing toys, trying on clothes, all with no plan of action—you might as well wear a button that says, "Rob me. I'm stupid." It's better to think, pray, decide, and attack. Get distracted and you'll be disappointed. Choose on the fly and later you'll regret it.

Now, you have something a lot more valuable than any birthday hoard or your savings from mowing lawns or sitting babies: your life. God wants you to spend your time and talents well. He won't leave you to panic. If you cry out for understanding, he'll give you all you need: "wisdom" (an ability to live skillfully), "knowledge" (brain capacity and insight into right and wrong), and "discretion" (being able to pick rightly between two actions or ideas). He'll keep you from wasting yourself in the mall of life.

For the Lord gives wisdom, and from his mouth come knowledge and understanding. He holds victory in store for the upright, he is a shield to those whose walk is blameless.
PROVERBS 2:6-7

Your Hand Looks Dead

The last time Lauren raised her hand to ask a question in class, her science teacher said her hand resembled something dead he had dissected in college. Lauren cringed and slipped both hands under her desk. When everyone had stopped snorting at Mr. Cooper's remark, she peeked at her hands. She flip-flopped them in her lap. They looked plenty alive to her.

Mr. Cooper had been mean to Lauren ever since she missed school for a week because of the flu. Even though she tried hard, she hadn't caught up. She was still a test behind the rest of the class, and Mr. Cooper was treating her like an idiot.

Now she needed help again. She couldn't decide whether to brace herself for another rude remark or to keep her mouth shut and fail more assignments.

Read James 1:5

How does God treat you when you ask for his help?

No one wants to look stupid or helpless. At school you would rather be bewildered than ask a teacher to explain the same point six times because you're still confused. At a party you would gladly cook all your CDs in an oven before you would admit that you don't know how to dance. And around home you would sooner get your head pounded inside out than let your mom fight off a bully for you.

Admitting to yourself that you need help takes guts. Actually asking for it is even harder.

Once you get up the courage, what you don't need is to be made to feel like a bonehead—like a teacher who treats you as though you're stupid in order to make you work harder. Or like a parent who roughs you up to make you tough for the real world. Or like an employer who never lets employees forget who's boss.

When you can't tell right from wrong, good from bad, or truth from lies, God has the answers. But knowing he's the Ultimate Brain doesn't do you any good if you fear he'll mock you for needing help.

God doesn't laugh. He doesn't scold. He helps.

If any of you lacks wisdom, he should ask God, who gives generously to all without finding fault, and it will be given to him. JAMES 1:5

Just in Case

Garrett knew that three months ago he could have asked God to show him how to survive Mrs. Weston's history class. He still wasn't sure, though, that he wanted to hear what God might have to say. So instead he whipped off a prayer at the end of his twelve-minute cram session the night before the final exam: "God, please make me do well on my history test tomorrow. I know you don't want me to flunk and develop poor self-esteem and spend my life sleeping in a gutter, so I trust you'll work on Mrs. Weston so I get an A. Thanks, God."

Praying made Garrett sure God would come through for him.

Well, not totally sure.

By the time Garrett started the test the next morning, he had figured a foolproof way to an A, in case God didn't deliver. Not only did Garrett have the encyclopedia of American history scribbled on his arm, but he had arranged to sit within easy eyeball range of the smartest kid in class. Between God, crib notes, and the son of Einstein, Garrett had things covered.

Read James 1:6–8
What's so bad about being "double-minded"?

If you constantly asked a friend for directions to her house—but always took your own route and then complained about getting lost—she would give up trying to tell you the way. Likewise, God knows that unless you're ready to listen and obey, showing you truth is useless.

God enthusiastically gives wisdom (James 1:5) to anyone who asks. He expects you to trust his desire and ability to answer your request. He expects you to believe him enough to act on the truth he shows you—to follow his directions, to walk his way, to do what he says.

Faith trusts. Doubt hatches backup plans. Double-mindedness picks and chooses. Part of you wants God's truth, part of you doesn't. Part of you wants to obey, part of you won't.

Don't assume that means you need flawless faith before God will answer you. No human being trusts perfectly. What God wants is a faith that shouts, "I do believe. Help me to believe more!" (Mark 9:24 NCV).

He who doubts is like a wave of the sea, blown and tossed by the wind. That man should not think he will receive anything from the Lord; he is a double-minded man. JAMES 1:6-8

Wasted Waiting

Andrew inspected his list: Three months of clean socks and underwear. *Check.* Extra toothpaste. *Check.* Razor and shaving cream in case of an unexpected sprouting of facial hair. *Check, check.* Skip the deodorant. *Uncheck.* He'd be alone on his quest.

It would be a long wait. But he was ready.

Andrew set out early one Saturday morning at the beginning of summer vacation. He figured he should climb a mountain, but he lived in southern Minnesota. He did the best he could. He found a high spot in a nearby cornfield and set up camp. After he pitched his tent he carefully arranged cornstalks so they spelled "HELP!" when viewed from above.

Andrew wasn't waiting to be seen by a search plane. He was waiting for God—for a vision, a dream, a lightning bolt, a talking bush. He didn't care which. He wanted God to speak to him, to tell him the secret of life.

Don't worry. Finding God's truth isn't that hard.

Read Psalm 119:9–16

Where do you go to hear God's voice?

You can find truth in lots of places. God lets you learn from parents whose heads aren't empty and from grandparents and other older people whose lives have been full. He allows you to study history so you don't repeat people's mistakes and to learn about science and the arts so you won't be stupid about your world. Sometimes you can learn from liars and lunatics.

But the Bible's truth is unique. It is "inspired by God." (Second Timothy 3:16 literally says it is "God-breathed.") So its truth is completely flawless. The Bible is a measurement for everything else that claims to be true—a friend's words, a musician's lyrics, a Web page, an author's ideas, a screenwriter's view of life. It corrects you when you're wrong and encourages you when you're right. God designed the Bible for you to read and apply with other believers so you can discover him and understand yourself and your world. It's how you get smart and steer clear of sin.

Scripture is God's perfect, reliable, written word. It's the first test of whom to listen to.

I have hidden your word in my heart that I might not sin against you. PSALM 119:11

But He Said He Loves Me

Wendy curled up on the living room couch to watch out the front window. She jumped at every passing car, and told herself that the snowy weather had made her father late. But he was already two hours overdue, and a dark thought crept into her head: *He's not coming.*

A few days earlier Wendy had received a letter from her biological father apologizing for running out on her and her mom ten years before. He promised to start spending time with his daughter. Wendy's mom warned her not to expect much, but Wendy's hopes ran wild. She was going to see her father again!

Now she sat staring out the window, blinking away her tears. *But he said he was sorry,* she told herself. *He said he loves me.*

She fell asleep waiting for her father, who never showed up.

Read 1 Corinthians 13:1–3
What does love have to do with truth?

It's hard not to believe in a parent who wants to come back and make things right. Any time *anyone* promises you something you really want, it's hard not to believe them.

But words aren't worth trusting if they aren't backed up by loving actions. From the Bible's point of view, truth is more than promises or bare facts or correct thoughts. Truth is something *lived.* Like 1 John 3:18 says, "Dear children, let us stop just saying we love each other; let us really show it by our actions" (NLT).

Truth without love is like poison in a Popsicle: sweet but deadly.

Scripture is the first test of truth. Love is the second. People worth trusting aren't necessarily the ones who know the most but the ones who combine knowledge with real-life love. People who love as God loves are the ones who have grasped truth.

You can't escape people whose brains are bigger than their hearts, but you can avoid being duped by them. Beware: Without love, words are worthless.

If I have the gift of prophecy and can fathom all mysteries and all knowledge ... but have not love, I am nothing.
1 CORINTHIANS 13:2

A Barf Bag Parachute

You settle into your seat. The flight attendant starts to rattle off the safety instructions. *Spare me*, you think. *Let's get this birdie in the air.* Just as she begins her speech, though, you interrupt and ask her why the plane is taking off late.

"Oh," she says, "we had an itsy bit of trouble getting a door shut. I think I fixed it." THE DOOR? your head explodes. YOU HAD A PROBLEM WITH A DOOR? YOU *THINK* YOU FIXED IT?! A few days earlier the same kind of plane dropped a door midflight and sixteen passengers were sucked out of the plane.

Your attention rivets on the flight attendant as she discusses sudden loss of cabin pressure and using your seat cushion as a flotation device. When she points to the plane's exits, you take it as a message from God. Better to deplane now than to skydive from forty thousand feet using your barf bag as a parachute.

Read Matthew 7:15-20
How can you spot a good person?

When you board a plane you assume it's been tested, retested and re-retested by someone who knows what to look for. Unfortunately, no one tests mouths for truthfulness. And that's a problem: Anyone can fake truthfulness for a while.

So Jesus suggests another test of truth. Scripture is your first test, and love is the second. But here's the third: consistency. Jesus says people's lives are like trees. Watching what people produce over time shows their real nature. An athlete's approach to life may seem fast and cool until he charges for autographs or beats his wife. Time makes it clear he's not what he seems to be. He's a skillful player, but he's not someone you want to act, talk, think, or smell like.

You wouldn't get on a plane if you thought it would crash. Why take death-defying risks with who you listen to? A plane ride lasts a few hours. Who you listen to affects your whole life. You're safest with people who are probably already around you—youth leaders, Christian friends, parents—people who have *proven* that they speak truth and love you like God does.

By their fruit you will recognize them.... Every good tree bears good fruit, but a bad tree bears bad fruit. MATTHEW 7:16-17

Stargazing

As she did every morning, Julia grabbed her favorite section of the newspaper out from under her dad's coffee mug. She couldn't start her day without reading her horoscope. Most days it read like the notes her mom tucked in her lunch box when she was little: *You'll have a happy day if you're nice to everyone.* But Julia relied on her 'scope to guide her life.

Once a speaker told her youth group that horoscopes were demonic, but she kept reading them religiously. If they didn't make her foam at the mouth or encourage her to kill her family with an ax, she didn't see anything wrong with them.

Horoscopes—like Ouija boards, Magic 8-Balls, divination (foretelling future events), witchcraft, spells, psychics, tarot cards, palm readers, contacting the dead, and channeling spirits—are attempts to tap into special supernatural power and knowledge that's hidden ("occult") from normal human senses (Deuteronomy 18:10-12).

Read Acts 19:13—20

What did the early believers do about their occult practices?

You could make a lot of touchdowns if you hid the ball in a sack, snuck out of bounds, climbed through the stands, and dashed into the end zone. Trying to find a shortcut to truth might be just as tempting. It might even work. But it wouldn't be wise if the stands were full of enemy fans ready to tear your head off.

God has ruled certain sources of knowledge out of bounds, a danger zone. It's obvious why. The seven sons of Sceva discovered that the evil spirits sitting in the stands are nothing to fool around with. The early believers admitted to God that they had stepped way out of bounds, and then they trashed many millions of dollars of occult materials.

Some occult practices are scams. Others call on dangerous satanic spirits. What's really wrong with the occult, though, is that it seeks advice and help from God's archenemy, Satan. That's not just dangerous. It's pointless. God never hides truth from his friends.

A number who had practiced sorcery brought their scrolls together and burned them publicly. When they calculated the value of the scrolls, the total came to fifty thousand drachmas.
ACTS 19:19

Get Smart

Justin dreaded seventh-grade gym class—mostly using the locker room. After a few weeks, though, he decided the locker room wasn't so bad—especially when the guys talked about girls. The hot topics sizzled his ears. He knew what they said wasn't good, but it was funny—like their plans to drill a peephole into the girls' locker room.

Justin had never had a girlfriend, but he started talking as if he had a lot of experience. The talk didn't stop in the locker room. Instead of talking *about* girls, Justin started talking that way *to* girls. He joked about what he wanted to do with them. The more he talked, the more he wanted. And the more he wanted, the more he tried to get it.

Read 1 Kings 11:1–11

Why did ultrawise Solomon lose his love for God?

News programs are full of I'm-not-that-stupid stories: Flood victims who perched too long on a housetop. Bodies charred because people didn't think a forest fire would reach them. Drivers dead because they assumed alcohol wouldn't affect them. They underestimated the danger.

You would never do that. Or would you?

If anyone had a right to say, "I'm too smart for that," it was Solomon, the wisest man in the world (1 Kings 3:12) and the son of Israel's most godly king. Yet Solomon's foreign wives pulled him into what he knew was wrong. He built temples to foreign gods, where idols were worshiped through prostitution and child sacrifice. Even Solomon wasn't smart enough. He listened to lies. He lost his love for God.

You're surrounded by a world that tells you lies, pulling you from God and his ways: *Adults are stupid. Money equals happiness. Trendy clothes and a perfect body make you supreme. Sex is a sport without rules. Treating people like trash doesn't stink.*

You want to think that you're wise enough to outwit the voices thumping your ears. But as soon as you think you're that smart, you're guaranteed to find out how stupid you can be (1 Corinthians 10:12).

As Solomon grew old, his wives turned his heart after other gods, and his heart was not fully devoted to the Lord his God.
1 KINGS 11:4

Morning Breath

You wouldn't think of facing your friends without scrutinizing your looks in a mirror.

You inspect your hair (to decide if it's a hat day).

You search for facial fuzz and ponder whether to save it or shave it (unless you're a girl—then you scream).

You take a pimple population census (to determine whether to go back to bed).

What you see in the mirror in the morning—good, bad, or utterly ugly—is seared in your brain for the rest of the day.

Looking in the mirror is a serious endeavor. And you don't just gawk. When your breath creates a green fog on the mirror, you make friends with your toothbrush. When light glares off your shiny nose, you get chummy with the soap. When your hair looks like your mom's high-school graduation photo, you get a grip on a blow-dryer and start repairing.

Basically, you do something about what you see.

Read James 1:22–25

What does it mean to totally pay attention to God's words?

Hearing God's voice by reading the Bible is like looking in a mirror that reflects perfectly everything you need to see about yourself and your world—what's great and what needs to change. God's Word lets you see yourself and everything else as God sees it: truthfully.

But *hearing* is only the first part of listening to God. *Doing* is the second part.

Paying attention to God means looking into the mirror of God's Word and responding to what you see. When you *listen* and *do* you will "be blessed." You'll find safety and freedom as you stay close to God.

God is the one Being in the universe who is totally powerful, totally smart, and totally loving. He's the One you can trust to be totally honest with you.

He's the One to listen to. And he's the One to obey.

Do not merely listen to the word, and so deceive yourselves.
Do what it says. JAMES 1:22

You're So Gullible

Matt saw the four-foot stuffed animal hanging in the carnival booth and knew that dog would win him Amber's love, at least for a day. All he had to do was shoot balloons with a BB gun. What could be easier?

"Everyone wins a prize!" the lady in the booth hollered. Matt unwadded a dollar bill and headed for the booth. His older brother knuckled him on the head.

"You're so gullible," Todd lectured. "It's a rip-off. See how you get three shots and then get a different gun? If you hit too many balloons you get a gun that doesn't shoot straight."

The lady running the game saw Todd whispering and pointing. "Hey, kid!" she yelled as they wandered to other games. "You chicken or something? If you're so good, get over here and show everyone."

You don't need a knuckle on your noggin to know that carnies don't run their games purely for your enjoyment. They want your money. They'll say whatever it takes to get you to play their games. But it's an uncheery thought to realize a carnival isn't the only place you're forced to sort truth from falsehood.

Read Isaiah 59:1–11

What are people like when they don't listen to and obey God?

Truth can be hard to find. Peers fib behind your back and then to your face. Sports stars inflate their images to sell you the goods. Musicians and media distort, deceive, and mislead. And if you hadn't noticed, even people who want to be honest with you make mistakes. There's one fact you can be sure of: People don't always tell the truth.

Without God changing our minds and words, people naturally follow the "ruler of the kingdom of the air" (Ephesians 2:2), who is the "father of lies" (John 8:44). Truth gets lost and life becomes a sticky spider's web, a shadowy darkness, a confusing carnival.

It would be nice to think you could accept as true anything that people tell you. But don't plunk down your money until you understand how the game is played.

Your lips have spoken lies, and your tongue mutters wicked things. ISAIAH 59:3-4

School Pictures

Merri opened her envelope of school pictures and gasped. Her hair looked more tortured than teased, her left eye was half shut, and her face looked like she had rammed her nose against the camera lens.

Her friend Brandi pretended to hide her own packet. Merri grabbed it, hoping someone else's picture looked as bad.

"Promise not to laugh, okay?" Brandi begged Merri. "I look awful!" Yeah right. Brandi's photo glowed like a model's, and Brandi knew it.

Brandi pulled out Merri's picture. "Ooooh. Merri, Merri," she said sadly. She handed the packet back. "I'm so sorry. Bad hair day, huh?"

That night in her room Merri studied her face in a mirror, wondering one thing: *Do I really look like my school picture?*

Read Psalm 139:23–24

How do you get an accurate picture of yourself?

If you actually looked as doofy as most school pictures, Congress would have passed a law to make you wear a paper sack over your head long before now. But that doesn't mean that some days you won't feel like a poster child for Uglies Anonymous.

Yet if you can't trust a photograph, how do you find out what you really look like on the outside—or more importantly, on the inside?

People's opinions can be wrong. An enemy won't paint a pretty picture: "Whadja do to your hair?" or "Nobody likes you" or "You priss." The portrait friends paint of you can be just the opposite—*too* pretty, like an airbrushed photo with all the zits gone: "It wasn't your fault at all" or "You're a perfect friend" or "Don't ever change."

The writer of Psalm 139 knew that only God—who knows us inside and out, even better than we know ourselves—sees us the way we really are. He prayed that God would examine his words, attitudes, and actions and show him the ugly parts of his life. Then God could make those parts better.

Being happy with yourself and being willing to let God fix the uglies starts only when you see yourself honestly.

Get it? It's God's view of you that's true.

Search me, O God, and know my heart; test me and know my anxious thoughts. See if there is any offensive way in me, and lead me in the way everlasting. PSALM 139:23-24

No More Doggy Bags

Sheena growled inside as she watched the kids at the park pick teams. *Those kids make me so mad! They always leave out the little ones.* When Sheena was small she always got picked last. When she got bigger she never got picked at all.

But now she could do something about it. What Sheena loved about her volunteer summer job at the park was helping the shy and small kids who got stomped on like she always did. She couldn't play ball—especially not with the kids who were almost her age—but she did know how to take the bunch who didn't get picked and start a whompin' good game of kickball.

Sheena glanced at the ball diamond and then at her little kickballers. They weren't leftovers. And neither was she.

Read 1 Corinthians 12:14–21
We're all different—is that good or bad?

You might glance around and conclude you're in a league by yourself. You're the first, the best, the greatest, the latest. *Too vain.* Or you might lean to the other extreme—you're a wretched slime, a leftover. *Downright warped.*

Your body wouldn't work if every part were the same. An ear can't see. An eye can't hear. You don't walk on your hands or eat with your feet. No part is better. None is a spare.

God put Christians together as the "body of Christ." We can't function without the gifts God packs into each of us—gifts of serving, teaching, leading, encouraging, and a bundle of other abilities. (Ephesians 4:11–16 and Romans 12:3–8 list even more gifts.) And gifts don't work just in church. What God has built into you shows up at home, school, when you work, and with friends.

Slamming others because they lack the gifts you have is like hacking off your hand. And hiding who *you* are is like lashing your other hand behind your back. Neither is smart—unless you like to feed your face with your footsies.

Now the body is not made up of one part but of many. If the foot should say, "Because I am not a hand, I do not belong to the body," it would not for that reason cease to be part of the body. 1 CORINTHIANS 12:14-15

Masterpiece

"Brandon! Jeremy! Tadd! Andy!" The cabin counselor jarred his campers awake. "Get dressed, gentlemen, we're going for a hike." At first the guys wondered why Jason was rousing them at three in the morning on the last night of camp. Then they worried about what he might have planned to retaliate for their obnoxiousness that week.

The four of them stumbled through the forest behind Jason until they stopped at the shore of a lake. The sky had exploded with stars.

Jason told them to sit down and enjoy the view. It was the first time they had shut up all week. "Makes you feel small, doesn't it?" Jason asked after a few minutes. The guys stayed quiet. Jason waited a bit before he said more. "God painted an incredible sky, didn't he? But it's nothing compared to what God made when he sculpted you. You guys need to stop acting like dirtballs. That's not who you are."

Read Psalm 8:1–9
What does God think of the people he made?

Bragging—that your high jumps are higher, your grades greater, your clothes classier, your looks more luscious—is pointless: God owns everything. He's the best at everything. And we don't have anything good that didn't come from him (1 Corinthians 4:7). Compared to God, the Maker and Master of everything, we're tiny mudsplats.

Yet that isn't how God thinks about human beings. He created us so that we would reflect his greatness the way the moon—which makes no light of its own—reflects the light of the sun. He gave each of us the privilege of knowing, obeying, and worshiping him, the God of the universe. He made human beings responsible for ruling our world.

Those aren't jobs he would give to mudsplats.

You probably look at stuff you make—a clay pot in art class, a napkin holder from shop, a report for English—and think it's stupid. But God was very pleased when he made you (Genesis 1:31).

So you're more than mud. You're God's masterpiece.

When I consider your heavens, the work of your fingers, the moon and the stars, which you have set in place, what is man that you are mindful of him? PSALM 8:3–4

Nowhere to Hide

No. Your stomach knots. *They didn't.* You were only gone a minute. *No!* *They couldn't have!* They did. They left without you.

Everyone from the school ski club had loaded up to go skiing, but you figured you had time to run to the bathroom. When you came out, everyone had left. Not one person missed you.

What do I do now? I could call home and congratulate Dad and Mom on being proud parents of a reject—maybe the school has a bumper sticker they can put on the van to tell everyone. No, wait. I could roll outside in the snow, get all wet, hide in the bathroom for the next six hours, and emerge just as everyone gets back. If I play it right, I can make everyone believe I went with them. Yeah, that's the plan.

Read Psalm 139:1–10
Where can you go to hide from God when you feel dumb and dumpy?

God always has his eye on you, but sometimes you don't want to be seen.

You might be terrified to realize that God knows everything you think, hears everything you say, and sees everything you do. You might feel like a criminal suspect—bugged, followed, and photographed by the FBI—or like a convict tracked by a radio transmitter welded to his ankle. Nowhere to hide.

It doesn't have to feel that way.

God's knowing you totally means he always knows where you are. He knows trivial things like the weight of the lint in your belly button and the progress of the pimple you've been tracking. It also means he knows huge things like your problems, hurts, and needs. Because God knows you completely, he can guide you with perfect wisdom. Because God is everywhere, you can rest in his protection.

God isn't the FBI, tracking your every move to catch you slipping up. Or Santa Claus making a list and checking it twice. God doesn't spy. He cares. He says that you matter, especially to him.

He's the best friend who's always right beside you. He'll never drive off without you.

You know when I sit and when I rise; you perceive my thoughts from afar. You discern my going out and my lying down; you are familiar with all my ways. PSALM 139:2-3

Yee-haw

Through thin walls Brittni heard what she wasn't supposed to hear. The school counselor told her parents that if Brittni's work didn't improve by the end of the year, she would have to repeat the grade.

Her parents' response burned in her mind. "We realize she's had problems," they apologized. "She's a little slow."

Slow? Brittni thought. *Why don't they just call me "stupid."*

At that moment—and forever—Brittni decided she would never let anyone say she was dumb ever again. She started studying with a flashlight under her blankets late at night and setting her alarm for 5 A.M. She wanted the highest grade in every class. A 95 wasn't good enough; she chewed herself out for not scoring 100.

Read John 4:34

What should you pick as the biggest goal of your life?

You probably like being laughed at: *You waddle when you run. You wear that shirt all the time. Your answer was stupid. You sweat buckets when you talk in front of class.*

Probably not.

Nothing is wrong with wanting to run faster, score higher, dress neater, or speak sweeter. There's a problem, though, if you think that winning the race, making your hair look perfect, or never wearing the same outfit twice makes you valuable and acceptable to yourself, to others, or to God.

Jesus knew that there was one great goal in life—and that if he kept that purpose in mind, everything else would fall into place. His big aim was to do exactly what his Father wanted, his "will." Jesus set his heart on nothing else. And the same goes for us. Ranking any goal higher than doing God's will is settling for less-than-best.

There's a problem if you make anything but the Father's will matter more than anything else: You've stopped chasing a good goal, and instead you're *being chased*—by a wild-eyed cowboy wielding a sizzling branding iron. When you think that brains, bucks, and beauty are the most important things you could ever possess, you know you've been branded with an attitude that doesn't come from God. You've been burned.

"My food," said Jesus, "is to do the will of him who sent me and to finish his work." JOHN 4:34

The Sign

A cold night rain pelts the rebel encampment outside the king's palace. You and a dozen other guerrillas warm yourself near a fire, waiting for your only meal of the day—tree bark soup.

Years of fighting have made you both tough and tired. Through the palace gates you can see bright lights and hear what sounds like a party. A sign on the gate reads *WELCOME. LEAVE YOUR WEAPONS OUTSIDE. ROYAL FEAST AT MIDNIGHT. COME EARLY.*

"What do you think the sign means?" you wonder out loud.

"It's exactly what we're fighting against," your commander hisses. "The sign is a lie! The king hates us. Why else would we be out here starving?"

"So why aren't the gates locked?" you ask.

"It's a trick. A trap." Your commander's bitterness makes you shiver. "You're not starting to believe the sign, are you?" He swings his automatic rifle around and shreds the sign with a spray of bullets. "Tomorrow we try again to storm the palace."

Read Psalm 5:4–8

What does God think of people who rebel against him?

Some enemies of God are easy to spot, as though they carry bazookas. Their wrongdoing—their sin—is obvious: They fight, kill, lie, or steal. They misuse sex. They disobey parents and beat up brothers and sisters. Or they hurt their own bodies by drinking or abusing drugs.

The sins of other people are harder to see. Even nice people with polite outsides, the Bible says, can have rotted insides. They may have a bad attitude toward God—by refusing to bow before his greatness or to applaud his absolute goodness. People make their own plans for life and mistrust God's wisdom. By that standard, God says that *all* human beings have messed up and sinned—including you. We're all rebels (Romans 3:23).

God can't stand evil. As rebels we have been kicked out of the palace (Genesis 3:22–24). But God doesn't hate us. He wants us close to him. And it's our own fault if we stay out in the cold, because God has created a way to welcome us back in.

Drop your weapons and come inside for the party.

You are not a God who takes pleasure in evil. PSALM 5:4

Inside the Palace

Outside the king's palace you wake to see the same sign that your commander had shot up during the night: *WELCOME. LEAVE YOUR WEAPONS OUTSIDE. ROYAL FEAST AT MIDNIGHT. COME EARLY.* It's freshly painted, the bullet holes gone. You spook when you see the king walking around the palace gardens with tools in hand. *The king himself fixed the sign.*

Suddenly you understand that the rebels are wrong. You slip off your firearms and ammo belt and bolt through the gate toward the king.

You had been told that land mines would mutilate anyone inside the king's gate, but when you reach the king you realize you haven't been blown apart. "The sign—" you gasp, out of breath. "It's true, isn't it?"

"It is," the king replies. "Welcome. I've been waiting for you."

Read Colossians 1:21–23
How can you stop being a rebel against God?

You probably don't try hard to be buddies with your enemies. But that's exactly what God has done. Even though the human race wasn't interested in a truce, God opened a gate back to himself through Christ (Romans 5:8).

We've all made ourselves God's enemies, deserving death—total separation from God—for our sins (Romans 6:23). Yet God sent Jesus as the welcome sign, your invitation to enter the palace of King God, and the gate back to God. You accept God's invitation by putting down your weapons, by admitting to him your sinfulness and need for his forgiveness: "God, you're King of the universe. I've rebelled against you by what I think, say, and do. My rebellion deserves death, but I know now that Christ died in my place." That's how you bolt through the gate back to the King. That's the beginning of being a Christian.

When you accept Christ's death for you, God says you're welcome back in his palace as his son or daughter. You've been "reconciled," made friends again. Your friendship with God and other believers starts now—and lasts forever in heaven.

The sign is true. It's up to you to respond. Are you still a rebel, or have you gone through the gate and become a child of the King?

Once you were alienated from God and were enemies in your minds because of your evil behavior. But now he has reconciled you. COLOSSIANS 1:21-22

At Our Ugliest

Mitch Stetson became quarterback when his coach discovered Mitch didn't need an offensive line. He was three years ahead of his time, so much bigger and better than the other boys in his grade that he could fend off opponents with one hand while he bulleted rib-busting passes with the other.

Mitch was the most popular person in school. Boys imitated the way he combed his hair at the rest room mirror. Girls gawked when he walked, spinning around quickly when he looked their way so he wouldn't catch them staring.

Then he got zits.

His face erupted into a million red, oozing volcanoes. Girls turned away to avoid gagging at Lavaface. Boys found other friends. Coach replaced Mitch with someone bigger and better. And one day Mitch stopped looking in mirrors. Even he couldn't stand to look at himself.

Read Romans 5:6–8

What can you do to make God look away and stop loving you?

Sometimes you feel like you have a blemish the size of a golf ball smack in the middle of your forehead, like a third eye. It's big. It's ugly. It's a flaw that makes you feel unlovable.

You might think you're stupid. You might hate how you look. Your flaw might be something you've done wrong or an embarrassing family situation. It might be a dark secret you hardly admit to yourself.

You might try to hide your faults from yourself, your friends, and your family, but you can't hide anything from God. He sees everything. And he still likes you.

He proved it. Not many people would die for a religious snob ("righteous" in Romans 5:7 probably means someone with right actions but a cold heart). A few people might give their life to save a good person or a friend. No one would think of dying for a reject, a flawed, sinful person, but God did. He proved his love for us by sending Christ to die for us not when we were perfect but at "just the right time," when we were at our worst.

God doesn't look away. Ever.

But God demonstrates his own love for us in this: While we were still sinners, Christ died for us. ROMANS 5:8

The Ultimate Coach

With bat in hand, the coach flipped a baseball into the air and hammered it toward right field. Rob backpedaled as fast as he could, but the ball still soared over his head and hit the ground before he reached it.

"GET IN HERE!" Coach bellowed, and Rob ran to home plate. "Who's going to get the ball if you don't, Robby?" Coach said sarcastically.

"No one, sir."

"Give me fifty. NOW!" Rob did fifty push-ups and ran back to right field. But then he missed a short pop-up, and a grounder skipped between his legs. It was a bad afternoon—lots of mistakes, lots of push-ups.

Read Romans 12:2
How does God change you for the better?

Every Christian starts out like a baseball player who needs to learn the basic skills of the game. Not one of us is perfect.

In fact, we need a *lot* of help. Without Christ, we have our caps pulled over our eyes. We stumble around unable to determine right from wrong—and we can't follow the ball of God's truth. We're out of shape—pretty much dead—and we've forgotten the sensation of God's life. We don't understand the game of life—we believe the lie that evil will make us outrageously happy, and we crave worse and worse things more and more.

God looks at us and says things have to change. When we come to Christ we put off evil thoughts and actions like a grimy, sweaty uniform and put on a new life created by God. That process starts when we become Christians, and it keeps on until we reach heaven.

And here's the good news: God isn't a nasty coach waiting for you to mess up so he can explode at you, kick you off the team, or punish you with push-ups while he looks on with a cruel grin. He works by changing the way you think and feel.

He gently remakes you from the inside out, teaching you that in the long run sin never makes you, him, or the rest of the world happy. Then you can respond to God out of love, not fear.

God respects you. He doesn't scream at you. He knows he built you a brain.

Do not conform any longer to the pattern of this world, but be transformed by the renewing of your mind. ROMANS 12:2

Bomb Squad

When the bus pulled to a stop in the tiny Texas-Mexico border town, Tiffany flew down the steps feeling like a cartoon superhero. She and twenty other supercharged junior highers were about to battle the forces of darkness—building houses as a way of demonstrating God's love.

Tiffany felt like a hero—that is, until her feet hit the ground. Then she didn't feel heroic at all. She wore jeans instead of blue tights and a T-shirt instead of a cape; her heart pounded with panic, and she remembered she couldn't speak Spanish. One whiff reminded her she was far from home. What was she thinking when she signed up for this?

Read Ephesians 2:8–10

What does God plan for you as a believer once you've accepted his "grace"—forgiveness through Christ?

Sinning isn't like flicking a firecracker that pops harmlessly on the ground. It's more like tossing a match at a truckload of dynamite, then sticking around to watch. You don't walk away in one piece. Some explosions—selfishness, jealousy, greed, anger—shred hearts one at a time. Other blasts—adultery, abuse, abortion, war, hunger—maim whole crowds.

Trusting in Christ's death for you makes you God's son or daughter. You don't deserve God's forgiveness—that's what the Bible calls "grace." But God doesn't plan for his children to just lounge around the palace.

Don't worry. God doesn't expect you to be a superhero.

He wants you on the bomb squad.

Your first mission is to let God help you love the people you see every day, so you defuse the explosives in your own life. Then you can start to befriend kids struggling at school, help older people in your neighborhood, teach kids at church, serve in the inner city, or go on a short-term mission trip. God will use you to prevent explosions and repair the damage sin has done to the world, by doing the things HE plans for you as a Christian.

You don't need special orders from headquarters. All believers are on the bomb squad. Just look around and get started. The bombs are everywhere.

For we are God's workmanship, created in Christ Jesus to do good works, which God prepared in advance for us to do.
EPHESIANS 2:10

He Has Plans for You

"Mom, I'd like to go hiking with Allison's youth group," Kristi said quietly. "It's right after school gets out. It's not very much money, and a bunch of people are going."

"You want to sign up for *what*?" Kristi's mom mocked. "Let me see that." She grabbed the brochure. "How far? In the mountains?"

"I know," Kristi pleaded. "I know it will be hard, but I want to try."

"Get that idea out of your fat little head," her mom spat. "You'd die out there. Who will roll your body back?" When her mom finished laughing she spat some more. "You know, this is just another one of your stupid ideas. You're useless. Maybe collapsing out in the woods would prove that to you. You'll *never* amount to anything."

It's awful to be declared worthless and tossed away. After all, even trash gets recycled. Even garbage has a future.

Read Jeremiah 29:11
How great is your future when you know God?

If you have no hope, you'll seek relief however you can find it—even in ways that bury you alive. You'll seek revenge—to show everyone how bad you can be.

When God's people were at their lowest low—taken as prisoners to a far-away land—God gave hope to people who felt like forgotten trash. They thought they were goners, but he had their future in mind. God had plans to make them flourish.

God doesn't promise to make you a bazillionaire or to snatch you from every sickness or hardship. Yet even when faith in God leads to tough times, a future with God is worth anticipating. Proverbs 3:5–6 puts it like this: "Trust in the LORD with all your heart and lean not on your own understanding; in all your ways acknowledge him, and he will make your paths straight."

You don't have to wait for God to fix your life. Your bright future starts now if you hang tight with him.

"For I know the plans I have for you," declares the LORD, "plans to prosper you and not to harm you, plans to give you hope and a future." JEREMIAH 29:11

She's Ki Nda Kyut

"Don't look." Mitch nudged Ryan. "She's after you again."

Ryan knew exactly who "she" was: Ki Nda Kyut, a new student at school. Wherever Ryan went, Ki Nda was there grinning at him.

"She wants to marry you," Mitch bugged. Ryan slugged.

Ki Nda did stare at Ryan a lot. Ryan didn't mind. Then rumors flew that Ryan liked Ki Nda Kyut. *That* Ryan minded. "You have to ditch her," Mitch warned him. "Don't you know that no one likes her? Everyone likes her sister, Ree Li."

So one day when Ki Nda was trailing him to class he yelled at her. "Quit following me!" Ki Nda ran off crying. She never looks at Ryan anymore.

But Ryan still thinks she's kind of cute.

Read Proverbs 30:18–19

Exactly why do guys and girls fall in total love?

The girls used to run from the boys. Now they chase them. Guys were afraid of girl germs. Now they want to get sick. True, some girls are still uninterested in boys and some guys still use girls as booger targets. That's okay. Sooner or later a trickle of curiosity about the opposite sex turns into a flood of fascination. How are you going to handle that?

Love is easy to appreciate but hard to understand. It's like a restaurant that everyone agrees has great food but where everyone picks a different favorite dish. Guys and girls are attracted to each other in baffling ways, like an eagle floating through the sky, a legless snake slithering across a rock, or a ship navigating the sea.

You never totally figure it out.

But it's time to start trying. You'll drown if you don't know that God has definite plans for how he wants you to get along with the opposite sex.

God isn't bashful. The Bible is blunt. And the parts of the Bible that talk about how girls and guys should get along weren't scribbled in by monks stuck at the monastery without a date. They were composed by the One who comprehends love best (1 John 4:7-8).

There are four things that are too mysterious for me to understand: an eagle flying in the sky, a snake moving on a rock, a ship finding its way over the sea, and a man and a woman falling in love. PROVERBS 30:18–19 TEV

Teased at the Table

"Conner and Cassie sitting in a tree, K-I-S-S-I-N-G..." sasses Jenni across the supper table. "I saw them holding hands at the park."

"Dad, make her stop," Cassandra begs. "I said it nice. I didn't say 'Shut up!'"

"What's this?" her mother smirks as she pulls out a crumpled note. "I have a little evidence *I* found in the pocket of Cassie's jeans. It says here, 'I love you, Conner.' With a big heart at the bottom. It sounds like *real* love to me."

Does she think this is cute? Cassandra wants to crawl under the table—and out the door and into the street and under a truck.

Cassandra can't say what she feels: *I'm not a little kid, Mom. Don't make fun of me. Conner is nice. I like him.* She can predict her mom's response. *"Sure you do, dear. That's so sweet."*

Read 1 Corinthians 13:4–8
What does true love look like?

You like someone. You decide to go together. You hold hands to show you belong to each other. You share a locker. At school you write notes and at home you hog the phone. People expect you to hang on each other. Some tell you to search for each other's tonsils with your tongues or grab what you can of each other's bods.

So what is love? How do you show it? How do you accept it?

Love is partly feelings. But a relationship won't last on tingles. Love is partly physical. But most of that is out-of-bounds until you're married. Real love is more than either of those. *Real love is a commitment in attitudes and actions to always do the best you can for another person.*

Still, it's harder to say what love *is* than what it looks like. People who love each other learn to be patient and kind. They avoid envy or boasting. They teach each other how to consider the other's feelings and to seek the other's best. They work to be slow to anger and to forget the wrongs they suffer. People in real love obey God. They protect, trust, and stick by each other.

Sound grown-up? Not exactly. It's the way all people should always act. And it's something you can practice now (Galatians 5:22–23).

[Love] always protects, always trusts, always hopes, always perseveres. Love never fails. 1 CORINTHIANS 13:7–8

Bagging the Best?

Eddie tried hard to get noticed by girls. His rough-and-smelly stage peaked in seventh grade. That's when he slugged girls he liked. Or he tickled. If she giggled even a bit—how could she help it?—he thought, *She loves it!* And when nothing else worked, body noises got him attention.

In eighth grade he upped his sophistication. He quoted geometric proofs and chemical equations and obscure dates from Roman history. The girls thought he was dumb.

In ninth grade he got cool. He showered in his dad's cologne, undid the top three buttons on his shirt, slung a gold chain around his neck, and said "Hey, baby" a lot.

He smelled better, but he was just as obnoxious.

Read Proverbs 3:1–4

How can you get noticed by the opposite sex?

Your brain won't overheat coming up with *bad* ways to get attention:

If you're a guy: Challenge a girl to a belching contest. Ask a girl if she wanted her makeup to look like that or if a dog licked her. Spit watermelon seeds in a girl's ears. Mess up her hair. Tell a dirty joke. Walk around with your neck muscles set at maximum flex.

Or if you're a girl: Get mad at a guy you like and make him guess why. Wear a skirt so tight you have to hop. Send messages through friends. Dye your hair a different color each week. Live to sit on boys' laps. Tell a guy you want to be "just friends" and then never speak to him again.

What's the alternative?

You might doubt God knows how to bag a boy or get a girl. So you worry: *If I do what's right I'll be a nerd. If I'm nice they won't notice me. If I act like myself people won't like me. If I tell them I'm a Christian they'll think I'm weird.* And what exactly does God say to try? Follow his commands and act loving and reliable toward everyone—which would make you secure, confident, loyal, and kind.

Sounds awful, doesn't it? Sounds like someone *you* would want to know. Others will too.

Let love and faithfulness never leave you.... Then you will win favor and a good name in the sight of God and man.
PROVERBS 3:3a, 4

Friends First

"We're not 'a thing,' " Aaron protested. "We're friends."

In band Jessica was first-chair trumpet and Aaron was second, a total humiliation to Aaron until she started helping him. He figured out she didn't care who was better. She liked that she didn't have to let him beat her and take first chair just because he was a guy.

Jessica had some explaining to do with her friends too. *He hasn't asked you to go anywhere? He hasn't bought you anything? Then why do you hang out with him?*

Read 2 Corinthians 6:14
What's the most important part of a guy-girl relationship?

When you're a prisoner to love you worry about what you say, what you wear, how you look. If you talk to another guy or girl, your cellmate goes nuclear. When you get labeled "boyfriend" or "girlfriend," you're best pals with some people and an instant enemy to others. And a guy-girl relationship feels like prison for another reason: When your sentence is up, you're out. Your friendship usually ends.

Few people are worth that. When you look back you wish you had a long-term friendship instead of a short-term relationship. So before you lock yourself up and eat the key, take a step back, go slow, and be friends first.

If you work at being friends instead of "going together," what's left?

Talking. Learning to not blab what you hear. Sharing hobbies. Surviving school together. Figuring out how to get along with his or her parents. Watching each other's games and concerts and recitals. Being friends with lots of friends, not just one. And most of all, growing together as Christians. Friendship is the most important part of a guy-girl relationship. And Christ is the most important part of the most important part.

God says never to "yoke" yourself—go together, date, marry, or even cling tight as best friends—to someone who isn't a Christian. You'd be like animals clamped together that plow in different directions. Your goal is to find a friend plowing toward Christ just as fast and hard as you.

Do not be yoked together with unbelievers....
2 CORINTHIANS 6:14

Sheer Delight

As the guys' gym class sat waiting for their pull-up test, Mark congratulated himself.

What timing! This is perfect. Mark knew he could do more pull-ups than any other guy. The girls' gym class was testing only a few feet away. *Julie can see me. She's going to think I'm so cool.*

"Mark!" the gym teacher hollered. "You're next!"

Tadd, the class thug, boosted Mark up to the bar. "Hey, Markie-poo!" Tadd snorted. "Julie's watching. Make her proud."

Julie turned when she heard her name. Mark did a pull-up. Two pull-ups. Three. The guys began to chant. "FOUR! FIVE! SIX! SEVEN!"

Then Tadd yanked Mark's gym shorts.

Mark was finished.

Read Isaiah 62:1–5

Does God ever think you're a reject?

Guys don't usually dream of their wedding day. They certainly don't picture themselves dressed in white from veil to toe, hitch-stepping down an aisle to "Here Comes the Bride," their beauty inspiring *oohs* and *aahs* and dropped jaws.

Yet even if you're a guy, that picture of a beautiful bride is one to hammer into your head. God cherishes you—girl or guy—as a groom cherishes his bride. No bride is ugly to her groom. No groom says, "Crawl back in the swamp and fix your face." No groom stands at the altar and offers to trade his bride for someone else in the congregation. God likes you—and loves you—when no one else does (Romans 5:8).

God's people—ancient Israel, called "Zion" and "Jerusalem" here—were labeled "lonely" and "unlovely" by their enemies. God renamed his people "the delightful one" and "my bride."

God promises that when you're mocked or dumped or rejected that you still reflect his blazing glory. You're "a royal diadem [crown] in the hand of your God." And he promises that one day everyone will see you the way he does.

For the Lord will take delight in you.... As a bridegroom
rejoices over his bride, so will your God rejoice over you.
ISAIAH 62:4–5

Hunks and Hunkettes

A voice echoed in Jennica's head. *Shouldn't you be studying?*
"I suppose," Jennica replied. "This is so much more interesting."
What's more interesting than math?
"Cutting out hunk pictures for my wall."
Why?
"I'm admiring their God-given qualities."
What do you think of boys when all they care about is how girls look?
"They're so shallow. I'm not like them. I don't drool."
How do you suppose the guys in the picture feel about you staring at them?
"They like to be looked at. I want them. And they're all mine."

Read 1 Thessalonians 4:1–8
What's it mean to "learn to control your own body"?

You don't run through a supermarket tasting all the soda and squeezing all the fruit. You don't open a box of cereal, take a bite, and spill the rest on the floor.

Anyone knows that isn't the proper way to shop. You don't taste, take, or wreck what doesn't belong to you. The Thessalonians, though, thought that when it came to sex they could ransack the supermarket, try before they buy, taste-test sexual love before marriage (called "fornication") or outside of marriage ("adultery").

Paul told them to control themselves. A footnote in many Bibles explains that Paul commanded them to "learn how to acquire a wife" in a way that pleases God. Anything less hurts not only the couple who disobeys God but their future spouses. (That's what Paul means about "wronging a brother.")

To hunt for a hunk or hunkette in a holy and honorable way means you don't treat guys or girls as objects (Job 31:1). You speak with respect about them (Ephesians 5:3–4). And you back off when guys want to grab and girls want to hold.

You probably don't even realize you're shopping for a husband or a wife. But you're maturing—which means you've been flung into the supermarket.

It's a long time until checkout. Be careful how you handle the merchandise.

It is God's will...that you should avoid sexual immorality.
1 THESSALONIANS 4:3

Nuke-Powered Toaster

The sweetie you met on the second day of summer camp makes you sweat. You hold hands at the campfire, and as the fire crackles you sneak an arm around each other. You decide you want to burn lips at the basketball court, the camp's after-dark spot. You want your first real kiss. Really bad. Your new friend hesitates, then says no.

What do you do? Multiple choice: (a) kidnap the nearest available person of the opposite sex and tie him or her to the basketball court; (b) pretend that kissing bores you; (c) hang out in the craft shop and make yourself a friendship bracelet; or (d) spit at the feet of the person who rejected you.

Read Hebrews 13:4
God made sex great. How great?

If you rate human experience from zero to ten, taking a bath with your hair dryer scores a definite zero—painful, scorching, and deadly. God intends sex to be *waaaaay* at the other end of the scale. But sex is only that great for those who wait.

To "honor the marriage bed" means to keep sexual intercourse—and the intense physical affection that precedes it—for marriage. Sex is God's wedding present to a man and a woman who seal their love through a public promise to stay together for life.

God's gift is hotter than a nuclear-powered toaster.

You don't want to power up now. Kissing starts a chain reaction God designed to end in an awesome explosion. If you feed fuel to the reactor *now*—in your thoughts, by what you look at and listen to, by heated kissing, by goals you set—you'll start a meltdown that you won't stop.

The fire and fallout from breaking God's command are deadly. You worry about *conception*—creating a baby. You risk *infection*. You face *rejection* when the relationship ends. And you won't escape *detection*. You strain your most important relationship—your friendship with God.

So what's your choice? Another option: (e) Ask yourself some questions: Why do you want to get to the basketball court? Whose rules are you playing by?

Don't try so hard for your first kiss. Wait for the best.

Marriage should be honored by all, and the marriage bed kept pure. HEBREWS 13:4

Dental Floss

Stephanie dashes from the changing house to a boulder along the beach—one not quite big enough to hide behind.

It's just like her new swimsuit—not quite big enough to hide behind.

Stephanie thinks: *I can't believe I bought this. But it's too late now.*

The guys think: *Come on out, Steph! We think your swimsuit is great.*

The girls think: *She's so cheap. Why does she get all the attention? I wonder if I should get one of those.*

Read 1 Timothy 2:9–10
Why bother to be modest?

When you were little your parents taught you not to let people touch your "private parts." Big news: Your private parts are still private. You're the proud owner of a God-designed, getting-grown-up body.

Your goal is *not* to give away as much as you can (Proverbs 5:15–23).

Girls: When Paul wrote that women should "dress modestly," he wasn't picking on you. He knew that people—*especially* guys—are tempted by what they see. When you choose swimwear spun from a single spool of dental floss you might as well mail the guys invitations to your birthday suit. To dress every day with "decency" and "propriety" you don't have to wear a bag. But you don't want to brag. Whenever you bait boys with your outward appearance, you're asking them to see less than the real you.

Guys: That's NO excuse for you to grab with your eyes or your hands what isn't yours. When you start to want what you can't have, stare somewhere else (Matthew 5:27–30): Turn off the TV. Surf somewhere else. Toss the magazine. Hang up the phone. Run away. Beg your girlfriend to cover up or find yourself a new girlfriend.

Back to both of you: When you buy a present for a friend, you don't wrap it up and then kick it down the street or hurl it around a crowd. You would never hand a friend a torn and dirty gift. And a half-unwrapped present spoils the surprise.

You're the gift. Your spouse is the recipient. Take care of the present.

I also want women to dress modestly, with decency and propriety.
1 TIMOTHY 2:9

Tale of an Idiot

So-called scientists in white coats brief you before the experiment. "We're testing a new brand of stay-fresh sandwich bags," they inform you. "We've constructed a bag big enough for you to crawl into. We'll zip you inside, place you in a cage with a person-eating tiger, and watch what happens. Rest assured, nothing will happen. You'll be perfectly safe. Our new bag is totally airtight, so the tiger won't catch a whiff of you. And tigers won't eat what tigers can't smell.

"Any questions?" they ask.

Just one.

Are you that stupid? Would you trust your life to a sandwich bag?

Read Romans 16:17–20
What did Paul warn the Romans to watch out for?

Your TV tells you to trust your life to a condom. Ads, friends, media—even some doctors, teachers, pastors, and parents—advise you to accept less than God's best.

They're like the people Paul warned the Romans against. They don't want what's best for *you*. They want to drag you into their disobedience, into following evil appetites instead of God, who is totally wise (Psalm 139:1–12) and totally loving (Psalm 145:17–18).

Paul says to flee from people figuring on feeding you to a tiger. But sometimes you don't even know you're being caged. No one ever bluntly told you how to tell good from evil.

Remember God's best: God made sex to be shared by a husband and wife in order to be physically and emotionally united (Genesis 2:22–24).

Run away from the rest: Sex isn't for people not married to each other. Sex isn't a party game. Sex isn't a dare or a contest to get as much as you can. Sexual contact isn't for people of the same sex. The sex God invented isn't selfish, hurtful, violent, or controlling. Sex isn't something adults or teens do to children. Sex isn't a spectator sport for the screen or a magazine.

God's kind of sex is never dirty. It's private, but never something you have to keep secret or be embarrassed to talk about with an adult you trust.

Don't be stupid. Don't let anyone toss you to a tiger.

For such people are not serving our Lord Christ, but their own appetites. ROMANS 16:18

This Means War

"Where are you and Brenda going after the game?" Tim's mom asked.

"I don't know." Tim shrugged. "We'll figure that out later."

Tim's parents looked at each other. *Say something*, they both silently said to each other.

"Are you planning to go out with anyone else?" Tim's dad tried to sound calm.

"I don't know yet."

"We don't think it's a good idea to leave your evening unplanned. We need to know where to find you," Tim's dad reasoned. "Why don't you call her now and ask what she wants to do?"

Read James 4:7–10

Why is it smart to plan—to decide ahead of time what you're doing and where you're going?

When you shoot rapids you don't shut your eyes and trust your raft to go where it should. You declare war on the river. You jam your paddle into the water, pull and push, and work as a team with other rafters. Only then do you avoid getting knocked around, hung up, or flipped out.

When parents ask your plans—with friends or with a date—they aren't prying into your privacy. They need to know you'll be okay. More than that, they want *you* to know where you're going. They don't want you to drift wherever currents drag you.

The same lesson fits all of life. You have to *choose* not to drift, and to fight to stay upright. And you need to decide while the river is calm, before hormones swamp you and peers push and spin your raft.

When you "submit to God" you give him your will. You say, "God, I want what *you* want." You declare that you're done drifting: You reject sin and get rid of "double-mindedness," halfhearted paddling.

Growing up is one of the wildest rivers you'll ever run. God wants you to decide *now* to follow him completely and, specifically, to stay pure sexually. You can write yourself a reminder of what you decide at the bottom of this page. Date it. Sign it. Celebrate it. And stick with it.

If you don't decide, then you've chosen to drift. And maybe drown.

Submit yourselves, then, to God. JAMES 4:7

Their Pain, Your Gain

"You're going to do *what*? Why?"

"I don't know. I've wanted to for a while," your friend explains. "I'm curious. I'll do it once and I'll know."

"Don't you think it's wrong?"

"I don't think God would let me get hurt. He wants me to fit in, doesn't he? Besides, my friends keep saying I can't say what they're doing is wrong if I've never tried it myself."

How do I answer that one? Maybe she's right.

"Besides, I know my mom did it when she was my age. She's always saying it was wrong. That's easy for her to say. She had her fun. She wants to spoil mine."

Read 1 Corinthians 10:1–12

How can you avoid making stupid sexual mistakes?

A friend climbs into a car and slams his hand in the door. One bash is an accident. Two bashes is a coincidence. But three bashes should make even a melonhead ponder what he's doing wrong.

After watching your friend's mishaps, how many times would you have to crush your own hand in the car door before you would be careful?

The people of Israel had awesome experiences of God. He saved them from slavery in Egypt and led them to freedom in a cloud and pillar of fire. He gave them Moses' leadership and fed them with bread from heaven. Yet they turned away from what they knew. They chased evil instead of God, making fake gods (Exodus 32:1-6), sinning sexually (Numbers 25:1-9), and grumbling against God (Numbers 21:4-6).

You don't have to try sin to know that it's wrong and that sooner or later it hurts. You can believe the Bible and your parents and other Christians when they say sin isn't the fun it's cracked up to be.

Experience is a great teacher—especially someone else's rotten experience. You're smart to learn from your own mistakes. But you're brilliant to learn from others' blunders.

Their pain, your gain.

These things happened to them as examples and were written down as warnings for us.... 1 CORINTHIANS 10:11

His Way or the Highway

"Would you rather stay here or run in with me?" your dad asks.

"Here. Just leave me the keys."

As soon as your dad is out of sight you clamber into the driver's seat, move the mirrors, and tilt the wheel. Best of all, you find *your* station on the stereo. You settle back on your throne. It's a moment of paradise in the quickmart parking lot.

In eight months and eleven days you'll take revenge on the world for being held back in kindergarten: You'll get your driver's license a year before any of your friends. It's a long wait, but you need the time to convince your parents to dump the family roadster and procure a car more suitable to your style.

Driving is your dream. So where ya gonna go?

Read Psalm 16:11

What does God promise when you travel his road?

You've got transportation. What's your destination?

You've got freedom. Where do you want to wind up?

Maybe you want to blast your car down curvy roads. That *would* be a blast—if you like to soar ditchward in a vehicle not made for flying.

God plans a kinder, gentler path for you if you know him. Suppose you trust in the Lord with all your heart—unlike people who aren't sure what they want (James 4:8). You don't live solely by your own brains. You seek guidance from the Smartest One. The result? God powers you straight and fast.

Another way of looking at it: You admit that compared to God you're not wise. You respect God's evaluation of good and evil. You choose his path. Once again—the result? Going God's way does your body and soul good.

God's way is a jolt of joy and pleasure, but it's not bump free. God's discipline jars you awake and keeps your eyes on his road, but it's still smoother than ramping off-road.

You can choose to drive in the ditch. But when you choose God's way over your way you find the path of life.

You have made known to me the path of life; you will fill me with joy in your presence, with eternal pleasures at your right hand. PSALM 16:11

Slam the Dumpster Lid

Matt was tossing trash into the Dumpsters behind his apartment when he spotted a stack of porn magazines under the garbage. Why not grab a look?

Mind garbage—it's everywhere. The Net, TV, videos, music, computer games, magazines, books—they're a lot like open Dumpsters, inviting you to dive in and play.

Some filth is easy to recognize. But some is "I-don't-think-it's-so-bad" junk we don't notice even when its stench suffocates us—the swimsuit issues and soap operas that warp our view of love and sex, the stars who make us feel subnormal if we don't imitate them, the peeks at the rich and famous that give us an unscratchable itch to acquire more stuff. Movies and TV can make violence and anger seem like good ways to get things done, and the ads that blip by us train us to be bored by real life. (Life, after all, is seldom as exciting as the frolicking fun of beer ad beach parties or as electric as soda commercials.)

And all these images seem to say life is happier and easier with God out of the picture. When was the last time God showed up in a commercial?

Read Philippians 4:8
What kind of stuff should you be watching and listening to and thinking about?

No sane person spends his day playing in a real Dumpster. Lots of people, though, play in mind garbage, often pulled in by the need for friends, for an escape, for some excitement. It takes guts to slam the Dumpster lid shut and go play somewhere else—to surf to a better site, switch channels, listen to a different group, find a different video, change magazines—but that's what the Bible urges us to do.

Anything that is good, praiseworthy, true, honorable, right, pure, beautiful, and respected—that is what should fill our minds. Read those words again. How much of what you read—and listen to—and think about—during a day passes those tests? What are you doing to slam the lid shut on things that don't—and to open yourself up to things that do?

Whatever is true... noble... right... pure... lovely... admirable—
if anything is excellent or praiseworthy—think about such things.
PHILIPPIANS 4:8

The Belching Llamgod

Shhhh—listen to the pagan drumbeat: BOOM-boom-boomp. BOOM-boom-boomp. Fiery lights flash from the Temple of the Llamgod as worshipers travel well-worn paths crisscrossing the dark jungle.

Worshipers devote hour after hour to accumulating sacrificial offerings before entering the temple gates. Without a sacrifice, worshipers can only wander the edges of the temple, adoring the temple riches from a distance and longing for the day they can charge into the frenzy at the Temple of the Llamgod. The temple attracts many young worshipers, who often slave in the kitchens of the Temple of the Llamgod to prepare lavish offerings.

At the temple, worshipers lay their offerings on ceremonial tables where their gifts are recorded. In return, worshipers receive gaudy trinkets as proof of their sacrifice. Oddly, the trinkets often lose their luster once removed from the temple grounds.

The drums summon worshipers daily, whipping up devotion that even rises in pitch during special seasons at the Temple of the Llamgod.

If a mall (llam) belched smoke or had an idol in the food court, it wouldn't be so hard to see that it can be a temple to a deceptive god: money.

Read 1 Timothy 6:6–10, 17–19
What should you think about money?

A mall's pulsating lights, colors, music, food, friends, and nice stuff stir excitement. They're fun, like the marketplaces in Bible times where people mingled and Jesus and other kids no doubt played.

But when scoping, snaring, and not sharing mall goodies controls your time, affection, and energy—then your favorite mall or big-box strip of stores has stolen your heart away from God and other important things. That's when the places you shop have become a temple for enlarging your greed—not a place where you shop to meet your needs. Ask God to show you if the things you buy fit his best plans for you—or if you're standing in line to sacrifice to the Llamgod.

But if we have food and clothing, we will be content with that. People who want to get rich fall into temptation and a trap and into many foolish and harmful desires that plunge men into ruin and destruction. 1 TIMOTHY 6:8-9

Mess Up Their Minds

Mike and Trevor had caddied through fourteen holes when they reached the spot where they had to walk ahead on the fairway a couple hundred yards to spot balls as they flew off the tee.

The caddies despised the guys they were working for. When the men biffed a shot, they cussed out Mike and Trevor. Mike's golfer even winged clubs at him. But Mike had thought of a fresh way to get even.

Mike and Trevor stepped behind some trees while they waited for their golfers to hit. Mike teed up half a dozen golf balls from his golfer's bag and pulled out a big wood to hit them.

"What are you doing?!" Trevor whispered.

"What does it look like I'm doing?" Mike turned to concentrate on his stance. "I ... *whack* ... hate ... *whack* ... this ... *whack* ... guy ... *whack* ... so bad ... *whack whack*." The balls flew off. Then Mike pulled a spare pair of golf gloves out of the bag and tucked them into his pockets. "That's because he tips bad."

Read Romans 12:17–21
What do you do when you crave revenge?

If you crave revenge because you think it will put an end to a bad situation, think again. Revenge only prolongs and intensifies your fights. You slam. They slam you back. Then you have to slam them again even worse.

When someone mistreats you—slugs you or pranks you or says stuff behind your back—your first job is to "do what is right" and "live at peace with everyone." Rather than getting even, try to fix the situation peacefully. The person you're battling with may make peace impossible, but you shouldn't. And if things don't change, leave revenge to God. Here's why: God promises to repay wrong better than you ever can.

"The best way to get rid of an enemy," an old proverb says, "is to turn him into a friend." If you really want to mess up your enemies' minds, love them. That's the only hope you have of disarming them and getting them on your side.

"If your enemy is hungry, feed him; if he is thirsty, give him something to drink. In doing this, you will heap burning coals on his head." Do not be overcome by evil, but overcome evil with good. ROMANS 12:20–21

Roadkill

You've no doubt studied this phenomenon in science class: When it's time for animals to die, they instinctively do an astonishing thing. Whether furry woodland creatures or city squirrels or bunnies, they mosey quietly to the side of a road, lie down, peacefully take one last breath, and expire.

Wrong. Those animals wander onto the road and get hit by cars. They're roadkill. Street pizza. Unhappy meals at the curbside café.

The sight of a cute animal dead on the side of a road is sick. And just as sad is seeing someone flattened by carelessly spoken words.

Read Ephesians 4:29

How do we know what is okay to say and what isn't?

Roadkill occurs when a driver moves so fast that he hits an animal before he can stop. Words kill when we nail our victims before we can skid to a stop.

Lots of times we speak without thinking—that's like not knowing where the brakes are. Other times we think hard ahead of time about nasty things to say—that's as bad as gunning the engine.

If we deliberately ran down animals, a judge would yank our driver's license. Unfortunately, no one is going to peel back our tongues and lips. We have to learn self-control. All we can do is practice being "quick to listen, but slow to speak" (James 1:19).

So what are your tests for the words you speak? Try these: Words should be helpful—not harmful—so if you say something negative, make sure it's to build up, not rip down. Laugh with people, not at them. Dirty jokes aren't great for our minds or for showing others respect. If you've got a problem, talk straight to the person, not behind his or her back. Using "God" as a swear word means you don't take God seriously. Complaining says you don't like what God has given you, so give thanks instead.

One other guideline. Just because an animal walks across the road doesn't mean you can hit it. Just because something is true doesn't mean you should say it. So slow down and let someone live.

Do not let any unwholesome talk come out of your mouths, but only what is helpful for building others up according to their needs, that it may benefit those who listen. EPHESIANS 4:29

It's Your Decision

Samantha felt a little uncomfortable wearing a long skirt to her first debate. Sam never wore "girl clothes." But it felt good to dress up. She had been picked to fire the first shots in a debate about how to protect endangered species. Sam's side would argue that the government couldn't use environmental regulations to seize private property.

Sam had tried running cross-country. She wheezed. She made cheerleading, but they just trailed boys they thought were cute and took stabs at girls who didn't make the squad. Sam didn't think there were any other Christians on the debate team, but the advisors and other students were fun. She got to stretch her brain. Finally she fit.

Once, after shredding another team and sending them home crying, Sam was asked to join a weekend tournament team. Great—until Sam realized she wouldn't have time for church for a few months. Sam's mom said she had to make her own decision. Suddenly it was Sam who felt like crying.

Read 1 Corinthians 10:13

How do you manage to do what's right when you're all alone?

You don't live in a bubble. Your world, you might have noticed, isn't very Christian. Your Christian friends aren't always around. You aren't even fitted with a pressurized space suit to keep you from exploding when you venture out alone into spiritual nothingness.

Like every other Christian, you'll face temptations to do wrong. (It's "common to man.") But it doesn't always come in scary offers of sex and drugs. The biggest temptation you'll likely face is this: To stop paying attention to God. To do well without him. To ease him out of your life. To be like the fool who says, "There is no God" (Psalm 14:1). The fool doesn't mean that God doesn't exist. He means that God doesn't matter.

Often it's you, God, and a temptation—no one looking, no Christian friends to pull you back. In those moments, the decision to obey God—to make him matter—is yours alone.

God always provides a way to choose for him. You might not see it at first. But choosing to hunt for his way out is the first step in choosing to make him matter. And it's a big part of total devotion.

When you are tempted, he will also provide a way out so that you can stand up under it. 1 CORINTHIANS 10:13

Keep Away With the Truth

Dad eyeballs you and your sister as you all stare each other down at a family meeting. One of you made a bunch of calls to a 900 number, and your pa just opened the whopper bill. Both of you deny it.

One of you is lying. Your dad has to figure out who.

Telling a lie is like playing keep away with a friend's shoe. She needs her shoe back, but you hide it behind your back or toss it over her head, around her side, anywhere that's out of reach. You have fun, but after a while your friend who can't get her shoe back stops laughing. She gets angry. Frustrated. And with good reason. It's tough to go anywhere or do anything with only one shoe.

Read Ephesians 4:25
Why is telling the truth important?

Lies never seem so bad when you're the one telling them. After all, liars can escape consequences (if you lie to parents or teachers), skip studying (if you cheat on a test), or avoid paying (if you shoplift or copy CDs or software).

But those benefits are deceitful. When people play games with truth the world grinds to a halt, just like when you can't get a shoe back. When people lie to you, it's hard to know what to believe or whom to trust, who's a winner or who's a loser, who deserves a reward or who deserves punishment, what's good or what's bad, who your friends are or who wants to hurt you. It's hard to live in a world where people lie to you—the shoe of truth you need in order to get on with life keeps flying over your head, out of reach.

You don't like being lied to, so don't lie to others. That's what Ephesians means when it says, "Speak truth, because you are members of one body." Truth is so important to the way the world works that God groups lying with sins most people would never do, like murder, sexual immorality, satanism, and idolatry (Revelation 22:15).

Playing keep away with the truth never wins.

Therefore each of you must put off falsehood and speak truthfully to his neighbor, for we are all members of one body.
EPHESIANS 4:25

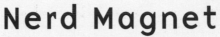

Nerd Magnet

Sally calls herself "the nerd magnet." Wherever she goes, she attracts a crowd of unusual people—you know, nerds. For some reason, misfits and social outcasts know Sally won't push them away like other people do. And you might squirm a bit when you spot someone like Sally being uncompromisingly kind to everyone she meets. She puts a disturbing question right in your face: Do Christians have to be nice to everyone?

"Favoritism" is judging people and choosing to be nice or nasty to them based on outward appearances.

Read James 2:1–9
What's so awful about playing favorites?

Note how the rich man received polite words and a cushy seat. The poor man got gruff orders to sit on the floor or stand in the back. That was more than a social boo-boo. James writes, "What are you doing? You are making some people more important than others, and with evil thoughts you are deciding that one person is better.... You are sinning" (verses 4, 9 NCV).

It's foolish to favor the popular while insulting the nerds. The world is like a tree. The most popular, wealthy, athletic, best-looking, and best-dressed people sit in the branches up top, and the nerds cling to branches at the bottom. And if you try to climb higher, the folks up top drop sticks on your head, kick your fingers, and laugh when you slip and plummet toward the ground.

The people in the bottom branches are special to God, however. Because they have less wealth or looks or popularity, they are often more hungry for God.

People you label "nerds" may make great friends. They like you and let you be yourself. You discover that they're *people*, not any more weird than you. (And if you befriend someone and find out he really does have problems, you can point him to help.)

Christlike love respects everyone, not just a favored few. It isn't wrong to show kindness to people who dazzle you. But it's sin if you don't show the same kindness to those who don't.

My brothers, as believers in our glorious Lord Jesus Christ, don't show favoritism. JAMES 2:1

Lumberjacks on Ice

You and your friend look like lumberjacks-turned-surfer-dudes as you trudge across the street in your flannel and baggies outfits, headed for the neighborhood hill.

With snowboards swung across your backs you're a little slow. Too tardy for the guy in the Corvette waiting at a light to make a right turn. He honks. *What's his problem?* He guns the engine and edges forward. As he turns behind you he nicks your friend's board and breezes your leg.

You pick up a hunk of ice and wing it at the Vette's back end.

Chink! Ice connects with window. No damage. But driver skids to stop. Driver blasts into reverse. Grinds to stop. Exits car. Chases snowboarders. Cop sees chase. Cop prevents your premature deaths. *Good thing.* Cop totally blames hip kids. *Bad thing.*

You find yourself in the backseat of a police car on the way home. The officer phones ahead. Your parents greet you at the door.

Read Psalm 33:12–19
Why be honest?

You blew it. You were caught in the act. Or you're at least the prime suspect. What's your first reaction to accusation?

Your gut no doubt tells you to flee like a prisoner who knows that the guards are snoozing. You try to sneak away. Or you blow a hole in the prison wall and tell a bold, bald lie. You point out the evil someone else committed and cover up what you did. You rave about the driver who went psycho but subtract from your story about the ice hunk you flung.

None of us likes to be wrong. It's easy to tell less than the whole truth. But God wants to lead you into *worship* toward him, *humility* toward yourself, *love* toward others, a *commitment* to do right in all circumstances, and *honesty* when you've sinned—it's what keeps you stuck tight with him. Dodging truth leaves you dead toward God (1 Thessalonians 2:10).

God knows the whole story—what you've done and what you haven't. If you ask him, he'll help you be honest with him, yourself, and other people. He'll help you admit your part—no more, no less.

From heaven the Lord looks down and sees all mankind.
PSALM 33:13

One Good Reason

In the dirt. *Ball one*. Into the bleachers. *Ball two*. Monica launches the softball toward home plate, and it barely misses the batter's back. *Ball three*. Bekah—the batter—tosses back a threat: "One more pitch like that, girl, and I'll push that ball in one of your ears and make a new hole to pull it out." Monica again sends the ball toward home plate—but this time it brushes the back end of Bekah's ponytail. *Ball four*.

In an instant Bekah is at the mound, and with one swift shove Monica is flat on the ground, Bekah pinning her down, arm cocked to punch.

"Give me one good reason why I shouldn't pound you."

Monica, unfortunately, isn't a fast thinker.

Read Matthew 5:7
Why be merciful?

Jesus told a story about a servant who owed his master a monstrous stash of cash. When the servant heard that he, his wife, and his children were to be jailed for the debt, he begged for mercy. In response, the master forgave the servant's debt and let him go. One day, though, the servant bumped into a man who owed the servant a relatively tiny amount of money. When that man couldn't cough it up, the servant had him tossed in prison. The master, on hearing this, understandably went berserk. He tossed his servant in prison after all.

Big point: "This," Jesus said, "is how my heavenly Father will treat each of you unless you forgive your brother from your heart" (Matthew 18:35).

You—and I—and everyone else on the planet—have done wrong. Sinned. Piled up a big, unpaybackable bill. Jesus, though, paid the penalty—death—that God decreed for your debt of sin (Romans 6:23). And forgiveness of your sin is free for the asking. John wrote, "If we confess our sins, he is faithful and just and will forgive us our sins" (1 John 1:9).

That's God's Good News. But it's silly to say you believe in your need and have said "Yes!" to God's mercy if you can't show mercy to others. Fighting back with fists or fingernails or foul mouths means you haven't figured out what God has done for you.

You'll get back what you dish out.

Blessed are the merciful, for they will be shown mercy.
MATTHEW 5:7

Chessheads

The only reason Luke dared join the chess club was that it met so early before school that no one knew he was in it—no one who mattered, anyway. Each morning he ducked out of the club meetings a few minutes early, snuck out the school's back entrance, and strode back in the front door. Perfect—until Miss Schaffhausen, the chess club sponsor, decided to take the club to after-school tournaments. Big problem: That's when Luke played on the school soccer team.

The soccer team was good. They knew it. And next to soccer their favorite sport was kicking clods they didn't like—like anyone in the chess club. When Luke was with his soccer friends he set the team record for rude chesshead remarks.

And then one day after school two buses sat in the school driveway, both full of people hanging out the windows screaming at each other, both waiting for Luke to board.

Luke contemplated crawling under the wheels.

Read Proverbs 6:12–14

What price do you pay when you change to fit your surroundings?

Before you go to battle in the desert you slip into sand-colored clothes and coil a rattlesnake around your head. If you fight in the Arctic you sport snowstorm white and hang icicles from your nose. And for combat in the jungle you wear green and black fatigues complemented by face paint and twigs in your hair. It's simple survival.

If camouflage is good for the marines it's good for you. Right?

You'll change a lot more than your clothes if your social survival strategy is doing whatever it takes to fit, belong, blend in. You pretend to like stuff you hate and detest stuff you love. You talk behind people's backs—out of both sides of your mouth. You get talked *into* and *out of.* And you chomp anyone you think resides lower on the food chain. With winks, nods, and inside jokes you're two-faced. Deceitful. A fraud.

But at least two people know the truth. You and God. When you hide the real you no one can mock you. But neither can anyone truly like you.

A scoundrel and villain, who goes about with a corrupt mouth...
who plots evil with deceit in his heart—he always
stirs up dissension. PROVERBS 6:12,14

Butchered Haircuts

"I guess it means that if I'm going to tell people I'm a Christian, I should act like one," Mark told his youth group. Toward the end of the semester, Mark had cut a class he hated. His teacher had found out, though, and reminded Mark how earlier in the year he had protested having to read a book that seemed anti-Christian. "I really blew it with Mr. Wallace," Mark said. "He called me a hypocrite. He's right. I can't stand up for Jesus one day and act as if I don't know him the next."

It's ironic. Mark didn't respect a person in authority, and it was that same person who pointed out an inconsistency in his life, a place where he needed to grow spiritually and get tighter with Jesus.

Read Romans 13:3–4
What good is authority?

Paul is blunt. He says that those who rebel against earthly authority rebel against God and that God will judge them. But he also explains why.

Paul doesn't claim that parents, teachers, coaches, police, bosses, pastors, youth group leaders, and other authorities are perfect or that their judgments are flawless. He does say that God uses authorities to help you, and because of that, he expects you to obey them.

God gives authorities power over you to keep you in line and to shape your character—even the police officer who pulls you over for speeding, the coach who benches you for sassing back, or the teacher who gives you a bad grade when you don't study. They teach you to respect others' rights, to work as a team, and to discipline yourself.

Submitting to authority hurts, but it produces results. Hebrews 12:11 says that "no discipline seems pleasant at the time, but painful. Later on, however, it produces a harvest of righteousness and peace for those who have been trained by it."

When you don't submit to authority, you're like a little kid running from a haircut. God uses authorities like scissors and combs and razors to make you look your best. The more you wiggle, the worse your hair turns out—and the more the process hurts.

Do you want to be free from fear of the one in authority? Then do what is right and he will commend you. For he is God's servant to do you good. ROMANS 13:3–4

Not Just on Mother's Day

With his mouth full of food, Matt outlined his afternoon plans. His mom glared at him coldly. "Aren't you forgetting something? Shouldn't we do something *I* want to do?"

"Why?" Matt asked and kept eating the lunch his mom had fixed.

"Here's a clue. It's Mother's Day today. You haven't even said 'Happy Mother's Day.' "

"Does that mean I can't go to a movie with my friends this afternoon?"

Matt's mom gave up. "Fine. Forget about me. Go do what you want."

At supper Matt flung a small bag into his mom's lap. "Here's your present. Happy Mother's Day." His mom pulled the unwrapped present out of the bag. It was a black coffee mug that read, *I'M NOT FAT. I'M JUST SHORT FOR MY WEIGHT.*

Matt grinned. "Funny, huh?" Mom wasn't laughing. Matt backpedaled. "All the other ones said stuff like 'I love you.' What did you expect?"

Read Exodus 20:12
Why should you honor your parents?

Honoring your parents means more than being nice to them on parental holidays. It means respecting, communicating with, and obeying them all day, every day. It means treating them the way you hope to be treated. Your parents deserve honor for giving you life and taking care of you.

You may not be impressed by the way they are parenting. You may even wish at times that they hadn't given you life. But God doesn't say to listen to and obey only parents who you think deserve respect.

In the Old Testament God told his people that he would give them an incredible place to live, the "promised land." God told them that by obeying his commands they would live long and prosper in the land. His presence and care would be part of their daily lives. God promised specifically to bless those who trusted *him* to guide them and shape them *through* their parents— even though parents aren't perfect. The same principle works now.

Believe that? Then trust God and honor your parents. Don't believe that? Then think about the flip side of the promise: Those who rebel against their parents will experience misery.

Honor your father and your mother, so that you may live long in the land the Lord *your God is giving you.* EXODUS 20:12

Mutant Daughters

Bad timing. You exit a store at the mall and right in your face is the school librarian. Earlier today you really made her nostrils smoke. Your latest little game is to ever-so-slowly tip your chair up on the back legs until she yells to put it down. Today you made her so furious she just about knocked you off your chair herself. And now there's nowhere to run—she's spotted you.

She's holding hands with some guy. *A husband? The monster's married?* And two girls are with them. *Daughters? She's reproduced?* You imagine her daughters as freaks bred to inflict pain on another generation of students. Then you blink. They're about your age, and they're actually pretty.

"Hi!" the monster waves. *Strange—she sounds friendly.* She introduces her family and then pulls you aside. She says she hopes she hasn't been too hard on you. She doesn't want you to get hurt, and she explains that the custodians are always after her for chairs breaking in the library.

As she walks away with her family, the library lady looks a little different to you. You had never noticed she was a human being.

Read 1 Timothy 2:1–2

What good things can you do to get along with people in authority?

God is King, but we don't answer just to God. Often he places us under the authority of people—parents, teachers, police, employers, the government—who in some way have the power to punish evil and reward good (1 Peter 2:14). At other times God places people under our leadership.

If everyone does his or her part, the world runs smoothly. Accept and obey what the authorities in your life require of you. That's job number one in getting along with authority: *submit.*

Submission, however, doesn't mean bagging your brain. At the right time, respectfully let them in on your point of view. If you want leaders to be an asset to you, assist them however you can. That's job number two: *help.*

And here's job number three: *pray.* Start by praying that they will lead wisely. Ask God for them to make it possible for you to live your faith fully. Pray for the leaders in your life to be responsive to God's leadership. Whatever you do, treat authorities as people. Even if you're convinced they're not.

I urge, then, first of all, that requests, prayers, intercession and thanksgiving be made for everyone—for kings and all those in authority. 1 TIMOTHY 2:1-2

Rule Busters

Within minutes after students heard that six of their favorite teachers would be laid off because of budget cuts, a plan had hatched. When the bell rang for third hour, students walked out of the school and planted themselves on the school's front lawn. The signs were unfurled. Students chanted, "NO MORE CUTS!"

When the students refused their principal's plea to return to class, they were suspended from school. The protesters fought with students who chose to stay in class. Parents whose kids were suspended complained that the punishment ignored students' rights to free speech. School administrators said the walkout wasn't the best way to protest the cuts.

It's natural to want to retaliate when a person or group in authority does something we don't like. But is it right? When is it okay to disobey someone you're supposed to obey?

Read Acts 4:13–22

The "they" in verse 13 is a group of Jewish rulers. Why did Peter and John decide to disobey those authorities?

Disobeying authority isn't okay just because you don't feel like following the rules. Disobedience is an option only when God's commands are directly challenged—and only when all other methods fail. Peter tried reasoning before threatening disobedience, and *then* he continued to preach because stopping would mean breaking God's clear command.

Most people—Christians included—agree that there are times when authorities are wrong and we should disobey them. Europeans hid Jews from the German Nazis. African-Americans broke laws that mistreated them because of the color of their skin.

If you choose to break a rule, or engage in "civil disobedience," be willing to suffer the consequences. Daniel went to the lions' den for praying (Daniel 6). Shadrach, Meshach, and Abednego went to the furnace for refusing to bow to an idol (Daniel 3:16–18). Their stands against ungodly laws pointed out the wickedness of the laws and gave God the chance to display his power. Yet at the same time, their acceptance of punishment demonstrated respect for the authorities God had established (Romans 13:1–5).

If you're going to be a rule buster, be ready to get busted.

But Peter and John replied, "Judge for yourselves whether it is right in God's sight to obey you rather than God." ACTS 4:19

Escape the Little Table

As grandparents, aunts, uncles, and cousins all crowd around for Thanksgiving dinner, you wonder where to sit. Your mom points: "Over there."

"Over there" is an orange plastic picnic table reserved for the kiddies. You have to sit sidesaddle because you can't squeeze your knees underneath. *Why am I always stuck at the little table?*

The moment your dad says "Amen," your eyes open to see the flash of a spud-loaded spoon wielded by a little cousin. "Incoming!" his sister squeals as they both let spoonfuls fly.

Splat. Potatoes in your hair. Stuck to your eyebrows. Glopping off your nose. All over your shirt. And being the oldest means you can't retaliate.

You want to split the little-table scene. When your mom finally invites you to the big table, you're pumped. But that's almost worse. The dads debate the merits of purchasing the family minivan versus leasing. *Who cares?* you think. The moms ooh and aah over the asparagus. *Get a life. All of you!* You ask to be excused. And you wish you were back at the little table.

Read Ecclesiastes 11:5
So how do you like being your age?

The massive changes happening in your body, heart, and mind are as untraceable as the wind. What God is making you is a mystery. You're dangling in that cool time of life between diapers and dentures—more precisely, you're in adolescence, caught between childhood and adulthood. You're stuck between tables.

If you goof off like a little kid, people shake their finger: "You're not a three-year-old, you know. Act your age." If you try to act grown-up, they shake in their shoes: "You're not ready for that. Act your age."

God knows exactly what's going on. He knows you're not a baby. He understands if the big table looks like a total bore.

God knew you well when you were a kid. He counts on being close to you when you're an adult. And wherever you're at in life, he wants you to hang tight with him. His love for you is unstoppable. And he has loads to tell you.

As you do not know the path of the wind, or how the body is formed in a mother's womb, so you cannot understand the work of God, the Maker of all things. ECCLESIASTES 11:5

Your Underwear Flyin' High

The image of your teacher waving a pair of underwear high overhead is frozen in your memory. "Class, do these belong to anyone?"

Your fourth-grade class was field-tripping to the middle school pool and you were terrified—of the locker rooms, showers, changing in front of other kids. So you hatched a plan. You wore your swimsuit to school under your clothes and hid your underwear—along with an enormous towel to change underneath—in a duffel. You had everything covered.

So when you saw the underwear waving in the breeze, you snickered. *What doof would drop a pair of underwear in front of the whole class?* Mrs. Burzloff kept waving the underwear, as if to flag down the owner. *What's she going to do next? Wear them on her head?*

Then you recognized them. You checked your duffel. They were yours.

Read Psalm 139:13–14

You look in the mirror and hardly recognize yourself.
What's going on?

You might still wish you could change in a locker. What you feel, how you think, or who you see in the mirror may be bewildering or embarrassing or confusing.

You're like a video image morphing from one creature into another. You know who you used to be. Now you only catch a glimpse of yourself in mid-morph motion.

The biggest unknown is what you're turning into. A werewolf? A beluga whale? A not-so-jolly giant? Or maybe someone is playing a cruel joke on you and you're never going to grow up.

Your Designer isn't worried or confused. God made you unique, just the way he wanted. God made your "inward being"—your brain and feelings. He "knit together" a cover for you—your body. That makes you "fearful" and "wonderful"—not scary but awestriking and incredible.

God has been caring for you since he put you together in your mom's womb. He has your present and future body, brain, and heart all figured out. And what he plans for you is good.

For you created my inmost being; you knit me together in my
mother's womb. I praise you because I am fearfully and
wonderfully made; your works are wonderful.

PSALM 139:13–14

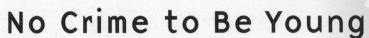

No Crime to Be Young

They might as well have torn down the store. The hangout was gone.

Old Mr. Robinson owned a quickmart next to school. He always said that he liked kids, which to him meant anyone under forty.

But students were his favorites. He knew most of them, even the ones who tried to rip him off before they figured out he was all right. When kids had problems at school or at home, they stuck around to talk with Mr. Robinson.

One day Mr. Robinson told his friends he was retiring and selling the store. Things changed fast. To the new owner, "student" meant "shoplifter." Everyone was guilty until proven innocent. Trying to guard the cash register and the candy aisle at the same time flustered the new owner, so he hung a sign on the door: *Only one student in the store at a time*. When kids still bunched on the sidewalk in front of the store he blasted elevator music through a loudspeaker to push them away. So they left.

Read Mark 10:13–16

If Jesus owned a store, would he chase students away?

Seeing Jesus was like going to get an autograph from a megastar, only better. Parents brought their children to Jesus for him to "bless" them, to put his hands on their heads and proclaim God's kindness and love for them. Get the picture straight: Some kids swarming Jesus were small enough for him to pick up—but not all. (The word Mark wrote here for "children" is used in Luke 8:42 to mean a twelve-year-old.)

The kids and young teens closing in on Jesus didn't even get close. Jesus' friends—his disciples—blasted them away: "Don't waste his time," or "He has things to do. People to see. All more important than you."

Jesus stopped his disciples and blasted *them*. Kids were exactly the people he wanted to see—not because kids are constantly cute or nonstop nice or because they always act the way God wants, but because they demonstrate how to depend on God. People need to accept God's love the way a son or daughter accepts a parent's love.

The only way to make sense of God is to think like a kid.

Let the children come to me, for the Kingdom of God belongs to such as they. Don't send them away! MARK 10:14 TLB

Size Twelve

"*Hoooo-weeeeee!*" Jason's golfer bellowed. "Look at that! Never seen anything like it."

The foursome of golfers and their caddies all whistled through their teeth at the sight of the third hole. Rain had made the whole fairway a water hazard. Everyone mumbled about skipping to the next hole, but Jason's golfer teed up and composed himself to whack the ball.

"Don't worry about it, gents," he said. "Haven't you seen the size of my caddie's feet? Hey, kid—what size shoe do you wear?"

"Twelve."

"Canoes! Just what I guessed. You can float out to fetch golf balls."

Read 2 Chronicles 16:9
What matters most about a person?

Some days it feels as if all anyone notices is how you look on the outside. So guys flex their biceps and wonder if the girls think they're manly. Girls flex their legs so their thighs *splurrggge* a half inch less.

God is interested in more than that.

Remember when God sent Samuel to find a king? Samuel was searching for that kingly look—maybe a camera-ready face fit for TV. God told him, "I don't look at the outside. I check out the inside. I want to see a heart that is good, one totally devoted to me." God picked David, the youngest brother, to be king. God said he was the one guy who was "the kind of man I want. He will do all I want him to do" (Acts 13:22 NCV).

You're at your best not when you're toned and tanned on the outside but when your insides are well-developed—when you're self-controlled, honest, unselfish, thoughtful, and thinking, when you respect God, yourself, and others.

There's a promise that comes when you're completely given to God. Your Lord is spying out those who totally belong to him. He's going to make you strong. Sounds like genuine babedom. Or hunkhood.

The Lord searches all the earth for people who have given themselves completely to him. He wants to make them strong.
2 CHRONICLES 16:9 NCV

Burst That Bubble

Jamie's head had blown into a big snotbubble ever since she got her driver's license.

"*Please*?" Rebecca begged. "Just to the mall. It's just me and Natalie."

"Not with us! Ride your bikes. I'm taking the car by myself."

"Dad!" Rebecca howled. "Jamie won't give us a ride to the mall."

"Jamie, give Becca a ride or *you* won't be taking the car."

Rebecca and Natalie jumped into the backseat. Jamie snarled at them, "I'm giving you a ride because Dad said I had to. When we get to the mall I'm dropping you off and we're going to the other end. Stay out of our way. We don't want to be seen with you little geeks."

Read 2 Timothy 2:19–21
What does it mean to be mature?

You might call it your lucky day if your older brothers and sisters cared as much about you as they did about the family dog. Parents can seem as if they've forgotten what it's like to be your age. And teachers often assume you won't be issued a brain until you turn thirty.

What do *they* know that you don't, anyway? Some seem so stupid.

You're right. A driver's license means someone can safely operate a car, not a mouth. A high-school or college diploma doesn't guarantee a person has graduated from the terrible twos. Maturity is more than having car and house payments and piling up birthdays.

So when the Bible urges you to become mature by being "made holy," like God—who's *reeeally* old—the thrill might not pump your bike tires.

God may be *reeeally* old, but he's also *reeeeeeeally* cool. And acting like him is the secret to real life. Maturity is being what God wants you to be when he wants you to be it. It's becoming like him in your attitudes and actions.

When you grow in obedience to your Master, running away from what's wrong and chasing what's right, then you're "an instrument for noble purposes," ready for the best God has for you (2 Timothy 2:21).

That's choosing to be precious gold, not a snotbubble.

If a man cleanses himself from the latter, he will be an instrument for noble purposes, made holy, useful to the Master and prepared to do any good work. 2 TIMOTHY 2:21

No Farmer Tans

You used to be such a nerd. Until you became a Wedunnawanna fammatanna, that is.

At the beginning you didn't even know what a 'Tanna was. You were totally tugged toward a group with jungle-print surfboards and coordinated swimsuits. They lay on the beach. They didn't say much. Just things like "Whoa, dude." Seemed serene.

You found out that 'Tannas didn't bathe. And they chain-smoked funny little cigarettes rolled fresh from weeds. "I don't do it myself," you told people who worried about your new friends. "They're melding their minds toward universal peace. It's so cool. They see stuff." No doubt.

You start reevaluating your friendships when your skin blisters and sprouts suspicious pre-cancerous growths, and then your hair gets gnarly and gnatted and you gnotice you can't get a comb through it. Bad scene.

Read Genesis 37:1–11

When is it stunning to have your own style?

It was ghastly that Joseph announced his family would bow to him. Joseph's older brothers decided to kill the dreamer, but it paid better to sell him as a slave.

But Joseph had a good side. He thought for himself. He spoke out, regardless of what others thought of him. He wanted to stand apart from his brothers, to lead, to be more than a seventeen-year-old shooing sheep.

Years after he became a slave, God allowed Joseph to interpret a dream predicting seven years of bad crops. He rose to power when he helped the Egyptians store food and avoid starvation. When his brothers went to Egypt to scrounge food, they bowed before a great ruler who fed them. That ruler turned out to be Joseph, the brother they were sure they had done in. Joseph realized that God hadn't made him different and given him power to pay back his brothers. It was so he could play a part in God's plans.

God wants you to think hard about how he can use you—to do right at school, to tell teammates about him, to reach out and feed the homeless, teach kids to read, or help the elderly do what they can't do anymore.

Dream big about what God wants you to be. Not to be strange. Not to be selfish. But to be significant for God.

Joseph had a dream. GENESIS 37:5

Whacky World

The argument got so ugly that everyone in the hall stopped to listen.

"You're acting like a baby," Mari spit.

"Really? Well, you *are* a baby," Ginny laughed nastily.

Mari gulped. "What are you talking about?"

"You know what I'm talking about," Ginny shot back. "You're a baby. You still wet the bed."

That was the secret Ginny had sworn never, *ever* to tell. Mari and Ginny met in third grade, and Mari stayed over at Ginny's house a couple times a month. She always brought blankets and sheets instead of a sleeping bag. Some weekends Mari had to toss her bedding in the wash or take stuff home in a plastic bag.

The girls were best friends. Mari's problem didn't matter.

Until now. And Mari was getting ready to remove Ginny's head.

Read Luke 22:47–54

How did Jesus react when Peter let his emotions overwhelm him—and whacked a guard's ear off with a knife?

With a kiss for a greeting, Judas—one of Jesus' twelve handpicked followers—showed the guards which man was Jesus.

Peter watched, horrified. For three years he had followed Jesus. He was one of Jesus' three closest friends. Now his friend and master was being seized by soldiers, torn away to be tried and to die. Peter was terrified and angry.

He lashed out (John 18:10). It felt like the thing to do. But it wasn't.

Your emotions say it's right, so you do it. A teacher gives you extra homework and you cuss under your breath. You slam your bedroom door in anger at your parents. You feel hurt and end a friendship. You see something you like so you take it.

But all the emotions that swirl inside of you—anger, excitement, hatred, jealousy, boredom, laziness—can't tell you right from wrong. Your sure guide is the Bible, with its calm, unchanging commands (Psalm 19:7–11).

"No more of this!" Jesus says. So think—don't just feel—before you act. Jesus isn't always around to reattach the ears you whack off.

But Jesus answered, "No more of this!" And he touched the man's ear and healed him. LUKE 22:51

Life Is a Logroll

A year ago when his mom remarried, Matt expected his life to stay put for a while. His biological father had started drinking again, so Matt decided to move in with Mom and her new husband, Joe. Matt hated switching schools, but it got him out of his father's yelling range. Besides, his mom's new husband had a pretty nice place.

Then last Tuesday his mom sat him down. "Joe and I are getting a divorce," his mom told him. "Things aren't working out. We'll need to pack up and find an apartment. We need to be out within a week."

"We're staying around here, aren't we?" Matt protested. He was sick of school shuffling.

"I don't know. I think I need some space. You understand, don't you?"
Sure. I always understand.

Read Hebrews 13:8
What one thing in life stays the same when everything else changes?

Life swirls: You switch schools. You move. Your mom might go to work and dad might lose his job. Your classes, schedule, and teachers never stay the same. Your world changes: Neighborhoods spring up. Malls multiply. TV shows premier and fizzle. You find a new favorite song. And besides that, *you* change: Your brain and body expand. You cut your hair and buy new clothes. You swap friends. You get a job. Your interests and hobbies and after-school activities come and go.

So even if your family isn't lurching, you still may feel as if you're logrolling. Life shifts, spins, and bobs, threatening your balance and leaving you insecure and powerless. Sometimes you give up and go in the drink.

Jesus never changes. Yesterday he showed himself to be God on earth (John 1:14). Today he's the one who won't leave you (Hebrews 13:5). And he prepares a forever home for you (John 14:3).

Jesus doesn't always stop the log from spinning. But if you ask for his help, he climbs on the log, holds your hand, puts cleats on your feet, and helps you dance.

And when life flips you into the water, he'll pull you back up on the log.

Jesus Christ is the same yesterday and today and forever.
HEBREWS 13:8

Game Master

"Breakfast was great, Mrs. Dahmke." Tabby groaned. "I'm stuffed. Thanks for letting me stay over."

"Thanks for coming, Tabby," Nicole's mom answered. "It sounds like you two had a good time. But I'll need to take you home now because I have errands to run."

Tabby whispered to Nicole. "But it's Saturday! Don't you want to watch videos or something? Then we could go to the mall."

"Sure, but Mom says she needs to take you *now*."

"I don't want to go. I always make sure I'm not home on Saturday mornings so I don't have to do my chores. My brother will do them. He's so juvenile."

"You *what*?" Nicole was amazed. "If I tried that my parents would never let me out of the house!"

Read Matthew 25:14–30

What does God expect you to do with the skills and strength that he gives you?

You don't get to play ball without practicing, have friends over without picking up, or be part of a family without doing your part. You can't split responsibility and privilege.

Jesus said his Father's kingdom is like a master who trusts his servants with astronomical amounts of money—not a student's measly allowance but more cash than you'll touch in your life, unless you can hit homers or skate a triple axel. Two servants work to increase the money entrusted to them. The master gives them even grander opportunities.

Yippy skippy. You do well, you get more work. Sounds like school.

Not quite. The servants hear their master's approval. They "share their master's happiness." Get it? It's like reaching the next level in a video game.

A third servant refuses to take risks. He hides what he has. He's tossed out.

God has given you vast riches, a lifetime to give back to him what he's given you. So how much do you have? What do you have? How can you wisely invest your life to serve God?

You have the next few years to figure that out. It's all part of the fun.

His master replied, "Well done, good and faithful servant!"
MATTHEW 25:21

Wheeling the Wrong Way

Sheri wanted everything perfect for her date. She puckered up to the mirror to get her lipstick right, then stepped back to check her outfit. *Just right.* She looked a lot older than she was. *My mother would hate this—if she bothered to notice.*

Sheri heard Darren pull into the driveway. Sheri hated the stunts Darren did with her on the back of his motorcycle, but she figured a few seconds of terror was worth the attention he gave her.

Sheri ran outside. She hopped on, hung on, and hoped.

Read Romans 8:38–39
How do you find total love and acceptance?

Trying to grow up too fast is like jumping on the backseat of a motor-cycle quickly heading the wrong way. Once you're on it's tough to get off.

Some kids fly down dead-end roads in their attempt to grow up—smok-ing, drinking, inhaling, or popping to feel cool; thinking they can get along without their parents; purging food or starving themselves; dating or hang-ing out with older kids. They push past the speed limit, thinking they can outrun the consequences of their actions.

But here's the surprise: We've *all* headed away from God (Romans 3:10-12). We've tried to act grown-up—*too* grown-up—trying to get along without God's closeness or commands, doing life our own way to feel big, strong, and independent.

There's a better way to feel important. In Christ, God offers us more love and acceptance and significance than we can ever make for ourselves. *Nothing* is bigger than God's love for us in Christ.

We need to stop trying to be something we're not—and enjoy being the people God made us to be. We can say, "God, I'm not all grown-up. I never will be. I need you. I want to follow and obey you because you love me. I'll never outgrow you."

That's how you get off the bike and accept God's love for you. It's like getting a ride back to where you belong.

*Neither death nor life...neither the present nor the future...
neither height nor depth, nor anything else in all creation, will
be able to separate us from the love of God.* ROMANS 8:38-39

They Call This Home?

"When are we going to leave?" Brent whispered not too quietly to his parents. He didn't get an answer—other than "*Shhh!*"

Brent loved Grandpa. Funeral homes gave him the creeps.

Brent got the message that he wasn't going anywhere, so he went back by the casket. Everyone remarked that Grandpa looked the best he had in years. Brent thought he looked like an old mannequin with its cracks and chipped paint puttied over.

In fact, everything in the place seemed unreal. Warbly church music played in the background as ladies cried on cue and men shook hands and talked baseball. Brent's little cousins darted in and out of the flowers around the casket. At the side the funeral director wore a well-rehearsed look of polite concern. He glanced at his watch a lot.

This isn't Grandpa, Brent thought as he looked back in the casket. He wondered where the real Grandpa was. He worried how it would feel to be in Grandpa's place.

Read John 14:1–7

What will the end of your life be like?

It's scary. You don't just morph and grow up. You grow old. Your skin wrinkles, your brain skips, and your body breaks. And you don't just grow old. You die.

God stays with you even if you reside in a nursing home (Isaiah 46:3-4). A funeral home or cemetery isn't your final resting place. Christians have a better home. When Jesus told his followers that he was "leaving" soon (John 13:33), he said not to worry. He was going to prepare a mansion for them. He knew his followers would arrive safely because he would come back for them (1 Thessalonians 4:13–17).

His disciples said, "Huh?"

Jesus had in mind a lasting home—heaven. His disciples already had directions how to get there. *Jesus* was the path. And the Father would welcome them in his mansion because they knew his Son, the true and living way to God.

Heaven is your forever home. And death on earth is just the door.

In my Father's house are many rooms.... I am going there to prepare a place for you. JOHN 14:2

Loves Me Not

You signed up for German because you thought the girl you like would take it, but she took Spanish. So you suffer through a teacher who spits on you when she says, "Ich liebe dich." If you plucked a flower it would slap you and say, *She loves you...not.*

Or you're a girl and the guy you adore from afar changes girlfriends quicker than you can change TV channels. He "goes with" a dozen girls a month. Never you. *He loves me...no*t.

Rejection—the person you like doesn't like you back. You wonder: *What's wrong with me?* You worry: *Everyone thinks I'm a loser.* You wallow in the unspeakable: *I'll spend my life as a nun.*

Read James 1:16–17
What does God have to do with finding someone for you?

God intends for most people to get married (1 Corinthians 7). That's probably what he plans for you. So the question most likely isn't *if* you'll find someone but *when* and *who*.

James says that "every good and perfect gift is from above." God knows what you need when you need it. You can trust him to give you the right gift at the right time, whether it's your driver's license, a date, or the guy or girl of your dreams.

That doesn't mean God doesn't care about you right now. He feels your rejection more than you can ever imagine, because he was rejected by the people he made (John 1:10–11). It's just that God's best gift to you might also be *not* letting you go with that guy or girl—or *anyone*—right now. Diving into the dating craze too soon or dating the wrong person messes up your other relationships and responsibilities. And it can make it harder to keep sex for marriage.

God sees your whole life. He wants you to be ready for a marriage devoted to him. The gift you might want him to drop on you is a quick date, but the gift he gives is patience, character, and—at the right time, almost for sure—trust him—someone you're so crazed about you want to spend the rest of your life together.

Every good and perfect gift is from above, coming down from the Father of heavenly lights, who does not change like shifting shadows. JAMES 1:17

On the Couch

Derek kisses Ericka awkwardly on the cheek, then the lips, and she kisses him back. Then he tries to touch her in ways that make her feel uncomfortable and excited at the same time. And now neither of them knows what to do. She's never been so close to a boy or felt so loved. She likes Derek's warm attention. And he wants more.

After a nervous minute Derek suddenly blurts out, "I love you." Ericka says the same. But both of them wonder what the words mean.

Freeze frame: Is love the reason why Derek and Ericka are mashing lips on the couch?

Doubtful. Ericka enjoys Derek's affection, which makes her feel as desirable as the other girls she knows. To keep him liking her, she's willing to do things she probably wouldn't do otherwise. So she's using Derek. But Derek is using Ericka too. Having a girlfriend shows him and his friends he's not a wuss. And he thinks groping Ericka is great fun.

Read Proverbs 5:15–23

What's God's awesome plan for sex?

Proverbs compares sex and love to water. In a desert, only a madman would carelessly spill the water he needs to survive. Marriage is God's way to protect sexual love as the priceless treasure God made it to be.

Love in marriage is for each other, not to look good for others or feel good for a few minutes. That's the God-designed setting where Ericka won't worry about Derek ditching her, and Derek can treat Ericka right, not just grab what he can. Real love between a man and a woman is billion-dollar stuff, but Ericka and Derek are trashing it like it's worth pennies.

But Ericka and Derek weren't having sex. And no one their age is ready for marriage. What about kisses and hugs? When are they okay? They aren't meant to be spilled all over either, because they're meant to lead to more. They're part of love, like a good warm-up band before the main concert.

Your parents—and your youth pastor or other Christian adults you trust—can help you *set and keep* limits that will stop you from wasting one of God's best inventions. After all, if your parents didn't understand the feelings you're facing as you grow up, you wouldn't be here! Talk to them.

Be faithful to your own wife, just as you drink water from your own well. PROVERBS 5:15 NCV

A Sea of Eyeballs

Tony thought Lindsey was fascinating—even in an ugly phys ed outfit.

Lindsey was, well, mature. The other guys made smutty comments about her, but Tony just contemplated how cool it would be if she was his girlfriend. He would be famous, or something like that, and more.

"You know you're dreaming about her," they yelled at Tony as he stood watching her. Dazed by Lindsey, he didn't hear. "Forget it, Tony. She thinks you're a moron." Still he didn't break his stare.

So the guys winged Tony the basketball to wake him up. The ball, however, didn't slam his chest or knock the wind from his gut. It smashed into his face, shattering his glasses and busting his nose.

Tony was in for a difficult time explaining to his mother why he missed the pass.

Read Matthew 5:27–30

How does Jesus want you to think about the opposite sex?

If guys or girls gouged an eye every time their thoughts got hot, the ground would be littered with eyeballs. Everywhere you look and listen—online, magazines, TV, movies, software, jokes, videos, T-shirts, billboards—your thoughts are shoved toward sex.

What Jesus calls "lust" isn't mere curiosity about the opposite sex. It isn't wanting a really close friend—or even, as you get older, having a body that feels sexually hungry. Lust is when you grasp for *what* you can't have *when* you can't have it.

The Bible is clear that "adultery," sex outside of marriage, is wrong (Exodus 20:14; Hebrews 13:4). But Jesus says purity runs deeper than that. You don't have to roam under clothes or get pregnant to have gone "too far." Real purity is booting from your brain even thoughts of wrong things.

That's what Jesus means by his hyped-up language ("hyperbole") about getting rid of things that cause you to sin. Jesus wants you not to mutilate yourself but to cut off evil—to exit situations that tempt you, look the other way when you need to (Job 31:1), and crowd out bad thoughts by filling your head with good ones.

But I tell you that anyone who looks at a woman lustfully has already committed adultery with her in his heart. MATTHEW 5:28

See Ya Later

Stefan and his friends crowded into the best baseball card store in town—an overgrown newsstand that sold everything from bubble gum and baseball cards to magazines and papers from all over the world.

But his buddies were looking for more than a Barry Bonds card.

"Don't think so hard, Stefan," they told him. "Just take it."

"It" was a skin magazine to be bought with a five-finger discount.

It wasn't that Stefan was an uncurious, hormone-free kind of guy. But he could think of a few fatal reasons to say no: (1) getting shot for shoplifting; (2) getting grilled by his parents for looking at porn; (3) the pledge he'd made to stay sexually pure—and porn-free was part of that; and (4) how awful he felt when he deliberately did something wrong.

Four strikes—his friends were out. Stefan walked away. "If you want it," he told them, "*you* steal it. See ya. I'm going home."

Read Matthew 5:6

Are you a fool to play by God's rules—like his rules about sex?

You want to do what's right. But lots of times cheaters grab better grades. Shoplifters score more stuff. Devious kids do wrong and then lie to get out of punishment. They all grab what they want for themselves—and they almost always get to keep it. You feel deprived.

God will smoke people who don't ditch sin (Revelation 21:8). But that's another topic—and besides, what's that end-of-the-world truth do for you? After all, right now you might feel like all you ever see is evil's spectacular success.

There's a great thing about doing good: If you do right, you have nothing to fear (Romans 13:3). That beats being filled with fear about getting in trouble. But there's another great thing: When you hunger for God and his ways, God fills you up so you can be wildly happy doing what's best. When you really want righteousness—right attitudes and actions, inside and out— he remakes you to want to be good not only for your own sake but also for the world around you to work right.

And whenever you want God's right thing in God's right time, he'll give it to you.

Blessed are those who hunger and thirst for righteousness, for they will be filled. MATTHEW 5:6

The Sleaze Queens

Heather had heard about "the Sleaze Queens" long before she graduated into her new school. And she spotted Amanda and Aimee her first day at the place.

Amanda and Aimee were twins who lived up to their wicked nickname. They had a reputation for being, um, sleazy—and from high atop their throne of popularity, they managed to control the entire social scene of their school.

They had decreed that any girl without a boyfriend was henceforth and forevermore a loser. Never mind that the boys knew more about the finer points of making armpit noises than they did about treating girls fine. Or that no girl or guy needs to get locked up in a relationship that sooner or later leads nowhere good.

Heather was—by the Sleaze Queens' quite official rules of the school—a loser. And know what? Knowing she was doing the right thing didn't automatically make her feel better.

Read Matthew 5:8

What does purity look like in real life?

You ache when you're left out for making right choices. If purity were just about doing rules for the sake of rules, you'd have reason to feel rotten. But it's better than that.

Yep, purity is about *performance—how you act.* It's about obeying and conforming to God's commands. But conforming isn't contorting—twisting yourself into a pretzel just because someone makes you.

Purity is also about *purpose—how you think and feel.* Jesus said that real purity starts with the heart (Matthew 5:21–22, 27–28). Being sweet-sixteen-and-never-been-kissed sure beats sweet-sixteen-and-never-been-missed—but not if your only goal in life is to hook up.

Get this: Purity is most of all about a *person—how you live close to Jesus.* It's no mystery. Jesus said that anyone who serves him hangs tight with him (John 12:26). Real purity wants right stuff and sticks close to Jesus' side. It's true: The pure in heart see God.

And having Jesus close by beats holding hands with an armpit-blasting boyfriend.

Blessed are the pure in heart, for they will see God.
MATTHEW 5:8

On Your Side

Shawna hadn't heard her twin brother's friend come into the house. When Andy shouted, "Anyone home?" she yelled, "In here!" She didn't think anything of it when he sat down next to her while she was doing her homework. They talked for a few minutes and she explained that everyone else had gone to a movie. Andy was always so nice.

Then he pinned her down and told her to be quiet.

Afterward he said not to tell anyone.

Shawna crawled down in the corner, stuck between the bed and the wall. She felt filthy. Numb.

Not much is such a horrible slap to God's plan for his world as sexual abuse—assault, date rape, incest, or being grabbed or molested.

Read Psalm 146:5–10

Where can a victim of abuse—any abuse—go for help?

Six Bible verses won't put life back together. God can.

Jesus was whipped and nailed naked to a cross. Jesus knows helplessness. No one rescued him. No one understood his pain.

God takes the side of the beaten down. He believes their side of the story. He wants them to feel clean, safe, and fearless; not dirty, threatened, and ashamed. Blessed ("peaceful," "happy," and "at rest") is the one who hopes in the Lord.

God doesn't leave the abused to suffer alone. When abuse steals the love God planned for his world, God wants to give it back through his family and other caring people. If you or a friend has been abused, tell a parent, pastor, school counselor, or a mental health telephone hot line what happened. They'll keep your story private but get you the help you need. *Don't wait.*

Abuse blends sex and violence and churns out helpless, hopeless victims, both guys and girls. It's a mess. But God knows how to put victims of abuse back together.

Blessed is he whose help is the God of Jacob, whose hope is in the Lord his God, the Maker of heaven and earth, the sea, and everything in them—the LORD, who remains faithful forever. He upholds the cause of the oppressed ... the LORD lifts up those who are bowed down. PSALM 146:5–8

ResQ'd or BarBQ'd?

Knock, knock. Bamm. BAMM. You open the door to your bullet-riddled apartment in a high-rise housing project. A fireman stands at your door.

"Excuse me," he says with polite urgency. "This building is on fire. You must have noticed the flames and heat and smoke from below. I'm here to rescue you."

"Actually, I hadn't noticed," you reply. "We're having a party."

"In there? In that smoke?" Your living room is a cloud.

"Smoke? What smoke?" You cough as you finish pouring yourself a soda.

"I can hardly see your guests. And look—the heat's melted your ice."

"Well, I don't want to leave. Everything I need is here."

"You don't understand. This building is burning down. I can show you the only way out. Just follow..." *Slam.*

Read Exodus 6:6–12

What did the Israelites think about God's rescue plan?

For years Israel had rotted in slavery, a life "bitter with hard labor" (Exodus 1:14). Egyptian masters beat them to make bricks for the Pharaohs' building projects and even tried to kill the Israelites' baby boys to prevent them from revolting as grown men.

Along came Moses, God's appointed leader. He brought a promise from God to save the Israelites from slavery, judge their masters, and guide them into a prosperous new land where they could live in peace as his people.

Here's the surprise: They didn't jump up and down with delight.

You might have the same reaction when God says he wants to usher you into a life of total devotion to him: *God, you couldn't possibly love me.* You're convinced you're too awful for God to love. *My life is too big of a mess.* You think your situation is too tough. *You don't care.* You suppose God doesn't understand the pressures you face. Or you may think, *My friends don't want to come with. I don't want to follow anyone. I don't know where God will take me.*

Here's another surprise: None of those feelings change the fact that God wants to set you free.

Moses reported this to the Israelites, but they did not listen to him because of their discouragement and cruel bondage.
EXODUS 6:9

Move

A message that passed secretly through camp told the prisoners to prepare to flee camp soon. And one night the POWs jolted awake as jets streaked over the camp an hour before dawn, destroying guard towers and the camp command. Half an hour later paratroopers stormed the prison itself. Cell doors swung open. The POWs were free. But they needed to walk out.

Crazed with fear, some prisoners wouldn't leave their cells. "We can't go out with no weapons! We're going to die!"

"Get out!" yelled the paratroopers, who knew they controlled the camp and a corridor to safety. "Trust us. Shut up and move!"

Read Exodus 14:10–18

What did God say to the Israelites when they thought they would die trying to escape slavery?

God sent horrible plagues—frogs, gnats, hail, and death—to force the Egyptians to free their Israelite slaves. And he had more miracles in store—like parting the Red Sea and drowning the Egyptian army. When Israel still doubted God knew what he was doing, he told them, "I mean it. I'll save you. Quit moaning and start walking."

To escape, they had to believe God. And they had to act on what they believed.

In Christ, God acted to rescue you. Christ died to bring forgiveness and a life close to God. But you won't ever feel freedom if you don't believe him and act on what you believe. You've got to get out of your cell.

You put your trust in him. Then you grab hold of what he's done for you. If you believe that God has forgiven and accepted you, then you talk to him confidently (Hebrews 10:19–22). If you're sure God protects you, then you fear nothing (Psalm 118:6). If you know that hardship is God's discipline, then you resolve to learn from tough stuff you can't change (Hebrews 12:11). If you accept God's love for you, then you love others (1 John 4:19). If you trust that God wants what's best for you, then you obey (Psalm 19:7–11).

If you don't act on good news, it can't change your life.

Then the Lord said to Moses, "Why are you crying out to me? Tell the Israelites to move on." EXODUS 14:15

Show Me the Way

David's parents wondered why he had helped himself to a clutchful of cash from a teacher's purse. "She's really stupid," he told them. "She always leaves her purse out."

"It sounds like you're trying to blame *her*," his dad said as calmly as he could manage. "What we need to know is why you took the money."

"I didn't do it for myself. There's this girl I know whose coat was swiped. It wasn't fair. Our teacher knew it and didn't figure out who took it. I was sort of getting her back. I gave most of the money to this girl so she could get a new coat."

"David, don't you realize that was wrong?"

"But I only kept five bucks. That makes it not so bad, doesn't it?"

Read Exodus 13:21–22
Why did God show up in pillars of cloud and fire for Israel?

God didn't abandon the Israelites to wander alone through the desert in search of the land he had promised them. He showed up by day in a pillar of cloud and by night in a pillar of fire, visible signs of his presence and protection. The people followed the pillar as it moved. It cleared their confusion and built their confidence.

God didn't stop at pointing out a route and rest stops. On a mountaintop he spoke to Moses and revealed ten commands that told Israel how to act toward him and toward people (Exodus 20:1–17). After Israel entered the land, God continued to speak through his spokespeople, the prophets.

We need the same assurance about where to go—how to live, what to do, and what not to do. It's not that we're dumb. But we need help to think right about wrong. Lying is bad, but we still find reasons to fib, exaggerate, jumble, and distort. Stealing is crooked, but we excuse ourselves when we shoplift, copy homework, or fill our hard drives with copyrighted music. Spin us around once and we're lost.

God doesn't dress in a cloud anymore, but he still guides us. He's given us the Bible to lead us where he wants to take us, to give us sure direction. It's our map. Don't leave home without it.

By day the LORD went ahead of them in a pillar of cloud to guide them on their way and by night in a pillar of fire to give them light. EXODUS 13:21

Just What You Need

Maurita screamed as Val walked away, "I don't know why I tell you anything. You always talk behind my back."

Val had been Maurita's best friend since kindergarten. At their small school where everybody knew everybody and they didn't have many other friends. When Val walked off, Maurita felt abandoned. Val was all she had. Where would she find another friend like her?

When a girl moved in next door, Maurita's hopes rose. But that went nowhere. Then Maurita's math teacher paired her as a study partner with the girl who sat behind her. Jen was quiet, so Maurita didn't know her well. She was nice, though. And after a few months Jen became a better friend for Maurita than Val ever was.

Read Exodus 16:9–20

How did God feed the Israelites when they thought they would starve?

Not long after the Israelites fled slavery, they faced certain starvation in the desert. Where could they find food for two million people?

They didn't expect it to fall from the sky. Yet it did. God sent "manna" (which means "What is it?"). It was God's unexpected solution to an impossible problem, a sign that God was looking out for them. If they didn't trust that God would provide again the next day, what they hoarded overnight stank and crawled with maggots. God made them gather manna repeatedly to remind them that they needed him every day.

You face times when you think you're going to die—that you're going to wither with loneliness, shatter from stress, melt with nervousness. One more ounce of pressure and you'll crumple. You know you need God. Yet you can't see a solution coming.

God will take care of you. Among other things, God promises to provide godly friends (1 Kings 19:14–21), encouragement (2 Thessalonians 2:16–17), and peace (Philippians 4:6–7), and to meet your physical needs (Philippians 4:19).

Where will help come from? God. What will it be? You never know. When will it come? On time. Expect it.

Thin flakes like frost on the ground appeared on the desert floor. EXODUS 16:14

Out Your Nose

Neil sat in the hall after Mr. Holtz booted him from Sunday school class. After a while Mr. Holtz came out and asked Neil what was going on with him in class.

"I'm bored," Neil answered. "I've been coming to this church for seven years, and I can't make friends here."

"Do you have friends at school?"

"Lots."

"What are your friends like at school?"

"They're fun. I suppose we get in trouble sometimes. But they aren't boring like kids here. My friends there are cool."

Read Numbers 11:4–6, 18–20, 31–34

What did the Israelites think of the food God miraculously provided for them in the desert?

Sure, God gave manna, the Israelites thought. *"It's good fur yah,"* he says. *Bet God doesn't eat bamanna muffins three times a day.* The Israelites' minds cooked up pots of fish, and their memories picked fresh fruits and veggies. They wanted Egypt.

What they remembered, though, was unbelievably better than what they ever actually had. And heading back to slavery in order to enjoy a bag of onions was like being a dog and wanting to go back to the pound because the biscuits taste good.

God wasn't upset that his people were bored by his menu. He was angry because they would rather be bound as slaves than walk with him. Their complaints rejected not only God's gift of food but God himself. So for a month God granted their request—enough meat that it came "out of their nostrils."

God gives gifts—family, church, work, school—meant only for your best (James 1:17). Your attitude toward all that God gives—however plain, simple, or even boring God's gifts seem—reveals your attitude toward God himself (Exodus 16:4). So don't whine for things you think are better than God's gifts. God just might give you what you want. You know how pleasant it feels when you spit milk through your nose. Imagine hunks of bird meat touring your nasal cavity.

But now we have lost our appetite; we never see anything but this manna! NUMBERS 11:6

Scared Off

During the trip with the kids from church, God seemed so real. So close. Everything made sense. Nothing, you decided, would come between you and God again. You wanted to trust and obey him the best you knew how. You were so sure.

But the last night of the trip you dreamed about your friends back home. The dream was like a normal day at school, except that every few minutes a friend told you what they thought about your faith in God: *You think you're better than us. That stuff isn't real. You were just hyper—you would have signed up for the circus if that's what they told you to do. Those people brainwashed you. Christians are geeks. Don't you know that being different is the kiss of death? I wouldn't say this if I didn't care about you, but...*

By the time you woke up you weren't so sure about following Jesus anymore. That day your own brain chimed in: *My friends are going to stop calling me. How will I survive at school? Everyone will mock me. Or ignore me.*

Read Numbers 13:26–33

What did the Israelite spies tell people about the land they saw?

When God brought the Israelites to the border of the land he promised to give them, twelve men went ahead to spy out the land. It was as good as God said, spilling milk and honey, bursting with globs of grapes so huge they took two men to carry. The spies saw definite possibilities.

Even so, ten of the spies focused on a problem: the thugs who ran the land. They forgot God's promise: the land was theirs for the taking. True, there were giants. But God said the Israelites could whip them, not with their own skill but with his strength.

There's no doubt that what God promises us is good. We look at it, we want it: friendship with the living God. Membership in his kingdom. Guidance and peace even in the middle of chaos. God's security, satisfaction, and splendor look mighty fine.

It's the giants that are scary—our friends' reactions, the things we need to give up, our fears and weaknesses.

Our eyes are fine. It's our hearts that fail.

Yes, there are giants in the land. But God is bigger.

And they spread among the Israelites a bad report about the land they had explored. NUMBERS 13:32

Stick or Get Stuck

The football team lined the wall of the school's main hall, looking cool on the first day of school. As Scott limped past, the team captain crooked his arm, cocked his head, opened his mouth, and flopped out his tongue. "Look, guys," Rick said as he drooled. "The retard is back! Everybody wave to the retard." The whole team copied Rick's cruel imitation.

Scott wasn't mentally retarded. Cerebral palsy slurred his speech and gave him little control over his muscles.

Not everyone thought Rick was funny. When he chased Scott down the hall, Rick's girlfriend stuck out her foot to trip Rick. He sprawled. And she yelled at him as he lay on the ground. "I'm sick of you making fun of Scott," she steamed. "You're so mean!"

Question: You're one of the guys on the football team. Do you applaud as Rick's girlfriend stomps on his chest?

Read Numbers 14:1–9

How did Caleb and Joshua and Aaron and Moses manage to stick up for what was right?

It's great to decide to stand apart from the crowd. But it's a lot more realistic to decide which crowd you want to stand with.

Everywhere you go you see two types of people. The first kind tries to do right. At school they want to learn, listen, do well. They treat others the way they want to be treated. At home they respect their families. At church they study to know God better and live what they know.

The other kind tests the limits. They do as much as they can get away with without getting busted.

It's true that the second group is often bigger. And that they often carry rocks.

That doesn't mean they're right or that they'll win. Joshua and Caleb stood up against popular opinion. They ripped their clothing to mourn the sinfulness of the others. They stood for God. They stood *together*. And because they did what God wanted, he made them leaders of a new, younger generation that stormed the Promised Land.

You may not have the guts to start the right crowd. But at least find a way to join them.

The land we passed through and explored is exceedingly good.
NUMBERS 14:7

You Asked For It

At her clinic appointment she screamed and cried, "NO! The test must be wrong!" In the next months as her stomach grew, she couldn't deny what she had done. On due day, when her abdomen wrenched with labor pains, she knew there was no easy escape.

That pain was nothing compared to having her baby whisked away to its adoptive parents. It was a perfect baby boy, the doctor said, but she didn't get to see him. Putting her baby up for adoption meant she could finish school and get on with life. But she wondered a thousand times a day what her baby was doing and how he was.

Even years later, when she had a husband and family, she still imagined what the boy looked like and pretended he was taking his spot at the table when she called for dinner.

Read Numbers 14:26–35
What happened to the Israelites when they decided to disobey God over and over?

When you rough up your little brother in the living room and knock a knick-knack off a shelf, sometimes you can glue the pieces together. But the knickknack you whacked won't ever be what it used to be. At best, it's cracked.

God does better than we can. When we sin and whack our relationship with God off the shelf, accepting God's offer of forgiveness mends the cracks. God fixes our relationship. The cracks vanish.

The Israelites, God said, sinned against him over and over (Numbers 14:22). When they refused to storm the land and accused God of plotting to murder them and their children in the wilderness—they even vowed to choose a new leader and return to bondage in Egypt—God was beyond furious. "How long will they refuse to believe in me, in spite of all the miraculous signs I have performed among them?" (Numbers 14:11).

Moses pleaded with God, and God forgave the Israelites (Numbers 14:20). So they lived happily ever after, right? Not quite. Forgiveness doesn't eliminate the results of sinful actions. Their guilt was gone. The consequences weren't. God gave the people what they asked for. He locked them out of the land. They missed the best of what he planned.

In this desert your bodies will fall—every one of you twenty years old or more...who has grumbled against me. NUMBERS 14:29

　　　　　　　　　　　　　　　　　　　　　　STAMINA

Comfy Cozy

Legs and arms flow in perfect harmony, a symphony of coordination and grace. As you admire your powerful stride you hum the tune, "O Lord, it's hard to be humble when you're perfect in every way."

Glancing over your shoulder you discover you're so far ahead of the pack that you decide to stop running. You congratulate yourself. *I deserve a break. Been training hard, looking fine. Yep, I'm good. So good.* You plop on the track and spread out your picnic. You bite into your hero sandwich. *Hero*—how appropriate, you think.

You lie back and fall into a deep slumber, dreaming of the gold medals and world records you're sure you'll win.

Sleeping contentedly, you rouse only when a truck driver rolls down his window and yells, "Hey, moron! Get outta the road!"

Read Deuteronomy 8:6–20
Why did God warn Israel against getting comfortable when things went well?

God saved Israel from some tough stuff—slavery, snakes, scorpions, and starvation, for starters. And the homeland he planned for them was sweet—filled with streams and springs, wheat and barley, grapes, figs, honey, sheep, silver, and gold. God had a worry, however—that his people would forget all about him when they settled in such a nice place.

It's no problem remembering God when life goes bad. You pray, you complain, you cry for comfort. But when you feel safe and satisfied, you're easily distracted, wrapped up in what he gives you. You're not alert and on track. You forget that everything you have and are comes from God. You dream that you've arrived at the finish line.

But your pace will speed up when you rouse yourself with the fact that God is still God, worth thanking and chasing even when life goes great.

The risk in slowing your pace in the race isn't that other runners—other believers—will pass you by. The real danger is that your pride will run you over.

When you have eaten and are satisfied, praise the Lord your God for the good land he has given you. Be careful that you do not forget the Lord your God, failing to observe his commands.... DEUTERONOMY 8:10–11

Onward

You spent the past week scribbling in yearbooks—things like *"You're a great person. Don't ever change."* Or *"Remember to call."* Sometimes you signed your name with *"F/F"* ("Friends Forever").

Gag. You didn't mean nine-tenths of that stuff. You wanted gobs of signatures in your yearbook, so you had to write something in other people's books.

Then eighth-grade graduation shook your brain awake. Middle school meant more than what you were scrawling in yearbooks. Because of middle school, life would never be the same. You started as goofy post-elementary kids, but you weren't kids anymore. You had made the grade and were moving up. You had a future to build.

Suddenly you started to miss the place. It actually seemed pretty good.

But you also looked forward to something more.

Read Deuteronomy 4:32–40

The Israelites were camped at the edge of the land God had promised, ready to enter. What did Moses want them to remember?

When Israel looked back at forty years of wandering in the wilderness, they had no problem recalling the difficulties they faced in the desert.

Moses feared they might forget how good God had been—and that God's goodness should make a difference in their lives.

The world had never seen anything like God's friendship with Israel. God conversed with them, and through pests and floods and fire and miracles, he rescued them from slavery to make them his people.

They had only begun to see what God would do. And what God had done for them, Moses said, should change their lives. They had seen that God was God. Now they should follow him.

God's acts were real, not mush made up to write in someone's yearbook. God's love for you is just as real. Through Christ he acted to rescue you. He's promised never to leave you.

What you've learned about God so far is just the beginning. And it should change you. God is God. Follow him.

You were shown these things so that you might know that the Lord is God; besides him there is no other. DEUTERONOMY 4:35

I Smell a Skunk

"Thawr's skuhnk in thuh pawrk, yuh know."

Skunks? *Yeah, right*, you laugh as you walk away. You aren't about to let a stupid park ranger ruin your fun. Anyone who talks that dumb *is* that dumb, you figure. So you ignore his advice to keep food in sealed containers inside a car so raccoons or skunks—or bears—don't ravage your camp.

You're a long way from believing the ranger. Before bed you spill chips and splash soda inside and out of your tent, and you tuck yourself in with a stash of candy under your pillow.

As soon as you lie quiet you notice animal noises in the woods. *Maybe that dumb ranger knew what he was talking about....Nah.* But you hide in your sleeping bag when the scratching starts on the side of your tent, and you run for your car when you hear claws shredding nylon.

Read Judges 2:6–15

Why didn't Israel rest easy in the land God had promised them?

As God had said, the Israelites who refused to enter the land died in the desert. Their children became the heroes—conquering most of the peoples in the land. In time, however, a generation grew up that hadn't seen God's miracles firsthand. That's when the trouble began.

Instead of serving God, this new generation of Israelites followed the gods, or *Baals*, of their neighbors, who were worshiped through prostitution and child sacrifice. When God saw Israel's disobedience, he allowed their sinful neighbors to survive. He let their presence test Israel, to see if they would be devoted to him or turn away.

Because Israel let sin stick around, sin became a sticky mess for them.

Doing wrong hurts you now. It's like choosing to get beat up. But it also hurts you later. God wants to chase sin from your life by changing how you think and act. When you don't let him, you let your enemy live. It threatens you. It teases you. And sometimes it wallops you all over again. God doesn't warn you for nothing.

Don't be surprised if you don't get the sugar out of your tent and you wake up wearing a skunk on your head.

Then the Israelites did evil in the eyes of the Lord and served the Baals. JUDGES 2:11

It's Okay to Be Alone

Tanya flopped on her bed, grabbed her pillow, squished her face into it, and cried.

After a while she rolled over and pulled out her diary and began to write.

LOSER! she scrawled in huge letters across two pages. *Dear Diary*, she started on a third page. *Today I made a total fool of myself. Jessie copied Michelle's test. Mrs. Williams found out and Jessie and Michelle got kicked off the volleyball team. Everyone thinks I told Mrs. Williams that Jessie cheated.* Someone *must have told—but it wasn't me.* Tanya had tried to defend herself at volleyball practice. No one believed her. At the end of practice the team walked away and flipped off the gym lights, leaving her alone in the dark. *Why are they treating me like this? I didn't do anything. I don't have any friends left.*

Tanya knew that wasn't true.

I still have you, God, she wrote. *Please get me out of this mess.*

Read Psalm 31:9–16
What do you do when friends ditch you?

It's no surprise when enemies lie about you, talk behind your back, leave you in the dust, or punch you in the stomach.

It's harder to understand when friends do those things. You do your best to be a good friend, you work out conflicts, you love like Christ loves—and a friendship still blows up in your face. Sooner or later it happens to everyone. You moan and groan with hurt and feel like a reject.

Yet if you trust God to get you through the hurt, you'll survive. God can make it okay to be alone, because *he's* still your friend. He sees what you need in the darkness or behind slammed doors—even inside your head or on a page of your diary: "The eyes of the Lord range throughout the earth to strengthen those whose hearts are fully committed to him" (2 Chronicles 16:9).

When you have God as your friend, pain is only part of what you write in a diary or journal, only part of what you think and feel. The last line you write—or the thought to focus on through an awful, lonely day—can always be, "God, I trust you. I belong to you. Help me."

But I trust in you, O Lord; I say, "You are my God." My times are in your hands; deliver me from my enemies and from those who pursue me. PSALM 31:14-15

He Ain't Ugly

Your life flashes before your eyes. There isn't much to see. With your cousin switching to your school, life is over.

Henry looks like a giant prehistoric beaver straight out of a natural science museum, minus the tail—beady eyes and teeth that would make a mamma beaver proud, topped by glasses like soda-bottle bottoms. You think about introducing him to a friend whose dad is a plastic surgeon, but instead you fake sick and stay home for the first three days he's at school. Then it hits you. *We have different last names. No one will ever know.*

Your solution works until someone swipes Henry's glasses. He's pitiful, with his teeth chattering as he whimpers.

"Give my cousin his glasses. NOW!" you hear yourself say.

Life is definitely done.

Read Ruth 1:1–16
Why be loyal?

While Ruth's husband lived she had a duty to her mother-in-law, Naomi. But then she *chose* to stick with Naomi—someone who had been good to her. She decided to follow God and to join a new nation.

You're "loyal" when you meet the obligations you should—to God (1 Chronicles 29:17–18), family (Exodus 20:12), country (Romans 13:1), people who have helped you (Luke 17:12–16), other believers (Galatians 6:10), and people in need (Luke 10:29–37).

And it's a mistake to misplace loyalty—to give it to material things (Matthew 6:24) or to people who hurt you (2 Corinthians 11:19–20). Being loyal doesn't mean you keep a friend's suicide note a secret or shield a friend who did wrong (Ephesians 5:11). Being loyal sometimes means you hurt a friend to help him.

So what deserves your loyalty—and how much—and why? Think it through: (a) your bratty sister; (b) your homely next-door neighbor who's been your best friend since kindergarten; (c) a popular peer who brushes you off like dirt; (d) your dad when he dresses dumb; (e) your favorite football team; or (f) your best pair of shoes.

Don't die for something dumb. But don't hide when something important deserves your help.

Where you go I will go. RUTH 1:16

The Price Is Right

"This one. Definitely the coolest." Paul's friends each grabbed a sweat shirt blazoned with their school's logo and headed to the cashier to pay.

"Aren't you going to buy one?" Chris asked. "We're all getting them."

"Nope. Maybe later."

"How come you never have money?" Chris nosed.

Steve sneered. "He doesn't make any money. He volunteers as a handy wipe at the nursing home. He changes old people's diapers."

"I don't change diapers," Paul fought back. "Besides, so what if I did? My job's more important than mowing lawns to make money for a sweat shirt."

"You don't get paid?" Chris was shocked. "That's stupid. Why work?"

Read Luke 21:1–4
What makes a gift really great?

Your dog won't know the difference if you stuff yourself silly *before* you flip a few measly scraps under the table.

But that's no way to treat people. Jesus says that when you love people you don't just give leftovers. Even though the gift the widow gave was tiny, Jesus said it was better than the bags of money the rich gave. She offered all she had.

Giving unselfishly might cost you *time*. Your gift might be to help little kids at church, volunteer at a latchkey program, or tutor during free time at school. Being a giver often costs *money*. You could choose to contribute monthly to provide a child with school, food, shelter, and clean water. Or you can give to projects where you live.

And giving a real gift can cost you *popularity*. Jesus says to target people who can never pay you back (Luke 14:12–14), to reach beyond your crowd of friends to the poor, strange, sick, or trapped (Matthew 25:34–36). You might not like those people. They might not like you. They probably aren't the people you normally hang out with. Loving unselfishly sometimes costs you even more. It can cost you everything—as it did the widow. But that's the kind of gift Jesus gave to you (1 John 3:16).

This poor widow has put in more than all the others. All these people gave their gifts out of their wealth; but she out of her poverty put in all she had to live on. LUKE 21:3-4

Just Kidding

He'll never talk to her, thinks Hugh. So he decides to help John out.

"John thinks you're beautiful," Hugh shouts at Danielle. She looks at John like he's a nerd on a stick. John clamps his hand over Hugh's mouth and drags him around the corner to slap him up. "Ha, ha, funny, funny," John says as he socks Hugh's stomach.

Later Hugh tapes a two-foot-high homemade valentine on Danielle's locker, complete with a drooly poem and candy wax lips and John's name signed in big letters. Half the school reads it before Danielle gets to school and tears it down. "Why did you do that?" John yells.

"It was funny," Hugh jokes. "You're so chicken."

John doesn't look amused. A lot of punches later both of them are wiping bloody noses on the way to the principal's office. Hugh still doesn't think it's a big deal. *Why can't John take a joke?*

Read Matthew 5:21–24

What can you do when you've made someone mad?

The passage you read pictures a person busily worshiping God ("at the altar") when he realizes he's angered someone. If that happens, Jesus said, the worshiper should go to the person he made mad and set things right.

Now picture this: You're sitting in church. You grow uneasy. A bit queasy. You break a sweat and dig for a motion-sickness bag in the pew rack. Suddenly you bolt screaming out the back to beg forgiveness from a person you hurt.

Highly unlikely.

When you blow it you might not even feel guilty, much less stabbed through the heart by the knowledge that you've done wrong. Jesus reminded his listeners that God hates not just "big sins" like murder but "small sins" like anger. It's all the same in his eyes. And you don't want to wait to fix wrongs until they're so huge you can't help but feel miserable.

Your problem isn't solved by a secret "sorry" tossed at God. He wants you to go to the one you angered and repair what you can.

Even tough guys need to go and apologize. And set the situation straight. And change.

First go and be reconciled to your brother; then come and offer your gift. MATTHEW 5:24

Somewhere Better to Go

Miki sat on the curb at the park, crying. "I don't want them to see me like this. I'm so sick of them.

"Shawna started it. She said I was ugly and laughed at me and talked behind my back, even though she said I was her best friend.

"She said I tried to steal her boyfriend from her. He and I had three classes together. I just talked to him. That's not illegal, is it? I'm not a flirt. She is.

"And then three weeks ago she said *really* bad stuff about me—stuff I wouldn't say about *anyone*." Miki started to cry again. "When I tried to defend myself it was even worse. It's been *three weeks* since any of my friends have talked to me. They all hate me now.

"And I hate *her*."

Read 1 Peter 2:19–23
Why forgive people who hurt you?

You trash your sister's boombox and she makes you buy a new one. You skip practice and get benched. You come tardy to school and get detention.

You got punished. You deserved it. Big deal. Take your lumps.

But you don't earn every bad thing that hits you—like when people lie about you, mock your beliefs, blame you for something you didn't do, or question your motives or friendship. Or when they rip you off or broadcast your smallest mistake.

Yep, Jesus said believers should "turn the other cheek" (Matthew 5:39). That doesn't mean you let people slap you up. Jesus said to confront people who pain you and to avoid them if they don't change (Matthew 18:15–17).

Even if you can change a bad situation, your hurts don't go away if you keep hating. Your enemies will still hit your heart, and hating them only ropes and gags you. You won't feel free until you forgive.

Jesus forgave by praying for the people who hurt him (Luke 23:34). Then he refused to plot revenge or toss back insults. He let God defend him.

By forgiving his enemies Jesus wrestled free from them.

Forgiveness gets you off the curb and back into life.

When they hurled their insults at him, he did not retaliate....
Instead, he entrusted himself to him who judges justly.
1 PETER 2:23

True Peace

Mayerly Sanchez remembers a close friend, Milton, buried two years before. "The day before he died," whispers Mayerly, "we had been playing soccer in the street." Stabbed in a gang fight in a suburb of Bogota, Colombia, Milton was one of thirty thousand people who died violently in his country that year.

At his funeral, Mayerly vowed to work for peace.

Mayerly now coleads a national peace movement of almost three million kids. Their work has influenced more than ten million Colombians to vote "yes" to a Citizen's Mandate for Peace that highlights love, acceptance, forgiveness, and work.

She discusses legislation with Colombian congressmen and speaks to conferences at leading universities. She's been nominated for a Nobel Peace Prize. She's fourteen.

Read Matthew 5:9

How can you make peace in a world at war?

Statistically, you can count on 98.6 percent of the contestants in any beauty pageant to stroll the stage and state that their deepest wish in life is world peace. (Right after acquiring big hair, manicured nails, and a beachside condo like Barbie's.)

They're blowing smoke to try to win a tinsel crown. Mayerly, though, does *real* stuff to try to stop the killing in a country with a murder rate fifteen times that of the United States.

To Mayerly, being a peacemaker is part of daily life. "We heard a lot about peace in the media," one fifteen-year-old Colombian said. "But Mayerly taught us that peace needs to be practiced. If we see two of our friends fighting, we need to intervene and try to motivate them to get along."

Mayerly's peacemaking didn't start with halting drug lords and their hired thugs. It began with how she acts at home and with friends. Your peacemaking begins with how you treat your bratty siblings and the pest who sits behind you in science.

You might not win a Nobel Prize. But when you spread peace among your ranting friends and raving family and raging enemies, you show them you belong to the Prince of Peace (Isaiah 9:6–7).

Blessed are the peacemakers, for they will be called
sons of God. MATTHEW 5:9

Fungus Among Us

Your mom's question was innocent enough. "How was the party?" she asked.

"Oh, fine," you lied. How could you tell your mom that the whole evening you felt as though you had bad breath, body odor, and an incurable foot fungus? Kelly kept looking around to see if there was anyone better to chat with. When you tried to talk to Craig, he left to fiddle with the entertainment center—six times during one song. Four times Cory ran off to get more soda, and Sheri was in the corner all evening with her nose stuck in some guy's ear, telling stupid jokes and nibbling.

What's wrong with you?

Probably nothing. But as long as you try hard to be in the inner circle in a class, at a party, on a team, even within your group of friends, you'll be unhappy with the results. There's a better way to find friendship.

Read Proverbs 18:24

What happens when you try too hard to be popular?

Seeking huge popularity ruins you. It forces you to fit the expectations of the ones you want to impress—to be someone you're not, to do things you don't want to do, and to say things you normally wouldn't say. Besides that, your popularity lasts for only as long as your beauty or brains are tops. Then you're out and someone else is in. It's better to find one good friend who "sticks closer than a brother" than a crowd of fans who control and use you.

You might not meet those close friends at parties. Jonathan and David met as young men after David walloped the giant Goliath and was brought before Jonathan's father, King Saul. They met because David did what was right (1 Samuel 18:1-4). Ruth and Naomi were stuck together by tough times (Ruth 1). The apostle Paul became Timothy's friend and mentor when Timothy began ministry as a teen (2 Timothy 1:6).

The crowd may never accept and appreciate you the way you are. But you can ask God to help you find one real friend in the midst of the crowd.

A man of many companions may come to ruin, but there is a friend who sticks closer than a brother. PROVERBS 18:24

Awash in a Pool of Drool

"The inverse of the common denominator is multiplied by the square root of the algebraic cosine," your teacher drones, "which of course demonstrates that if x is greater than or equal to y, then z is the negative product of an imaginary number."

The rest is a haze. Mr. Ultradull keeps lecturing, too slow to see you're losing consciousness in the back of his room. As you drift off to sleepy-bye you wonder if there are laws against a teacher being so boring.

Half an hour later the bell rings.

You awake. Your face rests on your desk in a pool of drool.

Through sleepy eyes you see the last of your classmates exiting the room. You stumble after them and wipe your face on your sleeves, only to notice that the front of your shirt has sopped up spit like a sponge. You're soaked.

You wish you could wake up. Only you're not dreaming.

Read Psalm 55:12–14

When have you been hurt by a friend? What's your best bet for avoiding that pain in the future?

You sass each other. You tell each other's secrets and talk behind each other's backs. You borrow without asking (aka steal) from each other. You fling teases laced with stinging bits of truth. You get in ugly moods and won't say why. Even the best of friendships often flip-flop between kindness and cutdowns, fondness and fights, cool times and cruelty.

They bite you. You bite back. That's life with friends. Or is it?

"A real friend," says Proverbs 18:24, "sticks closer than a brother." And Ecclesiastes 4:10 says, "If one falls down, his friend can help him up." So what's up when your friends stab you rather than stick close?

No one wants to go through life alone. But not just any old friend will do. You need friends who keep you from making a fool of yourself. Friends who keep you from destroying yourself. Friends who wake you up before you drool on the desk. And friends who stick with you even when your shirt is soaked. But you only get that kind of care when you get the right kind of friends.

If an enemy were insulting me, I could endure it; if a foe were raising himself against me, I could hide from him. PSALM 55:12

It's a Team Thang

"She needs an answer *now*!" Clayton whined, muffling the phone against his shirt.

"We've talked about this before," Clayton's mom answered calmly. "We don't think it's appropriate for you to go out with Mara alone."

"We're not going out. We're just going to the mall. Don't you trust me?"

"It's not a question of trust, Clayton. It's not wise to put yourself in a situation where—"

"The kids at church are going to a hockey game tonight," Clayton's dad broke in. "You said you might go to that. Why don't you invite Mara to go with you? We'll even pay. You can treat her."

Problem solved, Mom and Dad supposed. Clayton thought not. "I don't want to bring Mara around the kids at church. She'll think I'm one of them."

Read Proverbs 16:18

What happens when you think you can survive alone as a Christian?

You may not be tempted to watch toxic rental videos or surf to Web sites you don't want your mother to see or sneak into a casino to blackjack away your college savings. But at times you may dream of ditching your Christian friends for bigger and better things.

You might laugh if people—like your parents—think you're tottering on the fence between devotion and ditching God, between living as a Christian and wandering away from your faith. But most people who stop being Christians don't dash toward the fence and pole-vault over to the other side. They try to tiptoe along the top of the fence.

That's when they need other believers to call them back from the edge—when, for example, they want to date non-Christians, or they decide they'll do *anything* to be popular, or they choose to make minor stuff like clothes or money majorly important.

If you ignore the pleas of your friends and do a dance on the fence, sooner or later you'll slip. Don't be surprised if it hurts to body-slam into the ground on the other side. There's no one over there waiting to catch you.

Pride goes before destruction, a haughty spirit before a fall.
PROVERBS 16:18

Blow Your Locker Open

Your parents told you being a Christian was "the most important thing in life." No one else your age seemed to think so.

Your youth pastor said you were supposed to "live for God" at school and "take a stand." God would be with you.

So where was he? *If God loves me*, you've been wondering, *why doesn't he blow my locker open?* You know—with some mind-melting display of power. You twiddle the lock and suddenly KABOOM, your locker door hangs by half a hinge. When the dust clears, you see God's blinding shining face talking to you, giving you a message for your school. Light fills the hall and your classmates fall to their knees in awe of God and respect for you, God's spokesperson in their midst.

It would be most impressive.

Read 1 Kings 19:10–18
How did God help when Elijah felt picked on?

Only a month had passed since Elijah stood on Mount Carmel, one man against 450 prophets of the fake god Baal. At Elijah's request, God flung fire from heaven to torch a sacrifice—stone altar and all. Baal failed. God won. Elijah was a hit, for a while.

What did Elijah get for doing everything right? He stood alone, or so he thought. Everyone else in Israel, he said, had abandoned their faith in the one true God to follow idols. And Queen Jezebel wanted to kill him. Lonely and scared, Elijah fled into the desert. He wanted to lie down and die.

Elijah's biggest complaint was this: He was alone! God showed himself to Elijah—not in an earthquake, wind, or fire, but in a whisper. God gave him a partner—*Elisha*. And God told him he wasn't really alone. *Elijah had friends*—seven thousand other worshipers of God.

God wants to display his power in your life. But he also wants to give you another truly potent gift: partners in following him. But get this: You have to be able to spot 'em before you can join 'em.

Yet I reserve seven thousand in Israel—all whose knees have not bowed down to Baal. 1 KINGS 19:18

Waffle Vomit

The lead singer of the band Waffle Vomit stared down from posters all over Kurt's bedroom. "He has songs about prayer and stuff," Kurt told his older brother Jeff. "He's got to be a Christian."

Jeff rolled his eyes. "Sure, Kurt. He's foaming at the mouth because he's a rabid follower of Jesus. That's why he chews bat eyeballs for breakfast."

"That's just a ploy," Kurt explained. "No one would listen to him if he didn't act like that. Besides—we're not supposed to judge."

"We're not supposed to condemn people," Jeff corrected. "But don't you think we're supposed to be able to tell who's a Christian?"

Read Ephesians 2:1–5
How do you know who is a Christian and who isn't?

If a dead guy were propped up in an easy chair with a newspaper and slippers, it might be hard to judge from across the room whether he was dead or just relaxing. But the closer you get the more you know—a whiff or a poke tells you a lot. Other times it takes a pulse check or a search for brain waves. And there are a few cases—usually victims of tragic accidents—where only God can distinguish life from death.

It doesn't usually take the county coroner to tell a dead body from a live one, and you don't have to be a pastor to know a Christian when you see one. Being a Christian isn't going to church or being nice or talking religious. It's having God's new life.

Without God, the part of you that wants to be friends with God is dead. Even if you look good, propped up on the outside, your insides are dead in disobedience—you've done what *you* want, not what God wants. But when you become a Christian, God freely forgives you. He makes you his friend and jump-starts your heart. You start to follow the One who saved you.

Sometimes when a person is reborn (John 3:1–16) you don't see much life right away—you can't see the new friendship with God that's formed on the inside. But God's life doesn't take long to ooze to the outside to affect attitudes and actions.

You spot a Christian by the new life that's begun. Life grows. Life shows.

God, who is rich in mercy, made us alive with Christ.
EPHESIANS 2:4

Head Above Water

"I guess I never thought of that, Mrs. Dalbey," Halley mumbled.

"There's a reason God sometimes doesn't seem real to us, Halley," Mrs. Dalbey said quietly. "The wrong things we all do are a lot worse than we think. They're sins that separate us from God. They make us his enemies."

Halley listened closely as Mrs. Dalbey continued. "God says we deserve death—eternal separation from him—for our sins. Except that God's Son—Jesus—took that punishment when he died on the cross. If we admit our sin and accept the fact that Jesus died for us, God forgives us. That's how each of us becomes a Christian. When you get to know Jesus and act on what you believe, it starts to feel real."

Mrs. Dalbey let Halley chew on that for a while. Then she asked if Halley wanted to pray to start a new relationship with God. She did. "God, I know I need you," they prayed together. "I've sinned. Thank you that Jesus died in my place for my sins. I want your forgiveness. I want to follow and obey you."

Read Colossians 1:9–14
What does it mean for God to "rescue" you?

Christians aren't corpses. They're alive. But what does that look like? People, after all, can look alive but not be energized by God's new life. They're propped up and well preserved, but they haven't come to know God. They're still dead on the inside.

So what's the first sign of God's life? You know you're *rescued* by God.

If you're in water over your head and don't know how to swim, you can pretend for only so long that you don't need help. The beginning point in becoming a Christian is realizing that you're in water way past your eyeballs. The bad stuff you've done and the good stuff you've left undone has plunged you deep in sin. If you say you never sin, you're lying to yourself (1 John 1:8). And the penalty for sin is separation from God forever (Romans 6:23).

But God doesn't leave you to rescue yourself, to yank yourself to safety by your swimsuit. If you admit your sin to God, he forgives you (1 John 1:9). He rescues you from drowning.

For he has rescued us from the dominion of darkness and brought us into the kingdom of the Son he loves, in whom we have redemption, the forgiveness of sins. COLOSSIANS 1:13–14

It's Not a Small World

"That was truly wonderful," you say to your hosts. "I want to do it again."

With that, your tiny boat glides off on another spine-tingling tour. Multicultural munchkins brighten your day as they sing "It's a Small World After All" over and over—and over—in 687 different languages.

After your fourteenth trip, your hosts are exasperated. "May we suggest that you look at your map?" they urge. "Really. There are many other attractions in the park."

"This *is* the park," you protest. You slap at the map they offer and instead pull out some papers and wave them in front of the attendants. "This is it. The deed to Disneyland. My father gave it to me, and here I am. Enjoying it fully, I might add. Another round, please."

"Whatever you say," they reply, unwilling to force you to go where you don't want to go.

Read Titus 2:11–14

What does it mean for you to be "remade" by God?

If you owned Disneyland you wouldn't be content to float your boat and listen to motorized mannequins in la-la land. Within minutes you would be off on another ride. Within days you would know the location of every feature of the parks. And years later you would know every inch of your territory. But if you didn't look at your map and go exploring you might never know that more existed.

Being immature as a Christian is like staying stuck on the first ride you find. Sometimes those of us who are Christians—those who have let God rescue them—don't realize that God has more for us. A Christian is someone who is being *remade* by God.

Being a Christian—possessing "salvation"—is a lot bigger than having your sins forgiven. The word behind "to save" means "to be made whole." God wants not just to rescue you from drowning but to fix the injuries you suffered and teach you how to swim. He wants to train you to say "NO!" to evil and "YES!" to good. He wants you to be totally devoted to him.

For the grace of God that brings salvation has appeared to all men. It teaches us to say "No" to ungodliness and worldly passions, and to live self-controlled, upright and godly lives.

TITUS 2:11-12

Turn on a Dime

As Bryan swept the garage he felt sick to his stomach.

Last night Bryan and his brother Trent were having a quick snack before bed. Trent wouldn't stop teasing Bryan, and Bryan got so mad that he hurled a plate across the kitchen at his brother. He missed, but it gouged the cupboard and shattered on the floor. *What was I thinking?* Bryan was a Christian. He couldn't understand why he still got angry at his brother.

By the time Bryan finished mowing the lawn he felt even worse. He just couldn't shake what he had seen on his mom's face after the fight with Trent. She wasn't a Christian. And she looked at him like he was a mass murderer. She might as well have said it: "You phony! I thought Christians were supposed to be different."

What do I do now?

Read 1 John 1:9–2:6
How can a Christian stay close to God?

It doesn't take long to notice that Christians aren't perfect. That's clear even in the Bible. John writes that if we know God we obey him. A few verses earlier he argues, though, that we're kidding ourselves if we claim to be perfect. He writes so we won't sin, yet points out that Jesus' death (his "atoning sacrifice") means forgiveness is available to any believer who needs it.

Here's the scoop: As a Christian you're *rescued* from sin and hell. But you're not fully *remade*. In the meantime you need to be *responsive*.

A car that's responsive takes barely a twitch on the steering wheel to turn it. An old car with sloppy handling will hardly budge no matter how hard you crank the wheel. To John, a responsive Christian is one who admits his or her sin and asks forgiveness. Paul said it almost the same: A responsive Christian is one who gets up and goes on after falling down (Philippians 3:12–14).

That's *your* goal. And it's the best kind of friend you could ever find. If you want friends who really count, start by looking for the *rescued*—the ones who know God. Then look for those who are being *remade*—the ones who are growing. And if you find a friend who's *responsive* to God—one who turns when God says, "Turn!"—hang on tight.

But if anybody does sin, we have one who speaks to the Father in our defense—Jesus Christ, the Righteous One. 1 JOHN 2:1

More Than Skin Deep

Jennifer quizzed Eddie, "You're wearing your shirt tomorrow, aren't you?" Their youth group had all bought T-shirts with the group's logo. Eddie got one, but he felt stupid wearing it to church, much less anywhere else. As far as shirts went it was cool, except people always asked him questions he couldn't answer. But it would look bad if he didn't wear his shirt the next day. He was supposed to help advertise a concert that week.

"It's dirty," Eddie lied.

"Won't your mom wash it?"

"I do my own laundry," he lied again. "I won't have time tonight."

"Don't be a dirtball. We're all wearing them. How else will people know about the concert?"

Eddie was worn out. "Okay, okay. I'll wear it."

He showed up the next day with it hidden under a big flannel shirt. Jennifer saw him. She told him that didn't count.

Read Acts 2:42–47
What good are Christian friends?

Strange things pull friends together. *Good things*: sports, hobbies, after-school clubs. *Hard things*: alcoholic parents, busted-up families, tough homework. *Stupid things*: potty mouths, slamming people, drinking.

But at least *something* pulls you together. You have things in common.

God doesn't plan for Christian friendships to be a bad scene where you sit and stare at one another because you can't find anything to talk about. Yet he wants your bond with other Christians to go beyond wearing matching T-shirts. Your job isn't to stick out but to stick together.

The passage you read and the rest of the book of Acts details how the early church hung close. They clung to each other without becoming a clique. They took care of one another. They shared their stuff. They went around doing good. They got close to Christ. They told the world about Jesus. They were an always-expanding family.

They stood out for more than their shirts (John 13:35).

Every day they continued to meet together in the temple courts.
They broke bread in their homes.... ACTS 2:46

Pray for One Another

Why are you sitting here all by yourself?" Danay prodded.

Aimee crumpled into a cry. "My dad told us last night that he and Mom are getting a divorce."

"No way!" Matt laughed. "Your parents are great. You're joking."

Danay hit Matt. "She's serious, Matt. Stop it."

Aimee told Danay and Matt that her parents acted nice whenever people were around but walloped on each other as soon as they were alone. Matt apologized for laughing, and after a while he said they should pray for Aimee. Right there. Right then. So Matt and Danay prayed very simply for God to take care of Aimee and do whatever he could to help her parents.

Read Ephesians 6:18
How can you pray for friends?

You probably don't dissect your conversations with friends the way you slice and study a frog in biology class. You just talk. Prayer, though, might not be so easy. But in this one verse Paul dissects prayer to show how prayer—talking to God—is put together:

"Pray in the Spirit" is the hardest part to understand, but it says *how* to pray: Ask God to spark your prayers and to help you want what he wants.

"On all occasions" says *where* to pray: Prayer works when you're alone but becomes even more powerful when you pray with other Christians (Matthew 18:19–20). And hey—talking to God along with them isn't meant to be any more complicated than talking to one friend in front of another friend. Keep it simple. No frothy words.

"All kinds of prayers and requests" tells you *what* to pray about: Everything! "Always keep on praying" describes *when* to pray: As often as you breathe. "All the saints" says *who* to pray for: Start with your Christian friends.

One question left. *Why* pray? Paul doesn't say, because it's an assumption behind everything else he wrote. You pray because you and the people you know need God. Because they need his help. And because God wants to answer (1 John 5:14–15).

And pray in the Spirit on all occasions with all kinds of prayers and requests. EPHESIANS 6:18

Talk It Up

Janelle did the "secret angel" thing the whole retreat. She wrapped a small present and snuck it into the cabin of the girl whose name she had drawn. She wrote a page-long note detailing everything she liked about her "mortal." She slyly volunteered to clean up the breakfast dishes when it was actually her mortal's turn.

She had no idea who had her own name. She hoped it wasn't the girl who barfed on her in the dining hall. It probably wasn't the guy who decked her on the skating rink.

On the last night of the retreat everyone flopped on their stomachs in a circle, a single candle in the middle lighting the room. One by one, each person told whom he or she had drawn and said something kind to that person. Janelle described how she saw her mortal being kind to someone. Everyone clapped for her mortal. But no one said anything about Janelle. They had lost her name.

Read Hebrews 3:12–13

How can you encourage your Christian friends?

Encouraging each other isn't group hugs. It isn't forcing gooshy feelings the way you wring the last bubble of toothpaste from a tube. It's inspiring someone's confidence. It's helping a friend climb higher.

The writer of Hebrews warned that it's possible for any of us to be duped into thinking sin looks good and God looks bad. The remedy? Daily doses of reality dropped kindly on us by other Christians.

Encouragement means reminding a friend *who God is*: God never makes dumb rules (Psalm 19:7–9). He's good and loving in everything he does (Psalm 145:17). Encouragement means reminding a friend *what's right*: obeying parents (Colossians 3:20), gulping back gossip (James 1:26), speaking with purity about the opposite sex (Ephesians 5:3–4), plus lots of other things you know are right. And encouragement means reminding a friend that *you'll make it together* (2 Timothy 2:22).

You don't have to say much. But you need to talk it up. If you and your friends don't encourage one another, who will?

But encourage one another daily...so that none of you may be hardened by sin's deceitfulness. HEBREWS 3:13

No More Stinky Days

Your day stinks from the start.

As soon as you sweep into school, you get shaken down for your lunch money. Then you bomb a pop quiz. You get whacked in the jaw in gym.

When you arrive home, your day gets worse. Your dad doesn't like the mess in your room. You run out the door mad. You step where you shouldn't. You squish. "YEEEEUCK!" you scream. And without thinking, you do the one thing you could possibly do to make the stink worse: You wipe your bare feet on the kitchen rug. Your dad glares. Your brother gags.

"MOMMMM..." you wail. "NOBODY LIKES ME!"

"Well," she says calmly, "you do smell like dog poop."

Read Revelation 5:6–14
Does God guarantee people will like you?

You can get lost in the seals and bowls and thunder and trumpets of the Bible book of Revelation. But what you just read is unmistakably clear: God is building a people who belong to him, a gaggle of friends who rely on his care now and forever. And there's a crowd of people following God.

Any no good, very bad, horrible day will leave you feeling friendless. Everybody faces those days. But being a Christian might make your lonely days feel even lonelier. You get left out for making right choices in your quest to follow God. Yet Jesus has a promise: He said that anyone who leaves "home or brothers or sisters or mother or father or children or fields for me and the gospel" will receive "a hundred times" as much in "this present age" and "in the age to come, eternal life" (Mark 10:29–30).

If God rewards leaving fields for his sake, he for sure cares when following him means you lose friends. And Revelation pictures a whopper way God keeps his promise: Heaven will be full of people from every tribe and nation.

They're here. Right around you. Right now. What Jesus said means you'll see some of those new friends soon, in "this present age." And Revelation shows you'll also be hanging with a cool crowd for all eternity. If you follow God, you'll have friends forever.

With your blood you purchased men for God from every tribe and language and people and nation. REVELATION 5:9

Snow Forts

"You can't come in here, runt," Angie scowled. "Go build your own fort." Her brother trudged through the snow to the far side of their yard. He built his own snow fort and sulked in it by himself. He packed hard snowballs that froze into ice balls to lob at his sister and her friends.

Isn't Angie's fort just like a clique?

If you live where it snows, it's great to build a snow fort. If you build thick walls and a roof, you can stay warm even if it's cold enough outside to kill. Just like that, a clique can be good. Cold winds of insecurity, peer pressure, hormones, and potential for failure blow through your world. In a clique, you and your friends can stick together for warmth.

But a clique is cold agony if you're on the outside. You freeze to death because the clique won't let you in. Like a snow fort, a clique is toasty on the inside and freezing on the outside.

Read 1 John 4:7–12
If God built a snow fort, what would it be like?

God's snow fort is the group of people who believe in Jesus Christ. He has only one entrance requirement: friendship with Christ. God doesn't ice-out people from the wrong school or neighborhood, or people who dress wrong or who aren't quite cool, pretty, or popular enough.

God's snow fort can't ever get too crowded. He keeps ripping down walls and building rooms. He's always inviting more people in.

The only problem comes when people inside the fort decide they won't let any more people in. First John 4:19 says we can include people in our group because God has included us—we can love because he has loved us. That isn't always comfy. We may have to squish to let someone else in, but that's what makes God's snow fort different from Angie's.

So stay warm with your friends. That's great. But remember to welcome others in from the cold.

Dear friends, let us love one another, for love comes from God.
Everyone who loves has been born of God and knows God.
Whoever does not love does not know God, because God is
love. This is how God showed his love among us:
He sent his one and only Son into the world that
we might live through him. 1 JOHN 4:7-9

But I Like Fish Sticks

Elmer cleared his throat into a dozen microphones while flashbulbs popped from every direction. "Hi," he squeaked as reporters jostled for better positions. Then the president of the United States strode to the platform to join Elmer.

"I am proud to award this Medal of Courage to Elmer," the president said. "As the first student in our country's history to stand and bravely proclaim that he actually likes school lunches, he sets an example of bravery and courage all America should imitate." The prez turns to Elmer. "Tell 'em what you love, son."

"Um, the fish sticks, sir. I think they're the best."

Admit you like fish sticks, and you'll get almost that much attention.

Read Hebrews 13:15
What things make you willing to cause a scene?

Jesus pointed that whatever is on your mind is what gushes out of your mouth. He said, "Out of the overflow of the heart the mouth speaks" (Matthew 12:34). Yet it's tough to say what you think when your world forces everyone to be the same. If you're short, you get yanked by the hair to the "right" height. If you're tall, you get your head mowed off.

It's not worth inviting mob ridicule by climbing a lunch table to shout that you like school food. There are bigger things to stand up for.

Like this. The Bible says, "If you confess with your mouth that Jesus is Lord and believe in your heart that God raised him from the dead, you will be saved" (Romans 10:9 NLT). Honesty about your faith doesn't get you into heaven, but it does reveal what's in your heart. The fact that Jesus saved you is worth squawking about.

And if you never split your lips with that good news, others won't know how they can meet Jesus. Romans goes on to point out this truth: "But how can they call on him to save them unless they believe in him? And how can they believe in him if they have never heard about him? And how can they hear about him unless someone tells them?" (Romans 10:14 NLT).

God deserves to hear thanks for what he has done for you. And others need to hear the great news too.

With Jesus' help, let us continually offer our sacrifice of praise to God by proclaiming the glory of his name. HEBREWS 13:15 NLT

Not Snots

Heather moved across the country in December, and the rules at her new school allowed her to try out late for whatever group or team she wanted. The cheerleading squad didn't exactly cheer when she picked their group. After Heather did some routines from her last school, the squad told her they needed to talk alone.

"I think we should let Heather in," Jennifer suggested. "Have you seen her older brother? He's cute."

"I like our group the way it is," Trish announced. "There's no way she can learn our routines midyear. I think we should tell her to ..."

"Pop the big head, Trish," Stacy interrupted. "Our routines aren't that hard. We don't have any reason to leave anyone out. Admit it. You just don't like Heather."

In the end, the team voted "no" on Heather. Part of us thinks, *So what? Too bad, so sad.* Heather won't spend life sleeping in a gutter because brats bashed her self-esteem. *Everyone gets left out sometimes, right?* Another part of us knows it's not right to leave Heather out. We know that life done right is all about belonging—and inviting others in.

Read Matthew 28:16–20

In some of his last few words on earth, what does Jesus say to his followers?

What Jesus gives us as believers isn't just for us. He welcomes us into a friendship with himself. He wants us to welcome others into the same friendship. We can't act like the captains of a snotty squad, picking whom to let in and whom to shut out.

It's awful to leave someone off a team. It's beyond awful when we allow our nastiness—the tiniest bit of "Tough luck. I don't like you. I don't care about you"—to shut him or her out of friendship with God and his people, now and forever. Bad stuff.

When Jesus gathered his followers to speak to them, most worshiped him— they fell on the ground in awe. Some others doubted. Their faith in him was immature. Yet Jesus said the same thing to all of them: "I am Master of all. Go invite others to join our crowd. I'll go with you."

Therefore go and make disciples of all nations. MATTHEW 28:19

Happy and You Know It

Keith shivered in a sweat shirt, jeans, and blanket. After working on an African mission trip in hundred-degree-plus heat for a whole summer, he felt frozen.

His friends sat comfortably in the cool evening air. They thought he was crazy.

Keith quietly told how he had helped build a house at an orphanage, how he'd gotten to know the orphans, and how God now led his life.

Talking about spiritual stuff came easy. While Keith's body had been toasted in the heat, the experience of the summer had also lit his heart on fire. Keith burned to know Jesus. And obey him. He'd figured out that Jesus wanted to be his one-of-a-kind friend.

His friends sat comfortably in their spiritual coolness. They thought he was loopy.

The next day his best friend gave him a letter a bunch of people had signed. "We think you should stop talking about Jesus. We don't want to hear about that."

Read Matthew 10:32–33
Why admit that you know Jesus?

Some people think Christians are like telemarketers. They call during dinner. They grab your ear until your food goes cold. They sell stuff you don't want. If you're smart, you hang up before they start.

God isn't into obnoxious words of faith. You don't have to wear a sign, pin, bracelet, or T-shirt—or stick a fish onto the tail end of your family roadster. But you do need to be okay with being known as someone who belongs to God. Peter says that once you know God, you need to have some simple words ready: "Give an answer to everyone who asks you to give the reason for the hope that you have." But those words should also be kind: "Do this with gentleness and respect" (1 Peter 3:15).

Sometimes, though, even close followers of God quake when people slam their faith. Even Peter crumbled when a little servant asked if he knew Jesus (Luke 22:55–62). But Peter knew God. He got bold.

You know God. You belong to Someone great. Don't be afraid to say it, even when others think you're crazy.

Whoever acknowledges me before men, I will also acknowledge him before my Father in heaven. MATTHEW 10:32

He's Not Grave Dust

"It's a myth," Rick argued. "You know—all that junk about Jesus rising from the dead. People invented God when they didn't understand stuff like evolution—or astrophysics."

"Astrophysics?" Steve pondered. "Isn't that the dog on *The Jetsons*?"

"No, stupid," Rick spat. "That's *Astro*. Astrophysics is the study of bodies in space. Before you could have evolution you had to have stars and planets. It's okay to believe Jesus 'lives in our hearts.' You just can't say he's alive. He's dead. He's just a dead teacher. Like Mr. Zalinki."

"Dead like Mr. Zalinki," Steve grinned. "Good one, Rick."

"Where do you get this stuff?" Marie objected. "You can say Santa Claus and my grandma Estelle 'live in my heart.' Jesus did more than that. He rose from the dead. Really. Body and all."

Read Luke 24:36-49

Why does it matter that Jesus isn't dust in a grave?

If Christ wasn't raised, Paul wrote, our faith is useless (1 Corinthians 15:14, 17). And his early followers knew it. After Jesus was crucified, they hid in fear. They'd hoped Jesus would set up the new kingdom he had promised. But then he was dead. Nothing had turned out how they had expected. A few disciples claimed he was alive. They said that the grave was empty. He'd risen from the dead (Luke 24:6, 34).

It seemed too good to be true—until Jesus suddenly stood among them.

Jesus dared them to study the scars on his hands and feet where he had been nailed to the cross. He dined on a piece of fish. Jesus was no ghost, no figment from their wishes. He helped them understand that God had promised his resurrection all along.

So why does it matter?

By raising Jesus from the dead, God declared Jesus to be his Son (Romans 1:4). He confirmed that Jesus had paid in full for our sins (Romans 4:25). And get this: Because death couldn't keep Jesus in the grave, it won't keep his followers there either. He lives with us now. We'll live with him forever.

He lived for real. He died for real. He rose for real. So we can follow him for real. Now and forever.

This is what is written: The Christ will suffer and rise from the dead on the third day. LUKE 24:46

High Voltage

"I sure don't have anything to say," Maria sighed. "My parents are Christians. My grandparents are Christians. I grew up a boring Christian."

Maria's youth pastor, Monique, stuck her head in the door. "How's it coming?" she asked. Michelle had stuck Maria and five other kids in a room to make them brainstorm how to tell other students at school about Christ. An experiment, she said.

"We could have a visitor's night at church. We could have games, skits, and free pizza," Shelly bubbled. "We might even—"

Scott interrupted. "Nick thought we should have a Bible study before school," he jeered. "You couldn't get *us* to come to that." Nick turned red.

Monique glared at Scott. "Actually, both of those are good starts. Here's the next step. Both of those tactics mean that your non-Christian friends have to come to *you*."

Read 1 Peter 2:9–10
What qualifies you to tell others about Christ?

Picture you and your Christian friends. You've started hanging together. Praying for one another. Encouraging one another with kind words and actions—or at least working at all of that. You're charged up. But you'll short-circuit and blow a fuse if all that energy stays in one place.

When God formed the church, the first believers grew up. They also grew out. Jesus told his followers to "go and make disciples" (Matthew 28:19). They did. God "added to their number daily those who were being saved" (Acts 2:47). They told the world about Christ and his love—always with actions, often with words. Instead of becoming a clique, they became a family. Instead of turning inward, they spread out.

You might think you have nothing to tell. You probably didn't rack up a bunch of gory, sensational sins for God to save you from. Your decision to get totally devoted to Christ may have been quiet, made over time. But if you understand God's "mercy"—how God forgave, accepted, and befriended you—then you have a story. You belong to God. Tell people about the God who called you to live close to himself.

But you are a chosen people, a royal priesthood, a holy nation, a people belonging to God, that you may declare the praises of him who called you out of darkness into his wonderful light.
1 PETER 2:9

Sure

"You used to be nice." Sasha rapped David. "You're changing."

"Me? Changing?" David faked innocence. "I'm just not a dork anymore."

"At school you ignore me and everyone else from church."

"Oh—" David fought back. "So you're jealous of my new friends."

Sasha didn't answer right away. "That's not the problem," she said after a long silence. "It's bigger than that. You ignore everything about Christ."

"So?"

"See? You act like it doesn't matter. I'm not sure who you are anymore. I thought you were a Christian."

"So did I," David finally admitted. "Now I'm not so sure."

Read Hebrews 10:19–23

How do you know that you're a Christian?

Who you are is partly what you like. Partly the way you act. Partly how you feel. It's also what you believe. And most of all it's who you belong to.

We belong to God because he made us (Psalm 24:1-2). We belong to him, that is, except we decided we didn't. We *all* chose not to follow God— we chose to sin, to do wrong again and again, to distance ourselves from him (Romans 3:23). And the sentence God declares for sin is death—total, endless separation from him (Romans 6:23).

The Old Testament pictured that separation concretely. God's presence dwelled in the temple, in the "Most Holy Place." Only one priest could pass through a curtain to get close to God's presence—and only once a year. And that high priest dared come close only if he carried the blood of an animal killed as a sacrifice for the people's sin (Leviticus 16).

But an animal can't take our place and die for our sins. God's Son—Jesus— did. He was the perfect sacrifice for all sins for all time. His blood opens a new way for us to "enter the Most Holy Place" with confidence. His death means God cleanses us, accepts us, and removes our guilt—and gives us eternal life with him that starts right now (John 3:16).

Becoming a Christian begins by saying, "Yes, God, I accept Christ's death for my sins. I admit I belong to you." You don't run from God anymore. You run toward him. You don't choose to be far away. You choose to follow.

Let us draw near to God with a sincere heart in full assurance of faith. HEBREWS 10:22

Doing the 'Tudes

Kaitlin and Will glared at their youth pastor. They hadn't liked their assignment very much—to go ask a non-Christian what she or he thinks of Christians.

"I asked Mr. Riley whether he saw anything in me that made him want to be a Christian," Will reported. "He said he didn't buy what I was selling. He said he hardly ever sees me being kind to people—nothing like Jesus. I blow up all the time. He said I was a fake."

"And I talked to Miss Fernandez, my Spanish teacher," Kaitlin said. "My question asked, 'How are Christians different from other people?' She said, 'Can I be blunt? Christians aren't different—they're *weird*.' "

Read Matthew 5:13—16
Why would anyone be crazy enough to follow Jesus' teaching?

You want to do right. But not if it's hopelessly hard. Not just "because God said so." But some of the commands of the Bible might sound wacky and unworkable. Like the "Beatitudes," the words Christ uttered in Matthew 5:1-11, capped off with the passage you just read. Why "do the 'tudes"?

Reason 1: *Doing the 'tudes makes you happy.* Okay, maybe a different kind of happy than an amusement park whizzy-with-glee. But people who live by the words Jesus uttered experience both God and his blessings.

Reason 2: *Doing the 'tudes makes you a person who makes a splash for good.* You're spice—tasty flavor. You're light—a beam on God's right way.

Reason 3: *Doing the 'tudes shows off God's power.* He's making you spiritually hungry, honest about pain, gentle, merciful, pure, peaceful, and patient in persecution. Powerful stuff—and powerfully attractive, whether or not people realize it right away.

Non-Christians don't need our bumper stickers or T-shirts—they're looking for God's good stuff inside us. How we vote won't transmogrify the world—though voting is swell. We're not distinguished by our health or wealth—in fact, we search for better riches. And we don't rub our goodness in people's faces—that isn't what Jesus meant by being "a city set on a hill."

If you want to be happy, do good, make friends, and show off God, Jesus gave you the list of the 'tudes to let him build in you.

Let your light shine before men, that they may see your good deeds and praise your Father in heaven. MATTHEW 5:16

The Shock in Their Eyes

Jill glanced up from her Bible study notes and paused, startled to see Shannon standing at the back of the room. A horde of shocked faces said the same thing: Why is *she* here?

Jill had met "Shannon the Sleaze Queen" at a track meet. Even with a hacker's cough, Shannon still ran fast. Shannon, in fact, ran around a lot, Jill had heard.

"Hi, Shannon!" Jill blurted. Shannon grabbed a seat and listened quietly. A girl next to her helped her follow along in her Bible. At the end of the evening, she talked to a few people and then slipped out the back.

Jill found her the next day at track practice. "Did you see how they looked at me?" Shannon asked. "I knew they wouldn't want me there."

"But it got better," Jill reminded her. Shannon nodded. "They were just surprised to see you at a Bible study. You were a little shocked too, weren't you?" Shannon had to admit she was—and that she felt welcome. And that she wanted to go back.

Read Mark 2:13–17
What kind of people did Jesus choose to hang out with?

Your photo doesn't have to be plastered on TV ads that scream, "Don't let this happen to you" or "This is your brain on drugs" to be a wrongdoer. You don't have to be a sleaze queen or an ax murderer to have offended God. When you grasp that God is good and sin is evil and how totally repulsive *all* evil is to God—well, you can start to feel like rat chow.

Here's the good news: We walked away from God, but while we were still stuck in sin he took the first step toward us (Romans 5:8). He didn't make people get perfect before he would be their friend.

The religious leaders watching Jesus hated his friendliness toward sinners. They mocked his choice of a crooked tax collector to be his follower and despised his dinners with sinners. But those who sneered at Jesus for chumming with the bad guys were blind to their *own* badness. They didn't think they needed a spiritual doctor, so they pushed Jesus away. They stayed sick. It was the ones who admitted they needed a spiritual doctor who let Jesus near—and got well.

Jesus said to them, "It is not the healthy who need a doctor, but the sick. I have not come to call the righteous, but sinners." MARK 2:17

When Truth Clashes

No one was surprised when Nina's older sister got pregnant. But Micki was shocked when she heard about the abortion.

"She did *what*?" Micki looked at Nina with sick eyes.

Nina stuck up for her sister. "I don't know what I'd do. But I sure wouldn't want to have a kid."

"How can you say that?" Micki blurted.

"I think you have to be there to know what you'd do." Nina looked at Micki like she was unbelievably stupid. "You just can't make that choice ahead of time."

"There's not much choice," Micki fought back. "Abortion is wrong."

Read 1 Peter 3:15

What can you do when your beliefs clash with your world?

Most people look to something other than the Bible as their prime source of truth. They follow their feelings and do whatever feels good. They think technology has all the answers and decide God is unnecessary. They appoint their own brains as the absolute judge and decide for themselves what is right and true. They look to a host of other religions to save and satisfy them.

Some ask polite questions. Others criticize what Christians believe and how we live. Many will point out our hypocrisy, selfish narrowness, and un-Christlike attitudes and actions.

Sometimes they're right. Because we're imperfect, our view of the world and of ourselves is imperfect. Criticism is a challenge to grow in what we know, to look at ourselves in the mirror of the Bible and make sure we aren't a mess. We need to double-check that Christ is really in charge of our lives and that we understand him and his Word correctly.

Then what? Go ahead and answer people's questions and objections as best you can. Tell what you believe and why. It's okay to say "I don't know" and give an answer later, when you've had a chance to ask more mature Christians how to give the best answer.

Sharing Jesus is an enormous chance to express your devotion to Jesus. When you live for Jesus, questions inevitably come your way. So get ready!

Always be prepared to give an answer to everyone who asks you to give the reason for the hope that you have. 1 PETER 3:15

Step by Step

"Sure, I go to church," Jackie fired back. "Got a problem with that?" Kids had asked Jackie about God a couple of times before, and when she hadn't been able to answer their questions, they laughed. So this time she came out fighting.

Acting like a cornered dog that barks and bites to escape is one response to people confronting your faith—to kids grilling you, teachers asserting opinions you disagree with, maybe a non-Christian parent telling you to spend less time at church. Another reaction is hiding your faith—changing the subject or changing your behavior to fit your surroundings. Either way, fears crash in: *Will I lose this friend? I should know what to say. Shouldn't I stand up for God?*

Read 1 Peter 3:15–16
How should you respond to people who question your faith?

When Peter says to be prepared to explain your faith—back in the first part of 1 Peter 3:15—that sounds like a small step for Peter, a giant leap for you. But Peter gave you a reason to be unafraid—because Christ is Lord. *Jesus* deserves your deepest awe and obedience. Your first concern is what *he* thinks, not what others think (Luke 12:5). If you can stop your fears from ringing in your ears, you'll be able to hear the Holy Spirit help you know what to say and when to speak (Mark 13:11).

But having the right words is only half of sharing Christ. Nothing beats real love and the example of a changed life for demonstrating that God is real. Gentleness and respect goes a lot farther than loud classroom debates—and, after all, God is the one who changes minds, not you (2 Timothy 2:24–26). Your job isn't to put on a big show but to have a pure heart, "a clear conscience" that silences the lies of your opponents.

God will help you share about him step-by-step. Ask God for courage, then start by refusing to hide that you go to church, and don't duck when a Christian friend waves "hi" at school. Take the step of bowing your head to silently say a quick thanks for lunch—most school lunches need prayer anyway. Then work on inviting a close friend to church. Practicing the little steps gives you the experience you need to take bigger steps, like speaking up about Jesus to that friend or to others.

Do this with gentleness and respect. 1 PETER 3:15

Heimlich Maneuver

"What was her question today?"

"She asked how we know that God made the world and that we didn't evolve."

"Maybe that's her problem. She's an ape."

"She thinks too hard. We're just supposed to accept stuff. Aren't we?"

"All this started when her grandma died. She asked Pastor Lee if heaven was real and he gave her this big huge lecture. She feels really bad."

"Did you see Mr. Swenseid's face when she asked if Jesus really did a miracle to feed all those people? He stopped breathing. I swear he had a heart attack. That's one thing I don't like. I don't like it when they act like we're little and don't have questions."

Read John 1:43–51
Does God dislike people who question Christian beliefs?

You can't swallow food whole. Either the gastric guards in your esophagus forcibly expel the intruder or your stomach grinds to a halt when the goo in your gut asks who let the solids in. Or you choke and die.

God doesn't expect you to swallow truth whole. He wants you to chew.

Nathanael was skeptical. He questioned whether Jesus was who Philip claimed he was, God's Son come to save the world.

But Nathanael also accepted Philip's invitation to come and see. That's different from refusing to believe anything no matter what the evidence. That's different from acting too cool for Sunday school—writing off Bible study or youth group or confirmation class without even trying to understand your faith.

Jesus saw him under the fig tree—a customary spot for studying Scripture. Nathanael knew where to look for answers. He was like the Bereans (Acts 17:11), who heard the message Paul preached about Christ "with great eagerness and examined the Scriptures every day to see if what Paul said was true."

Nathanael wasn't crabby. He wasn't making excuses. He loved truth enough to ask questions, chew on the answers, and live (2 Thessalonians 2:10). Being mature doesn't mean you know everything. It means you know the One who does.

When Jesus saw Nathanael approaching, he said of him, "Here is a true Israelite, in whom there is nothing false." JOHN 1:47

Stand Downwind

As soon as they hit seventh grade, Brock and his friends started having weekly weekend parties. Back then the boys hid the dance CDs in the microwave so the girls couldn't find them. By eighth grade couples were tongue-wrestling on the couch. By ninth grade kids were sipping wine coolers and belching beers.

Brock told himself that other parties and places were a lot worse. Yet he had a queasy certainty he should have quit the parties a *looooong* time ago. But the kids who did the parties were his best friends. His only friends. All of his friends, actually.

And they told Brock the stuff they did was no big deal. When he said it was, they bagged him. And before he could stop going to the parties, they stopped inviting him.

Read Matthew 5:10–12
What's it mean to be "persecuted for righteousness"?

You're in a situation and you're feeling weird. You wonder if it's you—or if it's Jesus.

Get it straight: You can't blame all your own random weirdnesses on God.

When people look at you funny, look at yourself to see if it's something you can fix. You do a deodorant check. You flip a breath mint. You stand downwind when you chat. You do your best to act normal—within God's limits, of course. And you still wind up thinking, *Hmm…I don't fit here.* And you ponder, *Hmm…this is about right and wrong.* And you conclude, *Hmm…I belong to Jesus—and if I decided to disobey him, this problem would go away.*

Then it's about Jesus.

People all over the planet are persecuted—sometimes solely for their beliefs, sometimes for a nasty knot of ethnic and economic and spiritual issues. You might never be persecuted like that. You're not likely to be picked on like people in Christian movies who don't bow to the Beast and get guillotined. Yet you'll surely catch some "all kinds of evil against you." And a lot of times persecution for making the right choice means you get ignored with a fury. People don't mistreat you. They don't beat you. They just forget you.

Massive is your reward.

Blessed are those who are persecuted because of righteousness, for theirs is the kingdom of heaven…great is your reward.
MATTHEW 5:10, 12

Monkey Pile

"One-monkey! Two-monkey!" Ryan counted. Then he rushed. *Bam*! Ben lay flattened, walloped in a quarterback sack.

Ben jumped up and pounced back at Ryan. "Stop it! One more time and I'm quitting! It's *three* monkeys."

Ryan laughed at Ben. "Benny's such a baby," he taunted.

Next play. "One-monkey! Two-monkey!" Ryan counted—and again rushed early, knocking Ben even harder. When Ben kept moaning and couldn't get up from the ground, his dad came running and scooped him into their car and sped to the emergency room.

It took a CAT scan to show Ben's exploded spleen, and it took emergency surgery to save his life. When Ryan came to visit Ben at the hospital he saw the tubes sticking into Ben and started to cry. "Your dad told me what the doctors said," Ryan finally said. "I'm sorry I did this to you."

"It's okay, Ryan," Ben said. "I'm not going to stay mad at you. I forgive you."

Read Psalm 103:8–12

You blew it. You know it. Now what are you supposed to do?

You can't unrupture a spleen you bounced to shreds. Or reel nasty words back into your mouth. Or uncheat on a test. Nothing can completely undo what you did—whether it's a sin or a mistake or a bit of both. But you *can* do *what you can* to make things right: Say you're sorry. Talk nicer next time. Turn yourself in to the teacher and take a zero or retake the test.

But squashing people is only half our problem when we do wrong. So setting that straight is only half our job. Our sin also snubs God. "You are not a God who takes pleasure in evil; with you the wicked cannot dwell," David wrote. "The arrogant cannot stand in your presence; you hate all who do wrong" (Psalm 5:4–5).

God's anger is bone-crushing stuff. But his forgiveness is even bigger. When you blow it and you know it, tell God. If you admit your sin, he wipes it away—completely. He doesn't stay mad.

He's not giving you permission to be bad. He's making you blameless. And offering you a fresh start at following him.

As far as the east is from the west, so far has he removed our transgressions from us. PSALM 103:12

Are We There Yet?

"You're on my side!" your little sister whines, swinging her Barbie at you. Whack! The hard plastic head cracks you across the nose.

"OW!" you howl. "Stop it! MOM—that HURT! Make her stop!"

The backseat of the family car has gotten way too tight on a trip that won't quit. You've been riding for weeks. Each evening you write in your journal about *The Great American Road Trip*—under "Things I'd rather forget."

"This is so stupid!" you fuss. "Where are we going?"

Your parents don't disclose your destination. They won't trace on a map the route you're taking. "It's a surprise," they say.

One day you stop at a gas station. The clerk is nosy in a friendly sort of way. "You folks aren't from around here, are ya," she figures. "Where ya headed?"

"Wish I knew," you reply. "Ask them. This was their idea."

Read Philippians 1:9–11
Where is Jesus taking you as you follow him?

You won't enjoy a long road trip if you haven't a clue where you're headed. If all you're sure of is that your backside is glued to a car seat you'll feel duped, dragged to who-knows-where. And you'll yawn, snooze, and snore if you finally get to your destination and no one explains what you're looking at.

The White House is more than a house. The Grand Canyon is more than a hole in the ground. Following Christ is an adventure. But not understanding where you're headed—and why—and what you'll see along the way—turns the ride into a chore and a bore.

Paul flips through some travel pictures to show you your destination— actually, to show you what *you* will look like when your journey is done: Your relationship with Christ will change you completely. You will be "pure," "blameless," "filled with the fruit of righteousness." Your life will glow with God. People will see what he's done in you and worship him. And on your trip you'll stick with other believers and learn how to live best.

The trip has already begun. God is in the driver's seat. He guarantees he will get you to the goal (Philippians 1:6). And you don't have to guess where you're going.

And this is my prayer: that your love may abound more and more in knowledge and depth of insight. PHILIPPIANS 1:9

Starting Over

"It's not like I'm a murderer or anything," Mia told the girls in her Bible study. "But I have a potty mouth. I can talk pretty while I'm around my Christian friends, but other than that I swear all the time. If my little brother hits me, I swear. If a teacher does something I don't like, I cuss under my breath. It's a bad habit.

"But the real problem is I feel bad all the time about it. I know it's wrong to sin, so I imagine God glaring at me and giving me the silent treatment. I wonder if I'm going to hell. All Christianity does for me is make me feel like a failure. I don't want that."

Read John 7:53–8:11
What helped the woman caught sinning start over?

Sometimes we're legends in our own minds. We think we're perfect. We might be rotten people who never feel guilt, or we could be like the Pharisees in the Bible—nice church people who don't smoke, drink, or swear but ooze pride, anger, and selfishness.

At other times we admit we sin. But our honest guilt turns into fear that we do nothing right and that God won't forgive us when we blow it.

Jesus deals with the woman's sin matter-of-factly, like a doctor who says, "Yep, you're sick. But we can deal with that." Jesus doesn't hide her sin. The woman was caught sleeping with someone's husband. He didn't say she didn't deserve death, the punishment Jewish law prescribed. But he set her free. He says simply, "I do not condemn you.... Leave your life of sin."

God treats us the same way: He expects us to admit our wrongdoing because we all sin. But if we admit our sins to God he promises to forgive us, washing away our guilt and putting our friendship with him back on track (1 John 1:8–9).

That's what gives us the freedom to start over. And over. And over again if we need to.

Christians aren't perfect. Unlike cows and horses, we can't run as soon as we get out of the womb. Like little babies, at first we lie helpless. Then we flip, roll, scoot, crawl, and stand. Muscles and balance develop. *Then* we walk. But we never walk—or run—without getting up from the pavement a lot.

Go now and leave your life of sin. JOHN 8:11

No One Cried Foul

You worked so hard.

You got nothing for it.

Last year your entry in the 4-H amphibian fair—Bob the ninja turtle—didn't even place. This year your Lola wowed the judges with her swamp-green nail polish, lipstick, and tail bow, as well as the fake eyebrows you penciled on her to make her look like your aunt Beverly. And spectators loved Lola's snappy turtle wax coat, which you had buffed to a fine shine in shop class at school. Yet when you and Lola took the stand to bask in the admiration of fellow hobbyists, another contestant snuck in, charged the medal stand, hip checked you out of the way, and claimed Lola and your prize for himself.

No one noticed. No one cried, "Foul! Impostor! Unfair!"

Rip-off.

Read Hebrews 6:7–12

Is it worth working hard when hard work doesn't always win the prize?

Every action has two audiences.

Fans on earth are fickle. They seldom know when to clap. You study for an exam until your brain bursts, but a classmate who swipes the answer key gets the highest grade. You play tough all season long, yet the coach plays favorites when he gives the MVP award. Or you leave a party early to get home by curfew and peers jeer.

Fans on earth even clap for people who deserve to be booed to bits.

But your Fan in heaven is faithful. God always spots a job well done. He sees when you do something "spiritual," like praying or reading your Bible. But he notices *all* the ways you obey him—when you do homework and chores, listen to your parents, play hard, respect teachers, treat people great.

When you dedicate yourself to doing good you're like a patch of soil that soaks up rain and grows a bumper crop for its master. God won't forget that.

Trust him. Be patient and you'll enjoy the harvest.

God is not unjust; he will not forget your work and the love you have shown him as you have helped his people and continue to help them. HEBREWS 6:10

Just Do It Doesn't Do It

Derek and his dad returned from their hunting trip with a ten-point buck roped to the roof of their minivan. "It should have been Derek's," his dad told everyone when he bragged how they got the deer.

Derek faked a smile. He knew he should feel disappointed, but he wasn't sure he was.

He didn't know what he felt. Sitting in a tree stand with his dad waiting for deer, Derek pretended to be happy. When a deer finally wandered by, he wasn't sure he could kill it. He had never seen a deer so close, except for the stuffed head mounted above his grandparents' fireplace. But Dad had promised him the first shot, and Derek didn't want to disappoint him.

"Shoot! Just shoot!" his dad hissed. The buck's ears perked and Derek paused a second more, then finally pulled the trigger. All he hit was ground. When the buck bolted his dad quickly shot. Dad didn't miss.

Read Jeremiah 1:4–10

How did Jeremiah react to God's expectations of him?

When you fail—or you're scared you will—you try to shrug it off or make excuses or say it doesn't matter. But in the back of your brain the truth rattles around: You want to do well. So you're bugged. You're embarrassed. And you probably wouldn't admit your lack of perfection even to God without checking who's listening.

When God made Jeremiah a prophet—someone who would speak to God's people, the nation of Israel—Jeremiah was scared. God sent Jeremiah to go nose-to-nose with kings and leaders and the whole nation.

Jeremiah didn't think God's expectations fit him: "God, you're way off. I'm too young. I can't speak."

But God's expectations always fit us. He knows us. He knows how he made us. He sees more in us than we see in ourselves. And he knows he can make us able to do what he asks.

God let Jeremiah doubt for a second. Then God said, "Don't worry about it. *I* will send you. *I* will be with you. *I* will make you strong." He doesn't bark, "Just do it" or "Just shoot it." He works patiently with us until we get to his goal.

But the Lord said to me, "Do not say, 'I am only a child.' "
JEREMIAH 1:7

Faster, Higher, Stronger

Cheri anxiously awaited her turn at her first all-district gymnastics meet. *There are so many people watching*, she thought. Cheri did fine in her first two events, but in the floor exercise she missed a landing and bounced out of bounds. Her score dropped to the bottom of all the girls competing. She ran back to her teammates crying, furious with herself.

Her coach tried to encourage her. "Cheri, you did great. We'll work on landings and some endurance training and next time you'll..."

"I'm not going to do this anymore," she snapped. "I'm not any good at gymnastics. I made a fool of myself."

Read Hebrews 12:4-11
If God loves you, why does he let you struggle?

You didn't stop toddling when you banged your face on the furniture a few times, and you kept trying at math even though 2+2=4 bewildered you. And no doubt you'll do whatever it takes to keep growing up—to get your driver's license, rent your first apartment, and build a career and family.

Life is hard. Just because something takes effort doesn't mean you're stupid or lazy or uncoordinated or unspiritual. It means God is working on you.

God uses your struggles with school, home, sports, lessons, and relationships to discipline you—to *train* you—to make you strong, tough, and more like him. That's not necessarily because you've been bad but because he knows you can be better. God probably won't shoot lightning at your legs so you effortlessly win gymnastics meets. Nor does he zap your heart so you flawlessly obey him.

You practice to get good at anything. You need to practice to master life and to become a strong Christian. God doesn't put you into training because he's a cruel coach who laughs while you run laps. He knows what it takes to make you mature—when to go easy and when to push hard—and his discipline is always perfectly planned for your good.

Discipline hurts. But it works.

No discipline seems pleasant at the time, but painful. Later on, however, it produces a harvest of righteousness and peace for those who have been trained by it. HEBREWS 12:11

Mow Me Down

When Bill's older brother went off to college, he arranged for Bill to take over his lawn-mowing business. All Bill had to do was finish the last month and a half of fall mowing, then start the business up again next spring. He could make three times more per hour than any of his friends. He would be rolling in green stuff.

But he had to mow it before he could roll in it. After spending a whole Saturday mowing—and not finishing what he needed to do—he recalled that his brother was a foot taller and sixty pounds bigger. And it took him five years to build his business.

This was more work than Bill had figured.

His mom felt sorry for him. His dad said he couldn't quit.

Bill whined that this experience was going to ruin his attitude toward work forever, and he threatened to live at home until he was forty.

Read James 1:2–5

If you're supposed to persevere, when is it okay to quit?

Your swim coach expects you at practice three hours a night, five nights a week. You're spending afternoons squished on a piano bench with a lady teaching you to play hits from *The Sound of Music*. Your dance instructor yells too much. And you just aren't any good at track.

Quitting a team or an activity or a job doesn't always mean you're a quitter. You need to quit when you're hurting yourself—when you can't get enough sleep, you cry your eyes out nightly, or you don't get your homework done. You don't have much choice but to quit when you're forced to do wrong—by a crooked boss, for example. And it's okay to quit when you can do better at something else, *after* you've stuck it out and kept your promises. Commitments you made first—not the ones you like best—come first. Get help while you sweat it out, even if that means someone else takes some of your jobs.

Bad times force you to rely on God. From the frontside, trials are terrifying. But from the backside you can see how God cared for you—and how he brought you through.

Consider it pure joy, my brothers, whenever you face trials of many kinds, because you know that the testing of your faith develops perseverance. JAMES 1:2-3

Don't Play Dead

Part of Mort's job working the late shift at the funeral home was to whisk the ashes of cremated customers into brass urns. The job didn't pay well, but it presented certain, shall we say, golden opportunities.

Night after night Mort picked through the ashes of the day's dearly departed for a treasure of enduring worth: gold. A filling here, a dental bridge there. Once in a while he struck the mother lode—a shiny mouthful from an older lady or gentleman who had for decades successfully resisted being fitted with dentures. In time Mort accumulated enough extra income to retire early—on beachfront property in the Bahamas at age thirty-five.

The best part was that his victims never fought back.

Read Philippians 2:3–8

Does being a Christian mean you always play dead—and get torched—and let someone steal your fillings?

As Christians there is no better way to show love to others than to "lay down our lives" (1 John 3:16) by giving our time or our stuff sacrificially, by showing kindness to an enemy, by putting others before ourselves.

But we have only so much to give. So we give wisely.

If you left your school locker open with a sign on it saying *Look here! Steal my stuff!* you would foolishly have nothing left either for yourself or to share with people who really need it. If you let people take advantage of you, then you won't be able to give when it really matters.

Christ gave because he was strong, not because he was weak.

No one walked all over him. No one stole anything from him. He *chose* to give, in both life and death: He "made himself nothing." He "humbled himself." Here's a strange one: Even when he was about to be taken by force to be beaten and crucified, he made it clear to his killers that he was dying by choice (Matthew 26:53–54).

Being robbed and giving a gift have the same result. You pay a price. But when you give by choice, people don't see a fool. They see Christ.

Your attitude should be the same as that of Christ Jesus: Who, being in very nature God, did not consider equality with God something to be grasped, but made himself nothing, taking the very nature of a servant.... PHILIPPIANS 2:5-7

Fighting Forward

Tragedy struck today in northwest Wisconsin, the newscaster announced. *A Polk County deputy sheriff was critically wounded after he responded to a call for help in capturing a man sought for a shooting in Minnesota last night. Deputy Mike Seversen was shot under the chin at close range as he attempted to ...*

Three days later Mike woke up in a hospital bed.

He couldn't move.

But he was alive.

Read Philippians 4:12–13

What's the toughest situation you could face without shattering?

You probably don't think life ends when the air conditioning breaks or your VCR goes on strike. You probably don't doubt God's care for you when you blow a test or can't afford two-hundred-dollar tennis shoes.

But what if you were paralyzed from the neck down? What if you couldn't walk, talk, or breathe on your own? Or if your brain biffed? Life is over when you hurt that bad, isn't it? Then it's time to give up on God and life, right?

Wrong.

Mike still can't use his arms or legs. He knows what he's lost. He's no fool.

But he also knows what he still possesses. He has God. He fought to learn to breathe and talk again. His brain works well. He hunts, works on his house, jokes with his family and friends. He teaches people about God's care.

Paul, like Mike, realized he could thrive with a less-than-perfect life. He was tougher than he knew. God was bigger than he thought. From prison Paul wrote that he could be happy in any circumstance, with little or plenty, because God made him strong.

You probably won't be shot trying to capture a criminal. But you won't escape bad times (John 16:32). Your life isn't finished when it falls apart—when the race turns into an uphill battle against the wind, with flies in your eyes and gnats in your nose. That isn't time to quit. It's time to see how tough God can make you. You can do all things.

I can do everything through him who gives me strength.
PHILIPPIANS 4:13

Where's the Finish Line?

A herd of cows glanced up from munching brunch to stare at the students cycling down their bumpy road. The cows were utterly content. The bikers were crabby.

"Stopping!" Tom screeched from the back of the line. "Something's wrong. I've clocked eight miles since that last left turn. Shouldn't we be to another road by now? Hey, Eric—did you get us lost again?"

"Me? Don't blame me! You've got a map too."

Miles later Katie yelled, "Stopping!"

"Why are we stopping this time?"

"Jon's barfing in the bushes. He can't take the heat."

"Ryan, you lied to us," Jennifer whined to the ride leader. "You said this would be fun. We should have camped someplace where we could lie on the beach. I can't ride any farther."

Read Jude 24–25

When you follow God, what's your ultimate destination?

Christians who don't focus their minds on the finish line are like bikers wandering the countryside asking cows for directions. They wander. They hit bumps and *fwang* over their handlebars. They forget to enjoy the rush as they blow downhill. But knowing where and when you'll finish keeps you from quitting a tough ride. If you aren't sure that each push on the pedals propels you closer to the goal, you'll ditch. Sweat for nothing, and you'll find something better to do. Yet when ice-cold sodas, crystal lakes, and a soft sleeping bag wait for you, you can endure. As a believer, your destination is sweeter than anything you've ever imagined. You're heading upward. Toward maturity. Toward heaven. Toward your Lord.

And because of his strength, God promises to get you there "without any wrong in you." Not because you're perfect, but because you cling to his forgiveness. Not that you'll reach your home as an out-of-shape slob. Jesus is invading your life with his glory, greatness, power, and authority. Your faith will be fit.

God is strong and can help you not to fall. He can bring you before his glory without any wrong in you and can give you great joy. He is the only God, the One who saves us. JUDE 24–25 NCV

I want to extend thanks not only to my readers but to the people who equipped me to write:

Our Parents...
Roy and Lois Johnson, Tom and Pat Benson

My publishing pals through the years...
Gary and Carol Johnson, Charette Barta, Barb Lilland, Rochelle Glöege, Janna Anderson, Natasha Sperling, Steve Laube, Christopher Soderstrom, Dave Bellis, Ken Peterson, and Lynn Vanderzalm

The pastors in my life...
Leland Evenson, John Sanny, Peter Yang, Jim Maines, Stuart Briscoe, Kit Marter, Rick Rittmaster, and Steve Dornbusch.

INSPIRATION

VOLUME ONE

Learn about some of the biggest Jesus Freaks of all time: those who stood out from the crowd enough to be called martyrs. If Jesus was willing to give His life for me, and if these people, these martyrs, were willing to give up their lives for Him, how much does it take for me to truly dedicate my days on earth to Him?

Jesus Freaks by dcTalk and Voice of the Martyrs

REVOLUTION

VOLUME TWO

In this second volume, learn about those who stood against the culture of their day and made a difference. These individuals were not all martyrs, but they were all effective witnesses for Christ in societies that did not value the ways of Christ. These stories will not just inspire but challenge us with ideas of how we, too, can stand up against and change the culture of our day.

Jesus Freaks: Vol II by dcTalk

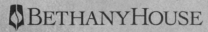